HARLEY GRANVILLE BARKER

HARLEY
GRANVILLE
BARKER

Man of the Theatre,
Dramatist and Scholar

by
C. B. PURDOM

HARVARD UNIVERSITY PRESS
CAMBRIDGE, MASSACHUSETTS
1956

Printed in Great Britain by Richard Clay and Co., Ltd.,
Bungay, Suffolk

A PREFACE
IN THE FORM OF A DEDICATION

My dear Edmund,

It was on a summer's evening just nine years ago as I listened to Desmond MacCarthy's tribute on the radio to Granville Barker's memory that the idea of this book came into my mind. I had known him and was well acquainted with his work, and I had admired him above all the men I had met in the theatre. You had then already started on your stage career, and you will remember how, two years later, we spent an afternoon on the Avon at Stratford while I talked about him. That was when you were playing at the Shakespeare Memorial Theatre, and I was trying, unsuccessfully, to get you reconciled to the smallness of your parts. You will remember that we spoke about the qualities that make the great actor, for the subject is one we have often talked about. Not that you were a great actor, except potentially, as I with parental partiality or critical insight thought, or that Barker himself was a great actor. He was a fascinating actor, whom I always thought it worth while to see, whatever he did. But he was a great man of the theatre, that rare combination of actor, producer, and dramatist. Above everything, he was a stage producer, by far the greatest of any whose work I have seen.

It is because I recognize in you the same meticulous, wholehearted care for acting that Barker had, and because you have the promise of the essential qualities of the actor, that I dedicate this book to you. Granville Barker's concern with the actor was because upon the actor the theatre depends. Without the dramatist the actor cannot work, and without the producer he may not perform the play as it is written, but unless he, the actor, is possessed of the energy that creates the actual presence of poetic reality by which the spectator is raised to the imaginative level on which the play lives, the theatre is nothing.

In discussing in these pages Barker's acting and producing methods, I have had you in mind. I have told the story of Barker's life, and examined his achievements and failures, his aims, his disappointments, and how he deserted the theatre for scholarship, for you and your contemporaries, but particularly for you. His is a remarkable story, not to be told without pain for what the theatre lost in him. Yet the sum of what he did was considerable and its quality high, so that no one interested in the theatre, and certainly no one whose future lies there, can afford to neglect its study.

v

Every account of the English stage in the first three decades of this century contains a tribute to Granville Barker as producer, dramatist, and critic of Shakespeare, and these tributes continue; but so far there has been no account of his life and no study of his work as a whole. This lack I have endeavoured to remedy.

It is said of him that Barker planned his life as ten years actor, ten years producer, and ten years writer; and it is a fact that from 1894 to 1904 he was an actor, a producer from 1904 to 1914, and a writer for the rest of his life. That is why I have divided the book into these three parts, with an intervening fourth part. Of course, his activities overlapped. He was a writer always, and an actor when he became a producer, though his acting ceased, and even when he had given up the stage he continued intermittently to produce to the end. I am inclined to think that when he spoke of the plan it was in retrospect. The important thing to note is that, as with all men, his life and work were one.

The lineaments of the later Barker are to be distinguished in the young, eager, and high-spirited young man, but there were also the lineaments of another man who might have been. We can see them in his longing for a National Theatre in London, and had that longing been satisfied he would have ended a different man. What wrecked his life was the indifference to the need of a National Theatre, and the impossibility of continuing his work on the stage without it. Through what he did and the efforts of others that theatre has now been promised by Parliament, but the need for it is as urgent to-day as when Barker longed for it, and staked his future upon it. Without a National Theatre the English-speaking stage is devoid of the artistic basis essential to its existence. I hope you will see that theatre, and that its coming will not be delayed.

Granville Barker cared little for films, and did not have the opportunities that have opened for you in that sphere. Had he been a young man to-day I do not know if he would have invaded Hollywood as you have done; I doubt it. It is unlikely that even the London film studios would have drawn him, though the realistic elements of his art would have had extraordinary scope there. He belonged to the theatre, as you essentially do. But in the sphere of the film the same principles hold good as in all the artist is called upon to do, to work with sincerity and with all his heart. You have often told me that your aim is to be a good workman; that is why I think this book will mean something to you. Here it is, with your father's blessing.

C. B. PURDOM.

Welwyn Garden City, Hertfordshire.
  31 *August,* 1955.

FOREWORD

AS one of the dwindling band who served with Granville Barker in those far-off Court Theatre days my remembrance of him is one of vital sensitive youth and energy, a lithe, athletic figure, warm brown eyes, thick red-brown hair, tidily parted till he pushed his fingers through it, and an air of relaxed concentration ready to spring in a flash to action or laughter. I remember the confidence he inspired in us all by knowing thoroughly every play before he began to rehearse it. He would start by reading it to us, more for its sense than for characterization or drama. There was no preliminary exposition and no touch of director's jargon or pretentious analysis. We started rehearsing without even being told more of our characters than the stage directions told us, to see what the actors themselves first made of them. Then he would start moulding us in the direction he wanted, using every device of witty illustration and metaphor to stimulate the actor's own imagination. If the actor's view of a character differed from his, but was still loyal to the author, he would frequently accept it and incline the whole production to meet it as far as necessary. I remember, for instance, his adoption of Dennis Eadie's reading of Henry in *The Return of the Prodigal* as " a man whose breath smelt ".

He always assumed that everyone was as keen as he on research into and expression of the author's meaning, and the motives, thoughts, and emotions of his characters, evoking the actor's enthusiasm and making everyone contribute his utmost. With his amazingly sensitive ear for speech and silence, his expressive hands and flexible body he could always help everyone to give clear expression to any ideas the actor or he wanted to convey. He would often demonstrate a rhythm or phrasing or emphasis, but seldom give an intonation, and always with the caution that it was given only to convey the thought, and must be made the actor's own before use. Then by detailed criticism he would make it subtler and more musical. This fine polishing went on right up to the last rehearsal, always by notes taken during the run of a scene, not by interrupting the flow. By the time the performance came, the whole piece was moulded into a musical and rhythmic pattern as definite as a symphony, where every word and phrase, every silence, every intonation had been scrutinized and accepted as the best he could achieve with his

vii

material. Careful over such matters as grouping, moves, scenery, and lighting, he was interested only so far as they directly affected the acting to which everything else was subordinated.

His death was a heavy loss to Shakespeare criticism and to the drama; but to us of the theatre, and especially to those of us who worked with him and for him and who learnt from him what the theatre meant and drew inspiration from his dazzling imagination and intelligence, the blow fell thirty years earlier when he gave up the struggle, threw off the dust of battle, and became a mere professor. To us it was almost a desertion, and we found it hard to forgive him. Always we would have left all and followed him if he had returned from his self-banishment; but it was not to be. Perhaps it was not his fault. The best theatre, always in advance of the public, seldom pays. There must be a patron, a subsidy, or some compromise with public taste. He came at a time when the wealthy patron of taste was dying out, and before the State had recognized the value and necessity of subsidy; and he would not compromise.

We few left that loved him and worked with him in those long-lost days still feel a loyalty to him and for what he stood for, and still try to carry on his tradition and the work he left. In our time, if ever, the theatre will not look upon his like again.

Mr. Purdom has made a fascinating story of his life and offers his own acute summary of his work, which is not only of historical importance to the English-speaking theatre but still continues to influence it.

LEWIS CASSON.

ACKNOWLEDGMENTS

WITHOUT the letters of Bernard Shaw to Granville Barker this book would hardly have been written and I owe great thanks to Lady Keeble (Miss Lillah McCarthy) for letting me use them, and for her papers and recollections, which she has made fully available to me. As the letters are being published independently, in London and New York, with a commentary by me, I have quoted them hardly at all in the following pages.

In writing the book I have relied upon personal knowledge, or upon documents, or letters, or statements made to me, or upon newspapers and books. As only very few letters by Barker have ever been published, I have printed many of his letters, and have relied upon them throughout to a great extent. I think it will be agreed that he was a good letter-writer. Unfortunately, except for two late ones, his letters to Bernard Shaw have disappeared: almost certainly they were destroyed. Most of his letters were undated, which presented certain problems, but they offer aspects of Barker of much interest.

I owe special thanks to Dr. Gilbert Murray for a large collection of letters, to Mr. Herbert Thomas for unpublished plays, written in collaboration, and his early memories, to Sir Lewis Casson for the Foreword and for much information, and to the late Allan Wade. Also to Mr. Nicholas Hannen, Sir John Gielgud, Mr. Harcourt Williams, Madame Cammaerts, Miss Edyth Olive, Miss Christine Silver, Mr. Michael MacOwan, Miss Maud Burt, Professor J. M. Cocking, Mr. Austin Gill, Mr. George Rylands, Mrs. Geoffrey Whitworth, the Right Hon. Sir Cuthbert Headlam, Bt., Sir George Barnes, Sir Kenneth Barnes, Professor G. B. Harrison, Miss Blanche Patch, Mr. John van Druten, Mr. H. F. Rubinstein, Sir R. C. K. Ensor, Mr. Malcolm Morley, Mr. Joseph Macleod, Messrs. Raymond Mander and Joe Mitchenson, Mr. G. W. Nash (Enthoven Collection, Victoria and Albert Museum), Mr. J. M. Granville, Maître Robert Martin, and Mrs. Georgina Masters, to all of whom, and to others unnamed, I am deeply grateful.

I am much indebted to Sir Max Beerbohm for permission to reproduce a drawing made for Barker, also for some verses he addressed to him.

I am also much indebted to Lady Cynthia Asquith for permission to print a number of letters from Sir J. M. Barrie, and for allowing me to quote from her book *A Portrait of Barrie* (James Barrie, 1954).

ix

Permission to include a letter from Dr. John Masefield, O.M., has been granted by him and the Society of Authors, and the Society of Authors and the Public Trustee have given permission for the publication of letters from Bernard Shaw.

After his second marriage, Barker hyphenated his name, but as it would be confusing to adopt two ways of printing his name, before and after hyphenation, I have decided to print his name throughout as Granville Barker, without the hyphen.

The List of Writings is the outcome of several years' labour of love by Mr. Frederick May and Miss Margery M. Morgan, and is as complete as it is possible to make it; unpublished work is included therein. I am indebted to them for enabling me to print it.

C. B. P.

CONTENTS

ILLUSTRATIONS

xiii

PART ONE

ACTOR

WITH the presence of Harley Granville Barker in the world of the theatre at the opening of this century there arrived new elements that are still developing in plays, acting, and stage production. He and his friends brought a new attitude to the stage, and, so far as England is concerned, he was the first of the modern producers. As dramatist and critic he was a product of the stage, for he earned his living there as a boy, and he was essentially an actor all his life. An account of his friendships, his work in the theatre, why he left it, and what he did afterwards, is not only a piece of theatrical history that needs to be preserved: it is a story of the human heart of immense interest.

In the year 1877, when Granville Barker was born, the drama was at a low ebb. In later life Barker once said he was disposed to write a paper on the theatre of the 'seventies " as it might have been ". He would have had plenty of scope; for while there was much talent, there was little result. Something like four new plays a week were performed in London's twenty theatres, but they were poor stuff, mostly adaptations from the French, and not one is remembered. The attention of imaginative writers was absorbed in novels, among whom Thomas Hardy, George Meredith, Samuel Butler, Robert Louis Stevenson, Anthony Trollope, and H. Rider Haggard tried their hands at plays without success. Money-making and religion were the main interests of the nation, riding high on the profits of the Industrial Revolution, and the arts had a low place.

The popular dramatists of the 'seventies were H. J. Byron, whose *Our Boys* was approaching the third year of its run, James Albery, Charles Reade, F. C. Burnard, Dion Boucicault, and T. W. Robertson; the latter had died, six years before Barker's birth, at the age of forty-two. Spectacular Shakespearian performances continued to be the glory of the stage. At the Lyceum, Henry Irving produced *Richard III* in January 1877, and the year before Alfred Tennyson's *Queen Mary*, while at the end of 1877 the early Gilbert and Sullivan comic opera, *The Sorcerer*, appeared at the Opéra Comique and, a year later, *H.M.S. Pinafore*. Otherwise dramatic poetry was represented by the works of W. G. Wills and Tom Taylor.

The stage was in the hands of Mrs. Bateman and Henry Irving, the

Bancrofts, John Hare, J. L. Toole, J. B. Buckstone, and John Hollings-
head; Charles Wyndham had appeared at the Criterion Theatre two years
earlier. There were managers, however, of whom Dion Boucicault had
written in an angry letter to his friend Charles Reade:

Few . . . could compose a bill of the play where the spelling and
grammar would not disgrace an urchin under ten years of age.

And a writer in *The Theatre* in August 1878 had said:

the career of the stage player is necessarily opposed to the conditions of
decent and decorous society; the actor is regarded as an outcast, the
actress as something worse.

The state of the theatre was always under discussion, some writers considering it to be "moving onward and upward", and in the same year,
1878, there was a strong plea, not made for the first time, for a subsidized
national theatre.

Bernard Shaw had come to London in April 1876, when he was
approaching twenty.

Harley Granville Barker was born there the year after, on 25 November
1877, at 3A Sheffield Terrace, a road that runs east and west between
Kensington Church Street and Campden Hill Road. The house disappeared some fifty years ago to make way for a block of flats. The
kind of house it was may perhaps be judged from the buildings on the
north side of the terrace, small, three-storied, stucco-faced, early Victorian
houses, by no means unpleasant to look at. Barker's early years remain
in obscurity, which he afterwards fostered; for, unlike his friend, Shaw,
who never tired of writing about his parents, childhood, and youth,
Barker dropped a curtain upon his origins. He never spoke about his
parents or his childhood.

Yet on the side of both his parents Barker had reasons for a little pride.
The Barker family has traced its descent from Randulph de Calverhall (or
Coverall), who was tenant of the Manor of Adderley, near Ightfield,
Salop, in 1200, though this is a matter of speculation. What appears to
be certain is that our Barker's great-grandfather, Joseph Gibbs Barker, was
born at Birmingham in 1774, lived and carried on business in the linen
trade in London, then, under the influence of Evangelicalism, gave up
business to become Lay Secretary to the London Society for Promoting
Christianity among the Jews, in which office he continued for sixteen
years, when he retired to live in Hereford; he died in 1864. He had a
son, Joseph Henry Barker, who was chaplain to the Hereford gaol and
infirmary and died in 1903 at the age of ninety-three. The Reverend
Joseph's fifth son by a second marriage, Albert James Barker, was born at

II Granville Barker aged 14

III Granville Barker's mother

IV Granville Barker in the sailor's suit he wore
for his recitations

V   Herbert Thomas

VI   John Masefield

VII   Granville Barker with William Archer

VIII   Granville Barker with Gilbert Murray a
Rosamund

Hereford on 30 January 1856, and became Harley's father. The name Harley was the Christian name of Albert's mother's father, Harley Thomas. Albert's eldest brother, Edwin, born in 1839, was an architect, and his eldest sister, Emily, born in 1838, also married a Hereford architect, Thomas Nicholson, and later Albert described himself as an architect. At the time of his son Harley's birth he got a living in London by converting houses into flats, and letting or selling them. Afterwards he was engaged in the disposal of land on the Howard de Walden estate at Bexhill-on-Sea. Albert James Barker seems to have made no success of his life, though proud of his family connections; he was of medium height, dark-haired, bald, with a black-pointed beard, thin-faced, active, nervous, excitable, an interminable talker, and consumptive. He died of that disease in France in 1909, aged fifty-three, when his son was already famous.

On Barker's mother's side a more colourful story can be told, for his father had married on 12 February 1877 Mary Elisabeth Bozzi-Granville, who was the granddaughter of a distinguished physician, Augustus Bozzi, born in Italy in 1783. Bozzi had assumed the name of Granville in 1806, when he was twenty-three, that being the name of his grandmother, born in Italy, daughter of Bevil Granville, a Cornish gentleman who had settled there. Augustus Bozzi was an ardent republican; he had the diploma of doctor of medicine from the University of Pavia in 1802, and afterwards became surgeon to the British fleet. He settled in England as Bozzi-Granville, married in 1809 Mary Ann Kerr, daughter of Joseph Kerr of Blackheath, became M.R.C.S. and L.R.C.P., joined the Anglican Church, was Vice-President of the British Medical Association and a Fellow of the Royal Society. He was a man of immense energy, lively, witty, and learned. He wrote many books, including his (unfinished) autobiography. In 1811 he published *Critical Observations on Mr. Kemble's Performance at the Theatre Royal, Liverpool*, where he lived at that time. This indicates a youthful interest in the theatre, and he records himself that he attended Mrs. Siddons for insomnia. His son, Augustus Kerr Bozzi-Granville, born in 1816, the fourth of seven children, was educated at Cambridge, and had no fewer than thirteen children, of whom nine survived infancy, the third being Mary Elisabeth, born in 1849. Mary Elisabeth was thus twenty-eight years of age when Harley was born, her husband being twenty-one. There was a daughter, Grace Alexandra, born on 30 January 1882, but no more children. Grace died in France of tuberculosis in 1917, aged thirty-five.

Mrs. Mary Elisabeth Barker gained a living as a reciter and bird-mimic, under the name of Miss Granville. She was a fair, stocky, charming, sentimental woman; her large repertoire consisted of popular poems, and she was something of a success on the public platform in this country and America at a time when poetry recitals were a regular form of cultural entertainment. Harley took after his mother in appearance. Indeed, there was a marked Granville family likeness in the shape of the head and his complexion. There appeared to be little of his father in him except volubility and delicacy of constitution. In fact, he cultivated the Granville side.

Mrs. Barker's tours were managed by her husband. She brought her son, Harley, with her, teaching him to recite, and he appeared on the platform in a sailor suit, glaring at the audience, while he recited " The Boy Stood on the Burning Deck " and other poems. As he grew older he was promoted to an Eton collar and to reciting pieces from Shakespeare, including " To be or not to be ". Though he must have hated this life, for he was a highly intelligent, sensitive, and not a very robust child, he got a taste for the stage. Popular as she was, Miss Granville was hardly in the front rank of artists, and worked usually in assembly rooms and small halls. When her husband was working at Bexhill-on-Sea they took the Kursaal for a summer season, when she appeared in straight plays, which gave some pain to her young son. She died in the South of France in 1925, aged seventy-six.

*

Barker could not have received much education, apart from poetry and Shakespeare, for his mother, upon whom the household mainly depended, was often out of an engagement, and there was very little money. In the spring of 1891, at the age of thirteen, he was with his mother at Harrogate and made his first public appearance in a play. According to the *Harrogate Herald* of 27 May, the part of Dr. Grimstone in Edward Rose's adaptation of F. Anstey's story, *Vice Versa*, at the Spa Rooms was taken by " – Barker ". He appears to have been given the part in an emergency in a company of juveniles organized by the lessee, Charles F. Dawson. It is said that, compared with the other players, he showed great confidence.

That he was an assiduous playgoer at that early age is shown by the programmes he kept of visits to the Lyceum to see Henry Irving in *Much Ado About Nothing*, *Charles I*, and other plays, and of Augustus Daly's season at the same theatre. That year, 1891, he was sent to Sarah Thorne's theatrical school at Margate to prepare for a stage career, as he had to earn his own living. Sarah Thorne, a famous name in late nineteenth-century provincial theatrical history, had many who afterwards became well-known players at her school, and to act in her stock company at the Theatre Royal, Margate, of which she was lessee and manager. On her programmes was printed, " The plays produced under the direction of Sarah Thorne ". Her company also toured the Kentish and Sussex towns. The Theatre Royal, which was opened in 1787 by authority of a royal licence, had its career as a theatre interrupted after her death in 1899. In her advertisements for pupils for her school, Sarah Thorne announced (in 1888) that she had thirty-five ladies and thirty-two youths.

Barker stayed with Sarah Thorne for a matter of months only, doubtless because there was no money to pay fees for him, but he went on tour with the company, playing, among other parts, Paris to Evelyn Millard's Juliet. At Margate, however, he became acquainted with Berte Thomas, nine years older than himself, who, having come into a little bit of money, was training for a stage career. Thomas, handsome, lively, and intelligent, had aspirations as a dramatist, which afterwards, when they met in London, led to suggestions to Barker that they should collaborate in playwriting, to the results of which we shall come. Barker, says Thomas, was then " always with his head in a book and always asking questions ". Their working together continued on and off over a number of years, but, says Thomas, though always very friendly, they were never great friends, for it was not possible to penetrate Barker's skin : he let people see as much as he wanted them to know about himself and no more.

After several engagements in touring companies, " Mr. G. Barker " made his first appearance on the stage in London on 19 May 1892 in the part of the 3rd Young Man in Charles Brookfield's musical piece, *The Poet and the Puppets*, at the Comedy Theatre. This was followed by " Mr. Granvill Barker " playing the part of Claudie in the same dramatist's piece, *To-day*. Though Barker afterwards spoke well of Brookfield, he was filled with disgust when many years later the dramatist was appointed Examiner of Plays.

As usual with young actors, Barker then disappears for some years from the records of the London stage. His cousin, the Rev. Francis W. Allen of Hereford, says in a letter :

I remember staying with his parents at Cheney Court, Chelsea, and finding him stage managing a play at Chelsea Hospital with absolute assurance when he was I think no more than sixteen.

In his book, *Miss Horniman*, Rex Pogson says that Barker understudied in the season at the Avenue Theatre in 1894 when Shaw's *Arms and the Man* was first performed, but although Mr. Pogson says Miss Horniman was positive about it, I think it unlikely, for he certainly did not come to Shaw's notice. He did, however, play in A. B. Tapping's touring company, in Lewis Waller's and other companies, and then joined Ben Greet's Shakespeare and Old English Comedy Company in 1895, when he was seventeen; at his mother's request he was looked after by Claire

Paunceforth, who played old ladies' parts and who was also in charge of young Edyth Olive; all three roomed together. In Ben Greet's company he met Lillah McCarthy, and played Paris to her Juliet. Barker took his work very seriously, was fond of walking, and read a great deal, especially the poets and Dickens. Ben Greet was at that time a strict producer, and everyone in the company had to work hard.

*

He had also started playwriting in collaboration with Berte Thomas, and a piece called *A Comedy of Fools* was completed, but after being offered unsuccessfully to a number of managements the manuscript was torn up. This was in 1895, and a year later another play was completed, a tragedy in four acts entitled *The Family of the Oldroyds*, which was never produced or published, though the manuscript survives. That year, 1896, he was at the Theatre Royal, Haymarket, playing with Charles Hawtrey in *Under the Red Robe*. In July the following year a performance is recorded at Kingston-on-Thames, when he played Hastings in *She Stoops to Conquer*, with Gordon Craig as young Marlow. He went on writing, however, and in 1897 completed with Berte Thomas *The Weather-hen, or Invertebrata*. There was no more recorded stagework until on 20 February 1899 Mrs. Patrick Campbell revived Pinero's *The Second Mrs. Tanqueray* at the Prince of Wales, Kennington, in which play Barker had the part of Gordon Jayne, M.D. "Mrs. Campbell's company certainly does not realize Mrs. Tanqueray for me", wrote the *Sketch* critic. This was followed by *The Notorious Mrs. Ebbsmith*, in which he had the part of Antonio Poppi. The company went on tour, when at Newcastle-on-Tyne on 15 March 1899 Barker read the part of Lucius Septimus in the copyrighting performance of Shaw's *Caesar and Cleopatra*, Mrs. Patrick Campbell reading Cleopatra. On 15 May they came back to London with *Mrs. Tanqueray*, with Barker in another small part in it. On 19 June Gilbert Murray's *Carlyon Sahib* was put on for a fortnight at Kennington with Barker as Selim, but the piece was a failure, and was taken off after a week. All these were small parts, but the last was important to Barker, for it brought him into touch with Gilbert Murray, who became one of his closest friends.

What was equally important was that on 29 June 1899 a matinée performance was given at Terry's Theatre of *The Weather-hen*, with Madge McIntosh in the leading part. It was so successful that the play was put into the evening bill at the Comedy Theatre from 9 July until the 20th. A. B. Walkley in *The Times* found it to contain "a well-worn theme . . . treated in a fresh and interesting manner". In the weekly critical paper, *The Academy*, St. John Hankin devoted a page article to it, finding the play perhaps "too clever for the London stage", but "wonderfully stimulating ". Barker was greatly pleased, and a fruitful friend-ship with Hankin was started. He was still actively writing with Berte Thomas, who was then in Mrs. Patrick Campbell's company, and that year they finished *Our Visitor to Work-a-day*, a melodrama with an unhappy ending, preserved in the British Museum, but not performed, and also started on a dramatization of Thackeray's *Henry Esmond*, which was never completed. In fact, the collaboration broke up, for the ways of the two men no longer ran together. It is hardly possible to overrate Thomas's influence on Barker at this early period, for while their talents were not on the same level, the elder man was a stabilizing as well as an encouraging element. Thomas first appeared in London at the Hay-market Theatre in March 1894 under Herbert Beerbohm Tree, and remained in Tree's company for some years. He wrote a number of plays, the last in 1923. Barker never forgot him. He had several parts in the Court Theatre productions, and appeared also in *The Dynasts*.

It was at this time that Barker, through Gilbert Murray, got to know William Archer. Murray and Archer had met in July 1895, when Charles Charrington (actor friend of Shaw's and early exponent of Ibsen, with his wife, Janet Achurch) had sent Archer the play, *Carlyon Sahib*. Archer wrote that it was " a curiously grim and powerful, though un-skilful piece of work, which interested me very much; then Murray came to see me, and we discussed the play, and he showed me another one, not nearly so good, and I sat upon it, and we struck up quite a friend-ship." [1] Murray was deeply interested in Archer's translations of Ibsen, and the two discussed at length the treatment of Greek tragedy, Archer " pressing the claims of verse and the more ideal treatment, Murray in-clining more and more to prose and realism ". The outcome was that Murray's next play, *Andromache*, " shaped itself somewhat on the lines of a rather more realistic Ibsen saga play ". It was performed at the Garrick Theatre on 25 February two years later and was highly praised: " an experiment that many people would be sorry to have missed ", said *The Times*. Barker developed his friendship with Murray and Archer, and both encouraged him in his playwriting. He also got to know the Charringtons, whose socialism and ideas about plays appealed to him.

He was working with increasing distaste upon the stage. Neither the plays he had to appear in nor the conditions of the theatre satisfied him. He made next to nothing, was poor and shabby; but this good-looking, thin, but highly attractive young man, impatient, critical, and keen to learn, was increasing his friendships. He understudied in a piece by C. B. Fernald entitled *Moonlight Blossom*, produced at the Prince of Wales

---

[1] Lieut.-Colonel Charles Archer, " Gilbert Murray and William Archer, 1895–1924 ", in *Essays in Honour of Gilbert Murray* (1936), p. 31.

under Mrs. Patrick Campbell's management on 21 September 1899, and afterwards had the part of Albert Bailey in *The Canary*, by George Fleming, produced at the same theatre on 15 November.

*

It was not surprising that Barker came into the orbit of William Poel, for the two men had much in common, and on the afternoon of 11 November 1899 he made his mark as an actor as Richard II in William Poel's production of Shakespeare's play at the Lecture Theatre, Burlington Gardens. His performance was highly praised by A. B. Walkley:

A fair all-round representation of Richard II was all that was expected. Yet the play had hardly started before it was clear that there was one player in the company whose talent would make the performance exceptionally interesting. A few months ago that oddly named piece *The Weather-hen* showed Mr. Granville Barker in the light of a promising dramatist. *Richard II* proved him to be also a well-graced and intelligent actor, with gifts specially fitting him for romantic drama. . . . Gay and princely in the first two acts, Mr. Barker played the later scenes with a decided sense of character, and with pathos that seemed to touch every section of his rather difficult audience.

The audience was difficult because Poel's methods were difficult, but they appealed to this young man, twenty-five years his junior, and more than thirty years after Barker wrote to Poel:

. . . such light as has shone for me upon WS dates from an earlier day on which you came to York Buildings to see me and shook all my previous convictions by showing me how you wanted the first lines of *Richard II* spoken.

In his biography, Robert Speaight relates how at one rehearsal of this play Poel " locked his actors in a room and declared that he would keep them there until they had mastered his inflections. They remained incarcerated for most of the night." There can be no doubt that Barker owed much to this tyrant of a producer.

*

He was now approaching a decisive year in his career. On 25 February 1900 he appeared at the third " meeting " of the Stage Society, formed the year before, in the part of Erik Bratsberg in William Archer's version of Ibsen's *The League of Youth* at the Vaudeville Theatre, produced by Charles Charrington. Here in the Stage Society he entered a circle of enthusiasts after his own heart, for their interest in the theatre was in its social significance : to them the drama was an art of high social value, which is what Barker himself thought. He was excited with the possibilities of the theatre in hands guided by aims different from the desire for personal exploitation and money-making. It was a great moment for him.

Early the next month, on 7 March, he took over the part of Lieutenant Maxon Wendowski, previously played by Albert Gran, in *Magda* at the Royalty. This was the occasion of a quarrel with Mrs. Patrick Campbell, for Gran came back into the play, and Barker lost his job. He claimed that in accordance with theatrical custom he was entitled to his salary for the run of the piece, and brought an action against the manageress. Mrs. Pat tells the story in her memoirs, in which she says:

I was interested in the idea of being in a court, and dressed myself in my best. Mr. Barker, on the other hand, seemed to me to appear in very shabby clothes and a much-worn straw hat.[1]

She lost her case, her stage manager not being able to remember what he had said at the interview when Barker was engaged, and Barker got £60. Her solicitor advised her to shake hands with the victor and congratulate him, but she records that " Mr. Granville Barker did not look as triumphant as I thought he ought to, and I will go to my grave believing that he owes me £60 ".[2]

None the less, Barker was making great strides in the direction in which he desired to go, and on the following 29 April he made his first appearance as a producer at another "meeting" of the Stage Society at the Globe Theatre, when three short plays, Maeterlinck's *Interior* and *The Death of Tintagiles*, and Fiona MacLeod's *The House of Usna*, were done. These Stage Society meetings were Sunday-evening and Monday-afternoon performances, so that they did not interfere with Barker's work in the theatre, but they meant more to this young man of twenty-two than perhaps to any other person connected with the society, with the exception of Bernard Shaw. For after another Stage Society performance in the part of Robert in Gerhart Hauptmann's *The Coming of Peace* at the Vaudeville Theatre on 10 June, he played Eugene in Bernard Shaw's *Candida*, produced for the society by Janet Achurch at the Strand Theatre on 1 July. The date is to be remembered as that of the coming together of these two men.

It is more than likely that Shaw and Barker had met before, but now they became firm friends. But Henry Arthur Jones[3] some years earlier had suggested to Shaw that Barker was the man for Eugene, having seen him in Poel's production of *Richard II*. Shaw had not seen that performance. Shaw found in the young Barker not only a mere actor,

---

[1] *My Life and Some Letters* (1922), p. 147.
[2] *Ibid.*, p. 148.
[3] *The Life and Letters of Henry Arthur Jones*, p. 205.

much as he valued actors who could perform his plays, but a sensitive, quick, and lively mind bursting with undeveloped energies, and inclined, too, towards the social outlook he desired most to encourage. He wrote to Henry Arthur Jones after his friendship with Barker had developed :

How do you get on with Granville Barker? Do you realize that he is a great poet and dramatist who feels towards us as we feel towards Sheridan Knowles? [1]

In his old age he wrote of the young Barker :

He had a strong strain of Italian blood in him, and looked as if he had stepped out of a picture by Benozzo Gozzoli. He had a wide literary culture and a fastidiously delicate taste in every branch of art. He could write in a too precious but exquisitely fine style. He was self-willed, restlessly industrious, sober and quite sane. He had Shakespear and Dickens at his finger ends. Altogether the most distinguished and incomparably the most cultivated person whom circumstances had driven into the theatre at that time. [2]

Shaw was vivacious and exhilarating, tall and lean, with a white face, pale blue eyes, reddish hair, and straggling beard. Barker, too, had reddish hair, not so red as Shaw's, nor was he so tall as Shaw, but very thin, with dark eyes and irrepressible vitality. Barker found in Shaw one who possessed dramatic creativeness of a new order in the theatre, who had, too, the skill to express a full mind on a great range of subjects outside it. Their major common interests were in the theatre, but the life of society and the reform of social conditions were regarded as the background to the theatre's life, as they shared in it and set out to transform it. At the same time as he got to know Shaw, Barker became acquainted with Dr. C. E. Wheeler, a famous homœopathic physician, who had translated (with Janet Achurch) the Hauptmann play performed by the Stage Society. Dr. Wheeler was a highly cultivated man, and Barker became a constant visitor at his house in Kingston, and a friend of Penelope Wheeler, his wife, who was interested in acting. In the Wheelers' house Barker was usually called " David ", which was his father's name for him, though his mother called him " Gran ". Shaw called him " Barker " – sometimes " G.B."

Bernard Shaw had gone to live in the Adelphi in 1898, where the lady he married had a flat, and when Barker got to know Shaw he took a room at 8 York Buildings, not far away, where his mother looked after him, for his parents went to live in rooms on the other side of the street.

---

[1] *The Life and Letters of Henry Arthur Jones*, p. 211.
[2] *Drama*, Winter, 1946.

Among Barker's other friends was the actress, Winifred Fraser, and her husband, George Foss, at whose house in Croydon he was a frequent visitor. Experimenting with his writing, he wrote for her a short play in what would now be regarded as verse, the dialogue being in short lines, entitled *A Miracle*. The following is an extract:

> We are forbidden to rise above ourselves
> We never sank below ourselves
> Body and soul inextricably commingled
> So when the little inch of wax is burnt
> Must not the light go out too?
> I have no faith in Heaven or care for faith
> It seems to me I am already dead
> Presently when I fall asleep
> Will begin my dissolution.
> As a dead leaf flutters from a tree
> So shall I put from the world.
> As a shell lies upon the sea shore
> So will my body be
> Death is extermination.
> Indeed . . . Indeed . . . I am already dead.

There are two characters, women, and the theme is love; but dramatically the piece is not clear. It was not done on the stage until seven years later, at a private performance by Miss Fraser, when Barker was famous, but he had nothing to do with it. Why he wrote in verse is not clear, for Barker displayed no verse-making gifts at any time. Perhaps it had something to do with Shaw's blank verse effort with his own novel,[1] made a little later; or Barker was in love.

Still in the commercial theatre, he had the part of " the licentious Earl of Rochester " in *English Nell*, by Anthony Hope and Edward Rose, at the Prince of Wales Theatre on 21 August 1900, in which Marie Tempest appeared as Nell Gwyn. He felt himself a slave in the field of theatrical commerce, but was soon to escape from it, and the closing year of the century marked his way of escape. Before the year ended, on 16 December, at the eighth " meeting " of the Stage Society, he appeared as Captain Kearney in Bernard Shaw's *Captain Brassbound's Conversion* at the Strand Theatre, afterwards at the Criterion on the 20th. From Shaw's correspondence it is clear that Barker did not want to play the part, and was more or less forced into it by his friend, who was by no means sparing of his criticism of the manner in which he rehearsed it – " Could you join an American Club for a week?" he asked him – and

---

[1] Shaw made his novel *Cashel Byron's Profession* into the stage play in blank verse – *The Admirable Bashville*.

was not pleased with the result. The correspondence shows that Shaw was already treating the young man on the basis of intimacy; he saw that Barker was not satisfied with what he was doing on the stage "in its present miserable condition". "Meanwhile", he added, "you give me the *quality* of work I want; and I hope to get more of it out of you before you get tired of it."

★

The eighteen-nineties, in which Barker had come to manhood, was a period of new birth. Holbrook Jackson, who was himself its product, wrote in his admired book, *The Eighteen-nineties*:

The awakening of the 'nineties does not appear to be the realization of a purpose but the realization of a possibility. Life aroused curiosity. People became enthusiastic about the way it should be used. And in proof of sincerity there were opinionated battles – most of them inconclusive. But they were not wasted on that account, for the very circumstances of idea pitting itself against idea, vision against vision, cleared the way for more definite action when the time ripened. It was an epoch of experiment with some achievement and some remorse.[1]

To that awakening Barker belonged. He carried on its enthusiasms and waged its battles into the new century. He never, in fact, lost the exciting atmosphere of the time so far as the theatre was concerned. The puritan objection to the theatre was still strong. Barker was a whole-hearted fighter against it, and undoubtedly his attack did much to undermine the prejudices that prevailed in the minds of earnest people in the late nineteenth century, who associated the theatre with loose living, late hours, drinking, and a gay time, so that good church and chapel people had to frown upon it. Many respectable families – including, I may mention, my own – went only to the pantomime at Christmas, which was regarded as less vicious than other forms of drama. Yet of this time, William Sharp, one of the founders of the Stage Society, wrote in his book, *Vistas*:

A great creative period is at hand, probably a great dramatic epoch. But what will for one thing differentiate it from any predecessor is the new complexity, in appreciation, in formative conception, in imaginative rendering.[2]

This was to look forward to more than the relaxation of prejudice, to a new drama, and a new art of the theatre. What characterized the drama of the new century was, indeed, the new moral fervour with which those who were engaged in it were imbued. To them the theatre was much more than a place of entertainment. For this conception the plays of

[1] p. 12.   [2] Quoted in Jackson, *op. cit.*, p. 7.

Ibsen, strongly assailed on moral grounds, were directly responsible. Those who attacked them as well as those who defended them did so on moral principles. To those who admired them, the theatre had become a school of morality, and it is now clear that, bitterly as the opponents of the new drama objected, and firmly as they were supported by the censorship, they had finally lost the battle though still in possession of the field. Of course, this quarrel in the name of morality had raged about the theatre since it was first established in London; the quarrel had never been resolved, and was continually flaring up. With the opening of the new century it entered a new phase, for there was a deep sense of the value of the drama as a means of culture. This inspired those responsible for the theatre societies, starting with the Independent Theatre, founded by J. T. Grein in 1891. This naturalized Dutchman had as his model Antoine's Théâtre Libre, founded in Paris in 1887, an amateur theatre, which Grein's was not, though the professionals in his society's performances were unpaid. He called his society an English Théâtre Libre. Literary and social culture was also the object of William Archer in the New Century Theatre in 1897, when Grein's society had died. It was the same with the Stage Society, formed in 1899 under Fabian Society influence.

I do not propose to discuss the work of the societies, as I have referred to the relevant facts elsewhere. Barker's association with William Poel brought him deeply into the new moral ferment, for Poel was an ethical reformer, as Barker, too, became, but the latter was never connected with the Independent Theatre or with Grein, except that in March 1901 he appeared in the second matinée of a light comedy translated from the French of Édouard Paillenon, *Le Monde où l'on s'ennuie*, by Grein and another, and given at the Comedy Theatre, where he played the part of Paul Raymond and was hailed by the *Star* critic: " Mr. Barker is a coming actor." This was under the aegis of the *Sunday Special* newspaper, with which Grein was connected, but the important point was that the producer was Max Behrend.

At another matinée under the same auspices the following month Barker appeared as the producer of an Israel Zangwill play, and as Napoleon in Shaw's *The Man of Destiny*, when he was greeted by Walkley in *The Times* as follows:

That clever young actor Mr. Granville Barker seemed to realize the situation and he made no great effort to create character. But both he and Miss Halstan spoke up briskly and kept the ball rolling *sans* intermission. The performance was certainly entertaining. . . .

Shaw's prompt copy of this production is in the Enthoven Collection at the Victoria and Albert Museum : there are many notes on the interleaved pages.

★

Always writing, Barker had completed another play by the beginning of 1901, entitled *Agnes Colander*, which he thought well enough of to keep for the rest of his life, though he seems never to have spoken of it or shown it to anyone, so far as the records go. He called it " An Experiment " and made up his mind to destroy it, but did not. It is in three acts, with six characters, and concerns the problem of what a woman is to do with her life. Having read it, I can say that it is no more than a first sketch of a play, and is unlikely ever to be printed or performed; but it shows Barker to be thinking fruitfully and working hard.

Throughout the early months of the year Barker was still engaged at the Prince of Wales Theatre in *English Nell*; in May he was with Charles Wyndham, playing Fergusson Pybus in a revival of *The Case of Rebellious Susan* at Wyndham's Theatre, and on 27 August he appeared again at the Prince of Wales as Mr. Wenham in *Becky Sharp*, by Robert Hichens and Cosmo Gordon Lennox. This was his last engagement for the time being in the commercial theatre.

He was greatly developing his friendship with the Shaws, being constantly at their house in Hertfordshire, Mrs. Shaw becoming exceedingly fond of what she thought to be a very self-neglected young man. During the year he joined the Fabian Society. He took no part in any production by the Stage Society, though he was elected to the Managing Committee in July, and there was talk of playing *The Philanderer*, but nothing came of it, as Shaw could not get a Julia to his liking. It was also intended to perform the censored *Mrs. Warren's Profession*, which Grein had refused for his Independent Theatre some years earlier, and, indeed, the performance had been announced for 8 and 9 December, but Frank Curzon, who had promised the Strand Theatre for those dates, withdrew consent when he learned that the play had been refused a licence. Barker was to play Frank. It was found impossible to get another theatre for the production, and only after superhuman efforts was it brought off on an improvised stage at the New Lyric Club, Coventry Street, on 5 January 1902. There was an uproar over the performance, the critics being solidly against it, one of the few exceptions being Max Beerbohm, who, in the *Saturday Review*, wrote :

Mrs. Warren is a powerful and stimulating, even an ennobling piece of work – a great failure, if you like, but also a failure with elements of greatness in it.

A. B. Walkley said of Barker's performance :

Mr. Granville Barker was not a bad Frank, though we think he might have been a little less sententious, a little more of an " agreeable rattle ".

Shaw was pleased with the whole affair, looking on the play then and afterwards as one of his best. He brought out an edition of the play with twelve photographs of the players, including the first published photograph of Barker. Shaw urged him during rehearsals " to soar, not gravitate " – good advice to all actors. " You seem," he said, " to be bitterly reproaching me all through for the flippancy of my dialogue." He wondered if anything could be done by getting Barker drunk, but doubted it, and wrote to him afterwards : " It is a question of feeding, perhaps . . . you must come to lunch oftener."

On 18 September 1901 Shaw had written to Mrs. Patrick Campbell suggesting Barker as a possible writer or translator of a fairy play, for he has " a very fine talent indeed "; but nothing came of the idea. Shaw made the proposal, he said, to enable the actress to heap coals of fire on Barker's head for his behaviour to her two years earlier! It does, however, indicate the direction in which Barker's mind was bent. He intended to be a writer. At this time he was always writing; both Shaw and Archer advised him, and read what he showed them. Undoubtedly, too, Shaw's influence was the stronger. He had read, and certainly greatly admired, *The Marrying of Ann Leete,* " really an exquisite play ", he said, which the Stage Society had performed at the Royalty Theatre, three weeks after the censored Shaw play, on 26 and 27 January 1902. This comedy in four acts, with twenty characters, was produced by the author, with Winifred Fraser as Ann. While the play mystified the audience, it was recognized that a dramatist of note had arrived. A. B. Walkley, in *The Times* (28 January), expressed the general view in a long criticism :

It must be difficult to write a play in four acts, four fairly long acts, the last in two scenes, and throughout them all to keep your audience blankly ignorant of the meaning of it. Many of those persons who sat throughout *The Marrying of Ann Leete* at the Royalty Theatre yesterday afternoon must have wished it were impossible. Granville Barker calls his piece a comedy. It might more suitably be termed a practical joke.
Something was expected of Mr. Barker, who was one of the authors of that capital play, *The Weather-hen,* which was seen some time back for a few performances and aroused a good deal of interest. After seeing his unaided attempt, one can only say that his collaborator must have been a very able playwright. There is cleverness in *The Marrying of Ann Leete,* abundant evidence of an agile mind, a good deal of humour, some observant sketches of character, signs of ability to write good, easy dialogue for the stage. But there is no trace of constructive talent, no skill in building up the framework of a drama, no coherency, no clearness. What seems

to have been in Mr. Barker's mind is the idea that the eighteenth century
had its "new woman" as well as the nineteenth. . . . On the whole we
prefer the "new woman" of a later date. She has her eccentricities,
but they are at any rate comprehensible, whereas the proceedings of Miss
Ann Leete utterly baffle the observer who tries to assign their causes or to
follow the workings of her mind. . . . It was a pity the play failed,
because the players did very well. . . . But without an explanatory
pamphlet, the effort to follow the wild catch-as-catch-can in which they
engaged could not but be barren of result.

Although not much thought of by the critics in general, the play was
admired, not only by Shaw, but also by other friends. It is indeed a very
engaging work, fresh, intelligent, sensitive, the product of a mind of
unusual quality. It was, however, dramatically weak, and has never been
performed since. Shaw wrote to Henry Arthur Jones on the 20 February
of that year :

I truckle to Granville Barker in order to conciliate him when he is forty.
He regards me as a vulgar old buffer who did my best in my day to play
up for better things – his things for example. In revenge I call him
"serious relief".[1]

Nothing of importance is to be recorded during 1902, except that in
July he had the part of Osric in six special matinées of *Hamlet* given by
Johnston Forbes Robertson at the Lyric Theatre during the successful run
of *Mice and Men*. He was working on another play. Early the next
year he took the leading part in W. S. Maugham's play, *A Man of Honour*,
performed by the Stage Society on 22 and 23 February at the Imperial
Theatre, a piece not liked by the society's audience ; it was, indeed, an early
effort that gave small indication of what was to come. Maugham himself seems to have felt out of place in the Stage Society, and afterwards
declared : "I wanted no such audiences as this, but the great public." In
The Summing Up, in which that sentence appears, published thirty-five
years later, he also says :

The attitude I found there was antagonistic to me. It seemed to me
patronizing and narrow. Granville Barker was very young ; I was only
twenty-eight, and he, I think, was a year younger. He had charm and
gaiety and a coltish grace. He was brimming over with other people's
ideas. But I felt in him a fear of life which he sought to cheat by contempt
of the common herd. It was difficult to find anything he did not despise.
He lacked spiritual vitality. I thought that an artist needed more force,
more go, more bluntness, more guts, more beef.[2]

Barker was, in fact, four years younger ; they did not meet again for

[1] *The Life and Letters of Henry Arthur Jones*, p. 211.
[2] *The Summing Up*, p. 117.

years. During 1903, on 26 and 27 April, at the Imperial Theatre, Barker played Barend, the son, in *The Good Hope*, by Herman Heijermans, giving a wonderful performance, and on 7 and 8 June at the same theatre produced a one-act play, *The Waters of Bitterness*, by S. M. Fox, in a programme that included Shaw's *The Admirable Bashville*, with which he had more than a little to do, it being in fact his first Shaw production, though it did not bear his name. Both plays were Stage Society productions.

In August the same year he played Edward II in Marlowe's tragedy of that name in a William Poel production at the New Theatre, Oxford. The production was of great interest, much care having been taken with it. A newspaper account (*The Pilot*, 15 August 1903) gives a very good idea of Barker's acting at that time:

Mr. Granville Barker, one of the very cleverest of the younger generation, deserves much praise for his careful study of the King. In the earlier scenes, arrogant, captious, self-willed, utterly regardless of his duties and the rights of others, and markedly epicene, he is as complete and truthful a figure as could be imagined. . . . The change to utter despair when hiding in the abbey is not altogether convincing. . . . The abdication is, I think, the weakest scene. . . . In the latter scene his conception is admirable. . . . He does not so much show physical suffering itself as the effect which intense physical suffering often produces on the mind. . . . The execution matches the conception, and the only fault to be found with it is that in the effort to produce a voice over which control has been lost, the actor becomes – and, it must be added, remains for lines together – inaudible.

The part was an exacting one; but Barker was engaged upon even more exacting tasks.

*

His friendship with William Archer was becoming fruitful, and Barker found the elder man, as had Shaw, a valuable friend. What the theatre owes to Archer it would be hard to estimate. Born 23 September 1856, barely two months after Bernard Shaw, he had when twenty-one and living in Edinburgh written in conjunction with his friend, R. W. Lowe, an anonymous illustrated pamphlet entitled *The Fashionable Tragedian*, severely criticizing the mannerisms of Henry Irving, shortly before that great actor was to open a season in the city. The pamphlet caused something of a sensation and by no means pleased the actor. Its importance to us at the moment is that the writers declared that Irving's faults pointed to the need for " a permanent school of acting in England ", and wound up with the words:

. . . the only remedy lies in a national theatre with good endowment, good traditions, good government. So long as actors have to trust for

training to their own haphazard requirements; so long as the one condition of their very existence is that they shall please a tasteless gallery and
still more tasteless stalls; so long as every artistic instinct in their nature is
liable to be ruined by a two hundred or even a thousand nights' run; so
long will histrionic talent, especially of the loftier orders, be unavoidably
doomed to the same destiny which has destroyed the unquestionable gifts
of Mr. Henry Irving.

This might have been a manifesto for Granville Barker, whose birth had
occurred a few months earlier, for what it contained he made the cause of
his life. As a result of his visits abroad, Archer had long been interested
in the idea of a National Theatre, and as early as 1873 was asking: " When
shall we in England have a National Theatre? "

When he and Granville Barker met in 1900, he at once filled the
younger man with enthusiasm for the idea, and the same year a meeting
was called at the artist Spencer Wilkinson's house to discuss practical
steps, and a committee was appointed consisting of Gilbert Murray,
A. C. Bradley, Hamilton Fyfe, Spencer Wilkinson, Archer, and Barker
to draw up a scheme. " I am sure ", said Barker, writing of that time, " I
looked forward to a National Theatre in being within the next year or
two."

As usual in such matters, the work fell on the two enthusiasts, who were
only too ready to undertake it. They prepared a detailed scheme, which,
after discussion with the committee and others, received the approval of
the seven most eminent actors and playwrights of the day, including Irving,
and was put into print with a stiff blue-paper cover for private circulation.
The " Blue Book " of the National Theatre, as it was called, showed that
£350,000 was required; but, despite Archer's efforts with his fellow Scot,
Andrew Carnegie, not a penny could be found from him or anyone else
for it. The National Theatre was still-born.

★

The impatient Barker was not to be discouraged, and on 21 April 1903
he wrote a long letter to Archer setting out a proposal " to take the Court
Theatre for six months or a year and to run there a stock season of the
uncommercial drama ", more or less continuing what the Stage Society
had been doing, but on week-day evenings. It was to be mainly a subscription theatre, the highest price 5s. or 6s., with a fresh production every
fortnight. He estimated the working expenses at £250 a week and
thought a guarantee of £5,000 would be needed. " Without doubt the
National Theatre will come ", he wrote, " so we ought to be getting . . .
ready . . . for when it does come." But after a long talk with Archer,
he wrote to say, " I don't think my Court Theatre scheme will come to
anything ", adding:

IX   Shaw and Granville Barker (Harmer's Green, 1901)

X   A trick photograph of Granville Barker taken by Bernard Shaw in 1904, and inscribed by him " The Two-Headed Nightingale "

XI   Bernard Shaw at the same time (1904)

XII & XIII   On holiday with the Shaws in Cornwall : (*left*) Shaw, (*right*) Granville Barker

I do hope the National Theatre will hurry up and that it will fall into Liberal or even Radical hands, and deliver us to some extent from the manager with the iron hand, before another generation of actors (mine in this case) has gone to the devil.

The Court Theatre scheme was nearer to realization than Barker thought. Later that same year, J. H. Leigh, a businessman friend of Martin Harvey and an amateur actor and Shakespeare reciter, purchased the lease of this very theatre, and put on a series of " Shakespeare Representations ". The productions started on 26 October with *The Tempest*, in which Leigh played Caliban and his wife (and one-time ward) Thyrza Norman, for whose sake the undertaking was embarked upon, was Miranda. Leigh, it may be noted, had bought a lease of the Prince of Wales Theatre, in 1899, for £25,000 to enable Martin Harvey to continue the performance of *The Only Way*, after its first production at the Lyceum Theatre the previous February, which had been backed by him; he lost heavily over it.

After another Shakespeare Representation at the Court, Leigh was dissatisfied with what was being done, and Thyrza Norman was told by William Archer, to whom she went for advice, to get the young Granville Barker for the next play. This pleased the young lady, so Barker produced the third play, *The Two Gentlemen of Verona*, on 8 April 1904, Barker playing Speed, Thyrza Norman Julia, and Lewis Casson Eglamour. Barker and Lewis Casson first met on this occasion; Casson, two years older than Barker, had become a professional actor the year before. The production and Barker's performance were both much praised. " It is very distinctly an endeavour in the right direction", wrote William Archer in the *World*. A. B. Walkley in *The Times* said : " I went with no little misgiving, and came away under so strong a charm that I almost told the cabman, ' To Mantua – by sea '." On Shakespeare's birthday a special matinée was put on composed of scenes from the plays, one of them being the balcony scene from *Romeo and Juliet*, in which Barker played Romeo to Thyrza Norman's Juliet.

As part of the consideration for his Shakespeare production, Barker had arranged with Leigh's manager, J. E. Vedrenne, that six matinées of *Candida* should be given, for which he would be responsible. Since the Shaw play has been done by the Stage Society, now almost four years ago, Barker had been anxious to present it to the London public, but Shaw did not want the Stage Society's production to be repeated, for he was not at all pleased with Janet Achurch's Candida, nor with Charles Charrington's Morell. He consented to Kate Rorke being engaged by Barker for the name part and Norman McKinnel as Morell; so the matinées started on 26 April, while *The Two Gentlemen* was still running. Shaw had warned

Barker that the whole thing would be " a hideous folly ", but it was a success. His advice to Barker upon casting the play shows his exact estimate of the capacities of well-known players and his acute sense of what was required in acting the parts. He told Barker that Eugene cannot be acted, ". . . it is a question of being the creature or at least having him in you : so that the casting of Eugene is either an insuperable difficulty or, as in your case, no difficulty at all as long as you keep your figure ". But Eugene, he declared, could not save the play, for without the necessary environment and support " the part would become harsh, ridiculous, and even violently unpopular ". However, the performances were more than justified, paid their way, and yielded Shaw £31 3s. Among those who had helped to finance the venture was Mrs. Shaw, without Shaw's knowledge.

Earlier this same year, 1904, Barker had produced *The Philanthropists*, a translation from Brieux, for the Stage Society at the King's Hall, Covent Garden, on 31 January and 2 February; and at the Court Theatre on 26, 27, and 28 June he produced W. B. Yeats's *Where There is Nothing* for the society. This ended his active work for the Stage Society. Leigh's last Shakespeare representation had been *Timon of Athens*, which opened on 14 May, in which he played Timon (" a purely elocutionary interpretation ", said a critic), but Barker had nothing to do with it.

In the meantime, Barker had produced Gilbert Murray's version of Euripides' *Hippolytus* for the hitherto dormant New Century Theatre, on 26 May, at the Lyric Theatre. William Archer wrote of this performance :

In the harmony and equipoise of its parts, the play is constructed like a noble piece of architecture.

It had, indeed, been a marked success, so that a suggestion came from Arthur Bouchier that he would like to take over the play; there was also talk of touring it. William Poel, too, was anxious to make an arrangement with Gilbert Murray, and in sending on a letter from him, Barker wrote to Murray on 5 June :

If I may advise, I wouldn't let him do it in London – for he may produce it in rather a cracked though clever way – not that that is so much a business reason as that there well may be a London revival in it as done just now. Also I'd be very sharp over your contract with him – for Poel is one of these limpid-eyed enthusiasts who sacrifices himself body, soul and pocket to his cause and expects and is absolutely unscrupulous in making everyone else do the same thing.

In fact, Barker did not want to let the play go, and to the same letter he added: "J. H. Leigh has expressed himself bitten with the idea of doing Greek plays. Not a word but he has talk anon."

★

The talk led to the most important development in Barker's career, to which we shall come in due course; but it will be convenient to consider here what he achieved as an actor, for in the performances as the Messenger in *Hippolytus* and as Eugene Marchbanks in *Candida* he displayed the qualities that caused me and many others to delight in his playing. He was no more than twenty-seven, and in the next ten years was to play a number of important parts until he gave up acting altogether, but nothing he afterwards did surpassed his playing in these two plays.

Barker's approach to the threatre and to drama from first to last was that of an actor. Though he was never, from his earliest days, merely an actor, for his mind was upon the play and upon production, as it was also upon life in the world, and as it was transformed in imagination, he handled drama in the terms of the actor. As we have seen, his training for the stage started early because, no doubt, he showed ability in that direction, but also because he had to be put in the way of earning a living. Before he had reached his middle teens, he was working in London under the direction of Charles Hawtrey, an able exponent of the Tom Robertson method of stage management. Then followed the season with Ben Greet, survivor of the old stock system, with unbounded enthusiasm for Shakespeare and old comedy, and soon he came under the influence of another enthusiast, William Poel, whose exploration of Elizabethan stagecraft and method of stage speech enlarged the young man's interests. He worked with Mrs. Patrick Campbell, the greatest romantic actress of her time, also for a short time with Charles Wyndham, and, what was more important, he encountered the German romantic actor, Hans Andresen, and the producer, Max Behrend, whose influence upon him was profound. Finally and above all, he was the friend of Bernard Shaw, the best critic of acting of his day. Thus was Barker grounded in experience under the best masters while he had the responsibility of earning his living. The theatre being what it was, there could have been no better preparation for his career.

As an actor his first notable success was at the age of twenty-two as Shakespeare's Richard II under William Poel's direction. Not a few young actors make a mark in Shakespeare's play, for it offers a chance for light, poetic, romantic playing of which actors with imagination can take advantage; the same can be said of Marlowe's Edward II, though a more exacting part, in which Barker made a great impression. But there can be no question that his outstanding performance was as Marchbanks in *Candida*, first given before he was twenty-three, and repeated on the public stage three and a half years later at the Court Theatre. Desmond MacCarthy wrote of this performance:

Mr. Granville Barker succeeded in playing Eugene Marchbanks where almost every other actor would have failed, because the representation of a lyrical mood is one within the peculiar range of his powers. His voice, too, can express a contemplative ecstasy. It possesses a curious individual quality, which, while it limits the range of his impersonations, gives particular intensity to some. When he repeats her name, " Candida, Candida, Candida ", there is not a touch of self-consciousness in the musical reiteration; he does not appear to be following the sound of his own voice, like most actors at such times, but to be listening, detached, to his longing made audible. It is in the representation of intellectual emotions that he excels, and so he excels in this part.

Barker's playing as Marchbanks was as near perfection in that part as one may ever hope to see upon the stage, and no other actor, in my experience, has even remotely approached the expression of lyrical emotion that he gave to it. Shaw never ceased to sing his praises, and had no criticism whatever, which was rare with him at that time. The part of Eugene, highly attractive to young actors, is more difficult than it appears, and they mostly fail. It can be played only by young men, and Barker himself did not continue to play it, for no doubt he felt himself already too old at twenty-six. Shortly after he was seen as the Messenger in the *Hippolytus*, which confirmed the high opinion of his acting. This short, exacting part demands rhetorical verse-speaking and descriptive powers of the highest order, and none who saw Barker play it lost the profound impression made upon them. The Messenger's speech is the play's climax, the culminating point of its action, describing the death of the hero, and contains narrative that must be delivered with passion, not naturalistically, but in lyrical, musical terms in which the poet addresses the spectators, bringing them to his own pitch of excitement. It is one of the finest speeches in dramatic literature. Desmond MacCarthy said that Barker's delivery of it " was the most memorable feature " of the play. Gilbert Murray said that Barker came to him at his cottage at Churt in Surrey the Sunday before the first performance and rehearsed the speech thirteen times straight off, which illustrates the young actor's seriousness.

Barker's acting was not notable for much play of feature. His expression was inclined to be set, except for his eyes, which were remarkably expressive. Variation of speed and inflection of speech were marked, however, and upon them he relied for the impression he wished to create. His voice was light; it has been unfairly described as adenoidal, but more fairly could be called high-pitched, with excited, ecstatic qualities, containing little depth or fullness, but musical and altogether distinctive.

His gestures were spare, his hands delicate, and his fingers sensitive. If his posture was somewhat stiff, his movements were quick, never extravagant, and always elegant.

The qualities his playing possessed were those of an unusually sensitive personality, but supremely those of a man of intelligence who had mastery of the essential nature of the character he was playing, expressed in a voice containing lyrical rapture sustained by elevation of manner. Bernard Shaw said of him in the letter to Henry Arthur Jones in 1902 from which a quotation has already been made that he was –

always useful when a touch of poetry and refinement is needed. He lifts a whole cast when his part gives him a chance, even when he lets the part down and makes the author swear.

These qualities might have made him a great actor, but he was conscious of deficiency in physical power, which to some extent, perhaps, accounted for a decided tendency to under-playing. This was by no means compensated for by over-subtlety in characterization. But it explains, perhaps, why he disliked acting, as undoubtedly he did. More particularly, however, it is certain that the demands acting made upon him were inconsistent with what he most wanted to do, which was to produce plays, but, above all, to be playwright in his own theatre.

That Barker was deeply concerned about acting, though he never treated himself as an actor-manager, was shown throughout his life. Acting was made the basis of all his work, not only as producer, but also as dramatist, and as critic of drama he looked upon plays from the actor's standpoint. What he thought about acting is expressed as well as he ever explained it in a passage from *The Exemplary Theatre*, after he had long given it up:

The histrionic mind, fully developed, carries a very particular equipment. It should be introspective, stopping short of self-consciousness; it may be sympathetic without principle; it must be observant, especially of the commonplace things that are apt to pass unnoticed; it must especially cultivate the power of induction – all dramatic interpretation is founded upon induction. I do not attempt to exhaust the list of qualities – all I want to affirm is that for the interpretation of modern drama a histrionic mind is becoming a more important asset than a histrionic body, and it is lamentable how few students, even if conscious of the existence of such a thing, pay any attention to its development.

By "induction" Barker meant understanding of the inwardness of a play by the actor. He was himself described as an intellectual actor, which means no more than that he played with his full intelligence; for he was certainly not a "natural" actor, one who plays with his subconscious mind, not knowing what he is doing. His mind was fully engaged and he played consciously, not self-consciously, for art requires self-forgetfulness, but knowing what he was giving it and how he intended to achieve it. That is why his acting was always to me, even when he failed in it, an exquisite delight.

*

To complete this Part, something must be said about Barker's interest in the organization of the acting profession, for not only were his friends mostly socialists, but he knew the need for organized self-protection in his profession. Up to the 'nineties of the last century theatrical business was largely a family affair, or financed among friends, but the development of the touring system by London companies, and the growth of speculation in theatrical properties, caused the theatre rapidly to become industrialized, and by the end of the century it was more and more in the hands of financial syndicates. Exploitation by landlords and others was brought to a high pitch. Thus the actor found himself at the mercy of economic powers much too strong for him. When the Actors' Association was formed in the mid-'nineties, Barker became a subscribing member, the subscription being 15s. a year. The association included managers among its members, for at that date theatre managers were almost invariably actors, but with increasing commercial control the position of actor-managers as instruments of financial management in an association of working actors made the effective working of the association alarmingly difficult. At the annual meeting of the association early in 1904, Barker as an ordinary member put forward a revolutionary programme :

That all salaries be paid on the weekly basis of six performances, with every additional performance paid for at the rate of one-sixth of the weekly salary. That special salaries be paid during rehearsals. That no actor or actress be employed in the West End in a speaking part, except as an understudy, who was not qualified to be a member of the Actors' Association.

These proposals, discussed at length, were ultimately shelved, but in June Barker was elected to the council of the association. But by now he was about to become a manager himself, so that his position was equivocal, for the feeling was becoming exceedingly strong that managers should not be included in the association. None the less, by 1907 he had become leader of a reform group, and at the association's annual meeting in February he with eleven others was elected to the council by a large majority on a reform ticket, which included a demand for a minimum salary of £2 a week. Barker proposed at the meeting that managers should be excluded from membership, which was carried by a large majority, insufficient, however, to change the constitution; but the managers, except Barker, retorted by retiring in a body, which made the association very weak, so that it well-nigh expired. Barker left at the end of 1907, when by great efforts the association had been put again on its feet. He took no further interest in the development of trade unionism among actors, however, or in the formation of British Actors' Equity twenty-two years later, when he had long left the theatre. The object of all these efforts was to improve the position of lower-paid actors, with whom Barker, having been one of them for many years, could not fail to be in sympathy.

★

In the next Part we return to the year 1904 and the great development that then took place in Barker's career.

PART TWO

STAGE PRODUCER

NO theatrical enterprise of this century has left a deeper mark upon the theatrical history of London than the Vedrenne–Barker management at the Royal Court Theatre in the first decade of the century. It followed directly upon and had relation to the efforts to get accepted the policy of a National Theatre. The management lasted under three years at the Court, though continued for a time elsewhere, but it brought into being elements that transformed not only the acting and production of plays upon the London stage, but also changed public attitude to the theatre. Its success was due to the collaboration of dramatists and actors, which is the necessary condition for theatrical achievement on the highest level. The major playwright whose works made the undertaking possible was Bernard Shaw; but the enterprise itself was Barker's, who was both actor and playwright: he with the actors he gathered around him and inspired carried out the work. Contributions were made by the business-like and astute Vedrenne, by the friends of both Shaw and Barker, and by the other dramatists whose plays were introduced to the public, as well, of course, above everyone, by Shaw himself; but it was to Barker that most was owed. I propose, while continuing the story of his life, to discuss the qualities of his work as producer.

The outcome of the successful *Candida* experiment in the spring of 1904, and of J. H. Leigh's interest in Barker's ideas, was that Barker discussed with him and with his manager, J. E. Vedrenne, the possibility of giving regular matinées at the Court, avoiding the usual matinée days at the London theatres. To this proposal Leigh gave his support as lessee, so, with the backing of small sums of money from friends, Vedrenne taking charge of the management, including contracts with artists, who were to be paid only the nominal fee of 1 guinea a performance, and Barker in charge of productions, it was agreed that the undertaking should start the following October.

*

Something should be said about the Royal Court Theatre, the scene of these activities. It had been built in 1888 on a site adjoining Sloane Square Station on the Metropolitan District Railway. There had been an earlier theatre on the other side of the square opened as the Chelsea Theatre on 16 April 1870, which was acquired by the actress, Marie Litton, who reopened it on 25 January 1871 as the Royal Court Theatre. John Hare drew the public there from 1875 to 1879; then Wilson Barrett took it over for nearly two years. It provided the stage for A. W. Pinero's first farce, *The Magistrate*, in March 1885. That theatre was pulled down in 1887, and the present building was opened on 24 September 1888. It seated 614 (206 stalls, 64 pit, 113 dress circle, 65 upper circle, 150 gallery, and 4 private boxes). After a number of successful managements, it had fallen on lean times. A pleasant little theatre, though not exactly in the West End.

★

Shaw took an active interest, though pretending to take no responsibility. As a good showman, he wanted the first production to be *Captain Brassbound's Conversion*, with Ellen Terry in the leading part. It is not surprising that she could not do it. Barker pressed for *Man and Superman*, which had been published the year before, but Shaw would not agree, for there was no Ann Whitefield in sight. Then Shaw dangled before him the possibility of starting with his new play, to be called *Rule, Britannia*, " a very advanced and earnest card in the noble game of elevating the British public ". But it was not finished, and as it had a political appeal he decided that it ought to wait until Parliament had resumed. Before this decision was taken Barker wrote to Gilbert Murray about the Greek play produced earlier in the year:

We mean at the Court to do *Hippolytus* second – that's to say, early in November – and we'd like an option to do it again in the spring – either for six more matinées or for some weeks in the evenings   And we can have another play for the spring – spring dates will be definitely arranged by Nov. 25?   I incline to the *Troades* with Genevieve Ward as Hecuba – I believe it is finer than ever if only I knew how to burn Troy. I have definitely come to the conclusion that the *Bacchae* won't do. By the way – will you have all the same people in November for *Hippolytus* – if we can get them, for I must be writing to them now? But Rosina Filippi *wants* to play the Nurse – and I don't want Aphrodite again.

In the same letter he wrote about another matter, showing how heavily he was engaged in the new enterprise, and how they were financing it; the play referred to was *Prunella*:

Now another matter of which I meant to write to you to-day. Do you still care to find me £200 for the production of the Housman–Barker play at the Court. It is to be done about Dec. 22 for 3 weeks certain – 2 performances a day. Its gross cost will be I think £1,400–£1,500, and £1,000 capital is being found. Leigh £600 – Vedrenne £200, myself £200. A quarter of this is to be called up at once (next week) to commission the music and pay an advance on the play – and I suppose partly book the theatre with. The terms I'd propose to you for the money – a first charge of 10% on the profits – to you. After that 4/5th to me and 1/5th to you until you have received 25%. This is the arrangement I have with my backer for the matinées and it seems to me equitable. However, I should tell you that a city man who was very willing to find the money balked at the limit of 25% and offered simply to go halves with me right through. But I stuck out about the 25% – it seems to me all a capitalist should get even on a great risk. The chances of this play doing well seem to me quite good as things go, but of course it is a risk – I am told that the Xmas play at the Court last year did quite well and paid – though it was an inferior sort of thing. This year too we shall have the advantage of any reputation the matinées will bring us.

You ought to see the play – or what there is of it so far: that I could send you. Better still I could read it you. But by Monday week (when I propose paying an afternoon call on my way bicycling from Bexhill to Bristol) it all ought to be settled. Indeed, I can't well leave Town till it is. Will you think it over and let me know as soon as you can – just what you feel inclined to do about it. This is a mightily long letter but I had no time to make it shorter (that *is* a good saying).

Barker was visiting his parents at Bexhill and cycling to Bristol, where he was still earning his living on tour with Mrs. Patrick Campbell. Writing to Murray in August when on tour in Blackpool, he said:

Ye Gods (and thou Poseidon!) have you ever been to Blackpool? Have you any conception how hideous humanity festers here? I leave at 9.30 on Sunday morning and count the minutes until then.

With as many as half a dozen productions to prepare for as well as collaborating with Housman in completing the new piece, *Prunella*, he was heavily pressed. It was to be the policy of the new management to put on plays for six matinées spread over two weeks, later to be increased to eight or nine matinées over three weeks. This meant a vast amount of work in deciding upon the plays, and in casting, designing, and rehearsing them. There was no relaxation in this heavy task; and in fact in the following year plays were run for six weeks in the evenings, in addition to the matinées of other plays.

The opening production was the Gilbert Murray version of Euripides' *Hippolytus* on the following 18 October for six matinées. Barker played the Messenger, while the handsome Ben Webster was Hippolytus, and Edyth Olive Phaedra. The performances were announced as:

Special Matinées under the management of Mr. J. E. Vedrenne. The Plays produced by Mr. Granville Barker.

John Eugene Vedrenne, with whom Barker now became associated, was at this time thirty-seven years of age and had been concerned with theatrical management for some years. He had met Barker earlier when managing the Comedy Theatre, but what interest he had in the new drama is uncertain. He was, however, as unusual as a business-man in the theatre as Barker was as an actor, and there is no doubt that his meticulous care for the business aspects of the partnership had much to do with maintaining it. He and Barker were never really intimate, however.

The matinées of the *Hippolytus* were reasonably successful. Then Shaw's new and unpublished play, renamed *John Bull's Other Island* (for the earlier title was " too frankly a jest "), was given the first of six matinées starting 1 November 1904. Arguments about casting had been going on for many weeks. Shaw was adamant upon getting the players he wanted, and his close familiarity with the London stage stood him in good stead. He was helped to some extent by the fact that the play was to be done at matinées only, when other theatres were not playing, so that it was possible to get actors who were otherwise engaged.

Shaw produced his play himself, giving attention to every detail, and was determined that Barker should play in it. Undoubtedly this was aimed at by Shaw partly in Barker's own interest, and because Shaw recognized his unique merits as a player. On the other hand, it is clear that Barker did not want to act. Yet his performance as Keegan in this play, though much criticized, certainly added to the play's distinction. It was, indeed, an admirable production, insufficiently rehearsed, judging from what some of the critics said, but the sheer brilliance of the dialogue, and Shaw's success in getting what he wanted from the players, made it an outstanding event. The crowded theatre was amazed and delighted, and the Vedrenne–Barker management was put firmly upon its feet. Mrs. Sidney Webb induced the Prime Minister, A. J. Balfour, to see the play; he was so pleased that he brought the Leader of the Opposition, Sir Henry Campbell-Bannerman, on a second visit, and another Opposition leader, H. H. Asquith, on a third, coming himself again on a fourth.

There followed six matinées of a play by Maeterlinck, translated by Alfred Sutro, *Aglavaine and Selysette*, starting on 15 November, in which Thyrza Norman appeared with Edyth Olive. Miss Olive had been one of the young players in Ben Greet's Company when Barker toured with it; her name will recur in the early part of this narrative. Miss Norman had first appeared on the London stage in 1900, and her name has already been mentioned here. She played one other part at the Court, and was divorced by Leigh, afterwards marrying a young actor, J. V. Bryant; she then seems to have disappeared from the stage. The Maeterlinck play was not much liked, and lost money. On 26 November, Shaw's *Candida* came

into the series, and was so popular that it was given four extra performances, including, for the first time, two evening performances. As I
can well remember, the winter weather was by this time showing up the
defects of the theatre, for heating was practically non-existent; everybody was complaining. At the first matinée of this play Shaw did not
appear in response to the demand for author by the audience, and
Vedrenne was reported to have said, " I am not Shaw " – or maybe he
said " sure " – " but probably you will find him on the platform of the
station next door." He had gone home to Adelphi Terrace to write a
letter to Vedrenne reciting a series of complaints about the cold, alleging
that the *Daily Mail* critic threatened to head his article, " A Frost at the
Court ". The theatre was then closed for three weeks, during which
the lessee had a new heating system installed, the stage improved, a new
scene dock and dressing-rooms added, and the lighting and equipment of
the public rooms improved, so that on its reopening the theatre was
claimed to be " one of the cosiest and warmest in London ". During
this interval, however, Berte Thomas, Barker's one-time collaborator,
gave a special matinée of a play of his own in which he appeared, entitled
A Little Brown Branch, with which Barker had nothing to do.

Then on 23 December Laurence Housman and Granville Barker's
" play in three acts for grown-up children ", *Prunella*, with music by
Joseph Moorat, was put on twice daily as a Christmas attraction for three
weeks. Much was hoped from this play. Barker had produced it with
the utmost care and played the leading part himself. Thyrza Norman
played the name part, and Lewis Casson the Statue of Love. The play
was, indeed, as William Archer said, " An exquisite and fascinating
entertainment . . . a thing of rare distinction ", and as he also said later
to account for its failure :

The critics and first audiences were disconcerted to find no Christmas
entertainment, but a pathetic, almost tragic fantasy, not without a touch
of bitterness.

There were, in fact, not sufficient grown-up children in London to
appreciate it, and it was above the heads of children not yet grown up,
who were taken instead to Barrie's *Peter Pan*, produced at the Duke of
York's Theatre four days later. So it was a dead failure.

How *Prunella* came to be written is told by Housman in his autobiography, *The Unexpected Years* (1937). He was living at Chipping
Campden in Gloucester :

. . . it was there, after a lecture by Granville Barker on the Shakesperian
theatre that I received my call to write seriously for the stage . . . out

of Campden, by Granville Barker, came *Prunella*, and after *Prunella* all
the rest. . . .

To help in financing the production, Barker had asked Gilbert Murray
the previous July for a contribution of £200, as we have seen. Murray's
response had been to send a cheque at once, receiving the following
acknowledgment from Barker :

July 12, 1904.
You are shockingly ignorant of the ways of theatrical finance. You
should have hummed and ha'ed and consulted your aunts and first cousins
and second cousins and my second cousins and your conscience and a
fortune-teller and then have said you'd think about it. However thank
you for the cheque (which wont be passed through for a few days yet)
and I'll write you further when things are quite complete – also about
plays. . . .

The fate of the play and Barker's agitations are disclosed in the following
letters to Murray after its production :

Dec. 29, '04.
Thank you for the £50. And while we're on this unpleasant subject –
prepare for the worst over *Prunella* – the *business* is *awful* – so bad that we
seriously discussed to-day whether not to close on Saturday and cut all the
loss we could. But it will cost so little more to keep open another week
that we shall do that – I cannot understand it – the people who come
seem most enthusiastic – yet so few of them come. One can only conclude that it's a real failure. I saw the first part of Act 1 from the front
this afternoon, and it is quite good – I enjoyed it. We've done our best
and there it is. Of course your loss is at worst limited to £200 – but oh
my dear Murray £200 ! I shall never forgive myself – I thought that
£50 was the most you might drop. Vedrenne will go delicately – like
Agag over the finance and by compressing the rent and so on may save
something. But really things are very bad. I won't go on to express
my feelings about them and you – you must imagine them.

Dec. 31, '04.
There is possibly a letter from you at home where I have not been for a
day (but at Hankin's to hear a play read). *Prunella* is picking up in a
microscopic degree but I don't see that we can possibly recoup on it – so
Vedrenne and I am devising schemes to get out of the wood if we can.
There is this one that a man should be found to take over the play and
production to another theatre, paying out the syndicate upon as good
terms as we can get – with a possible extra in the event of the play ultimately paying. This X must I think be an ordinary theatre speculator
who makes a business of such things. To get at him, a man like Addison
Bright seems to be indicated. In an ordinary way, Vedrenne or I might
go straight to Bright – but Vedrenne objects and I think he is right that

the moment you begin to hawk a play openly its value goes to zero. Still our case to be put to Bright and through him to X is a perfectly sound one.   We believe there's money in the play and everyone tells us so if we could spend the time and money to work it up – but apart from money it *isn't* worth our while to spend the time – because in five weeks we must take it off as the theatre is otherwise engaged – that is to say just when it would be beginning to pay well if it meant to.   And this, of course, is where the other man and the other theatre would come in. You'll have guessed that Vedrenne has suggested that if you've seen the play, that you might suggest to Bright that there's something in this for him to do – The point being of course that an outsider of weight making the suggestion will contribute to rather than depreciate the value of the play.   Once again – Vedrenne does not know that you are my unlucky backer – I have thought you'd prefer him not to – But of course I see why you can't go to Bright.   But now again – could Barrie be roped in? – You could put the entire business before him if you thought well – and then if he saw the play and thought well of it – though all would depend upon that – he could tell Bright all the business part of the matter and his word would of course carry great weight.   He might even know of an absolute X himself and speak direct to him, saying that owing to the circumstances of the theatre being let later we'd be willing to let the play go.   Tell me quite candidly what you think of this – It seems to me a possibility.   Of course I am very anxious that as much of this syndicate money should be saved as possible – Also I do honestly think that the play has a chance.   Our primary mistake and a costly one – has been doing it as an Xmas play, it won't go down as that and our usual public is out of town or has over-eaten itself.   However, we've this week to turn round in – while the play is still alive – and I really believe something can be done.

Wednesday night.

Prunella is petering out with dignity – more money in the house, not much – much enthusiasm.

Monday.

I'm glad you liked Act III.   £17 in the house this afternoon and 3 calls at the end of the play.   I cannot make this blessed public out.

However Bright may induce Seymour Hicks and his wife to do it – and then you'll see – !   What it wants is a few coon songs.

Monday, 16th.

Prunella made one final effort and had a last house of £60 so that one performance paid for itself.   So liveth Loxias, you are kind about the fizzle – But I hope the play isn't really dead.   I can't write collectedly.

The last performance of *Prunella* was in the middle of January, its failure being a bitter disappointment, but the play was by no means dead, as its subsequent history proved.   It has, indeed, been the most often played of all the dramatic works bearing Barker's name, and when published ran through fourteen impressions in the next twenty years. Addison Bright, referred to in these letters, was an author's agent who came to an unfortunate end not very long afterwards. J. M. Barrie did see the play, and was much impressed by it, but could do nothing; his friendship with Barker, however, soon became very close.

The matinées re-started early in February and a programme until the end of May was announced, to include six plays, all of which were done, with the exception of a version of Brieux's *The Cradle*. To restore their fortunes, the first of the matinées was a revival of *John Bull's Other Island*, which was given nine performances, starting on 7 February, followed by three short plays, including Shaw's *How He Lied to Her Husband*, on the 28th of the month, Barker playing the lover in that play. Shaw wrote to Gertrude Kingston, who played the lady:

you must forgive me for Mrs. Bompas, which was rather an outrage, but was perhaps pardonable as a sordid matter of business.

However, the actress liked herself in the part, for on 21 March the play was transferred, with the same cast, to the St. James's Theatre as an afterpiece to Alfred Sutro's *Mollentrave on Women*, which had opened there on 13 February. Also she persuaded Barker to play in it again at a special matinée at the Savoy Theatre a year later, on 8 March, when she was interested in two other short plays.

While the last programme at the Court was being done, a Command Performance of *John Bull's Other Island* for King Edward took place on the evening of 11 March, which set the seal on the management. All the same, the theatre did not recover its popularity, for the triple bill was badly attended; so were the next series of matinées of Gerhart Hauptmann's *The Thieves' Comedy*, produced by Barker, and praised by some critics.

Then on 11 April came Gilbert Murray's second Greek tragedy, *The Trojan Women* of Euripides, for which long preparations had been made. Hecuba was played by Marie Brema, Cassandra by Edyth Olive, Andromache by Edith Wynne-Matthison, and Helen by Gertrude Kingston. Barker had written to Murray a letter of great interest about the play earlier in the year:

Shaw has not only written to you but to Miss Kingston (he is a beast and a devil when he likes). Miss Kingston writes me to-night wanting to play and saying that her first appearances as an amateur were as Clytemnestra and as Penelope. Now my position is this – I was the original person I believe to think of her as Helen – then you told me Helen was something like Mrs. Bishop only more so and I cooled off. But now I am drawn to Miss Kingston for various reasons. For one – we're in I

think for Marie Brema – therefore we may as well have a really sporting
cast while we're about it – For another Gertrude Kingston can't but be
interesting and she would be very keen to do it.   But my real reason is
this – It seems to me that Euripides just does the pity and terror business
(Cassandra), then the temple and pathetic (Andromache), and then –
knowing that the real business of the play Hecuba and Troy is to come –
proceeds to brace up the minds of the audience to appreciate this by means
of a little intellectual exercise and so writes the Helen scene.   I felt and
found this in reading the play to Marie Brema.   That scene is an intellectual exercise and I think must be recognized as such and treated
accordingly.   Now G.K. *would* get the meaning of the speech and the
scene into the heads of the audience.   She is quite beautiful to look at –
in rather a serpent of old Nile brought up to date way – but she is clever –
she will be sure – and polished – very sweet – sweetness suggesting hard-
ness certainly – Mondaine describes her in modern things.   But that
woman has appreciation – principally of cleverness – no religion except
the Roman Catholic – which doesn't count, and great intention.   Just for
her cleverness I'd have her.

Now about Miss Farr – whom we shall settle with of course – I *dread*
that she may be writing tin-pot choruses – the formal ones I'm not so
afraid of but those bits with Hecuba at the last.   What is to be done?
Miss Farr is taking to discover on the psalter all sorts of progressives and
phrases which to her simple ear are quite effective and might be to ours if
the composer of the *Belle of New York*, not to mention Verdi and Wagner,
had not accustomed us to them for other purposes.   Now this is torture
to a musical ear (so I'm told).   You see, she really has a big subject to
deal with this time – far bigger than *Hippolytus* – one that mustn't be
wobbled or patheticized about.   Would it be possible to drop a little
sound musical advice on her head?   I am really worried.

This letter shows Barker's approach to a play as producer, and indicates
that he did not care (to put it mildly) for Florence Farr or her musical
ideas.   There are many letters in which he expresses his unfavourable
views about her.   For the production he depended upon Murray's help,
but the latter went away to the Mediterranean, returning just before the
performance.   A letter from Barker says:

Jan. 27, 1905.
I always like to impress upon authors that they are a confounded nuisance
and far better in Crete – I could make an awful pun about concrete and
abstract but refraining I pass on to say that I shall miss you from the
Troades rehearsals if you go and indeed if it were not that having absorbed
some of your ideas over *Hippolytus* I think I can't utterly neglect them I
would urge you to stay – but as it is though I shall miss you I think you'll
be safe in leaving it if not more – at the end of which wonderful sentence
I add Coward Coward – you are flying before the face of Brema and
Kingston – and you know it – Coward!

XIV   J. E. Vedrenne

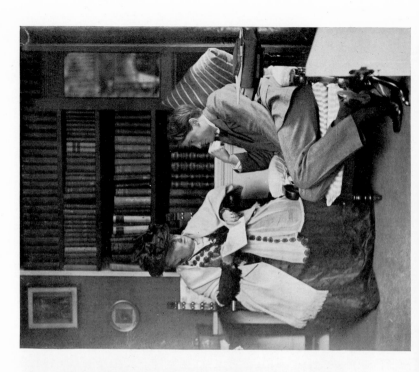

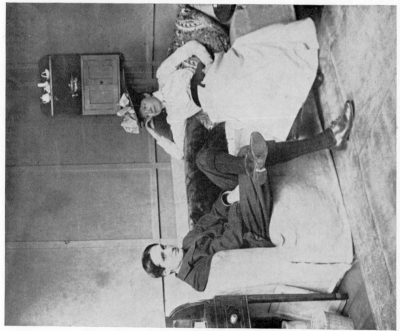

On reading the play some months earlier, William Archer had told Murray that it was "one of the noblest and most moving things I know". He then went on to say: "*But* don't let Barker seduce you into putting it on the stage." His reasons being, first, that the play is "not a complete and independent work like the *Hippolytus*, but an epilogue to an epic", and because "the experience of the *Hippolytus* seems to show that the male parts get over the footlights better than the female". This was good criticism; but all the same the four women made the audience feel all that Archer had said in praise of it.

After the first performance Barker wrote to Lady Mary Murray:

Thursday night.

Well, we've done our present best with the *Troades* but that best isn't enough for me – the truth is we're not big enough people for it. How it gives us away that our idea of representing grief is to weep and howl and that anyway we can grieve over a baby but we can't grieve over a city! But even now if you'd find me an ideal Hecuba I could do better with the play – for Oh it is a big thing. Well it's done and now there's the *Electra* and then the *Medea* – we'll have a classic drama in time. I hope this *Troades* will pay its somewhat costly way, for of course the future a little depends on that. I hope I haven't worked the Vice-Poet too hard this time. If I could do a little moral algebra and work out his relation to Euripides – but still the product is what concerns me and I doubt not that Euripides is plaiting up a bit of his crown ready for him when they meet. I wonder whether the old gentleman does know or whether he has been absorbed into the Greek Spirit. I try to absorb a little of that myself. I hope you know – for I think you'll like to know – what an education the *Hippolytus* and the *Troades* have been to me and I value that more than anything. One opens out to work like this. Certainly I behave like an ill-tempered schoolboy in the theatre too often, but when I've ceased to rasp at the acting and the scenery I go about singing the play inside me and it makes very good music to work to.

Always yours sincerely,
H. G. Barker.

Bernard Shaw wrote to compliment Miss Kingston:

Helen was magnificent; nothing else in the whole affair is really classical.

The production was, in fact, an impressive affair and, without being a popular success, was fairly well supported and added to the reputation of the management.

*

Immediately after the Greek play, on 1 May, *John Bull's Other Island* was put on for three weeks only, every evening at 8.15, with a matinée on Wednesdays. This meant that the company had to be paid something more than nominal fees, though the salaries were still very low for leading players. A serious drawback from the actor's point of view to accepting engagements at the Court were these low salaries; but as the Court set a new standard of acting and production, which appealed to serious artists, and as the plays themselves were on a level unreached by the commercial theatre, there were compensations. A stock company was engaged which included then, or later, Lewis Casson, Norman Page, Edmund Gwenn, Trevor Lowe, C. L. Delph, Frederick Lloyd, Allan Wade, Dorothy Minto, Hazel Thompson, Amy Lamborn, and Mary Barton, each of whom was paid £3 a week. The arrangements were somewhat flexible. The rule was adopted that no production was to cost more than £200.

The cast of the Shaw play was substantially the same as at the first performance, except that Lillah McCarthy played Nora in place of Ellen O'Malley. This was Miss McCarthy's first appearance at the Court, and, as she was to play a leading part in Granville Barker's career for the next ten years, it is necessary to say something about her at the time at which she entered it. She was already known to Barker, for he had toured with her in his youth in Ben Greet's company; and Shaw, too, had met her, for he had written in the *Saturday Review* on 25 May 1895 an account of her performance as Lady Macbeth, when she was a young girl and an amateur, which has become famous. That performance and Shaw's praise had at least something to do with her becoming an actress. As Lady Macbeth she was "bad", he said, "but it is clear to me that unless she at once resolutely marries some rich gentleman who disapproves of the theatre on principle, she will not be able to keep herself off the stage". He advised her to get experience. That particular performance was given to help to raise funds to erect a statue to Mrs. Siddons in Paddington. "I went from door to door selling tickets for it," she says. She recited a prologue at the performance, written by a good-looking young man, J. B. Harris-Burland, a Newdigate Prize-winner at Oxford, whom she had known from childhood in Cheltenham, and to whom she was then engaged. The prologue of seventy-two lines started:

> I looked into the darkening glass of years
> And saw the shadowy pageant move along . . .

Miss McCarthy had earlier the same year read Romeo at the Steinway Hall for the Shakespeare Reading Society under William Poel, and the month after Shaw saw her she played Olivia in *Twelfth Night* at the Burlington Hall, the first production of Poel's Elizabethan Stage Society. After Shaw's article appeared, she went to see him, and he told her to go away and become an actress. Then she went to Ben Greet, with a view to joining his company. He had seen her as Olivia in a flaxen wig, and when she turned up, a dark-haired beauty, he at first refused to believe she was the same girl. She was too young, he said: she was in fact nineteen. He asked her to speak some Shakespeare, so she said young Arthur's speeches from *King John*. "Now," Greet said, "do something you have not been taught to say." "I was never taught," she replied, but he gave her another part to read, and engaged her on the spot as leading lady in place of Dorothea Baird, who was just leaving the company, the leading actor being young H. B. Irving. She played many Shakespeare parts with Ben Greet, and a year later was engaged by Wilson Barrett for *The Sign of the Cross*. She went to America in that play, and afterwards to Australia, and returned to London to do a number of other engagements; then rejoined Wilson Barrett as leading lady in 1900, and was with him playing all over the country, in South Africa, and again in Australia, until he unexpectedly died in July 1904. Wilson Barrett had intended setting her up in her own company, for she had become, he said, too powerful a leading lady for him, but these plans vanished with his death. So she went back to the West End stage, and in 1905, almost ten years after Shaw's criticism of her as an amateur, went to see him as an experienced artist. As soon as Shaw saw her, he recognized his long-sought-after Ann Whitefield, and gave her the part to study. In the meantime, at Barker's suggestion, he offered her the part of Nora in *John Bull's Other Island* to be going on with, as Ellen O'Malley was not available. He wrote to her (25 March 1905):

Can you talk real broad Irish, like Miss O'Malley in *John Bull's Other Island*? We cannot get her for the evening performances of that play (have you seen it?) in May. If Tree has not snapped you up for the rest of the season in the evenings, I should like to know whether you know the part and whether it attracts you at all. In a year from this you will be so famous that you won't look at my little plays and matinées; so I may as well make the most of you whilst you are still attainable.

Different as she was in almost every way from Miss O'Malley, Miss McCarthy was an instant success, and the Court Theatre company was strengthened in its first venture (apart from *Prunella*) upon regular evening performances by the addition of a youthful actress of much experience, who was still anxious to learn. Although she did not cut herself off from the commercial stage, for she had to make a living, she was thereafter in her life and stage career bound up with Shaw and Barker and the dramatists inspired by them, and, as she says in her memoirs, "a new life began for me; a new life of the Court Theatre and of the new woman . . .".

*

The day the regular evening performances started, 1 May, a partnership agreement between Vedrenne and Barker was signed. It was to last for three years, until 1 May 1908, subject after that date to six months' notice by either partner. The capital was to consist of " such sums of money as shall be required " for carrying on the business, and to be contributed by each partner in equal shares, but no sum was mentioned. The partners were to share equally in the profits or losses, and were entitled to draw £20 a week each in anticipation of profits. Vedrenne was to be responsible for the business management and Barker for the artistic management; fees were to be paid in respect of any interest in plays, and for acting in any play. Otherwise there was nothing special in the agreement, which continued in force as long as the partnership lasted.

*

After the Irish play went into the evening bill, Shaw's *You Never Can Tell* started upon a series of nine matinées, with Tita Brand as Gloria, Granville Barker as Valentine, Louis Calvert as the Waiter, and Mrs. Theodore Wright as Mrs. Clandon, an altogether different cast from the Stage Society's production in 1899. The theatre was thus occupied every afternoon and evening, except for two afternoons, with Shaw's two most popular plays – a feast of delight! This was continued for a further three weeks from 22 May with *Candida* in the evening bill, *Man and Superman* having the first of twelve matinées the day after. Granville Barker was, of course, in both plays: Eugene again in *Candida* (otherwise the cast of the previous year's matinées, with only two small changes), and John Tanner in the other play.

On the previous Sunday the first performance of *Man and Superman* had been given at the theatre for the Stage Society. The following announcement appeared in the programme in which the dramatist's hand can be detected:

Messrs. Vedrenne and Barker beg leave to explain that the acting version of *Man and Superman* now presented has been prepared solely by the author. None of the omissions by which he has brought the performance within the customary limits of time have been made or suggested by the managers. They do not regard a complete performance, occupying both afternoon and evening, as impossible or unacceptable. But as Mr. Bernard Shaw designed the play from the beginning so as to admit of the excision, for practical stage purposes, of the scene in which John Tanner's motor-car is stopped in Spain by brigands, of the philosophical episode of Don Juan in Hell, and of the disquisition on the evolution of morality as a passion, they feel that they can present the rest of the play as a complete comedy in three acts without injury to the artistic integrity of the work, or violation of the author's wishes, which have been unconditionally complied with on all points.

With *Man and Superman* the Vedrenne–Barker management reached its high-water mark, to be touched again, but never exceeded. The casting of the play was superb; Lewis Casson and Edmund Gwenn making their reputations, Florence Haydon a delicious Mrs. Whitefield, while Barker, made-up to look like Shaw, and Lillah McCarthy as Ann Whitefield, gave performances that no subsequent production ever approached, let alone surpassed. There was afterwards a splendid John Tanner on the Court stage in Robert Loraine, after his fortune-spinning experience with the play in the United States, but to my mind, much as I admired Loraine, Barker's performance had the gay and shining quality of an original stage masterpiece, while Lillah McCarthy's Ann was a marvel of beauty, assurance, and expression of the emotional subtleties of the character. Certainly, what she accomplished with Shaw's greatest comic heroine has never been surpassed by any other actress. Both parts were exacting, making the severest demands upon the technical skill of the players, as well as upon their understanding of what they had to do, and under Shaw's direction they gave performances that none who saw them could ever forget. The love-scene at the end of the play is not only a remarkable piece of writing, but calls for remarkable talents in the players. Miss McCarthy records that at the end of one of the rehearsals of this scene, Louis Calvert, who was not in the play, said to her, "You would be a great dramatic actress – a great tragedienne – away from plays like this." He was right, though not in the deprecating final words, for Calvert resented the devastating wit of Shaw, which was beyond his comprehension, excellent actor though he was in Shaw's plays; but Lillah McCarthy, like all good tragedy players, could reach heights of true comedy, the opportunity for which is only too rarely offered, and she was able to attain them in this play.

A. B. Walkley would not have it that the play was a play. He devoted a long, critical review to discussing what he called the action-plot and the idea-plot; he considered that Shaw, like his master, Shakespeare, had sacrificed action to idea. But, he said, "the acting is quite admirable". Barker was "a born interpreter of his talent", and Miss McCarthy turned the impossible woman, "the walking theory . . . almost into a genuine character, and entirely into an agreeable woman". The *Illustrated London News*, following Walkley, referred to ". . . the so-called comedy". And the *Westminster Gazette*, in a long, complimentary notice, said:

. . . that prodigious, psychological, physiological, esoteric, propagandist drama which with its appurtenances occupies a stout volume has just been presented as a short, merry, farcical comedy. . . .

The critic thought Barker " too young and pretty for the part, but acted, as always, with a great deal of skill ", going on to say : " Ann's part is of great difficulty; Miss Lillah McCarthy played it brilliantly."

After the ninth performance of *Man and Superman*, on 12 June, there came for the first time in the evening bill, for three weeks, *You Never Can Tell*, with the same cast as in the previous month's matinées; then Barker went for a holiday with Gilbert Murray.

*

The first season had lasted from the middle of October until the end of June, when twelve plays new to the London public had been performed, four by Shaw, one by Barker and Housman, two translated from the Greek, one from the French, and one from the German. The last two months were wholly Shaw's, and there was no doubt that he was the Court dramatist. A regular audience had been created, and, without making any money worth speaking of, the season was a success. The policy had been short runs, six or nine matinées or three weeks in the evening bill, no advantage being taken of a play's popularity, except to give it a short revival.

All the plays were announced as " produced by Granville Barker ", although Shaw's plays were largely produced by himself. I say " largely " because he rehearsed them, and had them done as he wanted, but the burden of production was upon Barker. When the second season started in September, and thereafter, no producer's name appeared on the programmes. The relations between the two men were very close, for Shaw depended much upon Barker, as his letters show, while at the same time he was teaching the younger man. Shaw had not, of course, Barker's stage experience, but he knew the theatre with the closest intimacy, and was himself a performer on the public platform, having mastered the art of public speaking, so that there was nothing any actor could teach him about how to woo and, if necessary, to arouse an audience. Shaw and Barker were temperamentally opposed, but as their aims were identical they worked together with fruitful results. Barker, indeed, had such confidence in his friend that he followed him closely, though not, as events proved, blindly, in much of what he did. They both talked to the players a great deal, both read their play to the company in the first instance, and nothing pleased them better than to get the company to sit around a table to discuss it, as Poel had invariably done. Both talked quietly and confidentially to individual players, and both made a practice of handing or sending them notes on their playing. But Shaw sought for bold and large effects, while Barker was for expressive detail. That Barker was in the school of Charles Hawtrey (that is, of T. W. Robertson) cannot be denied, but he went far beyond anything aimed at by that able artist, because he went to life for his inspiration, not as actors lived it or thought of it, but as men occupied by the world lived it. Furthermore, his poetic vision was not the same as reproducing or creating an illusion of everyday experience. Shaw, however, wanted to get right away from the Robertson tradition and from the " gentlemen actors ", Hawtrey, Wyndham, and du Maurier. He wanted actors who worked as creative artists. That is why he treated his plays as musical scores, a notion Barker took over from him. Shaw was for going " all out " for decided movement, for the top notes, but Barker tended towards the muted, subtle, sensitive, and delicate air. In short, Shaw's fault was to encourage overplaying, while Barker was constantly in danger of getting underplaying. " His style and taste were as different from mine as Debussy's from Verdi ", declared Shaw.

The inherent fault in Barker's stage method was understatement, under-emphasis, a tendency even towards what seemed to be inarticulateness, so that the rhythm appeared to go underground. That is what aroused Shaw's fury, for it was the opposite of what he rightly considered appropriate to the stage. But he recognized Barker's sensitive feeling for detail and truth, which is called his realism, and was without stint in praising his work publicly while privately he rebuked him. The effect Barker got from his players was that of extreme ease. What he succeeded in did not seem difficult, yet no other producer was ever able to repeat his results.

*

After the nine months' season, Barker was in great need of a holiday and had been discussing a trip abroad with Murray, with whom he felt wholly at one; also he was working on another play and wanted to get on with it. A series of letters between the two friends shows how they made up their minds. The spelling and punctuation in his own letters are Barker's.

From Granville Barker to Gilbert Murray

Friday [May 1905].

What I can get abroad is a fortnight or three weeks – though if I found a place where I could quickly finish my poor play – then a little longer. I have just been at an Atlas and there seems lots of places in the world. My heart goes out to Papayanni a little bit – should I be ill all the time? I have had a great shock at hearing that Rodjestvensky's men after going all that way were mostly seasick during the voyage (of course it may have been funk – however!). Also would it be very hot and would there be the flies of Egypt? But my real fear on board any boat is that the moment we are out of sight of land someone will come up to me and say " Surely you acted in *John Bull's Other Island* at the Court Theatre – what a *nice* play – how funny Mr. Bernard Shaw is – was it your own hair you wore or a wig? " – I should have to go overboard. But now – shall we try the mild Mediterranean? For mountains – their great advantage being that they don't rock much and that you can step off them – my soul certainly goes out to a mountain – I had not thought of Switzerland and *table d'hôtes* – no – no – I had had the Austrian Tyrol in my mind – there's Venice and Triest and a funny part of the Adriatic to the South and there are more mountains and Bohemia and Vienna to the North – and just beyond Vienna the Carpathians. I suppose Pau and the Pyrenees would be too hot – what about the Basques?

Then Desmond MacCarthy tells me of the pine forests of the Jura looking towards Strasbourg on one side and France on the other – Shall we walk – shall we bicycle through the Pine Forests of the Jura?

Near home there is Brittany but that's only a foreign Cornwall. Oh not England – Murray not England an you love me. . . .

We might go to Troy and see how it looks without Marie Brema – or to Tauris. But the risk of Papayanni turning out a failure being too great – I can't decide this in my own mind, do you say what you think (Patras and Corfu sound awfully fine). I can't help thinking that the Tyrol has points.

One should in a way go to a place where the people are nice where they rob you politely and only murder you in your sleep. Then again these Pyrenees loom large. By all of this – done on slippy paper with a slippy pen – otherwise not done at all you'll gather that as long as on SUNDAY JULY 2 I shake the dust of Sloane Square London off my poor tired feet I'll go quiet anywheres. The last phrase used in recognition of your exploits at Bow Street. Now must go and " Candid ".

Tuesday [June 1905].

I hope there was more fun in your plans for a Papa Yanni [*sic*] steamboat or a mountain or a plain or summat. Do come away with me on July 2. I'll go where you will and stay how long you will. I don't know what sort of a companion I'll be but you Murray will come as a boon and a blessing.

Also there's this – I am now carrying on a sort of semi-business flirtation with Mrs. Campbell. Now would you like her for *Electra* ? If not who is your alternative – Shall I mention its existence to her at all (by the way I am going to dine with her on Thursday) and how is it getting on? When will it suit you for us to do it – early spring, February or so – or what? I also want to discuss an evening bill – *Hippolytus* and *Troades* or *Electra*. I want it to be two plays. When are you in town. I hope you're not getting to like Oxford. To be a mere number in a mere street !

From Gilbert Murray to Granville Barker

June 10 1905.

O Man,

It is dawning upon me after painful reflection, that perhaps we want rather different things. You see, my first object is to avoid Hay Fever;

which implies either 1. a sea voyage; 2. a sandy and barren seaside, not very far away, because of the railway journey; 3. a very high mountain, or a glacier. And 3 is further complicated by the conditions that the railway journey will start my disease, and secondly that I can't make ordinary genteel expeditions or walk in meadows or bicycle about. I could, for instance, take a railway journey straight to the Rhone Glacier and there sit admiring the works of the Creator until they bore me, but I could not play about in the Jura or the Vosges. Nor could I go as far as Trieste.

Now an English or Breton seaside is rather boring to the young and adventurous, though they might do well enough for me and my falling leaves. (I am doing a lyric passage to-day, in the *Electra*.) A sea voyage seems the possible meeting place. On it I would offer the following remarks.

1. It is a very concentrated holiday, very restful, very full of change, and you come out fat at the end of it.

2. Sickness will pass after about a day, but you will never feel absolutely free from a suspicion of biliousness. You will dislike the food, were it the food of angels. (Angels, by the way, were believed by Liebig to live on chocolate until he invented his patent food: then they took to that.)

3. Your opinion of me will sink very, very low.

4. The weather will probably be something heavenly and rapturous, though dashed slightly by smells of oil or cooking. It will not be too hot at sea, though it will be in the ports. But you will be too lazy to mind.

5. You will try to work, but you will be too stupid.

6. When you get home again you will give thanks in a loud voice and leap like a young lamb just discharged from penal servitude.

7. On board the fashionable passenger steamers there will be people who have seen *John Bull* and *Candida* – duchesses, in fact; but on Papa-Yanni there will only be about six passengers altogether and none of them will ever have heard of Shaw or seen any play but musical comedies in Liverpool and Benson's Shakespeare. There will be a man travelling in rope; a married couple going as missionaries or perhaps consuls to Beyrout, and a young Scotchwoman going to be a governess in a Russian family in Odessa. There will be a lady secluded in her cabin, and an elderly person who clamours intempestively for sheep's head. . . . Here my vision fails me.

8. There is of course a bare possibility that you may be one of the few people who remain seasick a long time. Then it would be hellish. But this is very unlikely. I am one of the worst sailors in the world.

9. For "pure gaiety and diversion" I do not recommend it; far from it. But it is a wonderful rest and change, and the new strange places are interesting to see and to remember.

I have been looking up other possible voyages, but the dates are very bad. . . .

My wife advises you to go your own ways to the Jura, without me.

She thinks the Papa would be too risky for you and the Jura bad for me. I, if left alone, shall probably go quietly to Holy Island and live in a cell, thinking of my friends' sins.

From Granville Barker to Gilbert Murray

Monday [June 1905].
Oh Murray – when I have worked myself up into a state of bravery about Père Jean – reminding myself that no one has really ever died of seasickness that quarantine never lasts more than 21 days then you descend on me with suggestions of cowardly mountains. Well I put it on you – I have never done more than cross a channel and I have prayed fervently for a channel tunnel. If I die you must play Keegan and Tanner in the autumn and otherwise help to run the orphaned Court – But I will spend a morning with Cook to-morrow.

About Mrs. P.C. I will talk to her seriously about *Electra* – as to whether or no she can do it simply and without mannerisms and reminiscences of the attitudes she thought Burne Jones liked.

Tuesday [June 1905].
Archer says why don't we go to Norway – they'd very probably make you king he thinks you'd look very well – Certainly you would. Yes there's Norway – is it hay feverish? – I have been told Finland is the place to go to. I send you the information I got about Brittany (Britanny). The seasick weary Barker (Romeo and Juliet both) will probably spread her bones there when Padre Giovanni has racked them his worst.

Let me tell you Sir that your method of drawing a cheque and leaving me to decide is a coward's method – and it shall not avail you – you'll receive dozens of letters yet.

From Gilbert Murray to Granville Barker

June 11 1905.
Your letter was forwarded to a wrong address by the New College porter who must have gone temporarily mad. Hence it did not reach me for six days, and my other letters were not answers to it.

Pleasure first. If you don't trust Father John or fear quarantine, why not come straight to Chamonix, or Murren or Bel Alp or the Rigi or Riffel Haus? It is very simple; get into a train on July 2, and there you are. Places will not be crowded so early. Or again, why not go to some almost uninhabited seaside, the Lizard or Macrihanish. Though perhaps Switzerland is more amusing. A holiday is always an awful thing. Or you might call at Cook's and ask about shorter voyages, to the Fjords, &c. I want some day to go on a wherry on the Norfolk Broads. Unless anything really good turns up, I recommend Switzerland. If you had more time, and I also, I would say Dalmatia.

Business second. February will suit me as well as any time: and I think on the whole the *Electra* will shape into a goodish play. It is both exciting and psychologically interesting, though it never sweeps you away. I am now about halfway through, and hope I may finish it before I have to begin preparing lectures for next term.

As to Mrs. Campbell, I think on the whole she is the best person we can get. But 1. will she do what we want? 2. If willing, can she speak a long, continuous speech? The main effects, as usual, depend on long speeches, and I have just a fear that she may be too restless and scrappy in her methods. She could not face the long speech of Phaedra at all. Still she would be splendid in some ways; and on the whole, if we can get her, we ought to be thankful.

Bradley was lecturing on Antony and Cleopatra yesterday; and his account of the latter – highly appreciative – reminded me of Mrs. Campbell at every turn.

I don't think Miss Olive would be very safe for *Electra*; and another point is that, if Mrs. Campbell did *Electra* and liked it, she might afterwards do *Medea* for us – a part that no one else whom I can think of could touch! But of course *Medea* is not ready, and she ought to act some other Greek part first to get comfortable in the convention.

I dreamed last night that I was being tried for some offence or other which was entirely due to hay fever. The magistrate said he had never come across a genuine case of hay fever, though it was always being offered as an excuse in that court; but he knew all about Drink, and so saying gave me six months! It was horrible.

From Granville Barker to Gilbert Murray

Sunday [June 1905].

Micawber have I deserved this – I who never have deserted you – who never will desert you Micawber! Let us risk Pappayanni – At the worst – if I live – I can but get off at Gibraltar and make my way back through Spain a broken man while you hold your Ulyssean course for the East. Shall I see about berths or will you?

Should this fail – yes a seaside place in Brittany will do me quite well. But if your heart really draws you towards Holy Island, there I will not come, for there I can – and shall – get newspapers and telegrams – then I would mount my Arab bicycle and set forth alone.

But I will risk all and Papyan Eastwards – Syracue – C'ple—yes I want to see them.

From Gilbert Murray to Granville Barker

Whit monday [1905].

. . . By the way, will you, in engaging berths, mention that you are a vegetarian, and that you expect to be properly fed, on milk, eggs, cheese, macaroni, porridge, fruit, and not fish or flesh? If you are particular, you can say it is me, and not you. That is less simple; but perhaps more effective . . . a vegetarian friend, deeply diseased and with a devil of a temper. If one warns them beforehand, I think it is all right.

On the voyage Barker wrote to Lady Mary Murray a letter worth preserving:

> S.S. *Lily of Cambridge*
> Somewhere near Gibralta on Sunday evening [July 1905].
>
> Dear Lady Mary,
> Five days at sea have reduced me to a state of pudding-headedness which just lets me tell you that my fellow-traveller is well (just a little sun-burn as to the nose) and that I am well and that the ship goes well and that Life is Laziness incarnate. I know – though I don't quite believe it that I have to revisit England sometime – but how or when I mean to get back the fellow traveller – who really is wider awake than I am – must decide.
> I hope you're well and have found a little holiday yourself (oh it's unkind to quote to you) – now that we're gone and there is peace! I now look out at the sea and my brain fogs over again so I finish ingloriously.
>
> > Very sincerely yours,
> > H. G. Barker.

*

When the holiday ended, the arrangements for the new season and the completion of his new play occupied Barker. The possibility of doing *Captain Brassbound's Conversion* was considered, but Ellen Terry was still not available, and Vedrenne was told " to put the play out of his head ". On 11 August, Shaw wrote to Tita Brand from Ireland:

> The Court people announce no further performances of Y.N.C.T. It is agreed on all hands that you and G.B. are quite impossible as lovers; your open and vigorous hostility to one another makes the whole thing absurd. There is no difficulty about G.B.; I can hurl him out of the part and get Ainley; but it is not so easy to get anybody to do the other side of Gloria. . . .

When the play was done eleven months later, Shaw had found another Gloria and had got Ainley in it, who showed, excellent as he was, that it was not so easy, either, to get anyone to do the other side of Gloria's lover.

The theatre reopened on 11 September with *John Bull's Other Island* every evening for six weeks, William Poel playing Keegan, for Barker had struck at last; and on the 26th of the month the young St. John Hankin's comedy, *The Return of the Prodigal*, had the first of the usual six matinées. Produced by Granville Barker, this mocking play was a marked success with A. E. Matthews (he looked a boy) as the prodigal son:

> The Prodigal's Return! The Fatted Calf! A father softened, a mother in tears! The virtuous elder brother scowling in the background! So I came here. Back to the Old Home, you know.

When he had joined the Fabian Society, Barker was much in demand for lectures, mainly on social aspects of the theatre, and was no less popular as a speaker at Sunday meetings of the London ethical societies. He was, indeed, a fascinating lecturer, always sure of a good audience. Among his Fabian friends were the Webbs, particularly Beatrice, and he became a frequent visitor to their house in Grosvenor Road. She was charmed by his brilliance – " the intellectual actor " she named him – and in her diary under the date 5 October she made the following entry:

On Sunday afternoon G.B.S. and Granville Barker dropped in and spread out before us the difficulties, the hopes, the ridiculous aspects of their really arduous efforts to create an intellectual drama. Granville Barker has suddenly filled out – he looks even physically larger than a year ago – he has grown extraordinarily in dignity and knowledge of human nature. But he dislikes the absorption in mere acting and longs to mix with persons actually in affairs or intellectually producing.[1]

The first Ibsen play to be done at the Court followed the Hankin play on 17 October, *The Wild Duck*, in William Archer's translation, Granville Barker producing and playing Hialmer Edkal. " I am wild-quacked to death ", he wrote to Gilbert Murray. After three performances he gave up the part, for *Man and Superman* came into the evening bill for the first time on 23 October, with a few changes in the cast, but with Barker and Lillah in their original parts.

*

For two years Barker had been working on a new play, *The Voysey Inheritance*, which was at last given its six matinées, starting on 7 November. This was a notable event, for the play was hailed as a masterpiece of the new drama, and was given a perfect production by the author; its cast of eighteen included A. E. George, Florence Haydon, Dennis Eadie, Henrietta Watson, Frederick Lloyd, O. B. Clarence, Edmund Gwenn, and others who afterwards made their mark. With this work Barker established himself as a leading dramatist of his time, as well as its outstanding producer and an attractive actor. While the play showed Barker's skill in craftsmanship, it is extraordinarily dry in emotional content, and gave him the reputation of writing intellectual exercises. A. B. Walkley called it " *triple extrait de* Shaw ", and went on to say:

All this notwithstanding, *The Voysey Inheritance* has great merits. It has fresh and rare observation, subtle discrimination of character, sub-acid humour, an agreeable irony, and a general air of reality. That is the important thing.

[1] *Our Partnership* (1948), p. 310.

He continued with an admirable analysis and appreciation of the piece. Max Beerbohm in an enthusiastic review said:

Mr. Barker is an exceptional person, in whose presence I bow. . . . On him, somehow, the blight of the theatre has not fallen. He has continued to keep himself less interested in the theatre than in life. . . . May his bright intellect never grow dim. I may have to suggest anon that he is too purely intellectual to be perfect. For the present, though, let there be nothing but praise.

This emphasis upon intellectuality is not surprising, for it is an element strange to the London stage, but there was more in the play, as both these critics agreed. Barker displayed in this play, as in the plays that followed, with the minimum of separation from actuality, the fact that he was concerned more with the reality of the characters and their situation than with surfaces and the transient moment. The best description of the play's impact was written by William Archer seven years later in *The Old Drama and the New*, when he said, referring to the afternoon of its first performance:

I should not be surprised if this came to be regarded as a noteworthy date in the history of the modern drama. At all events it is a red-letter day in my own experience; for on that afternoon I realized (utterly against all expectation or hope) that I could actually understand and enjoy a play by Mr. Granville Barker. I had known Mr. Barker for several years, and he had done me the honour of submitting to me in manuscript three or four of his youthful efforts. I saw in them a queer sort of originality, but I laboured under the disadvantage of being wholly unable to make head or tail of them. At last, tired of writing plays which were Hebrew to me, he declared he would write down to my intelligence; and the result was *The Marrying of Ann Leete*. He succeeded in a sense: it was written in a language not wholly unfamiliar to me; but . . . candour compels me to own that, after repeated attempts, I have not yet acquired a taste for it. . . . Therefore when the curtain went up on *The Voysey Inheritance* that November afternoon, I had not the least idea what was in store for me. Imagine my delight, then, when I found myself from the first interested and absorbed; when I found that I understood almost every word, one or two super-subtleties excepted; and when, at the end, I realized that here was a great play, a play conceived and composed with original mystery, and presenting on its spacious canvas a greater wealth of observation, character and essential drama than was to be found in any other play of our time.

I submit that, in *The Voysey Inheritance*, we have an English family group presented with a mastery of draughtsmanship and a depth of colour that remind us of a canvas of Rembrandt or Franz Hals, while at the same time the dramatic movement is sustained with subtle and original art. . . .

This judgment Time had not reversed; the play has often been revived, and is now firmly established in the English repertory of plays of the century.

Then came another Shavian masterpiece, *Major Barbara*, on 28 November, which had no more than the normal six matinées, ending on 15 December. Barker played Adolphus Cusins, modelled on Gilbert Murray – though the latter had written to Barker for Shaw to note, " If people call me Adolphus they do so at their peril ". There was difficulty with the censor over the play, who would not let it go forward until he was satisfied that the Salvation Army had no objection. In fact, the Army was delighted and was strongly represented at the first performance, although normally barred by their rules from attending theatres. Another thing that troubled the censor was Barbara's use of the words " My God : why hast thou forsaken me ? " in the second act, when she is overcome by a sense of failure. But after Barker had assured the censor that the words were a quotation from the Psalms, and as the Army found no fault, the censor was satisfied. Mrs. Sidney Webb found the play " a dance of devils ", and noted in her diary that Arthur James Balfour, who saw the play with her, " was taken aback by the force, the horrible force of the Salvation Army scene, the unrelieved tragedy of degradation, the disillusionment of the Greek professor and of Barbara – the triumph of the unmoral purpose . . .". A day or two later she called on the Shaws and found him alone in his study, and she goes on to say :

He was perturbed – indeed, upset by the bad acting, as he thought, of Undershaft and generally of all in the last scene – and by a violent attack on the play in the *Morning Post*. Calvert, he said, had completely lost his nerve over Undershaft – could not understand or remember his part and was aghast at what he considered its blank immorality.[1]

No one who saw that excellent actor on the stage could doubt that he was at a loss, and not for the first or last time was Shaw dissatisfied with his actors. All the same, the play caused the year 1905 to end in a blaze of glory that put the Court in the first place in the London theatre.

On New Year's Day, 1906, the theatre reopened with *Major Barbara* in the evening bill for six weeks only, with a few changes in the cast, the most important being Lewis Casson as Adolphus in place of Barker. It does not appear that Shaw was particularly happy with the state of affairs, for he wrote to Vedrenne on 10 January :

Your partner sent me word through the telephone that I could see him if I desired, on my way to Battersea, though it would not be particularly convenient to him. As I never expressed the smallest inclination that

---

[1] *Our Partnership*, p. 314.

way, and in fact, after the paltry remittance for which I enclose my receipt, never desire to see anyone connected with your wretched 7½% theatre again, I was at a loss to understand the communication.

The moody Barker was heavily engaged upon the production of Gilbert Murray's version of the *Electra* of Euripides, the matinées of which were to start on 16 January, and in which Edith Wynne-Matthison played the name part, Edyth Olive was Clytemnestra and Harcourt Williams Orestes. The music was written at the last moment by the conductor, Theodore Stier, who wrote:

It was done by a committee of three seated side by side upon the piano bench: Gilbert Murray, Granville Barker, and myself, each phrase as I played it being subjected to the close analysis of the other two, and accepted, rejected, or modified according to the joint decision.

There had been negotiations over this play since the previous August with Florence Farr (not to have her again as leader of the Chorus) and Mrs. Patrick Campbell (to get her for the name part). Mrs. Pat wanted the play for an American tour, to do with it as she pleased, and also the *Medea*, in which to tour both England and America. Vedrenne–Barker were willing to undertake to tour the plays in the United States with Mrs. Campbell, but only with their own production. Furthermore, Mrs. Pat would not undertake " to study and create the part for merely six performances at the Court Theatre ", her manager said, so Vedrenne–Barker agreed, if it were a success, " to put it on for a regular run of Tuesday and Friday matinées throughout the season ". But the lady could not get her own way, and did not appear at the Court. Part of the correspondence between the translator and Barker, with Vedrenne interposing, follows, with an opening reference to Shaw's play and continuing references to Barker's trouble over Florence Farr:

Granville Barker to Gilbert Murray

Saturday [August 1905].
Shaw writes that Adolphus Cusins quotes whole screeds of the *Bacchae* (I knew it'd be the *Bacchae* – blow the *Bacchae*!) What are you doing – the *Electra*? When am I going to see that? Have you any further ideas about the music – who is to break the matter to Miss Farr? Someone must steal her psalteries first for we shall want them. Of course, I'll *ask* her to come and play and chant someone else's music. She won't even answer.

Gilbert Murray to Granville Barker

August 19 1905.
Primo, I have finished the *Electra*, though there are still some bad bits, and there are no stage directions yet. I shall do it over in the next few days.

XVII   Lillah McCarthy

XVIII Lillah McCarthy (aged 15) as Lady Macbeth

Secundo, as to Miss Farr, I do not see our way clearly. (As to the *Bacchae*, I think we should only give her permission to perform as a last resort, in case we get into difficulties with her about, e.g. the music of the *Hippolytus*.) I agree with all your letter, subject to the following remarks. 1. Is it wise to be off with the old Chorus-Leader before you have at least some idea of a new one with whom you wish to be " on "? I agree in being dissatisfied with Miss Farr, but I have no person or system in my mind who would be better . . . nor, as far as I can see, as good. 2. On thinking things over, I am clearly against making the choruses more *musical*. . . . I mean, against sacrificing the words to the music. I would sooner get the words clear than have even a very good unintelligible song. I think you agree. This is a serious consideration in approaching any musician. 3. As to the leading of the chorus, the actual leading, on the stage, I think there is rather a disadvantage in the second *Hippolytus* arrangement – I mean in having Miss Farr, who has composed the music, in the ordinary chorus, and someone else leading and directing her. But really everything depends on your substitute for Miss F.

How are the Voyseys? I have just been hearing of a similar case in Carlisle. Only there the thing was found out at the father's death, and the honest son, who knew nothing about it, was taken as partner in the house that had wound up the father's affairs and exposed him. That is more in the style of the old-fashioned drama.

The post blares at me!

Granville Barker to Gilbert Murray

Sunday morning [August 1905].

As to Miss Farr – the question is a little serious. From my point of view there is the free-trade or protection question – complicated by the further question, what good or harm will a production – an archaic – or archaotic production by Miss Farr do to the Greek play cause as a whole? I think she may well get a more " beautiful " production than we do at the Court because Beauty is her sole idea – But I fear that it would be quite outside the theatre scale (so to speak) while I want to make the plays come as naturally to the theatre as possible, and also I have an uneasy feeling that all through – to get good results – Miss Farr lowers the standard. This is a device that is least easily seen through and it is most dangerous I'm sure. For Heaven's sake – she mustn't play about with Maskelyne and Cook transparencies. Then there's the question how time and space will cohere and jump. I want the *Electra* in the Spring at matinées, and thereabouts if possible an evening bill of *Hippolytus*, *Troades* (?) and the *Electra* – following up its matinée success which it has got to have. Now I don't really want to get rid of Miss Farr at all – at the very least I want her psalteries. But I want someone to replace her jejune harmonies with something better, and her muddling with a little real training of the chorus.

Miss Farr's music for the *Hippolytus* and a chorus properly trained with or without Miss Farr. Which music for the *Troades*? Someone else's music for *Electra* with chorus properly trained – with Miss Farr? With

E

Miss Farr's psalteries? But not with Miss Farr as *leader* in either of the three plays (but that doesn't involve Tita!). This wants much discussion – the peace negotiations at Portsmouth aren't in it. It seems to me that at the slightest of these proposed changes, even the *Electra* one, Miss Farr will throw us over – I wonder! But we must make our plans very soon, for there's work in this. Let me know about what time would suit you best to have *Electra* done – between Jan. and Easter.

Saturday [September 1905].

This is too belated to be called an answer to your letter. I've heard nothing further from Mrs. Campbell – *and* I haven't yet got *Electra* – But I will tell her that she should let you read it to her – But she refused to let *me*!!!

I think I have discovered a way out of the chorus difficulty – Percy Pitt to arrange matters. But also I want to try how simple speaking together would sound. I could get Miss Lamborn, Miss Thompson and another to try it. Will you be in town any time? You ought, in fact you *must* hear it. Also I want to "study" you.

J. E. Vedrenne to Gilbert Murray

Sept. 26. 1905.

I confirm your proposal as to Author's fees on the performance of the *Electra* at this Theatre. 5% if the gross receipts do not exceed £450 for the said six performances and 7½% on the total gross receipts if they exceed £450 for the said six performances. As to Mrs. Patrick Campbell, I hope she will play for us and we shall certainly be most happy to put the piece on for a run of four weeks in the evening should its success warrant it (as I expect it will). On the other hand, if she acts with Tree and is unable to play in the evening at the time which we have in our minds, I think we should give the matinées with her just the same and bottle the piece up for a revival as soon as Mrs. P.C. is available, or should she not be, do the play with someone else. She wrote me a very charming letter the other day and I am under the impression that she is anxious to play. She is asking for a delay of one or two weeks and we are therefore expecting to hear from her again.

Granville Barker to Gilbert Murray

Sept. 27 1905.

I also saw Mrs. Campbell that day after you read the play to her and she is I think really anxious to do *Electra*. We are now going to make a proposal to her of the 6 matinées in January and of 18 more matinées right through the London Season. This we think would be financially sound and probably an arrangement she would be able to accept at once, as it would not interfere with any evening engagements she may have.

She told me in her childish way that you were quite willing that we should hand the rights of the play over to her. I replied in my childish way that however willing you might be I had no intention of doing so.

Now I would be very careful about giving her any American rights.

It seems to me the important thing is that the first time the plays are done in America (and indeed every time) they should be done according to our design and your approval. It would be quiet easy for us to arrange with Frohman or with Mrs. Campbell, or as it would probably turn out in practice with both, to send a production to America, that is, the scenery, the chorus, the costumes the cast and the business arranged as you and I have done it, with Mrs. Campbell as Electra – and why not as Phaedra? – and could she play Hecuba? I think this would be a better game than letting Mrs. Campbell loose to do what she liked with the play; for one thing my experience of her as a leading woman producing plays is that she sends all the other actors into a Lunatic Asylum before the curtain ever rises. It would certainly be more satisfactory to us. Of course we must take care that no deadlock results from trying to make this arrangement, but I think that could be managed.

Monday [October 1905].

The point of all this is of course that these *Greek* plays must not be put into a repertory [with other plays]. It seems in the case of *Electra* – Mrs. P.C. as a star, the rest of the cast as it happens and the chorus anyhow (for a repertory company cannot manage a Greek chorus). Now you cannot book the *Electra* alone for an American tour and therefore if Mrs. P.C. gets this one piece to play about with – part of a repertory is its only fate. So I want to arrange matters that the 3 plays we've done so far may be tied together (with Mrs. P.C. in the centre by all means if she'll do it). That will make it worth while to send out a special company to play them – you can afford for 3 plays what you can't afford for one – or if we can't bring this off I want to let her have the *Electra* only on such conditions – as to chorus, scenery – cast – as will ensure a proper start for Euripides-Murray in America.

I hope you think I'm right in this and will back me up. *I think* she means to play the part here and I very much hope she will – but I shouldn't break my heart if she didn't, and anyhow she's not a lady to give way to – I saw her yesterday. She's intelligent about it of course, but too precious – she doesn't see yet I'm sure where the real point of the thing lies – but she'll get to it.

Wed. night [October 1905].

I want her either to go to some trouble over the play – which she'll do if she makes a success here or to leave it alone – which she'll do if she doesn't. But I think to let her have it carelessly to use or let alone as she likes would be bad policy. But I take it that you are in agreement with me that she ought to reproduce the Court production as we arranged it – otherwise of course the position we take up on the matter is not sound from your point of view – but this is so isn't it?

October 13th, 1905.

The other day I saw Mrs. Campbell. She asked me if we would give up the *Medea* in order to let her produce it in London for some matinées in November and take it to America in the Spring. She asked me if I would attend five or six rehearsals and apparently help her to produce it, but I said at once this was out of the question, for I cannot produce Greek plays in five or six rehearsals, as you know, and also I am nothing like ready with it.

On the main question of letting the play go, I have spoke to Vedrenne and our position is this: We should very much regret losing the play and breaking the continuity of your association with us. But at the same time we feel that we ought not to stand in the way of what you may consider a more advantageous chance. What we can guarantee you is this – a production for eight matinées some time during 1907, and a Medea of whom you approve. Mrs. Patrick Campbell . . . if she would come on reasonable terms and make her arrangements a reasonable way ahead, but as it seems impossible to induce her to be at all businesslike I should say this practically means *not* Mrs. Campbell. Now you must consider if she can go one better.

Vedrenne and Barker being now in competition cannot offer you any advice on the subject, but Barker can and does. It is only this – that you should consider very carefully the sort of production you will get from Mrs. Campbell at short notice, with no ideas as to the chorus and with a fair percentage of her American modern comedy company playing the parts. Against this danger there is the great asset of her personality and her obvious liking for the play. I am not sure myself which way the scale dips, but that is what you have to consider.

Nov. 21st, 1905.

Also how about Ainley for Orestes? I do not think I ought to play in the piece. My acting is getting worse every day and the production is so important and my mind will be upon that and not upon a part.

Dec. 5th, 1905.

Surely Miss Olive is too young for Clytemnestra. I fear you are cultivating a conscience about Miss Olive. This is wrong, however, I will dispute that matter further in a moment. I had thought of Miss Frances Ivor, who is the rather battered woman of 45 that I suppose Clytemnestra should be. That or something like that will, it seems to me, be a professional and businesslike piece of casting. The Miss Olive idea strikes me as a little amateurish. Orestes is most difficult, I never for a moment thought of anybody like Hearn, and I think the rejected Hippolytus had not anything like enough experience. I am inclining towards Harcourt Williams, who can speak verse, and although he is rather inclined to strain after his effects he is about the right weak-strong personality.

After all this, the play was not done by Mrs. Patrick Campbell. She was, however, to become associated with the Court Theatre later. The Greek plays were the Court's greatest stage innovation, but Barker did not solve, either then or later, the problem of the chorus.

A decided failure then occurred, for on 6 February a three-act comedy by Robert Vernon Harcourt, *A Question of Age*, was produced by Barker, the programme filled out with a one-act piece by Frederick Fenn, *The Convict on the Hearth*. The last little piece was attractive, though conventional, but the Harcourt comedy was altogether too thin a play: it was accepted, no doubt, because of the great anxiety to introduce new dramatists, but was so complete a mistake that, intended to have six matinées, it was taken off after two. The play really collapsed at the first performance owing to Fanny Brough in the lead cutting two pages containing the essence of the plot. Cleverly written, it was not up to the Court Theatre standard.

Major Barbara, which was in the evening bill, completed the matinées. Then *The Voysey Inheritance* followed the Shaw play on 12 February for four weeks only, with Barker for the first time as Edward Voysey, a part that suited him exactly.

But the next series of matinées, consisting of two plays by Maurice Hewlett, *Pan and the Young Shepherd* and *The Youngest of the Angels*, in both of which Lillah McCarthy reappeared on the Court stage, were also failures. Both charmingly written, they were essentially undramatic, and could not be made to hold the stage, despite Barker's delicate production. The takings fell to £13. Then on 12 March the *Electra* was put into the evening bill for two weeks, followed by the *Hippolytus* for a further two weeks, but they, too, spelled financial failure, for at the second performance of the first play the takings were no more than £15 6s., the week's total being £189 10s. 3d., the second week doing better at £280 18s. 9d. *Hippolytus* was even worse, taking £181 13s. 9d. and £193 1s. in its two weeks.

Shaw was furious at Barker's choice of the matinée plays, and at what he considered to be essentially untheatrical pieces. Yet his fury came after the result, not before the performances, when he was noncommittal; in fact, he was aroused more by Barker's production than by anything else. He talked openly about bankruptcy, making no secret of his displeasure. It was under such conditions that Ellen Terry was at last induced to appear in *Captain Brassbound's Conversion*. There were six matinées, starting on 20 March, while the Greek play was occupying the stage in the evening.

Ellen Terry's entrance on the Court stage was a great event, but the star was highly nervous and not sure of herself. At a rehearsal Vedrenne asked Shaw, " Is Miss Terry speaking the lines as you wrote them? " Shaw, making the best of a bad job, replied, " No; but she's speaking the lines as I ought to have written them."

The story is told by Theodore Stier in his reminiscences, *With Pavlova Round the World* (1929), in which there are many good Court Theatre stories, for Stier became music conductor at the theatre soon after the

Vedrenne–Barker opening. He was a young man then, and they gave him his first chance, paying him at the start their usual 1 guinea a performance. With Stier's aid, a feature was always made of the music at the theatre, so much so that Vedrenne complained that the audience remained in their seats during the intervals and the bar receipts fell seriously. Stier tells an excellent story about the incidental music for Shaw's play. It occurred to Barker that a chorus of sea chanties could be introduced into the second act with advantage, and he asked Stier to get them. He was not successful, but on reporting the fact to Barker was told that it did not matter, as a boy had come into his office that day who had been a deck-hand on a windjammer and had made a hobby of composing sea-songs, so Barker had made an appointment for the boy to come to the theatre the next day to whistle the tunes. This is Stier's account:

And sure enough at the appointed time on the following day a slim, poorly dressed, and very shy young seaman insinuated himself through the door of my sanctum. "Mr. Barker told me to come and whistle to you," he said diffidently, twirling his cap in his hands. "That's all right," I said. "Sit down and let me hear those sea chanties I've heard so much about." So, very stiff and upright in a chair, the young sailor went through the tunes that in his spare time he had composed in the forecastle of a wooden sailing ship. When he got up to go, obviously relieved that his ordeal was at an end, I asked him his name. "John Masefield," he said.[1]

Masefield's lasting friendship with Barker followed, and before the end of the year he was writing to Barker about the production of *The Campden Wonder*: his first sight of the stage had filled him with ambition.

After *Captain Brassbound's Conversion* had been put into the evening bill on 16 April for twelve weeks, the longest run yet given to any play at the Court, but by no means a profitable one, there started eleven matinées of *Prunella*, with W. Graham Browne as Pierrot and Dorothy Minto as Prunella. This time the piece took on.

*

But on that day, 24 April, Granville Barker and Lillah McCarthy were married at the West Strand Registry Office (where Shaw had been married in 1898) in the presence of his solicitor and her father. The month before she had still been more or less engaged to her Cheltenham friend, and had told Barker she was going to marry him, but Barker said, "No!" So she gave up the other man, and as, in fact, she was madly in love with Barker, got engaged to him, and they were married. It was quickly carried out. On the day of the marriage Barker wrote to Murray:

---

[1] *With Pavlova Round the World*, p. 265.

April 24 [1906].

Now see the result of your having this operation. In an hour's time I'm going to be married. If you'd come for another holiday with me it might never have happened. Lillah McCarthy – whom you don't know – do you? – is the unfortunate victim – Pray for her, Murray, and that I may be given one or two of your qualities to help me to make life good for her.

Yours on the brink,
H. G. B.

It was a secret from everyone, except Shaw and Vedrenne. Shaw was away in Paris, sitting to the sculptor, Rodin. The married couple went there after the ceremony, and had luncheon with Shaw and the sculptor. "You intriguing miss," said Shaw to Lillah. They went off to Germany and the Tyrol for their honeymoon. When Shaw got back home he said to Vedrenne, "Now Lillah will have all the best parts" – a mischievous remark, which Vedrenne took to heart.

While in Berlin they saw a Reinhardt production of *Caesar and Cleopatra*, which, when he heard of what the producer had done, caused Shaw to declare, "May the soul of Reinhardt scream through all eternity in boiling brimstone," because of a serious cut. Later, Barker wrote to Lady Mary Murray:

Hotel Vier Jahreszeiten, Munchen.
Friday [May 1906].

My dear Lady Mary

It isn't in me after much journeying to and from – Paris – Mainz – Berlin – Dresden and here – think of it and pity my poor wife, who is not nearly so tired as I am though – it isn't in me to say all I want to say to you and G.M. I was very glad to get your letters. The "in an hour" was literal – we kept it all quiet because I cannot bear the conventional merrymaking and congratulations. One marries in fear and trembling and drops one's dearest possession (the latest M.S. say) into the Thames to propitiate the gods.

I want you to know my wife and to like her. But if you don't – and why should you because I do (though perhaps that is a reason) I hope you'll just dislike her frankly and not like me any the less or let there come any differences between us.

She says she'd like much to come to Oxford and see you. We're back in June – I leave again in July but she stays on to work.

Is the patient better still. I owe him a letter – but tell him that business pursues me even as it did round "the blue Mediterranean where we lay". Thank you for all you write to me.

Yours,
H. G. Barker.

He also wrote to her husband, Gilbert Murray, two letters, in one of which he disclosed that even on his honeymoon he could not cease playwriting:

> Hotel Ginstermunz, Tirol.
> May 19, '06.
>
> I have just written a perfect pamphlet to Lord Lytton on the 'orrible economic conditions of the theatrical profession – therefore I am dashed if I will write a long letter to you *in* my 'orrible condition (when I've worked for two days – and done precious little I get a headache). *But* I will simply enquire will *Medea* be ready by the New Year? We are talking our arrangements now, Vedrenne and I. I am nearly through the life of Gladstone. I haven't been so fascinated with a book for years. It is cheering to discover (1) how consistently unpopular he was because (2) no one ever understood him. And very interesting to see – not what he got to but what he came from. I wish Morley wouldn't talk about his " four-score years " quite so much. My homage to you all.

> May 20 [1906].
>
> I'd like to write you a really proper and well-spelt letter saying all or most of what I think and feel towards you – 3 vols Qto it would be. But I will now content myself with hoping that you've escaped the witch doctors at last – that your operation for hay fever (apply ice to the feet for a cold in the head) has been entirely successful – by stating that this is the most beautiful place I have ever seen, that I have just begun to tackle seriously my play, that I have not yet beaten my wife with a red-hot poker (there are none in the Tirol), but otherwise am only an average husband – by enquiring after *Medea*'s health.

The Barkers went to live at 3 Clement's Inn, to which Barker had moved from the Adelphi some months earlier, the rooms having been taken for him by Mrs. Lee Matthews and furnished for him by her. Mrs. Matthews was much attached to Barker, who owed a good deal of his knowledge of music to her. They engaged additional rooms and built a spiral staircase from the upper floor to the lower floor taken for Lillah: there they remained for several years. Lillah also looked for a house in the country, and found a place at Fernhurst, near Haslemere, in Surrey, a delightful spot where they lived for some time, though it was very inconvenient for the theatre. The Shaws gave them as a wedding present a Bechstein piano with a pianola attachment, which Barker played a great deal. The members of the stock company presented him with his first comfortable armchair, giving him, possibly, as Lewis Casson remarked when telling me the story, " a taste of the luxury that led eventually to his downfall! " Barker seems to have needed much looking after, for he neglected his clothes and his food, and was in a poor physical state. He suffered much from gastric trouble, and sometimes lay on the stage in pain during rehearsals. Lillah was able to see that he had regular meals, and she insisted on a cottage in the country for his health's sake, and to give him quiet to work at his plays. He was inclined to be moody and irritable; a delicate, excitable man at that time. There is a significant remark recorded by Beatrice Webb in her diary after Barker had been taken by her, following his marriage, to see Lord Milner. As they left, Barker said to her, "He would have been made by being loved." Barker was being loved as never before.

Unfortunately, Vedrenne had taken Shaw's jest seriously about the manager's wife having all the leading parts, and thereafter he was insistent that Lillah should be treated on what he (Vedrenne) considered to be her merits, which meant that she was usually objected to. This, however, was as much a resistance to his partner as to the actress, and, as the objections increased, the increasing strain under which the partnership was continued is indicated.

One of their closest friends was J. M. Barrie. He liked to come to the rehearsals, admiring both Barker and Shaw at work, and both were more than pleased to have Barrie there, that master-craftsman of the stage. But it was Barker to whom Barrie gave most of his attachment, and both he and Lillah were frequent visitors to Barrie's house.

*

On 9 July *You Never Can Tell* followed the run of the Ellen Terry play, with Lillah McCarthy appearing for the first time as Gloria and Henry Ainley again as Valentine, for a limited number of weeks. It was followed on 17 September by a six weeks' run of *John Bull's Other Island*, with William Poel as Keegan and Ellen O'Malley returning as Nora. The matinées were resumed on 25 September with a first play by a new dramatist, *The Silver Box*, by John Galsworthy. This production showed Barker's realistic manner of stage production to perfection, and the play made a great impression. I shall say more about Barker's realism as a producer later; here it is sufficient to say that it made the play, giving it a poetic tragedy–comedy quality, utterly different from the naturalistic treatment it has since received. On 23 October it was followed by St. John Hankin's comedy, *The Charity that Began at Home*, another Barker production, which was nothing like so successful as the preceding piece. *Man and Superman* returned to the evening bill on 29 October, with Barker and Lillah in their original parts.

While this superb piece was still being played, another high-water mark was reached on 20 November with Shaw's *The Doctor's Dilemma*, which was allowed eight matinées, Barker and Lillah playing the Dubedats. To some extent, Shaw had Barker in mind when writing the part of the artist, Louis Dubedat. It was not a portrait, but an exaggerated presentation of certain aspects of Barker. His performance was much criticized Desmond MacCarthy, however, praised him for acting the death "naturally and realistically", and defended him against the charge of making the artist die "in a pose", which, again, is what Shaw intended That the dramatist borrowed something from Barker can be seen from his description of the character:

. . . pretty, though not effeminate. He has turquoise blue eyes, and a trick of looking you straight in the face with them which, combined into a frank smile, is very engaging. Although he is all nerves, and very observant and quick of apprehension, he is not in the least shy . . . he moves among men as most men move among things, though he is intentionally making himself agreeable to them. . . .

Barker's eyes were not blue, as were Shaw's, but the description might otherwise have applied to him. His performance had elevation of thought and emotion, and for that reason, in addition to the fine, rhetorical speaking, it was a marked success.

This play followed *Man and Superman* in the evenings, on 31 December, for six weeks only. By this time Barker and John Masefield were firm friends; Masefield wrote to him on 20 December suggesting a Christmas pact for the coming year that they should lunch together one day in each week.

The new year saw the final six months at the Court, with everyone, despite the Shavian brilliances, much depressed, for the Ellen Terry venture had landed them in a loss, and there had been too many other, though much smaller, financial failures. Indeed, the first matinées with which the year, on 8 January, opened repeated the failures. They consisted of a very light comedy, *The Reformer*, by Cyril Harcourt, and a short play in three scenes by John Masefield called *The Campden Wonder*. Both were admirably produced by Barker, who found the young actor-author of the first piece very fussy about his play; but the programme did not please, for the Harcourt comedy was altogether too light and empty for such digestions as the Court Theatre had trained, and the Masefield play was too much even for them, though praised by Shaw and others. An imperfect dramatic piece, it appalled most playgoers by its horror, and putting it in the same programme as the Harcourt triviality was an unfortunate managerial decision, for the plays were not for the same audience. After the experience with his first play, Masefield would not allow it to be played again, though it was printed in a limited edition. Vedrenne could never be got to consider a Masefield play again. Masefield was, however, fired with the idea of playwriting, and sent Barker the synopsis of a proposed farce based on a story told him by a sea-cook. That Masefield became a dramatist of considerable distinction, the fore-runner of modern verse-dramatists, came out of this first effort and Barker's enthusiasm for his writing. His second play, not in verse, was produced by Barker later on, as well as one of his first verse plays, as we shall see.

Although Shaw admired the Masefield play, he stormed round and round the little foyer of the theatre when no one but the staff was about, exclaiming against the smallness of the houses and the financial results, for which he blamed the theatre, the management, the production, the acting, the methods of publicity, the critics, and the play especially, if it were not his own; but he never blamed the public. The public was never at fault, though everything else might be. He wooed the public, flattered it, scared it, insulted it, but never despised or was afraid of it.

He was insistent that his belittled early play, *The Philanderer*, should be done. He had great belief in it, and considered it could be made " a humming success " given the right actress for Julia, which he believed he had found in Lillah McCarthy. Barker was not keen on the play, neither was Lillah on the part, but in face of all objections the rehearsals went on, Shaw protesting against the lukewarmness he had to overcome. At the dress rehearsal, however, Lillah was taken off to hospital with a miscarriage, and on the day after, 5 February, the play had Mary Barton, her understudy, in the part. It is not surprising that the piece was coldly received. A photograph of Lillah as Julia appeared in the *Sketch* on 6 February. Fortunes were recovered by a six weeks' revival of *You Never Can Tell*, starting on 11 February, with Grace Lane as Gloria and Granville Barker, forced back by Shaw into his original part; this was the last time Barker was seen on the Court stage.

At last Mrs. Patrick Campbell appeared in Ibsen's *Hedda Gabler*, which was given seven matinées only, starting on 5 March. The production dis-played the actress's powers at their best, and had the integrity the play demands for its full dramatic effect. In her memoirs, Mrs. Pat wrote grudgingly of Barker:

Mr. Barker attended the rehearsals and sometimes Mr. Bernard Shaw; their " basso-relievo " methods fidgeted me. However, as far as I remember, they left me alone.[1]

She says that she spent well over the salary she received on Hedda's wardrobe, and because of the success of the matinées she wanted them continued, " but Messrs. Vedrenne and Barker were adamant "; they told her the Court Theatre was not for stars. She did a provincial tour,

[1] p. 212.

however, and afterwards took the play to America, but, not being allowed to do the Gilbert Murray *Electra* there, she played Arthur Symons's version of Hofmannsthal's play of that name.

*

Mention has been made of a little-noticed verse piece by Barker called *A Miracle*, which was now given a public matinée performance on 23 March by the Literary Theatre Society at Terry's Theatre, produced by Robert Farquharson. The two characters were played by Winifred Fraser (to whom Barker had given the play years before) and Gwendolyn Bishop. This tiny medieval play had costumes and setting by Charles Ricketts which gave it some distinction. In the same programme a version of *The Persians* in a prose translation by B. J. Ryan was produced by Lewis Casson. Barker had nothing to do with his own play: he had called it " an experiment ", and it was, indeed, an early experiment in modern verse drama.

In sending Barker a copy of his collection of stories, *A Tarpaulin Muster*, at the end of March, Masefield said that Barker must tell his friends that he (Masefield) had had very little sea experience, and added:

But you must tell them also, that an artist is only hampered by experience; and that it is no more necessary to be a sailor to write about the sea, than it was necessary for Shakespeare to keep a brothel, or to poison his father, in order to write parts of *Hamlet* or *Measure for Measure*.

*

At the Court in the evening bill on 8 April, *The Silver Box* appeared for three weeks only with the original cast, save for a few exceptions, and the Ibsen play was followed on 9 April by Elizabeth Robins's *Votes for Women !* This topical piece provided one of Barker's easy triumphs as a producer, showing him to be a master in handling crowd scenes. Then *The Return of the Prodigal* was given the evening bill from 29 April, but was so poorly received that the Elizabeth Robins play was substituted for it after two weeks. Shaw was angry over the St. John Hankin play, despite the praise it had earlier received, declaring it to be a poor piece and the production no credit to Barker. He had bitterly complained in a letter to Vedrenne about Barker: " He won't act himself, and drives out of the theatre, on one pretext or another, everyone who could take his place." Shaw was always free with his criticism of Barker in particular, because he thought it was good for him. He went on in the same letter to point out to Vedrenne what he had done for the management:

I have given you a series of first-rate music-hall entertainments, thinly disguised as plays, but really offering the public a unique string of turns by comics and serio-comics of every popular type.

haw took Barker's seriousness very seriously indeed – not that Barker
cked a sense of humour, for he certainly did not, but, because he took
bstacles too heavily, was too readily discouraged, and could not let off
team so easily as Shaw. But Shaw's railling only made Barker more
erious than ever. Shaw told him to go and take a holiday, which he
id early in May, spending a few weeks abroad.

Before that, however, on 7 May, eight matinées of *Prunella* started, to
neet again with success, and as the last evening bill *Man and Superman*, on
7 May for five weeks only, in which Robert Loraine played Tanner,
nd, finally, the last eight matinées from 4 June, consisting of Shaw's
ream scene from *Man and Superman*, entitled *Don Juan in Hell*, and the
ame dramatist's early one-act piece, *The Man of Destiny*. There had
een talk of doing the *Don Juan* scene as long ago as the end of 1905,
vhen Florence Farr was interested in it and came to see Charles Ricketts
vith Shaw to discuss the proposal, as Ricketts records in his journal;
ut Shaw put up objections, as he did not then see a cast for it, particularly
or the part of Ana. It was now played by Robert Loraine, Lillah
McCarthy, Michael Sherbrooke, and Norman McKinnel – a splendid cast
or a dramatic *tour de force*, brilliantly played, beautifully staged, and
naking a deep impression. Shaw took immense pains with it, Barker
ooking after the stage management. Charles Ricketts, writing to Lillah
fterwards, said of Shaw's production:

was delighted with his method of training by lucid pieces of acting and
xplanations of difficult passages; and he avoided interruptions and noisy
xclamations so usual at rehearsals, in this respect he is nearer the French
tandard, where speech is even over-studied; in England too much
ttention is given to business.

Ricketts' costumes were magnificent, and the cost nearly broke Vedrenne's
neart. Shaw referred to the performance in one of his letters to Mrs.
Patrick Campbell five years later, saying about Robert Loraine:

. . when Ricketts did that magical production of the hell scene from
Man and Superman, he (Robert) was simply wretched in his exquisite
ilver dress, and thought that Ricketts was making him ridiculous instead
of immortal.

The production of the second piece, played by Dion Boucicault as General
Bonaparte and Irene Vanbrugh as the Lady, was not on the same high
evel; neither was the acting.

None the less, the season closed in a blaze of glory. The last per-
ormance was on Saturday, 29 June. An era in the history of London
Irama was ended, for, while the management continued for some time,

its great contribution to the twentieth-century stage had been made in the two years and nine months at the Royal Court Theatre. Thirty-two plays by seventeen authors had been performed, twenty-eight for the first time, and 946 performances had been given, five performances having programmes of more than one play – four double and one triple bill.

*

A complimentary dinner to Vedrenne and Barker took place at the Criterion Restaurant on 7 July, when Lord Lytton was in the chair and 150 friends assembled. The dinner had been arranged in the name of a number of distinguished people, the executive work being done by Frederick Whelen, W. Hector Thomson, and John Pollock. There were two menus, one vegetarian. In proposing the health of the guests Lord Lytton said that " they have given us . . . something of which, as Englishmen, we can justly be proud ". He expressed the fear that America would rob the country of Mr. Barker, which, he said, would be a " severe blow to the English drama and an abiding disgrace to this country ". He concluded by saying that he hoped that before long they would meet again " to congratulate our two guests of to-night on the completion of their experiment in the establishment of a real National Repertory Theatre ".

In reply Vedrenne gave a simple expression of thanks to all who had helped them – authors, actors, theatre staff, brother managers for lending artists, and the Press. Barker, in a modest speech, began by saying that they were standing on the shoulders of older men, mentioning J. T. Grein, William Archer, and William Poel. He claimed that the significance of their work was the system on which they produced their plays. They had by no means started a repertory theatre or anything like it, but had introduced a system " which may prove the artistic necessity of such an institution " :

We have opposed to the long-run system the short-run system. It has many disadvantages, perhaps, but it keeps the plays fresh. . . . I think we can claim that the plays are more value now both from a business and an artistic point of view than they would have been had they simply been run callously to the fullest limit of their popularity.

Barker thanked the authors, and, in the presence of Herbert Beerbohm Tree, threw a stone at the actor-managers. Tree followed in a long speech, twice the length of Barker's, proposing the health of the authors and said :

It has always been a source of deep regret to me that the conditions of the theatre over which I now preside have precluded my devoting my whole-hearted energies to the modern drama.

In a reply for the authors, of equal length, Shaw attacked the Press, " which from first to last has done what in it lay to crush the enterprise . . . by grudging, petulant, ill-conditioned disparagement ". At the end of Shaw's speech the proceedings were brought by the management of the restaurant to an abrupt end, the time for closing having passed.

*

This is the moment to survey what had been accomplished at the Court. The aims were to find new dramatists and to create a new audience.   For these aims Bernard Shaw and Granville Barker were jointly responsible. Though not technically part of the management, Shaw was an essential factor, for without his encouraging support, energy and advice, little or nothing would have been achieved.   His attention to every aspect of the enterprise was unremitting; he was an inspiration, and at the same time a candid and disturbing critic.   Fortunately, he and Barker had aims in common, and fortunately, too, Barker accepted the leadership of the older man.   The relations between the two were as intimate as between father and son, and as full of conflict and disagreement, with the same firm attachment that could not (it seemed) be broken.

Vedrenne as a business-man was fascinated by his two associates, " like a man trying to ride two runaway horses simultaneously ", said Shaw. Writing to Shaw after the dinner to the two partners, Charles Ricketts said :

I was at the dinner . . . to find out, incidentally, if Vedrenne really existed : like all men, I had viewed him as merely a smart impersonation of Barker's, done with a wig and a pair of blue spectacles.

All who had business relations with the partnership knew Vedrenne, but to others he was unknown, though Ricketts was voicing a general impression.   Vedrenne possessed not only caution, but also maintained a standard of highest reliability in the firm's business transactions.   He was thirty-nine when the Court season finished, and after his death on 12 February 1930 Barker wrote of him :

It was a pretty precarious enterprise; and its capital, in the sense that was his chief concern, consisted almost literally of his aplomb (the French word naturally fits), his shrewd ingenuity and his sense of reality in business, when all the talking was done for the moment, when he was left alone to add up his figures. . . .

He was fundamentally the most cautious of men, always knew to a shilling where he was, and every shilling he spent brought its shilling's worth – and more !

There was a particular contract of which the party of the one part received a blue copy, the party of the other part retaining a white one, that was usually known as the Seidlitz Powder.[1]

Shaw did his utmost to induce well-known writers to turn to play-writing, among them H. G. Wells, Conrad, Kipling, Maurice Hewlett, and G. K. Chesterton. Wells afterwards proved himself to have no gifts as a dramatist; neither had Conrad, though he tried his hand, nor Kipling, and Hewlett's efforts were failures. Chesterton showed dramatic talent, but too late for the Court. The new audience was required because regular playgoers had been spoiled by the false values of the London theatre, and, as Coleridge said, poets have to create the taste for their work: appreciation of the new drama had to be aroused and cultivated. That was not all, for, above everything, both Shaw and Barker intended to establish a new standard of acting and production.

The aims were in fact realized. Dramatists of importance in John Galsworthy, St. John Hankin, Laurence Housman, John Masefield, and Granville Barker himself were introduced to the English stage, while Greek drama was for the first time made practicable for modern audiences in the verse translations of Gilbert Murray. Among foreign dramatists, works by Ibsen, Maeterlinck, Schnitzler, and Hauptmann were brought before the public. Bernard Shaw, though by no means a new dramatist, was established in the forefront of English playwrights. When all is said, of course, his plays were the major element in the enterprise. Before Vedrenne and Barker had got together, Shaw had not been adequately presented to the London public, for, apart from Miss Horniman's effort ten years earlier with *Arms and the Man* and the Stage Society's " meet-ings ", the Shavian drama was virtually unknown on the stage. A number of plays, it is true, had been toured in the provincial cities by various people, but Shaw would allow none of them to come to London, because none was good enough. Vedrenne and Barker gave him his opportunity, as surely as the partnership gave Barker his opportunity. Without them, Shaw would still have waited; without him, they could not have started. It was, indeed, Shaw's practical theatrical sense as well as his plays, to say nothing (as nothing was ever said) of his money, that provided the basis for the undertaking.

Not only were there new plays, however; the achievement in produc-tion and acting was such that people were able to say, with new meaning, how excellent London actors are. In short, the question can rightly be asked: Where would the commercial theatre be to-day without the work of Vedrenne and Barker at the Court Theatre? What Max Beerbohm

[1] *The Author*, April 1930.

wrote eighteen months before the end was an accurate evaluation of what the management had achieved:

People often ask, quite innocently, with a genuine desire for information, why the acting at the Court Theatre seems so infinitely better than in so many other theatres where the same mimes are to be seen. One is that the mimes at the Court are very carefully stage-managed, every one of them being kept in such relation to his fellows as is demanded by the relation in which the various parts stand to one another – no one mime getting more, or less, of a chance than the playwright has intended him to have. The other reason is that at the Court Theatre are produced only plays written by clever persons who have a sense of character and who are thus enabled to create characters which are human, and which, therefore, repay the trouble that the mimes take in playing them.

In her memoirs, *Myself and My Friends*, Lillah McCarthy confirmed this, agreeing that there was loss of power when the same actors went to other theatres and played for other managements. She went on:

There was inspiration, originality, and discipline in the Court productions. When we went elsewhere, the part was everything; but at the Court . . . any of us would cheerfully take a small role, for we knew that even so we should not have to be subservient, negative and obsequious to the star. . . . We were members of a theatrical House of Lords; all equal and all lords.

Barker's own acting in parts that suited him – Marchbanks, Keegan, Valentine, Tanner, and Dubedat in Shaw's plays, and Edward Voysey in his own – was unforgettable. He played all these parts as if they had been written for him, and everyone who saw him in them will I think agree that no other actor has approached what he did. He had a lyrical quality, an elevation of spirit, that was extraordinarily exciting. But, to repeat what has already been said here and will be said again, he did not care for acting, and avoided it when he could. His enthusiasm and understanding, however, never (or shall I say, seldom?) deserted him; and from that fact the enterprise gained more than can be said.

It is natural to compare the Court with the Abbey Theatre in Dublin, founded a few days earlier the same year. While the first depended mainly on Shaw with a widening base of other dramatists, the other depended on Yeats, Synge, and Lady Gregory. The Court lasted less than three years; the Abbey remains. Yet the two enterprises, though akin, with aims not essentially dissimilar, were very different in the conditions they accepted. The one started as an amateur effort, on a comparatively modest scale, but had a building of its own. The other was in competition with the London West End theatres, on a scale that such competition demanded, with obligations financial and otherwise

F

with which those of the little Irish theatre did not compare, and it was without the money to acquire a suitable theatre had one been available. For every pound spent in Dublin fifty were required in London. Had it been practicable to make the Court a permanent home, the capital demanded would have been a large sum; but it was not practicable, and from Barker's point of view was not even desirable, for in his eyes that theatre was but a makeshift, and, indeed, cosy as it was in the stalls and dress circle, was a very inconvenient building. Both enterprises were alike in depending upon dramatists, and both were alike in making important, even revolutionary, contributions to stage production, for both also depended upon actors. What Barker contributed as actor and producer to the Court, the Fays contributed to the Abbey. The combination of dramatists and actors is, indeed, essential to the theatre at all times, most of all in times of change.

What had been done had left its mark. The stimulating effect of Shaw's plays the stage was never to lose, and the foundation of his great fortune was laid, and Barker as producer had set a standard of acting and production that has not since been surpassed. Barker had the teaching ability and the technical knowledge of the stage, for he was himself an actor and was able, when necessary, to demonstrate what the play demanded of the player. He never adopted type-casting, and each player was expected to use his brains. Creativity was looked for in everyone, and though Barker knew exactly what he wanted, he was no autocrat. He was insistent and determined, reasonable and charming in manner, but fell out with players who were self-opinionated or unimaginative. Every actor in every part was expected to give of his best, and Barker spared no effort to develop even the smallest character to the full extent required by the play. The leading character was never treated as a star part in which the attempt is made to exploit the actor's personality to the fullest degree, no matter at what sacrifice of other players or the play. The work of individual actors was limited by, and was not allowed to go beyond, the requirements of the play as a whole. Thus the stage had life at every moment, and the play had full justice done to it. There was never anything mechanical, or brittle, or merely clever in any of his productions. He was always able to get from his players acting that had life and interest, even when the play had a trivial theme, but he was limited by the theme, never seeking to transcend it.

Although it is often said that the Court Theatre was a financial failure, the facts are that both Vedrenne and Barker drew their salaries as managers week by week, Barker being paid in addition as actor and author, and, despite the poor returns from the performances of *Captain Brassbound's Conversion*, at the end a small balance remained to the good.

*

To bring the work that had been done right into the West End of London, a lease was taken of the Savoy Theatre, in the Strand, from Mrs. D'Oyley Carte. At the same time a proposal was made to convert the management into a limited company, with Shaw a member of it, but he would not have anything to do with such an idea, for, he said, nothing would be gained, and it would lead to trouble. He made it quite clear that he was not a member of the partnership, either : "I am not going into partnership : I shall simply act as a usurer." On those terms, he put up the sum of £2,000 at 5 per cent. interest to enable the Savoy season to start, Vedrenne and Barker putting up £1,000 each, Shaw saying : "This will be a real proceeding on my part, and a purely paper one on yours." Under this arrangement, Vedrenne and Barker were each to continue to draw salaries of £1,000 a year, to be charged as expenses, with Barker receiving a salary as actor and fees as author in addition. "My own salary, another thousand," said Shaw, "is to be taken out in moral superiority." There was talk by Barker of doing Congreve and Shakespeare, but Shaw was dead against it. He was full of complaints against Barker, "because", as he wrote to Vedrenne, of "his reluctance to tackle anything but easy plays and easy people – easy, that is, to his temperament". The qualification should be noted.

However, the Savoy Theatre season proved to be little more than a flash in the pan after the blaze at the Court. Conceived with some enthusiasm the previous autumn, when the inconveniences and limitations of the Court Theatre were conspicuous, the move to the West End was regarded as necessary for getting full recognition of what the partnership was doing. After all, the Court was an out-of-town theatre, and though very handy for those who were near to the Underground railway, it was two miles from the centre. On the other hand, the Savoy was a famous West End theatre, and about twice the size of the Court. It was, however, at that date, though only twenty-six years old, a rather uncomfortable building, and, somehow or other, the regular Court Theatre audience found itself not at home and never became at home. Also by the time the season was to start a strong feeling of uncertainty had grown up in the partnership itself. Barker was more moody than ever, and was more and more doubtful that the work they were doing was leading anywhere, and Vedrenne had his mind upon a new theatre in Shaftesbury Avenue, then nearing completion. Shaw was highly sceptical about the whole affair, but that was always his way when other people were determined upon anything.

It was intended to follow their well-established system : a play for short runs in the evening, with the usual matinées, and a series of special matinées on Tuesdays, Thursdays, and Fridays. The first play was a revival of the old favourite, *You Never Can Tell*, which opened the season on 16 September 1907, with Harcourt Williams as Valentine and Ellen O'Malley as Gloria. The first of the special matinées was John Galsworthy's second play, *Joy*, called "a play on the letter I", on 24 September. Nothing more commonplace than this sentimental comedy could have been found. It shocked all who had seen and been moved by the writer's first play, and its triteness surprised the West End playgoer, expecting something unusual from this much-talked-of management. Barker produced both plays. The Shaw play seemed to sparkle less than before, and the Galsworthy play was a disaster. Then followed in the evening bill, on 14 October, Shaw's melodrama, *The Devil's Disciple*, produced by Barker, with Shaw coming in only at the last moment; and though the piece had the popular Matheson Lang as Dick Dudgeon, Edith Wynne-Matthison as Judith, and Barker as General Burgoyne, it was by no means first-rate. Barker himself gave an exquisite performance, but Lang was self-conscious, and the whole thing lacked distinction: Barker, in fact, failed in the production, as Shaw kept on telling him he would, for his mind was divided. Max Beerbohm, in the *Saturday Review* on 26 October, supposed that Barker's name in the programme was a printer's error. He went on mischievously to say:

I find myself distracted between my sense of the fact that the production of *The Devil's Disciple* is a thoroughly bad one and my distaste of decrying anything done by Mr. Barker. . . . I am convinced that *The Devil's Disciple* was cast and stage managed by Mr. Vedrenne alone.

Vedrenne was highly annoyed about this criticism and wanted to answer it, but Shaw dissuaded him, saying that it was only Max's joke, but that if he really insisted on replying he (Shaw) would write the letter for him. Thyrza Norman had been cast by Barker for Essie, but she did not play it. "Bigamy will be the next move," was Shaw's comment when he heard of the proposal.

The second of the matinées was Gilbert Murray's version of Euripides' *Medea*, starting on 22 October, with Edyth Olive as Medea and Hubert Carter as Jason. Received with respect, this production, for which Barker had long been making preparations, was sincere and workmanlike, but uninspired. The result of the six performances were reasonably good, the total receipts being £587 18s. 3d., which yielded Murray £44 1s. 8d. The following letters from Barker to Gilbert Murray, starting in the previous October, throw light on what had been happening about the Greek play:

Oct. 11, 1906.

It goes very much against the grain with me to postpone indefinitely any play because it seems impossible to cast it on that ground. Half the plays would never get done at all. And of course abandoning it is out of the question. You don't mean that do you? But I think it would be wise to make up our minds to do it at the most convenient date in 1907 that is compatible with a good Medea. Certainly Constance Collier is in it. She is tiring for two hours but she has a certain amount of devilry. Mrs. Campbell definitely says she is going to America in the Spring, so we are now tackling her about the Autumn.

Tuesday [October 1906].

I want to read *Medea*, talk it all over with you, think a day and then decide, that's what I want to do. Shaw casts as he sometimes thinks . . . *in vacuo* (is that right?).

Sunday [October 1906].

I wait to hear how the Greek *Medea* struck you. I will get at the play myself as soon as I can for casting, and I am setting Mrs. Lee Matthews on to the choruses . . . if she definitely will, and I am discussing with Vedrenne its place in the Autumn bill. Meanwhile will you send him direct your suggestions for a Medea, for that is the crux of the matter and the sooner it is settled the better . . . send them to me too, but to him direct. My *Statesman* progresses slowly. . . . I am not really good at drafting disestablishment bills; you must give advice.

Monday [October 1906].

One thing I must know before I see Mrs. Campbell . . . do you stick to your decision about the American conditions . . . are the plays to be performed there as here or not? I of course feel I must advise you to stick to the condition, your financial tenure in America is already precarious . . . your artistic tenure may become more precarious still. But on the other hand we can apparently offer you no immediate alternative. If you decide to make no effective restrictions as to her method of performing them, I very much wish that you need not hand her over unrestricted powers until you have at least seen what her own performance is like; and do in any case insist on a strict time limit . . . entire surrender of rights if she doesn't perform within a year or something.

Oct. 15th [1906].

I am very glad indeed at your letter and so is Vedrenne. I rang him up to tell him this morning. But I still don't quite feel with you as to the comparative easiness of casting *Medea*. However, now I shall start to study it more or less and I may see whose failings in the part will matter least.

Now will you please write *yourself* to Mrs. Campbell and inform her that we have played the game by putting the matter before you and we

will in turn make her a final offer of the part if she will give us any idea
as to when she will be in London. This if you think wise.

Sunday [October 1906].
It is good to hear you are back. When do we meet? . . . you are tied
at Oxford I suppose. . . . I am busy here. There are all sorts of pros
and cons about *Medea*, which I must write to you; they concern the
wisdom of opening with it and the safeness of Miss Olive. I want if
possible to open with something which could not have been so well done
at the Court, something sensational if may be and something the success
of which hangs rather on the ensemble than on one person. I had hoped
for *Peer Gynt*, but there are difficulties. I wish the *Trojan Women* were
still to do with a good Hecuba!

2nd Nov. [1906].
This bring us again to the *Medea* for the Spring, and if that reduced us to
Constance Collier, which Vedrenne and I for the moment feel that it
does, then, if she is still with Tree, he may not let her play for us, and that
postpones any classic till the autumn which is a nuisance. Or is there any
alternative Medea in Edyth Olive? My thoughts have been towards her
a little bit, but of course I want to read the play again more carefully.

The *Statesman* referred to in one of these letters was, of course, the play
later to be called *Waste*. After the production of *Medea*, Barker wrote to
Miss Olive:

24 Oct. 1907.
I hope you feel you did well, as we do; and remember if *everyone* does
not at once acclaim you as the only legitimate successor to Mrs. Siddons,
how very few people there are who could play the part at all.

You did all I asked you, you did a lot of other things that you hadn't
done before and that were quite good, only the opening of Part II found
you a little unprepared and your new drapery tempted you to use more and
vaguer gestures than you should have. Once or twice they lacked
meaning.

But, to go back a little, it seems that Lillah McCarthy wanted to do the
part. She had written to Gilbert Murray telling him how much she
wished to play it.

I find myself getting very anxious as the time is drawing for the production of the *Medea*. *I want to play Medea*. I have studied her and *know*
I can bring out her barbarian savagery, do please put on me the burden of
playing her. Mr. Vedrenne has decided not to cast me for parts at the
Savoy unless the author wishes me.

Mr. Shaw wishes Miss O'Malley to play Nora in *John Bull* and Gloria in
You Never Can Tell on tour, which will necessitate her playing both

parts in London, and Miss O'Malley refuses to do this unless she also plays *Major Barbara* at the Savoy. These productions will be followed by *Caesar and Cleopatra* with Forbes-Robertson and his entire company, so that there will be no part for me at the Savoy in the coming bill.

This is all by the way, and nothing to do with *Medea*. But I want you to know that Harley cannot cast me for parts, as I am his wife, and Mr. Vedrenne prefers not to unless it is the author's first wish.

If you really want me for *Medea* you must ask for me.

We are both very well. I am here just for to-day. I am playing nine performances a week at the Court but come here in three weeks for a long summer holiday. I am looking forward very much to seeing you and Lady Mary when you are at Hindhead.

But Vedrenne was adamant that she should not act in the play: he did not intend to allow Barker's wife to have the best parts. It nearly broke up the partnership, and Barker's half-heartedness at the opening of the Savoy season was partly due to this cause. Lillah then tried to get Charles Frohman to finance her in an American production of the play. Julia Marlow, the American actress, afterwards saw it at the Savoy and wanted it for America for herself in association with her husband, E. H. Sothern. Murray preferred that Lillah should have the play, but in the end nothing came of either proposal. Neither did anything come of an idea that Lillah should play the part for Miss Horniman in her new Manchester Repertory Theatre, for Miss Horniman was not ready.

Barker's distraught state was due even more to his struggle with his new play, *Waste*. By the time the production of *Medea* took place, Barker knew that his play, the matinées of which were announced to start on 19 November, was banned. It came as a great blow, and may be said to have virtually killed the management. The censor wanted the play amended—in particular, the references to an abortion left out. In his evidence before the Joint Committee on the Censorship eighteen months later, Barker referred to the matter in the following terms:

I have had one play censored, *Waste*. This is an exceedingly painful play, a tragedy springing from illicit sex relations between a man and a married woman. Mr. Redford demanded alterations. I asked him to specify them. He said it was "not necessary . . . to indicate particular lines", but that I "must be prepared to moderate and modify the extremely outspoken reference to the sexual relations". I replied that I considered in such a play sober plain speaking to be the only honest course, that innuendo would be indecent, and that while I naturally could not admit that I had written anything unfit to be spoken in the theatre and it was difficult to delegate my responsibility in such delicate matters to him, still if he would name the particular phrases which he objected to I would consider their alteration. He paid no attention.

And further he demanded that I should "eliminate entirely all reference to a criminal operation". I had myself produced at the Court Theatre a few months before under the Lord Chamberlain's licence a play the plot of which partly turned upon a criminal operation which was quite openly referred to on the stage. What was I to do? What is any playwright to do in parallel circumstances?

Barker had put the best of himself into the play, and the rebuff was severe. Despite what he said in his evidence before the committee, it is clear that Barker was averse to discussing his work with an official. He put his objection to the committee with great feeling. The idea that artists do not mind their work being censored is mistaken. When the work is killed by authority, the artist suffers not only financially and in his reputation, but also in mind and heart. There can be little doubt, however, that the play's political setting was the fundamental reason for objection to it. No doubt the censor concentrated upon the objection to the abortion, but the fact that the leading characters were party politicians must have weighed most with him. The hero, Henry Trebell, is a lawyer-politician who has drafted a Bill for the disestablishment and disendowment of the Church of England, on the strength of which his party hopes to get into power at a forthcoming General Election. At a political house-party a woman guest seduces or is seduced by the hero, and as the consequence of a momentary infatuation she becomes pregnant. As the woman is married, an action for divorce would ruin Trebell, and possibly the party's hopes of success. Trebell acts like a gentleman; but the woman does not want the child, and has an illegal operation, resulting in her death. Although the facts are kept secret by the connivance of the woman's husband and the party leader, Trebell is thrown over by the party, and shoots himself. The emphasis throughout is not so much upon the personal affair as upon the political situation, and it was no wonder that the censor, whose office was set up to prevent attacks on the stage upon politicians, would not license the play. Nothing was said about this aspect of the matter, but it must have been the decisive one.

A private performance of *Waste* was given by the Stage Society at the Imperial Theatre on 24 November, when Barker at the last moment had to take over the leading part, as Norman McKinnel, who had rehearsed the part, was refused permission to do it by Lena Ashwell, for whom he was playing at the Kingsway Theatre. Such a performance was no more than a makeshift for a play written for the public stage and the dramatist's own theatre. Barker's state of mind is reflected in a letter to Gilbert Murray:

30 Nov. 1907.

Waste has wasted me, and I am finding it difficult not to leave undone the things I ought to be doing. One is writing a letter to you.

By the way – this not being exactly what the letter's about – I read the *Greek Epic* for a night-cap all the time I was working hard, and it kept me sane more or less. May I suggest, asking to be corrected, that a man did not feel disos for his slave, or rather he felt just the same sort of disos that one would feel for a thousand-pound motor car, and for the same reason. I also wish that over the introduction of " spurious " passages you had taken the parallel of the modern pantomime-writer, whose formula is: " Now I think I see a chance to introduce my little song and dance." What parallel could be closer?

A committee meeting luncheon party, present Barrie, Cannan, Galsworthy, self, and hosts took place at the Shaw's on Friday. Two things were mooted: (1) the formation of a playwright's Society, Cannan to sound the Seventy and One on their attitude towards a general treaty. (2) Suggestions of Barrie's that we should now proceed to get as many signatures of important and celebrated persons as possible to a version of the manifesto adapted to them and not to playwrights. He wished in some way he didn't make clear to hand this job over to you. Use to be made of the document, I suppose, about next February when C.B. will be receiving the deputation. What he wants you to do I don't quite know; I suppose to get as many signatures as you can. Anyhow will you let him or me know what you think.

The " Seventy and One " were the signatories to a letter to *The Times* for which John Galsworthy was responsible, demanding an inquiry into the working of the stage censorship. The Prime Minister, Sir Henry Campbell-Bannerman, agreed to receive a deputation, but there was delay in his doing so. In the meantime a Committee for the Abolition of the Office of Dramatic Censorship was formed, with Magdalen Ponsonby as honorary secretary, to get the signatures of distinguished literary people who were not dramatists to a memorial to the Prime Minister supporting the dramatists in their demand for ending the existing system of censorship. Many signatures were secured, but as many others were refused because the memorial went too far or not far enough, one of those who thought it too drastic being Robert Bridges. Vedrenne was by no means at one with Barker and Shaw in this attack upon the censorship.

*

As at that date stage copyright in a play was secured only by public performance, what was technically a public performance was given at the Savoy with the omissions required by the censor, which had been obtained from him by Vedrenne. The programme read as follows:

SAVOY THEATRE

Tuesday 28 January 1908 at 11 a.m.

WASTE

As licensed by the Lord Chamberlain

LADY DAVENPORT	Mrs. W. P. Reeves (of New Zealand)
WALTER KENT	Mr. Gilbert Cannan (of the *Manchester Guardian*)
MRS. FARRANT	Miss Magdalen Ponsonby (by kind permission of Lord Althrop)
MRS. O'CONNELL	Miss Charlotte Payne-Townshend (Mrs. Shaw)
LUCY DAVENPORT	Mrs. H. G. Wells
GEORGE FARRANT	Mr. St. John Hankin ("The Campden Wonder")
RUSSELL BLACKBOROUGH..	Mr. Joy Galsworthy (his First Appearance)
A FOOTMAN	Mr. Allan Wade (his Original Character)
HENRY TREBELL	Mr. Laurence Housman
SIMSON	Mrs. Granville Barker (her First Appearance in this Character)
GILBERT WEDGECROFT ...	Mr. H. G. Wells (of the Theatre Royal, Sandgate)
LORD CHARLES CANTELUPE	Professor Gilbert Murray, LL.D.
THE EARL OF HORSHAM ...	Mr. Bernard Shaw (late of the Theatre Royal, Dublin)
EDMUNDE	Mr. Arthur Bowyer
JUSTIN O'CONNELL	Mr. William Archer (his Last Appearance on any Stage)

Neither the Costumes nor the Scenery have been designed by Mr. Charles Ricketts.

After the reading, for it was no more, Gilbert Murray wrote to Barker:

By the way, I meant to tell you that I was more than ever struck by the goodness of the writing of *Waste*, when we read it on Tuesday. It impressed me greatly. Perhaps that is one of the reasons why we made so comparatively few mistakes in emphasis.

The shy J. M. Barrie would not take part in the performance, though his young secretary, Gilbert Cannan, did so. By this time the Barkers were accepted everywhere in London society, she for her beauty and talents, he for his leadership in the intellectual theatre, and his charm, he naturally wearing the same air of unconscious superiority as the important people they got to know.

In the meantime, negotiations had been going on with Iden Payne,

Miss Horniman's manager in Manchester, about the production of the Euripides plays. This new repertory theatre was to be run on lines similar to the Court, and some of the Court plays were made available, though Payne was searching for dramatists of his own, and found them. Barker had suggested that Lewis Casson, in whom he had great confidence, should be engaged to do the Greek productions on the lines of those done by him. He wrote to Murray on 2 December :

2 Dec. 1907.
Mine is the hand concealed behind the Iden Payne proposal. They have also engaged Casson and I put him on to making them do Greek Tragedy, and if possible letting him produce them as well as play Messengers. Their enterprise is of course much better than Neilson's, though it wont remain so if Iden Payne insists on managing, producing, and playing every leading part himself. Actors will be fairly keen to go to the Gaiety Theatre, Manchester; their tours from there are so far rubbish.

We start rehearsing *Arms and the Man* this week. I wish I were away writing another play.

Harold V. Neilson, who for some years had been touring plays by Shaw and Ibsen, was anxious to include *Hippolytus* in his repertory, and uneasy negotiations had been proceeding with him for some time. Murray went to Manchester and had talks with Payne and " the Helen-like Mona Limerick ".

Among the Barkers' friends and most ardent supporters was old Lady Ponsonby, and a letter written to her at Christmas 1907 by Barker from the Savoy Theatre deserves to be preserved :

Thursday night.
My very dear Friend,
I won't sit down to tell you – describe to you – the joy that your Xmas letter gives me, nor will I go putting on paper the love I have for you – its a particular sort and kind that I haven't for anyone else in the world – though this is a time when one is allowed to come nearest to saying these things. I'm sure you know – you know so many things that can't just be learnt by rote. But first this – it is my wish that you have a corner in your heart for me.

I like much the bookcase – I wish it meant I was to travel for a whole year.

There is to be a photograph of me for you – it hasn't come in time for Xmas though. Lillah asked to-day if I hadn't written you a love-letter in its place. I can now reply that I have.

I have been owing you a letter about *Waste* for more than a month – it has not been the letter that was difficult but the subject – I've not been able to look at it since it was done. With the New Year though I must get at it. I hope now for a talk with you instead of a letter. May I come down to Gilmuire just for lunch one Sunday? – if the roads would behave I'd bicycle over from Windsor.

My love – till then – and a good New Year.

Yours
HGB.

There was an idea for an Oxford Repertory Theatre, which did not come to anything. Murray wrote to Barker:

[February 1908.]

My dear B.

Two Dons have been talking to me about the possibility of getting up a stock company for Oxford and some other towns, say Birmingham, Leamington, and Cambridge. We get first-rate music here in unlimited quantities; and it looks as if here was an almost equal interest in drama if we could get good drama. But we mostly have only musical comedies. It is a cheap theatre, and I believe we could raise a goodish guarantee fund, or form a society on the Benson model, enough to fill the theatre for three weeks a term, i.e. nine weeks a year, if we could be offered a varied programme. We should want Hauptmann and Suderman and Maeterlinck and stuff to make us feel cultured. I wonder if this could be hitched on to Payne, or if anyone else could form the nucleus of a stock company of the sort.

Yours ever,
G. M.

To which Barker made the following reply:

18 Feb. 1908.

As to your University Theatre, Payne is the natural solution, but I should strongly advise you to wait and see how he gets on for a bit. My mind is not easy about him yet. Perhaps hold this out as a bait that he may become really efficient. Anyway, I've no doubt I could find someone who could do the work decently at any rate, and undoubtedly it should be done. But drama costs more than music, remember.

Then the Prime Minister agreed to receive the dramatists' deputation on the censorship on 21 February, but he became ill and it had to be put off. Instead, they were received four days later by the Home Secretary, the Right Hon. Herbert Gladstone. Barker wrote to Murray:

It's a nuisance we have to go before Gladstone, who I am convinced is an ass, but it can't be helped. Nothing happened at the meeting to-day, except that I came to the conclusion that we must leave Pinero and Gilbert alone to do the job as best they can. They, but especially Gilbert, are so terrified at being mixed up with the disreputable drama, that at the word " Shaw " so to speak they perform evolutions suggestive of flight.

The deputation was introduced by J. M. Barrie, supported by a large attendance of playwrights, but all the Home Secretary could say was that he would put what was laid before him to the Prime Minister. The dramatists got no satisfaction.

Arising out of all this, the question was raised of forming a society for dramatists, but it was decided to keep the subject a sub-committee of the Society of Authors. Later, in March 1909, a Dramatists' Club was formed, with A. W. Pinero as first President: this was a luncheon club confined to dramatists of established reputation; everyone else was excluded. Barker was a member, with Shaw.

On 25 November 1907 Johnston Forbes Robertson, who had been touring Shaw's *Caesar and Cleopatra* in America and the English cities, came to the Savoy for a five weeks' season. Originally the play had been intended for Forbes Robertson, and Shaw had rehearsed him and his company before they went to America, where it had been a great success, but Barker had no confidence that the production with the kind of company the actor-manager considered suitable would do any credit to the theatre, and he was right. The arrangement was carried through, however, *The Devil's Disciple* being transferred to Vedrenne's new theatre, the Queen's, with Barker playing the hero. There it remained until towards the end of December. This character was not one of Barker's outstanding efforts as an actor. The Forbes Robertson season was a financial failure, and did the Vedrenne–Barker management no good, though that management had nothing whatever to do with it. "The conventional mind was quite upset", said the famous actor, but so was the unconventional mind of the old Court congregation. Forbes Robertson, however, revived the play later with success in his farewell season at Drury Lane.

Then for the first time in London since its original production in 1894 came *Arms and the Man*, on 30 December for six weeks only, with Robert Loraine as Bluntschli, Lillah McCarthy as Raina and Barker as Sergius. It was a good cast throughout, but there was trouble because Lillah hated her part and did not like playing with Loraine, and Barker did not care for his part either. Shaw was displeased. The production was largely in Barker's hands and lacked the pronounced operatic character Shaw wanted. He wrote to Barker before rehearsals started: "Strictly between our guilty selves, if I can get Lillah into the play to walk in beauty like the night, I do not care a twopenny – or say a tenpenny – damn what she plays." One of Lillah's troubles was the salary. Loraine had been offered "splendid terms" to come back from America, and she was offered a wretched £20 a week, a quarter of what she normally earned, to do a part she did not want, "with the ice-eyed Bobbie, who will simply play her off the stage as if she were a concrete wall at rackets", as Shaw said. She was beguiled by Shaw into accepting £25, as he gleefully told the reluctant Vedrenne. Shaw's tempting suggestion was that Miss McCarthy should be got to play the secondary part of Louka with Barker's Sergius. "The question is, dare you, as a married man, propose it?" Of course, it could not be done, even if proposed, much as Shaw valued his secondary characters, and even though he said: "I had myself rather play Sergius than Bluntschli."

Charles Ricketts wrote later to Lillah recalling her performance and the costumes for which he was responsible:

Concerning *Arms and the Man* I have nothing to say save in praise of a superb all-round performance, my contribution being confined to your two dresses. This was the first occasion when the bustle was revived on the stage; to-day no Cochran revue can do without it. I think, at the time, you were a little frightened, Shaw rather neutral, but when worn by you this fashion proved so charming that its success was immediate with the charladies who were dusting the seats during the rehearsal. "Ain't she lovely!" they exclaimed and I have ever since considered the employees of a theatre the soundest judges of scenery and dresses.

The play ran on past the six weeks, until 14 March, when the tenancy of the theatre ended. There had been talk of doing a pantomime at Christmas, "a real pantomime", said Shaw, but nothing came of it – the spirit was not there: certainly not in Barker. What a pity, however, Shaw's idea was not taken up, for certain elements in pantomime were daily bread to him! Indeed, William Archer had declared long before that the new Aristophanes would almost certainly write pantomime; but "its ingenious nursery babble", in Archer's words, though well within Shaw's scope at all times, was outside Barker's in his then state of mind. In other circumstances, Barker's natural high spirits might have led to something that might have transformed the Savoy situation; for as has been said, to suppose that he was devoid of humour is a mistake: he bubbled over with it. But not, unfortunately, at that moment.

Altogether the Savoy venture had been a failure. Shaw had no new play, Barker's play was banned, and Galsworthy's effort was a frost. Gilbert Murray's Greek play was weakly cast. There were no new dramatists. Vedrenne would not have the new Masefield play, which was ready and would have done something to restore at least the artistic status of the enterprise. In fact, the two partners were seldom in agreement. Nothing was added to artistic reputations. In an interview published in the *Pall Mall Gazette* on 14 March, Barker said among other things:

The important thing for the public to consider is this, that if they want anything in the shape of a theatre like this they cannot have it under the present conditions that obtain in London of enormous rents. If the public want even so much of a repertoire theatre as we have been running, the building must be kept rent free. As theatres are now run in London it comes to this, that when you get a success you have to extract every ounce of money out of it you can in order to put by for the next failure, and that involves running a play to death.

The first thing we did was to struggle against this long-run system, partly because we wanted to produce a lot of plays and partly because we disagreed with it. It is bad for plays and bad for acting. It also means, what is more serious still, that you are constantly looking for plays that may run, if successful, 200 or 300 nights. You have no right to expect every play to do that; but I do really think that if you are looking for those plays you get this sort of play written.

Now, we wanted another sort of play written. And you see the whole vicious circle of the system. If you are going to have various sorts of plays which will appeal to various sections of the public, you must alter your present system.

He added:

I have my living to earn, and that may mean a certain amount of producing, but I hope I shall not have to act; for personally, I find it impossible to manage a theatre and act satisfactorily at the same time.

The management was now bankrupt, and Shaw had the painful experience of meeting the greater part of the loss, for everyone was paid. Barker was left penniless.

Although more work was done, as we shall see, the Vedrenne–Barker management virtually ended with the Savoy season. It had suffered a great disappointment, but sufficient has been said to indicate why failure occurred. The magical atmosphere of the Court Theatre had not been re-created, due partly to the theatre, which could not accommodate it, and partly to the management itself. The undertaking could not establish a basis for success on the divided minds of those responsible for it. What had carried it through at the Court – enthusiasm for a new thing – had to be replaced by another motive, which was not found. In fact, the finance for repertory was required, but was not forthcoming; for nothing but repertory would fully carry out what Barker and Shaw had in mind. Vedrenne, on the other hand, was afraid of repertory, and set his mind firmly against it. All the conditions of the London theatre were opposed to repertory enterprise – not merely the high rents (though they paid less than £100 a week for the Savoy), but also the commercialism to which the theatre was wholly subject. There was no possibility of reconciliation between the idea of drama as an art and that of the theatre as a commercial enterprise, as subsequent events demonstrated. Looking back, no such reconciliation has been nearer realization in the period now approaching half a century since the Vedrenne–Barker management was defeated.

*

Immediately the Savoy season ended, Barker went to the United States in company with William Archer to look at the new theatre in New York, nearing completion, which the responsible committee was anxious for him to direct. He had been pressed to go for some months past and had dallied with the idea. He was promised a great welcome and a large salary. He found the theatre too large for the drama he wanted to produce, being more suitable for opera or spectacle, and he turned the offer down. This was no less a disappointment to Barker than to the American committee, and he returned home at once with Archer, who agreed with his decision. The latter, however, accepted the post of adviser to the management on European plays. Winthrop Ames was afterwards appointed director. There is a letter from Shaw to Vedrenne written when Barker was on his way home:

9/4/08.

Vedrenne and Barker are enough to drive any reasonable man to destruction between them. Here is Barker's cablegram. It so happened that Lillah turned up here this morning for the first time since he left and informed me that he had chucked the American people; that the 15th mentioned in the telegram is the 15th of the month, so that he will be in Paris next Wednesday; and that his plan of life, so far as she knows, is to write plays at his ease, and occasionally – say three or four times a year – act as producer for a fee of three hundred pounds or so. Did you ever hear such blasted nonsense?

Before all this took place, the Barkers had found a small Elizabethan house at Stansted in Kent, near the Pilgrims' Way, Lillah being determined that he should live out of London as much as possible. This was a charming but neglected farmhouse called Court Lodge, for which they had a twenty-one years' lease at the rent of £37 a year. At first there was little money to spend on doing up the building, and they went in as it was, but while Barker was in America, Lillah had some work done, and did more later, uncovering the original oak panelling and fireplaces. It had a large garden and orchard and some stabling. There Lillah made a real home – "house-proud" she was, according to Lady Mary Murray. The front door opened into the dining-room; on the right there was a sitting-room; upstairs, the largest room, facing west, partly panelled, was Barker's workroom, a cheerful room, full of sunshine; there was also their bedroom and a guest-room, with another small guest-room on the landing, which Bernard Shaw favoured, he being a constant visitor,

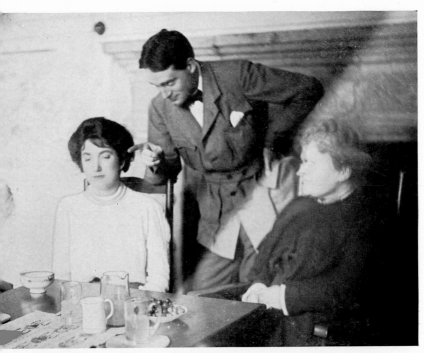

XX   Lillah McCarthy, Granville Barker and Barker's mother at Stansted (1912)

XXI   John Galsworthy, Lillah McCarthy and John Masefield at Stansted (1912)

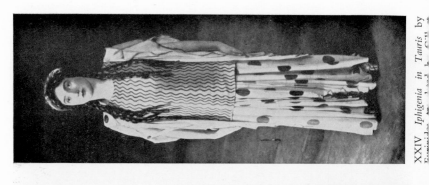

XXIV Iphigenia in Tauris by
Euripides re d und b CVI th

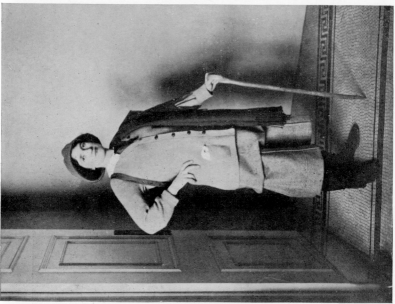

XXIII The Master Builder by Henrik Ibsen (Little Theatre, 1911) :
L'ula McCarthy as Hilda Wangel

XXII The Tragedy of Nan by John Masefield
(Royal Court Theatre, 1908) : Lillah

usually with Charlotte. There have been a few small additions since the Barkers had the place, but it remains substantially as it was, a little gem of a home. The hamlet is very small, with a church (St. Mary's) and a public-house, right away from the heavy motor traffic to the coast. Two miles north of Wrotham, to which there was a reasonably good train service on the Maidstone line from Charing Cross, Court Lodge was convenient for the West End, though not for some years were the Barkers able to afford a motor car.

★

While Barker was away in America arrangements were made for a demonstration in London at the Lyceum Theatre on behalf of a National Theatre as a Shakespeare Memorial, which took place on 19 May, with Lord Lytton in the chair, and the National (Shakespeare Memorial) Theatre Committee was set up, which got laboriously to work. The committee held many meetings, and the scheme had many distinguished friends, but there was no money. In a private " letter to millionaires ", Shaw argued that the Court Theatre enterprise had demonstrated the need for a National Theatre, and pointed out that the Court, though financially successful, had traded " on a windfall unprecedented in the commercial history of the stage " – his own plays. But this, he said, had prevented the management from pursuing an impartial policy. It was suggested to Lillah that her persuasive powers might be usefully devoted to a certain wealthy gentleman interested in the theatre, and interested also in getting a title. She was therefore invited to a party at the gentleman's house, with the result that she secured a promise of £70,000 for the National Theatre. This generosity made it possible to believe in the practicability of the scheme, and Barker was heartened at the prospect of its realization. No further large subscriptions were, however, attracted, though to look after the £70,000 and to enable other sums to be added to it a trust was created on 20 May 1909 and an appeal was made for £500,000. There is no need to follow the fortunes, or misfortunes, of this affair further here, but the failure to make progress with the National Theatre was Barker's most bitter disappointment to the end of his life.

★

Lillah had been ill, and when Barker returned from America he produced the rejected Masefield play, *The Tragedy of Nan*, for her for the actors' play-producing society, The Pioneer Players, at the Royalty on 22 May. This was a success that provided Lillah with a part that took her back to her childhood. Barker had some trouble with the production, for he was not at one with country people. At one point he said, " I'm not going to produce this play. The players know more about these peasants than I do. I have always been a Londoner, and leave it to them."

G

Nan was, however, after Lillah's heart. "I was the living Nan," she said; "it was not acting. I was dead, the character was alive." For the dress rehearsal Barker invited everyone, Shaw, Murray, and all his friends; but Lillah forgot her lines and gave a dreadful performance. But Barker knew she was all right. Barrie said to her: "You have a dual personality. You are never Lillah McCarthy on the stage." Here was one of the differences between Lillah and, say, Mrs. Pat as an actress. Lillah never played herself; she did not know she existed. Mrs. Pat made the part herself – *she* was the creation in the dramatist's mind. This play was a great advance on the author's first work, larger in scope and more mature in treatment.

Even after this success Vedrenne would have nothing to do with the play. Shaw wrote to him on the 25 May:

I went to see *Nan* last night at the Pioneers. There is no doubt at all that we should give at least three or four performances of it. Lillah is very fine; and the quality of the play is unmistakable. . . .

Vedrenne still being obdurate, Shaw wrote again the following day, pointing out the danger of forcing Barker out of the partnership, especially as Vedrenne would not consider repertory:

You and Watson (who makes no pretence of having any patience with our silly game of the advanced drama) opposing me and Barker, with Harrison doubtful, but evidently quite ready to play the forward game (which is also the most prudent one) if we were solid on it ourselves! If you are putting the drag on simply as a man of business insisting that the artistic partner must cut his coat according to his cloth, then it would be all right. But here you are acting as the anti-artistic fashionable manager preferring to wreck a sinking ship sooner than let it have a last shot at the enemy.

In this letter Shaw was referring to a proposal for a joint management with Frederick Harrison at the Haymarket Theatre.

It is clear that Barker himself had wanted to end the partnership altogether after the Savoy season; but Shaw had persuaded him not to do so, for he considered there was more work before it. But Barker had had no idea of continuing in London, as he had told the representative of the *Pall Mall Gazette* in the interview already quoted:

I do not think there is any likelihood of its being resumed on the same lines. . . . For my own part, I have other things to do, and I believe Mr. Vedrenne has too.

None the less, *The Tragedy of Nan* had a number of matinées under Vedrenne and Barker's joint management with Harrison at the Haymarket, starting 2 June. This new venture had been carried out while Barker was away by Shaw and Vedrenne with the main object of putting on Shaw's new play, *Getting Married*, for a series of matinées. These had started on 12 May. The play was afterwards put into the evening bill. Shaw had paid attention to every detail of the production, designing the set and even writing out the billing. He was most anxious for success, for the partnership's sake as well as his own. He had wanted Barker to play the Bishop, but he had refused, which caused the angry Shaw to add to the letter to Vedrenne already quoted:

Barker must take the part, or else definitely withdraw from Vedrenne and Barker altogether. In which case he will be busted and the new drama will be busted too.

In fact, the part was played admirably by Henry Ainley. Before the first performance Shaw wrote to Vedrenne on a subject he would never let alone:

26/4/08.

. . . We must convert Harrison on the question of deadheads. I shall pay for my two dress circle seats; and I protest against the admission of a single soul without payment apart from the press and our own immediate belongings. Remember that the West End routine is fatal to us: the deadheads are our worst enemies: our real friends all pay.

Shaw did his utmost to arouse public attention to the performances, employing his publicity arts to the full, but in vain: the weather was exceptionally hot, and sufficient support was not forthcoming quickly enough, and, despite Shaw's frantic protests, the run ended, and with it the management, with Shaw losing quite a lot of money. Before the end, Laurence Housman and Joseph Moorat's *The Chinese Lantern* was given eight matinées, starting on 16 June, which added to the losses.

Thus Vedrenne–Barker ended in London. Barker had nothing to do with the plays at the Haymarket except *Nan* and the Housman play written earlier, with Barker coaching the author. Barker could not have been very pleased with it, for Shaw complains to Vedrenne that Barker would not let him see the MS. But Shaw thought highly of it when he saw it on the stage. Barker was getting ready to go out on tour with *Arms and the Man*, playing Bluntschli, and *Man and Superman*. *John Bull's Other Island* and *You Never Can Tell* had been toured since the late summer of 1907, when Nigel Playfair, Harcourt Williams, A. E. George, J. D. Beveridge, William Poel, Agnes Thomas, Ellen O'Malley, and others formed the company. Wherever they went, they were advertised as the Vedrenne–Barker original productions. "The play is sure to be extremely novel, the treatment novel, not to say daring, the acting so good as to have won the reputation of being the best in London ", read the four-page announcement to playgoers in the provincial cities. In the glowing terms of that green-covered announcement which said that the plays "swept the London stage", "captured the paying public", "never . . . a wrong selection", the hand of Vedrenne can be seen. The object of the tours was to retrieve the firm's lost fortunes.

*

For some months Barker had been working on a new play, which will be heard of later. Despite the rebuffs he had received, his spirit, though flagging, was not quenched. Two letters to Gilbert Murray while Barker was on tour should come here:

Harrogate . . . Friday [September 1908].
Good. . . . Good . . . good. My address next week is at Mrs. Walker's, 10 Wright Street, Lime Grove, and there I will expect you Saturday. I don't know the rooms so I will wait till Monday, when I arrive to take them on for you for your week . . . is it not so? You see . . . if they are not good and you have to be found others . . . theatre ones . . . you could not go into them before a Sunday afternoon . . . so you can come to me on the Saturday anyway. I could not get in at Knutsford . . . and perhaps it is as well. . . . I have found the journey out here every night rather tiring . . . though it is good to get out of Leeds.

Dammit . . . as my friend Mantalini remarks . . . come to Manchester. I am very good for a cold. And look you I have to leave for Cardiff early on the Sunday morning whatever, and how shall I get a chance at all of telling you what I think of the *Hippolytus* rehearsals if I have seen any. Not to mention that there is a scheme of Lillah's about the *Bacchae* of which you will have heard by then and which we may be able to do some good by discussing. Oh . . . lor yes . . . come on Friday. Casting the *Bacchae* . . . that cannot be done under one day.

About the tour, Sir . . . ? Well, I went for a very enjoyable twelve-mile walk yesterday over the Yorkshire moors . . . which are inhospitable places . . . down to Bolton Abbey . . . which is very beautiful.

Wednesday [September 1908].
Churton Collins used to do all his work at night I hear and drink strong tea to keep him awake for it. Then he got so that he couldn't sleep, I suppose, and then . . . But I don't really write to tell you that but to say . . . Cannot W[illiam] A[rcher] now have that Professorship of English Literature? Can't it be worked somehow? I don't know yet where I stay in Manchester next week, but wherever it is will you come and stay with me for the day or two that we are there together. . . . Do. My exile . . . oh my exile. Casson gives me quite exciting accounts of the *Hippolytus*. . . . I hope to see something of a rehearsal of it while I am there. How are you all. My love and homage.

" My exile . . . oh my exile " are significant words. While on tour in Dublin in November, Barker was taken ill with typhoid fever and nearly died. Lillah was sent for and arrived to find that a homœopathic doctor was not being successful, and she sought Lady Gregory's aid. Together they tried in vain to find another doctor to take over the case, and in desperation Lady Gregory went to the Abbey Theatre doctor, who immediately attended to Barker and pulled him through. While he was lying ill in Dublin, George Moore came to see him, and Barker gave Moore a copy of his banned play. Moore records this in his *Conversations in Ebury Street*. " Every evening ", he says, " I read an act and every morning I came to tell you how much I admired the construction, the dialogue, and the characters." But he found faults; in particular, so he says, with the shrubbery in which the incident occurred on which the play turns, but more especially that the politician kissed the lady only once : " In writing *Waste* you do not seem to have remembered that to kiss a lady once is most impolite." Barker had met Moore earlier, for the latter was a frequent visitor at the Court, and he was, of course, a friend of Shaw's. Barker was ill in Dublin for some time.

★

A few days before this event, Lillah had put on Gilbert Murray's version of Euripides' *Bacchae* (on 10 November, at the Court) for a number of matinées, which she had been anxious to do for some time, but it was without much of Barker's help. When he was able to leave Dublin, the Barkers were lent a cottage near Guildford by Edith Lyttelton. He had no money, though, fortunately, Lillah was playing. He was not fit again until after the end of the year. Writing to Lady Mary Murray on 26 December from the Wells's house at Sandgate, he said : " I progress like anything – the difficulty is to resist the temptation to behave like the ordinary human being one begins to feel. However, another month will see me one – and no more being waited on – please Heaven." He did not return to the tours, which continued for another two years.

★

It will be as well to break off here to complete the account of the Vedrenne–Barker management. The partnership ran on until March 1911. It ended in debt. There was cash in the bank amounting to £484 3s. 10d., but Shaw had advanced no less than £5,250, so he accepted the cash together with what the other assets fetched, which was not much, and wrote the whole thing off. He had, in fact, made a profitable investment, as he well knew, though generosity was not absent – especially generosity to Barker, whom he looked upon as a son. Vedrenne and Barker had already gone their separate ways, which never met again. Vedrenne died at the age of sixty-two on 12 February

1930, leaving £25,630. He had continued in the theatre; one of his future partnerships being with the actor, Dennis Eadie, their outstanding production being Edward Knoblock and Arnold Bennett's *Milestones*. In the organ of the Society of Authors, *The Author*, for April 1930, Barker paid a tribute to Vedrenne's memory, from which a quotation has already been made. "How much of the work done at the Court was to his personal taste I never quite knew", he said. The two men were utterly unlike, but Barker, who had no sense of money, needed the man who knew what money was, yet had sympathy with what was more than money. "He had imagination", said Barker. An admirable account of the man was written by W. MacQueen Pope in *Carriages at Eleven* (Hutchinson, 1947):

Vedrenne was very acute. His sharp-pointed nose, which dominated his dark face, was a keynote. He worked to schedules, he was alarmingly punctual. He made appointments at odd times. . . . But mostly Vedrenne's method was that of the open hand, open heart, and complete confidence. He would almost weep when terms were being discussed. You gathered from what he said that he had no margin of profit and that the demand you had made would make all the difference to him between solvency and bankruptcy. He would take you into his confidence – he would, in his own phrase, "lay his cards on the table". He would speak gently and pityingly of risks, of the terrible gamble of the production, of the mutability of human affairs, and his strange voice carried a covert hint of tears. He would offer you – if you were an actor – what were known as "summer terms" – salaries taken at a time when most theatres were closed. But he would stress the fairness. He would declare he would not bind you, he would not stand in the way. As soon as a better offer came along – if any – you could have your release and take that salary which you now began to regard as extortionate. Far be it from him to hold you up, to prevent you getting what he knew was your real worth, but which he, a poor man taking such risks, could not afford. You took his terms and very seldom did you leave the play before the end of the run. Those cards on the table were mostly trumps.[1]

Vedrenne was said to have been the model for the theatrical manager in Lady (Arthur) Lever's comedy, *Brown Sugar*, produced at the Duke of York's Theatre on 7 February 1920. Mr. Edmundson, the manager, appears in the last act only: he shows himself to be astute but generous-minded when he gets his own way. "I'm not out of the top drawer," he says, "but I have my code." Vedrenne's son, Laurence, is a novelist whose first novel, *The Closed Wall*, published in 1924, was dedicated to his father; it is about a boy at school and the First World War.

*

[1] p. 194.

One of the mysteries connected with the Savoy enterprise was why John Galsworthy's trivial piece, *Joy*, came to be produced when he had already completed one of his major works, *Strife*. This play was now taken by Charles Frohman, at J. M. Barrie's urgent suggestion, for a series of matinées, the production being by Barker. A letter from Barker to Gilbert Murray may find a place here: it refers to Miss Horniman's Manchester company as well as to *Strife*:

2 Mar. 1909.
I seem to remember you vaguely. You represent Oxford in the Liberal interest, I think. Howsumdever, *Strife* is struggling to its birth amid bursts of incompetence and despair. I'm getting on all right.

No reason at all that Payne shouldn't do the *Voysey* and many reasons that he should. I told him he might a year or two ago, but wanted to be satisfied as to the cast. But now Galsworthy reports a very good company of men for *The Silver Box*, and that's the important thing for the *Voysey*. I don't think I need produce it entirely. To begin with it's very difficult to get the time, but I could see two or three rehearsals and put a polish on. That would be enough I think.

You're coming up to see *Strife*, aren't you? Can we meet then?

Strife appeared at the Duke of York's Theatre on 9 March 1909, and more than restored the earlier reputation of the dramatist, for it was a masterly work. Furthermore, it enhanced Barker's fame as producer, and gave Lillah a fine opportunity for the display of her powers. It was an admirable effort, and support was enthusiastic if not overwhelming, sufficient to allow the play to be put into the evening bill at the Haymarket for a week, and afterwards to be transferred to the Adelphi. Bernard Shaw wrote to Barker after the first performance saying that it was " an important event in stage history ".

*

Earlier the previous year Barker tried his hand at fiction in a longish short story entitled *Georgiana*, which was published in two instalments in the February and March 1909 issues of Ford Madox Hueffer's *English Review* when that remarkable magazine was serializing H. G. Wells's novel, *Tono Bungay*. This effort, no doubt, persuaded Barker to keep out of the field of the novel. The story opens well, on a scale that promises much, but tails off in the second instalment, possessing nothing but a commonplace development, suggesting that its author had small gifts for sustained storytelling. The method adopted is that of a monologue by the principal character, a difficult form of storytelling. Although not a success, it has great interest, coming from Barker's hand. Why, however, should one who had to perfect his skill in an art in which he had proved ability expend his energies on another art in which there were already many able practitioners?

★

During the year an enthusiast named Alfred Wareing set out to establish a Scottish National Theatre Society on a repertory basis in Glasgow. Barker's aid was sought, for the impetus had sprung from his work, and he would have gone there towards the end of the year to play in *Man and Superman*, but was checked by Shaw, who reminded him that for him, as Tanner, an Ann the equal of Lillah was required. The Glasgow scheme did in fact open in April and continued for some years. Barker played there and Lillah did play Ann, though not with Barker.

On the initiative of Frederick Whelen, who was Beerbohm Tree's reader of plays, the latter had ventured into the higher drama at His Majesty's Theatre the previous November with what was called the After Noon Theatre, which repeated the Vedrenne–Barker system of Tuesday, Thursday, and Friday matinées. After Shaw's *The Shewing-up of Blanco Posnet* had been announced for 4 June 1909, the play was censored, which aroused the still-seething opposition to the censorship, with the result that the Prime Minister, Mr. Asquith, appointed a Joint Select Committee of Lords and Commons on 19 July to inquire into the working of the dramatic censorship.

Reference has earlier been made to the dramatists' deputation to the then Prime Minister (Sir Henry Campbell-Bannerman) two years before (which the Home Secretary had received) after the banning of Barker's *Waste*. The resentment against the censorship, though not a matter in which the majority of citizens concerned themselves, was deeply felt by dramatic authors, as the letter signed by seventy-one of them in October 1907 had shown. As the subject figured greatly in Barker's life, somewhat extended reference must be made to it.

A play censorship had existed from Elizabethan times, when a printing censorship was also imposed, but it was exercised as a royal prerogative, in the hands of the Master of the Revels, who also licensed the theatres. Twentieth-century stage censorship was in the form given it by Parliament in 1737 to prevent political satires from being staged; the provisions of this Act having been incorporated in the Theatres Act of 1843. Strange things had been done in the name of censorship, for the application of the Act depended mainly on the vagaries of the Lord Chamberlain's reader of plays. In the early years of this century, however, considerable latitude was allowed to playwrights, apart from blasphemy, references to royalty, and to the representation of divine or living persons upon the stage. In carrying out the duty to prohibit plays that in their " general tendency contain anything immoral or otherwise improper for the stage ", the rule had been made that an illegal obstetric operation must not be mentioned, or incest, or venereal disease.   Among plays recently prohibited according to that rule were *Waste* and Edward Garnett's *The Breaking Point* (which had been refused by Barker for the Court).   Shaw's *The Shewing-up of Blanco Posnet* offended because of supposed blasphemy, and there were also banned Sophocles' *Oedipus Tyrannus* (in translation), Shelley's *The Cenci*, Ibsen's *Ghosts*, Maeterlinck's *Monna Vanna*, D'Annunzio's *La Città morta* (in Italian, with Eleonora Duse), Rostand's *La Samaritaine*, Brieux's *Maternité*, Laurence Housman's *Bethlehem*, as well as Shaw's *Mrs. Warren's Profession*.   The prohibition of masterpieces was felt to be an outrage upon the theatre, as indeed it was when French farces, suitably glossed over, and trivial, even immoral, English farces were readily accepted.   It was on this ground that objection was taken to the censorship.

Under the chairmanship of the Right Hon. Herbert Samuel, Chancellor of the Duchy of Lancaster, the Parliamentary Committee held its first meeting on 29 July, and continued to meet until 2 November.   Forty-nine witnesses were examined, including the Speaker of the House of Commons, the censor himself, and officials from the Home Office, dramatists, actors, managers, critics, and others.   Among the ten members of the committee were Lord Gorell and A. E. W. Mason, who were dramatists, also Robert Vernon Harcourt, one of the Court Theatre dramatists, who had himself not long before presented a Bill to abolish the censorship.   The first of the non-official witnesses were William Archer and Bernard Shaw.   The latter had prepared a long statement and circulated it, by permission, to members of the committee, with copies of his censored plays, but when he appeared the committee refused to admit his statement as part of the evidence or allow him to read it, and he was simply asked a number of questions.   He argued against the censorship because of his abhorrence of anarchism, declaring, " I want the drama and authors to be brought under the law," which he considered was not done if censorship depended upon mere opinion.   " I have no objection whatever if you will make a law that I shall not mention certain subjects.   If you pass that law, I am prepared to obey, or to be guilty of breaking it under conditions under which a man is a martyr.   What I object to is that there is no law."   He contended that his censored play, *Mrs. Warren's Profession*, was "a profoundly immoral play, more so than many of the people who have written about it think ".   He also asserted that Ibsen's plays " were certainly immoral ".   By these statements he meant that his and Ibsen's plays " challenged existing morality ".   The next day he appeared armed with a pile of documents, but the chairman told him, after the committee had conferred in private for twenty minutes, that

they had no further questions to put.   This was annoying, and next day
The Times printed a summary of the rejected statement as well as an
indignant letter of protest from Shaw.   He printed the statement in full
in the Preface to *The Shewing-up of Blanco Posnet* when the play was
published two years later.   On 5 August, Granville Barker gave evidence
as actor, manager, and author of plays.   His statement of evidence,
from which I have quoted, was a moderate but feelingly expressed
objection to the idea of censorship.   He declared himself, in answer to
questions, to be absolutely opposed on principle to the censorship of
plays, which " has indirectly retarded the advancement, and especially
the development of the drama. . . . The result has been to narrow the
field which the drama covers in England."   He said that when *Major
Barbara* was to be produced Mr. Redford, the censor, asked him as
manager to see him, and inquired if he thought the feelings of the Salvation Army would be outraged, and it was only because he assured him
that the Army regarded the play as an excellent advertisement that the
play was licensed.   He was questioned about his own play, *Waste*, and
said that the correspondence with the censor had been conducted by his
partner, Vedrenne.

The difficulty of forecasting the judgment of the censor was part of
Barker's objection.   He considered that managers who offended should
be proceeded against under the ordinary law, and agreed that grossly
obscene plays and also plays that outraged religious feelings and plays
containing libels should be proceeded against, but he thought action
should be taken after performance.   He thought local authorities should
have power to object to plays, and was much questioned on that notion,
which Shaw had previously put forward.   Asked if he would be driven
to abandon playwriting were the censorship not abolished, Barker
replied :

I only mean that I have passed through one period of uncertainty during
which I did not know whether my plays would be accepted by managers,
and I am not prepared to go through another period of uncertainty as to
whether they will be passed by the censor.

Questioned further about *Waste*, he affirmed that the censor refused to
indicate the particular passages he wished removed or altered.   He was
further asked :

You remember *Dear Old Charlie*.   A reference was made in that play to
a prohibited piece by a Mr. " Bleater ", entitled *Sewage*.   Did you see
any personal reference there?

I thought it might have a personal application.

" Bleater " being " Barker " and *Sewage* representing *Waste*?

Quite so.

Did the Examiner of Plays confer with you?

No.

But you would call the reference personal?

I think so.

At the close of his evidence, Barker submitted a statement (prepared by Barrie) from Charles Frohman, who was out of the country, opposing the censorship. The message declared that " in America we have no censor, and I do not see that the absence of one causes any inconvenience to managers ". Frohman went on to say:

No censor can prevent the appearance of numbers of plays that are vulgar and of low aim. Those are common to all countries whether there be a censor or not. The strictly immoral is another matter, but what seems immoral to one person may to another be not only not immoral but highly immoral, and I would trust the public here as in America to decide in such a matter at least as readily as any single official. . . .

Without a censor you would probably have religion among the subjects of the stage. To this I can only reply, Why not? . . .

Anyone who, like myself, has been in close touch for many years with the modern play must be aware that the drama as an art and as a criticism of life has made great strides forward since, say, about 1890. We are nearer the really good than we have been for about a century. We have a body of dramatists of real ambition, and there is every sign that they are firing the youth of intellect to follow and to aim high. Surely it would be well to encourage these men instead of heaping an obstacle in their way.

Barrie did not appear before the committee. He wrote to Barker saying why:

Is it essential? To assist from the background is my passion. Of course, I'm very anxious we should get some result.

But Barrie was going through the agony of arranging to divorce his wife; he got a decree *nisi* the following October.

Of course, Shaw's evidence and letter to *The Times* had upset some of the dramatists' committee, including John Galsworthy, who wrote to Barker on 6 August to say: " Shaw seems to have queered the pitch. I was afraid of his blessed pamphlet." Galsworthy was in favour of keeping the Lord Chamberlain " as a mechanical issuer of optional licences ", and proposed that no play should require a licence, but that if, after six public performances, public protest had not caused the local authority to threaten not to renew the theatre's annual licence, or neither manager nor author had been prosecuted by the Attorney-General, a licence should be given for the play.

A month before giving his evidence, Barker wrote to Gilbert Murray a letter referring to the matter and to his new play, *The Madras House* :

Saturday night [July 1909].

I have this day done the last bit of the first draft of a new play – and there's lots wrong with it – principally I know that its philosophic flats are not joined – I seem to have said something quite different from what I set out to say – and I'd rather like to inflict it on you – if you'd bear it and that were possible – and get your sentiments. I'm free, oh now for a week or two – until Lillah gets off, then I hope to dash away with her abroad somewhere – oh by jove no I have to give evidence on August 5 or summat – and of course now I'm going to spend time in preparing censorship ammunition. But I think I could make a dash down to Aldeburgh for a night – and the rest of this letter is therefore to Lady Mary to ask if she'd like to see me on such an errand.

Oh by the way – I don't know how much this censorship business may keep me by the leg next week. By the way, I don't think this new play is quite Redfordilus prensque.

Oh me ! I've never been depressed at finishing a play before.

This was followed by another letter, undated as usual, but written early in August :

Dear G.M. [writer of a letter to H. Granville Barker, Esq.]

How do me so you do – for I have to be here all this week – or rather every day this week on Committee of one sort and another. I give evidence Thurs. And on Saturday Lillah and I galumph away. We had thought of Brittany, then we thought the weather there would be just humerous, then we thought of a ship – we still think of a ship – We thought of Norway – then I could have paid an afternoon call at C.H. *en route* – but I couldn't bear the idea of evening dress on a " pleasure cruise " and besides Norway in this temperature. So now we think of an Orient liner on Saturday to Naples – and back (if alive). I'm not at all sure that I ought not to stay and watch over this blamed censorship business (I send you by the way an (uncorrected) copy of my proof) – But I don't know what I can do – it is hard to see just which way it will turn – Well – when will you hear that play, I wonder – it is not what it should be and it certainly does want the light of your intellectual morality and moral intellectuality turned on it.

Gilbert Murray gave evidence at the eighth sitting of the committee on 20 August, and said that he regarded the censorship as totally indefensible on principle, for the censor did not state a definite objection that could be argued out, but merely decided in the vaguest possible terms that he did not approve of it. He thought the duty of an examiner of plays should be " to consider whether a play breaks any known law ", and, if necessary, " to put the Attorney-General or the Director of Public Prosecutions in motion ". Barker sent a postcard to him:

25 : 8 : 09.

Oh – and I must add this to say I read your evidence – I thanked Zeus, Sir, that you were there to come after the popinjay A.B.W.[1]

Another letter to Murray on the same subject is interesting because of a reference to *Waste*:

Of course, I have now for the first time got hold of the official report of your compromise – now I'm rather clearer about it than I was – I want to talk – I've things both to say and ask.

A. Is this the time for working a round-table conference – or after the report comes out and a bill is framed.

B. Theatre people are the worst committee men in the world – I verily believe.

C. You only propose of course that the cachet given to a play should give it customary protection and the managers have sought to ask for more – but can you express that in drawing up an act? Must you not either give definite protection or not and you can't compromise – Again this way that only a public official may prosecute what another public official has passed – that would be dog eating dog.

D. I'm not sure that anyhow the Common Informer must not be done away with – otherwise managers will be so chary of producing " doubtful " plays and even then——

E. We should have to make a league to put on all our contracts : this play must not be submitted to the Censor.

F. That's bears hardly on the new author(?).

G. Would you like to have me at Oxford the week-end, the 18th. Lillah goes to Glasgow the Tues. before that to play Nan and Ann – I'm rehearsing *John Bull* on tour from next Monday.

H. I think what Butler says about *Waste* is most just and true. The worst of it is it is faults of execution, not conception. I have him all right in my head. The man of no religious ideas who when he gets one at a great crisis in his life is so superstitiously possessed by it that it drives him monomanical and kills him – That's all right I believe – but I've not done it ! ! !

I. All the more reason you hear and judge this play before it is quite run into mould – it has points – but a lot wrong. I've just read it over.

J. I *must* read *Iphigenia*.

K. I go to town to-morrow for *Lear* – back here Friday.

Shaw wrote to Barker from Ireland on 2 October that he had –

. . . formed a combination with Hall Caine (who was going to support the censorship). I have written a smashing preface to *The White Prophet*

[1] A. B. Walkley.

– so smashing that the *D. Telegraph* didn't dare publish it – and given H.C. the occupation's head on a charger. At last we are getting combined. Pinero and the Dramatists Club, the Sub. Comtee. of the Authors, and now Hall Caine. If I can only keep you youths from turning up your noses and your elders from delighting to bark and bite, we shall presently have something like a profession.

While the report was being drafted, Barker wrote to Murray:

I've hear of no differences. But Harcourt was prepared to accept Samuel's draft (when last I saw him) which is the optional business, subject to one or two minor but important points. The word licence should be abolished, because its use in present head-leases (" no unlicensed play shall be performed, etc.") might make the concession quite nugatory for years to come. Also – any penalties should be directed against lessee and/or licensee and not against the building – since many theatres are owned by widows and orphans, maiden ladies and syndicates and head leases would be made impossible again. I understood that Samuel had all his committee in rough agreement with the draft before he put it on paper – but I don't know.

I'm seeing a good deal of Barrie – he's very down – very. Happened to say the other day that you are one of the few people he'd *like* to see – so if you're up in town do manage to see him; he's at present at Mason's flat – 17 Stratton Street. Best of course if you'd get him to Oxford for a week-end, but he might shy at that. He'll get through but it's been a devil of a time for him. This quite private to you of course – he'd loathe to think I talked about him – but as he spoke of you like that I thought.

Lillah condemned to be on her back for two months and see no one but her nurse and me and an occasional doctor. What a year!

A study of the evidence given to the committee showed that while the dramatists and critics were against the censorship, most of the managers were in favour of it, a situation that continues to-day. A good deal of uncertainty was expressed by some of those giving evidence on both sides. The committee's report, issued on 11 November, recommended that it should be legal to perform plays without licence, but that plays could still be submitted for licence. The compromise was unsatisfactory, for in a commercialized theatre the Lord Chamberlain's licence was an asset to the managers; the outcome was that there was no change in the law, but the Examiner had (for a time) a committee to advise him.

*

During the year 1909 the Barkers had moved their London home from Clifford's Inn to 20 Alexander Court, Queen's Gate, but as much time as possible was spent at Court Lodge, though visits were paid to the H. G. Wells's at Sandgate and to the Galsworthys at Manaton in Devonshire. As will be seen, Lillah had been ill in the spring. In the summer Barker and Lillah went to Italy for a holiday, and on a picture postcard of Pompeii, the Teatro Maggiore o Scoperto, he wrote to Gilbert Murray:

I wouldn't have missed this for anything. I stood on the stage and tried to remember a bit of the *Troades* for Lillah at the back of the gallery! But it was too hot. I am going on to Passtum now. She has gone back to Sorrento. . . . I fancy the censor business goes well for us.

When they returned, Lillah was still ill. Masefield wrote a sympathetic letter to Barker hoping they would soon meet, adding:

"All we have here is our lives": and it is rather awful to think how short, and how full of unutterable opportunity, they are.

While the censorship business was on, Barker wrote an article on " Repertory Theatres " for *The New Quarterly* (November 1909) on the text that –

a civilized man needs a home; a sensitive nature needs change. To complete the civilization of the drama, homes are needed for it, for its sensitive interpretation there must be constant change.

A repertory theatre, he argued, " is a place frequented by people who take an interest in its work as its work, not visited occasionally for the sight of a popular success ". Therefore it must have an audience interested in its normal work, for it can exist only in closest relation to the everyday world.

*

In the spring of 1909 two repertory schemes were announced in London simultaneously: one by Herbert Trench, in association with Frederick Harrison, at the Theatre Royal, Haymarket, the other by the American manager, Charles Frohman, at the Duke of York's Theatre. Both appeared with a great blare of trumpets before the not easily startled London public, and it was strange on the face of it that there should be this coincidence of repertory fervour. The explanation is that Lord Howard de Walden had been persuaded the year before by a lady interested in Barker to finance a repertory at the Haymarket Theatre in which he, Barker, was to be re-established in management. But Barker considered that he would not have effective artistic control and too much to do with the lady, and refused to become associated with the scheme. For another reason, which had nothing to do with Lord Howard, the poet Herbert Trench was then brought in as director. This appearance in the theatre of a man who had hitherto shown no interest in it and who was supposed to have no knowledge of its workings remained a mystery.

Barker, writing from Stansted, had mentioned Trench to Gilbert Murray in an undated letter inviting the latter to a performance of *Strife*:

Sir. . . . Come right along. Favour the official . . . Box-Office Manager Cyrus O. Skute who so urbanely presides over the Thespian Temple of Martin's Lane . . . favour him I say Sir with a copy of your birth certificate on Toosday next and if he does not immediately fork out a brace of fauteuils for you and the honorable Lady Murray . . . draw a bead on the skulking coyote . . . hold him up, Sir in the sacred name of Liberty.

I shall be down here I expect so shan't see you . . . but do you and Lady Mary look round to Lillah's dressing-room after the performance . . . she will be so disappointed she says if you don't. I have been conversing in the utmost secrecy with a certain Tr–nch . . . at his request giving him advice . . . which he probably won't take. But I feel that we ought to combine to push him into the repertory game. Nothing else matters now I feel. Everybody wants to do something good. . . . Tree would swear to that for himself . . . but it is the system . . . the system . . . the system in a thousand ways that will continue to handicap us. All our lot of dramatists are slacking off in production because they can't be sure of anything but matinée audiences . . . lucky if they get that. It is hard work to push push push at the blessed old English . . . and repertory is our salvation. I don't want the final advance to be over the corpses of most of us . . . therefore repertory as speedily as possible.

Before anything was announced, J. M. Barrie had taken the initiative in interesting his friend, the manager, Charles Frohman, in establishing a repertory at one of his theatres, with Barker in charge.

A letter to Murray towards the end of the year refers without naming it to the Frohman scheme and has reference also to lecturing, of which Barker was called upon to do more than he really cared to undertake, and to another Greek play:

Dec. 13.

Well, I showed it to Barrie and he thinks quite strongly that nobody ought to do IT before we do it!!! When do I have a copy? Do you come to town – How are you?

About lecturing I'll answer in a day or two.

I've found your letter, and I am answering about the lecture now.

Well, I've promised – or half-promised to lecture to the New College Essay Society in March. And I've only one lecture anyhow! Don't you think they and the Drama Society had better toss for it?

Thus it came about that on the same day in April 1909 Herbert Trench and Charles Frohman announced their intentions. The poet-manager was to be responsible for a combination of repertory and long run: repertory for the first half of the week, a play put on for a run for the

The Twelve-Pound Look by J. M. Barrie (Duke of York's, 1910). Lillah McCarthy and Edmund Gwenn

VI *The Sentimentalists* by George Meredith (Duke of York's, 1910). Lillah McCarthy with Godfrey Tearle

XXVII *John Bull's Other Island* by Bernard Shaw. The special performance of Act III at N
Downing Street in the presence of King George V and Queen Mary (1911). Lillah McCarthy, '
Fay, Agnes Thomas, Louis Calvert and Granville Barker

XXVIII *Androcles and the Lion* by Bernard Shaw (St. James's Theatre, 1913). Designs by Alb
Rutherston. Act II, Scene 3

second half; the repertory was always to include three plays: a new play, a revival, a classic play, performed on Monday, Tuesday, and Wednesday respectively, with one matinée. This programme was never carried out, nor even attempted. On the contrary, when the Trench–Harrison theatre opened on 9 September 1909 with Shakespeare's *King Lear*, produced by Frank Vernon, it was for a run, and there was no talk of repertory ever again, though there was flirting with Gilbert Murray for a Greek play, with, possibly, Barker as producer, but it came to nothing, Trench being very jealous of Barker. The management remained in existence at the Haymarket for a year and ten months, then faded away, having been indistinguishable from an ordinary commercial venture except for the presence of the poet.

*

Earlier in the year, in June, Miss Horniman's Manchester Repertory Company gave a season at the Coronet Theatre, Notting Hill, for a period of three weeks, presenting eleven plays in twenty-four performances. Miss Horniman had started her Manchester Repertory Theatre in 1907 while the Savoy season was on – " the first repertory theatre in England ", she called it, opening at the Midland Theatre and moving the year after to the Gaiety Theatre, which became its home. With Barker's co-operation, Lewis Casson was engaged for Gilbert Murray's Greek versions and for Shaw plays, and in 1911 he took over the direction. Although the word " repertory " was used, Miss Horniman's was never a repertory theatre, except in London, for she instituted the system of weekly runs of plays with a stock company. She did, however, keep the plays alive, and revived them from time to time. In 1909, also, as I have said, Alfred Wareing had started the Scottish Repertory Theatre in Glasgow, the opening performance being Shaw's *You Never Can Tell* on 5 April; this, too, was not repertory, plays being given for a week. But repertory was in the air.

*

That there was more than a little vagueness about even the Frohman scheme is indicated in a letter from Barker to Gilbert Murray (undated) in which reference is made also to the work being carried out at the Barkers' home at Court Lodge:

The carpenters still banging at shelf-putting-up – me with such a bad cold in my head and not within a mile of doing any work so just starting for London. Still this is a gorgeous place – anything like the flowers in the woods I never did see and when we've done with the ramshackle house I believe it may be comfortable.

Your portrait on my new mantelpiece faces that of W.A.[1] Oh

[1] William Archer.

H

images of rectitude.   Lives of great men all remind us, etc.   I have pu
them there for inspiration.

I am wondering if you approve of the Frohman scheme, and 3 days ag‹
Barrie did say to me – he did – I hope we shall get something fror
Murray – I bethought me of *Iphigenia* – and then there is the *Troja*
Women.   Well sir – well?

I think it is all – well " maybe " a big step forward.

Barrie also wrote to Barker about the matter showing how strongly h‹
was behind his friend:

17.7 [1909]

F.'s plan as you have it is all wrong.   I'll see him to-morrow and wil
propose something like the enclosed scheme.   I feel that we must fi‹
our character at once by being repertory in the second week and with
sufficient company it should be practicable.   If my play is ready it coul‹
take the place of one of the six.   I have invented titles for Shaw an‹
Murray.   The X and Y are what I spoke to you about, too private t‹
mention to anyone else.   It would play an hour, and I put it with *School*
mistress under the impression that the latter is short.   I may be wrong
All is of course subject to alteration.   A different order might be better
Probably I have put one-act plays in programmes sufficiently long with
out them.   The precise number of performances of a play in any par
ticular week might be altered.   Results must guide us a great deal.   Wha
I offer is just a sort of general idea.   Perhaps the first four programme
would carry us thro' season.   How does it strike you?

There is another letter from Barker to Murray:

Friday

No, I suppose we can't tackle Barrie just for the moment – though th‹
sooner we can the better – for *him* don't you think?   But I am writin‹
to Frohman by to-morrow's mail asking him to send a formal confirma
tion of the arrangement Barrie made with you.   Will this do or do yo‹
want something more definite?   We none of us (Shaw, Galsworthy, an‹
I) have anything more definite about our plays – nothing on paper tha‹
is.   In case he makes no answer – or too vague a one – he'll be over i‹
November.   But if that delay will be too long – then I shall certainl‹
take it on myself to make a definite arrangement with you, sooner thar
let nibbles (the impudence of these *other* people) become bites.

Yes, I know all that is wrong with the play (mine).   I'm battling witt
it.

Shaw wrote to Ellen Terry about the possibility of Gordon Craig
taking an interest in Frohman's venture in the new drama.   He said:

Cant E.G.C. be coerced into coming along and doing a man's work witt
Barker and Barrie and myself at the Duke of Yorks?   Barker writes tha‹
it is not good enough for him.   And it is good enough for ME . . ‹
Laziness!   Infinite dishonourable laziness!   Tell him I said so.

To which Miss Terry replied that " Ted is not in the least lazy ", but he
' imagines you don't like him ".

While the preparations were being made, Barker paid a visit to Glasgow
Repertory Theatre to give support to that enterprise by a lecture on " The
Citizens' Theatre Ideal ", which greatly impressed a large audience. He
urged the need for civic support, for all the good cannot, he said, be got
out of the theatre by individual enterprise.

Plays by Shaw, Barker, Murray, Barrie, Masefield, James, Maugham,
Pinero, and others had been announced by Frohman – some new, some
revivals. Shaw had written to Barker suggesting that *Peer Gynt* should
be added " to the list of Frohmannatial Theatricalities ". Unfortunately,
Barrie's domestic troubles had flared up, and his contribution came to be
a small one, and though with great difficulty, because of illness, Henry
James completed and cut *The Outcry*, it was never done. The Murray
version of *Iphigenia in Taurus* was among other plays announced but not
done. Murray did get a contract for the play, however.

The repertory opened on 21 February 1910 with John Galsworthy's
tragedy, *Justice*, in place of the announced play, *The Eldest Son*. This
masterpiece of production by Barker put the enterprise in the front rank
artistically, and was received on the first night with unparalleled enthusiasm; but its reception by the critics, though respectfully admiring,
led the West End playgoer to suppose that the repertory was not for
anyone out for an evening's entertainment. After the performance,
John Masefield wrote to Galsworthy, " Good God, it is a revelation " –
as it was. " A great play", wrote Beatrice Webb in her diary, " great in
its realistic form, great in its reserve and restraint, great in its quality of
pity." There followed much public discussion of the play's theme and
the effect of solitary confinement in prison, and Winston Churchill, as
Home Secretary, went to see it.

Two nights later, in accordance with the repertory programme, Shaw's
new play, *Misalliance*, followed, a complete contrast to Galsworthy's in
lightness of heart and frivolity, but none the less a play demanding more
from the playgoer than he reckoned to give, and the critics, as usual with
Shaw, were extremely severe with the dramatist for not attempting to
write " a play " at all.

He had written to Barker the previous November when the play was
finished, " Frohman, who expects a melodrama, will be dumbfounded
and will most likely throw up the whole affair ". He asked Barker to
bring Barrie to hear it, " but it will lacerate his soul ". It did, indeed,
lacerate almost everyone who saw the performance. Shaw had wanted
Lillah for the leading actress, but she was not available. In fact, he
demanded an all-star cast. He was staying with his wife's relations in

the Midlands over Christmas and was bombarding Barker with post
cards. He thought he was sure of Robert Loraine for Tarleton, th
principal male character, though he doubted "whether he will throw
himself into the repertory company to be cast for anything you please"
He even thought of Martin Harvey and H. B. Irving, which wer
interesting suggestions, showing how Shaw viewed the acting of his play:
On 29 December he said: "The play has gone to the printers, and as soo
as they get it through we shall be ready for Redford." Shaw wante
Mona Limerick for Hypatia, but she was not available for rehearsal
until 7 March: he was always a great admirer of that strange actress
He would not have Mrs. Patrick Campbell: "Stella has not the drive
the zest", he wrote to Barker on the last day of the year. By 2
January they were getting rather desperate, as no one had been engage
for the part and rehearsals were due, with Shaw down with one of hi
recurrent headaches. However, they got Frederick Lloyd and Miriam
Lewes for the two parts, with Mona Limerick appearing in the last thre
performances.

Shaw had called his play "a debate in one sitting", and, despit
abundant wit, audacity of method, and exaggerated characterization
it did not please. Max Beerbohm considered the characters "perfunc
tory":

Throughout the play, indeed, I had the impression that Mr. Shaw ha
not done his best – that the work had been thrown off in the interval
snatched from lecturing and speech-making and organizing this or that.

The Times was severe, declaring the play to be "the debating society of
lunatic asylum – without a motion and without a chairman . . . it i
madness . . .". The *Standard* was equally outspoken, asserting tha
written by anyone else it would never have been seen upon the stage
"The dialogue is full of sophistries, paradoxes, wisdom, and arran
nonsense"; while the *Globe* thought it to be "absolutely his wors
play". Indeed, the critics were furious, and the public bewildered
The second week a triple bill was added, consisting of two new plays by
Barrie, *Old Friends* and *The Twelve Pound Look*, produced by Dio
Boucicault, and an unfinished comedy by George Meredith entitled *Th
Sentimentalists*, produced by Barker. This fragment, part verse and par
prose, had been found among Meredith's papers after his death and wa
handed to J. M. Barrie to arrange for performance; he added nothing o
his own. Altogether it was a confusing programme.

Indeed, the repertory, exciting as it was, was altogether confusing, no
relieved when a week later Barker's new play, *The Madras House*, wa
done. I record here a remark made by Lillah that when Barker had firs

read his play to a small company, including Shaw, the latter sat grinning throughout the evening and went away and wrote *Misalliance*. A resemblance between the two plays is unmistakable. It was produced and acted to perfection, which gave full expression to the play's irony. Max Beerbohm wrote of it:

Every character in the play is a true study made by a man with a lust for accurate observation, and with an immense talent for sympathy.

Masefield in a letter called it " very noble and very beautiful ". Beatrice Webb, while admitting its cleverness, found its obsession with sex " intellectual but dull " and could not stand it. This play, which is to be regarded as a major dramatic work of its time, was offered to a theatre and an audience not capable of appreciating it.

In the sheer brilliance of its writing, the play is remarkable, one astounding act following another. Although the dialogue appears to be inconsequential, it has direct bearing upon the developing situation, and does more than merely create atmosphere: it contains the action. There are many playwrights who write light and witty but dramatically inconsequential dialogue, which leads nowhere, as though dialogue exists for its own sake: it is a kind of journalism. That was not Barker's way. Every word contributes to the dramatic action. Thus, his is true dramatic dialogue, while much that we have to listen to in the theatre is nothing of the sort. Neither is dialogue that merely unfolds character to be regarded as dramatic dialogue; for unless related to the action it is redundant, and, even when entertaining, it actually weakens or disintegrates the dramatic qualities of a play. There is no such dialogue in this or in any of Barker's plays. Yet it must be admitted that nothing can hide or make up for the weakness of the leading character, which is the reason for the play's incomplete success. This was the cause of William Archer's puzzled though appreciative criticism.

Coming into the repertory after Shaw's brilliantly nonsensical play of parents and children, its balanced and acute summing-up of rather a similar problem was disconcerting, which had something to do with the strong objection taken to it. What Barker owed to Shaw was brutally (and rightly) pointed out, but the play's own outstanding qualities and the debt Shaw owed to Barker were overlooked.

The following sets out the repertory programme for the first three weeks:

Monday	21 February	*Justice* (first performance)
Tuesday	22 February	*Justice*
Wednesday	23 February	*Misalliance* (first performance)
Thursday	24 February (Matinée)	*Justice*

Thursday	24 February	*Justice*
Friday	25 February	*Misalliance*
Saturday	26 February (Matinée)	*Misalliance*
Saturday	26 February	*Justice*
Monday	28 February	*Misalliance*
Tuesday	1 March	*Triple Bill* (first performance)
Wednesday	2 March	*Justice*
Thursday	3 March (Matinée)	*Justice*
Thursday	3 March	*Triple Bill*
Friday	4 March	*Misalliance*
Saturday	5 March (Matinée)	*Triple Bill*
Saturday	5 March	*Misalliance*
Monday	7 March	*Triple Bill*
Tuesday	8 March	*Misalliance*
Wednesday	9 March	*The Madras House* (first performance)
Thursday	10 March (Matinée)	*Misalliance*
Thursday	10 March	*Justice*
Friday	11 March	*Justice*
Saturday	12 March (Matinée)	*The Madras House*
Saturday	12 March	*Triple Bill*

A true repertory system was adopted throughout, the programmes being announced two weeks in advance. It became certain before the three weeks were up, however, that the repertory needed an audience of its own, which would take time to create; but in the commercial theatre there is no time for such an undertaking. Had Frohman dared, he would have stopped at once, but he was committed, his reputation was at stake, and he went on losing money. He was, he was assured, though not by his business associates, gaining prestige. The Duke of York's was in fact a thoroughly unsuitable theatre for repertory, for it had no accommodation for scenery, which, after each performance, had either to be left outside or taken to a store across the river !

A bad-tempered onslaught upon the repertory was made by the novelist-dramatist Gilbert Cannan, who had his own reasons for attacking anything with which Barrie was associated. He wrote after the first three weeks, though the article did not appear until June in *The English Review*, and said :

If this Repertory Theatre fail, it will fail not because it is a Repertory Theatre, but because it is conducted by men who are under a misconception as to what is and is not serious drama. A Repertory Theatre can only succeed if the public are convinced that whenever they enter it they will be certain of finding more or less of the pleasure which it is the function of the theatre to provide, of never being actually bored or offended. In the first four programmes presented by the management of the Repertory Theatre there was offence and there was boredom, because the plays presented as serious were not serious, but intellectual without being imaginative.

Cannan attacked Shaw's *Misalliance* because in it he " seems to have a desire to have it both ways, to be both a charming liar and an apostle ", and in the struggle he " seems to have been consumed and broken ". He attacked Barker as " intellect divorced from imagination " and said that his play " possessed neither sense of the theatre nor dramatic sense ". He concluded with the reflection that a theatre that pretends to provide " spiritual food . . . and provides nothing but nauseous draughts of patent medicines cannot gain support . . .". There was much in what Cannan said, though he was writing as an enemy, not a friend, and did not trouble to take into account the uncertain conditions under which the repertory was being carried out.

A return to normality was made on 5 April, when A. W. Pinero's comedy, *Trelawny of the Wells*, was included. Admirably produced by Dion Boucicault, it gave general pleasure, and was certainly worth a place on its merits. Barker and Housman's *Prunella* was revived on 13 April, and thereafter, except for one more performance of *Justice*, the repertory continued to be *Trelawny* and *Prunella*, with a trifling piece by Anthony Hope and Cosmo Gordon Lennox *Helena's Path*, produced by Barker on 3 May for two performances only, until Elizabeth Baker's *Chains* was produced by Boucicault on 17 May to run to the end of the season.

The Shaws were away on holiday in France with Charlotte's sister; Shaw was very unhappy: " I have not written a word of anything dramatic ", he wrote to Barker from Amiens at the end of April. " Charlotte positively loathes me ", he adds, " and is, as usual, pathetically unable to dissimulate." But he complains most of having to sleep in damp sheets every night. He is writing, as usual when away from home, on a series of eight picture postcards, and goes on to refer to the repertory, about which Barker was keeping him fully informed. But he cannot make out what " Helen's Path or Pathé " is. Barker was even contemplating dropping the whole affair. Shaw says they have no choice in the matter, for they " undertook to propagate a higher drama ". He goes on:

Charles has not played the game for a single moment. I dont blame him: I dont see how any manager who has the other game open to him as an alternative *can* play our game; but that does not alter the facts: the R.T. is not an R.T. in our sense; and all we have succeeded in doing is to prove the impossibility of a high-class theatre under a commercial management.

This letter shows how uneasy the association had become and exposes the essential weakness of the Frohman scheme. It was not surprising that

Shaw followed with a letter to Barker on 9 May, " The bolt has fallen on
Frohman ", meaning that he had definitely quarrelled with him for
" holding up my plays (especially *Blanco* and *Barbara*) " in both London
and America. " The Shaw–Frohman combination is off ", he declared,
" his power stops at the commercial frontier." The next day Shaw
wrote, " he is chucking the Repertory altogether, as from now; also the
devil (meaning you and me) and all his works ".

After ten weeks the repertory collapsed on 17 June, following the death
of King Edward VII on the previous 6 May, the management having a
good reason for closing in the general theatrical slump.

The Duke of York's was, however, while it lasted, a true repertory,
and proved that the system was practicable, though unfamiliar to modern
London. Its failure was due to confusion of aims, as Shaw had pointed
out, and because a much longer time was required than commercial
management is able to allow to establish a theatre with purposes not
wholly commercial. Barker added to his reputation, but was disappointed and discouraged, not only at the short life of the enterprise, but
also because his own play was not comprehended. He did not act in the
repertory; neither did Lillah: she was ill. In October she played in
Somerset Maugham's *Grace* at the same theatre, when it had reverted to
its familiar function.

Charles Frohman was an enterprising manager, but the repertory was
entirely outside his experience, even contrary to it, and its practical sense
was much questioned by all his managerial associates and friends. To
maintain it after what to him was initial failure went utterly against the
grain, but he did so to save face after his fervid declarations until given an
unmistakably good reason to stop. Yet he was afterwards for the rest of
his life proud of what he had done. His biographer gives the repertory
much attention and says :

Had he done nothing else than the Repertory Theatre he would have left
for himself an imperishable monument of artistic endeavour.

William Archer gave a criticism of the entire repertory in a long article
in the *Fortnightly Review* (October 1910), in which he dealt very sensibly
with the reasons for its failure, which, as a critic, he thought to lie in the
lack of single and responsible direction, the absence of a careful budget,
the attempt to run a repertory theatre with a star company, and no
selection of plays at all " in the sense of an endeavour to reconcile the
claims of art with those of the treasury ". Although he declared that he
had no inside information, there can be no doubt that in this respect he
was expressing Barker's own point of view. An admirable detailed

account is contained in P. P. Howe's *The Repertory Theatre : a Record and a Criticism* (1910).

★

The following letters from Barker to Gilbert Murray, while the repertory was working, on the subject of Murray's projected Greek play and *The Madras House* are worthy of record : the punctuation of some of these letters is normal, as Barker had now a secretary :

Mar. 12 [1910].

I go back, I think, on my idea of one scene – well; I go back I think to this extent : could we have one platform and one set of seats for the chorus and then vary the background? This not so much for the sake of cheapness as in order to standardize the arrangements, for I am convinced that there is only *one* best way, and I am trying to wipe my mind clear of what we've done before in order to discover that one. At present I incline to setting them up and down stage on each side, like the stalls in the choir of a cathedral.

Then ought there not to be an altar in the middle of the stage? This seems more or less indicated in *Iphigenia*; it could be used in *Hippolytus* with effect, I suppose, but there is nothing to it in *Electra* or *The Trojan Women*, is there? I do believe it would be a magnificent effect to have a life-size bit of the Temple of Paestum as a scene. I shall part from the idea with great reluctance.

Yes, I rather think with you, I'm afraid, that the revival before *Iphigenia* is bad. The notion sprang from several rather confusing currents of events; one thing that was in my mind was, as we had Casson in the company, to let him repeat for a few performances his production of *Hippolytus*. I very much want to get in some other producers than myself. But there's the casting difficulty again and the powers that be didn't jump at it. I also thought we might try some of the people we have got upon a thing that after all had its show and was known more or less at its best; for the real *Iphigenia* difficulty is the cast, and Lillah's health is by no means the only point in it.

But to take her position first, it will be a great disappointment to me if she doesn't play it, and more than disappointment, indeed a bitter grief, to her, for she has been studying it and knows it already, she is that keen. Putting that aside as the personal aspect of the matter, she may be able to do it by the end of May. She is sure she could, and I think she could. The doctors won't say yet, indeed Christopher shakes his head. But she picks up quite marvellously. We shall know in another fortnight. By the autumn of course she would have fifty per cent. more strength to give to it. I see I harp on the personal question but you'll understand and forgive that.

But supposing it is done without her, who is the substitute? Frankly, I practically know that they won't consent to Penelope doing it – they don't consider that she has weight or authority enough for it. My half-formed plan for *Hippolytus* has included her as Phaedra and there was

immediate doubt about that. I fear I don't think that she could carry off
Iphigenia either, though of course there will be an awkwardness in
expressing my opinion, and I only do so now to you.

Then what are the other alternatives? – there's Lena Ashwell who
seems, to judge by one performance she gives for us, hopeless in anything
of the sort; there's Violet Vanbrugh, wandering about in music-halls,
but really I don't advise her. Still somebody might be found, but, for
the rest of the cast : – I have no Orestes; Bryant would be hopeless in it –
he is rather a disappointment to us so far; Valentine could play Theas,
and Casson one of the Messengers, but – here is the real point – if it were
to mean special engagements outside the company for Iphigenia, Orestes,
one Messenger, perhaps Athena, and at least two-thirds of the Chorus,
it makes it very expensive at two performances a week, which is what it
might average.

A little shifting is going on in the company which might make matters
easier, but it hasn't so far. My hope is in the autumn when we shall have
one or two robuster plays to do that we may have collected more likely
people; the only way of forming this company, (it isn't really formed yet)
not quite ruinously, is to engage people for two or three plays.

I write this at great length and rather confusedly – I wish I could talk
to you, for there are many complications and I am not, of course, in any
absolute authority. But what principally ties me up over an immediate
production is an Iphigenia – bar Lillah – and an Orestes. (I want Forbes-
Robertson, a pleasant sort of want – none of these young men do – they
are all either too thin or too fat – none of them fate-haunted.)

Well, write and let me know what you think. I must stop now or
Wade will strike.

Wed. [March 1910].
First – personally. Thank you ever so much about Lillah – it would
have been a bad smash to her to have missed it. Impersonally – I hope
you won't regret the wait and I don't think you will.

But shall we wait if we need not and produce in June if we can? I'd
a little bit rather wait for October. You can certainly have an approxi-
mate date – I will speak to Frohman – and I don't see why we shouldn't do
one more during next season – say *Troades* – but that I must discuss with
them. I suppose we have none of us had any agreements by the way – I
do not even know yet what royalties I have for the *Madras House* such is
the adventuresome way we have done it all – (I have much to tell you).
And when can I see you by the way, for I cannot write about that scene
and chorus question; a possible Orestes looms in H. E. Anson – do you
remember him—a part in a Sutro play – Dick in *Nan*.

I must stop now for the post.

I hope you will see the M.H. I did not think a play could have been
so misunderstood even by " mean sensual men ".

Tuesday [March 1910].
Thanks about M.H. and Lillah and the cornland – that's given me an
excellent idea. I ought to have sat at Margoliouth's feet a bit more.

One thing else, State (the American) . . . the vagaries of the female mind – have they laws? – are those laws discoverable? I recall a passage in Epictetus – I want the passage, please – I ain't particular to Epictetus – the bit should be some much translated classic – Can you suggest anything?

Lillah has been having rather a bad time – she is steady now, if not better – and cheerful in herself. We shall have to watch and nurse her carefully for a bit.

After Frohman's decision to put a stop to the repertory, Barker wrote to Murray:

Sunday [May 1910].
The effect of the shock has now rather worn off with me: you will imagine the particular feelings with which I hand it on to you.

But now before you decide anything I wish we could have a talk – about this – as to what is the way round it that best suits you – and about the whole situation rendered a little critical by the action of Frohman. I think it is possible – when and where?

The Barkers, by the way – Lillah and H.G.B. – have developed a sudden desire to hear Roosevelt's Romanes lecture – Is that possible or *not*?

I shall be in town Tuesday, otherwise I'm here trying to get *Madras House* ready for printing – awaiting Frohman's decision about my last – his next production.

While the repertory was still in being, Barker gave a lecture in London, on 10 June, on " The Theatre: the Next Phase ", which was published in the July number of *The English Review*. In the course of it he said:

I have come to the conclusion that a Repertory Theatre cannot be made to pay in the commercial sense of the word.

He paid testimony to Charles Frohman:

Whatever has been done or left undone, gained or lost, at the Duke of York's Theatre since last February, the practicability of modern repertory has been proved, and the public now knows by demonstration what a Repertory Theatre is. . . . As far as my thanks go, I want to render them publicly to Mr. Frohman, and to say that I am proud to have taken a part in his enterprise.

He expounded what he meant by " normal drama ", and wound up by an attack on the critics for lack of open-mindedness, and referred to the sayings of " a person called Aristotle ", in whose name, he asserted, dramatists were " terrorized ". He was really arguing against A. B. Walkley, and against those who declared that the plays he and others were writing were not plays. " We are breaking new ground," he said, " enlarging the boundaries of the drama, fitting it for every sort of

expression. When we deserve it a new dramatic genius will arise."
Nothing, of course, will do but a National Theatre. "Ought it not",
he asked, " be opened at the very latest the day after to-morrow?"

*

There was a proposal that summer to revive the Court tradition at the
Coronet Theatre, Notting Hill, with Shaw willing. He wanted *Misalliance*
to be done again, with Lillah McCarthy as Lina, the part originally intended for her, and Barker as Lord Summerhays, and he urged a revival
of *The Madras House* at the same time. Barker wanted *Man and Superman*, but Shaw had promised it to Loraine. Barker sought to get financial
help without success. Lord Northcliffe was approached without result.
John Galsworthy was not eager for it, "Don't run your head against a
brick wall", he advised Barker. It came to nothing, and Barker played
John Tanner in Glasgow, but not with Lillah. Neither this production
of the play nor Loraine's in London pleased Shaw, for he considered
justice could not be done to it without a good Ann, which, in his
opinion, neither production had.

When the Frohman repertory closed, there was an idea that the
manager would put on Murray's version of *Iphigenia in Taurus*, for which
a contract had been completed with the translator. Lillah was keen upon
the play, and negotiations went on for some time with the half-hearted
Frohman, also with Granville Bantock for the music and Margaret Morris
for the dances, but all in vain, for the play had to wait another two years,
until Lillah herself was in management. Some letters from and to Murray
are of interest. There was talk of Beerbohm Tree doing Murray's version of *Oedipus*, and even a proposal that Trench might put it on at the
Haymarket. Also an idea of Greek plays in New York at the theatre the
direction of which Barker had turned down. All came to nothing.

Gilbert Murray to Granville Barker

July 8 1910.

I have at last got off here, after an increasing whirl of work which has left
me dull and sodden, and just fit for this health resort.

Frohman sent me two beautiful contracts, bound in blue borders. He
signed them "Lestocq", which I understand is one of his aliases. It is
to be matinées in the autumn, produced by you (or Lestocq is to commit
hari-kari) or else evening performances in the spring. This I take it
means the autumn. Anyhow, that is what Bantock ought to be ready for.
It is not likely he will risk evening performances if he can help it.

If not produced by the spring, in the evening by you, Frohman under-
takes to scalp Lestoq, subscribe £10,000 for the maintenance of com-
pulsory Greek, and pass Smalls. I have hay fever and a game eye.
Otherwise I am doing *Oedipus* lazily, and having my portrait re-painted
by One who before made me look like the Corpse of Aegisthus.

Granville Barker to Gilbert Murray

Tuesday [July 1910].

This is a belated comment on your last. I feel sure that if you want *Iph:* done in the autumn you must intimate the same to Frohman – who will otherwise from pure inertia and looking on (and after) stars let it drag till the spring repertory. And as you know, my most secret thought is that he won't do it at all – but will pick out his Snagsby's half-crown. This would be a pity, for there seems an autumn opening – thereby (not for Frohman, who has theatres of his own – but for them as hadn't). Marie Brema is to do more opera at the Savoy (so she'll be busy, she couldn't act herself), but there will be the theatre loose for matinées and a certain amount of chorus-y people to hand – would you like, say, the *Hippolytus* done again? Shall it be thought of?

You see I can't rest with things undone though I do my best to make other people do them. Oh my poor new play!

How are you? – When comes *Oedipus*?

Tuesday [July 1910].

My own belief has always been that Frohman won't do *Iphy* or indeed touch anything repertory again with a pair of tongs – but I have absolutely no evidence to bring on the subject.

If Payne writes to him personally, he probably won't answer. If Payne goes to Lestocq – he might get provincial rights for a consideration if there were any to give – but you've no detailed contract with Frohman, have you?

Frohman might well consider that a previous country production absolved him from a London one – he is funny – a little – about these things and probably would. On the other hand, he'd probably act quite squarely over the £200 – though if it got left with Lestocq he (L) would save him (F) every penny of money he decently could. My opinion is – on the whole – that as Payne has many undone *Euripides* to choose from – as far as Manchester is concerned it would be safer to let him do one of these and not disturb the Frohman arrangement in any way – as to matinées at Easter. Also – a Payne " 2 nights " at the Coronet would wreck its chances for the home with any London management whatever. Whereas, things being as they are, you are quite sure of £200 or its equivalent – and reasonably sure (I think) of the £200 and then of a series of matinées in London.

Bless you, I can't get to no John the Looses.

W.A. has been here – says you were lunching with Tree on Monday – not where you eat Sir but where you were eaten. What result?

Monday [July 1910].

Well – about *Iph:* so far so – as good as may be. But now about Bantock. He said he could do the music for the autumn – I asked him about business arrangements – he asked me to propose them (then came the standstill). If I write to America and ask for authority to go on with the matter I shall either get the vaguest of answers or none. On the other hand, it is no use trying to get that music done at a month's notice – which is what Frohman will give – and the same remark applies to Miss Morris, whom I wanted (who I wanted) to arrange the chorus movements. What am I to do? To Bantock I suppose either I or you could say that you would consider his music a necessary part of the production as long as his business proposals were reasonable. With Miss Morris it is more difficult. But to get that chorus right we ought to have at least 10 weeks' notice of the production. How to get it?

Gilbert Murray to Granville Barker

July 19, 1910.

Evidently Bantock must be put to work at once. I should think it was quite safe. Frohman must know – or can be shown – that it is necessary to have the music and the movements for the chorus carefully settled.

Can't you 1. agree with Bantock and set him going? 2. Write to Frohman and tell him you have done so and assume that he approve unless he cables to say that he does not? 3. Explain this to Bantock, promising to let him know instantly if F does object?

I think you might do just the same with Miss Morris. But anyhow they ought to be set going at once. Is the fee a difficulty?

Oedipus's eyes are just rolling on to his beard. There will be an awful mess if I don't attend to them.

Granville Barker to Gilbert Murray

Wed. [July 1910].

Well – I'll write to Bantock and Frohman, but I doubt if F. will authorize me to make any business arrangement with B. However B. will most likely go ahead without.

The difficulty with Miss Morris is that she must have the people engaged to train 8 weeks ahead and I know F. won't give us that notice. ? how to make him.

I see your Academy is announced. I have a perverse desire to throw a stone at its study window. Oh by the way Lillah has perhaps written to you to-day. I want to work it that Ames does one of the Euripides at the New Theatre this autumn.

(*a*) I think he ought.

(*b*) I'd like Lillah (if you approve) to get a smack at it.

(*c*) I want to go over and produce. I find I *can't* produce rot. I ruin it – show it up – even if I get that to do in the autumn and I must earn some money somehow.

Have you any views – have you had any passages with Ames?

Gilbert Murray to Granville Barker

August 6, 1910.

All right about *Iphigenia*. The spring is as good as another time. Only that will involve Frohman putting it on in the evening, and then no one will come: though perhaps he would also come in the afternoon. I have just finished a first draft of *Oedipus* and may at any moment send you a copy to read. But this is not imminent, as I have not got a copy made. I do not really in my heart believe in the music for choruses, but we had better try it again. The O.T. chorus consists of old men like me, with lumbago and several false teeth. Such persons are considered very attractive.

Granville Barker to Gilbert Murray

[August 1910.]

Bantock wrote saying he must give up doing the music. I wrote dissuading him and committed myself to the statement I underline in his letter because I thought that if I were wrong – we'd be no worse off than with his refusing altogether – for who else is there to trust to do the music – knowing – having experience that is the sort of thing wanted? But see if I have done wrong.

No word from Frohman. I committed him (F) to a guinea a perf. in fees for the music. I thought that couldn't hurt.

Before Barker went off to carry out an engagement at the Scottish Repertory Theatre, where he produced, in addition to *Man and Superman*, Masefield's *The Witch*, he wrote the following letters to Gilbert Murray :

Thursday.

I go up to Glasgow tonight – Royalty Theatre until Monday fortnight.

Tree, I hear, wants to do an *Oedipus* – Shall I tell him you have translated it or would you sooner I killed you at once.

Don't you feel that on Oct. 11 and 12 it will really be necessary for you to go to Berlin for a week to talk things over with Wilamewik and see the German drammer – I have a reason for asking.

No good sending you polite telegrams.

You know I suppose that the Little Theatre opens with the *Lysistrata* – blessed by Redford.

I don't get that copy of *Oedipus*, but there . . .

Glasgow [September 1910].

Just finished *Oedipus* – a whacking fine play – doesn't it wake up? Can't quite fathom the end – what Creon means – why doesn't Oedipus go wandering after all? Do they mean to have another go at Loxias? Of course I can't help feeling that their daughters are dragged on – at least feel it until the scene is well under way and its horror has got you – then it justifies itself – until then I feel – Ah – Euripides didn't work things this way in the *Troades* ! And oh I say – Enter a stranger ! Enter Sardou with a telegram ! Let us write a Greek play with the aid of the telegram. One character or at most two and four telegraph boys – or gradually swelling chorus of telegraph boys. (I say – how fine the scene with the old shepherd is though.) There's nothing in the choruses to touch the other gents to my mind, though " The white brides of Helicon laughed for delight " is a gem of a line – dashed if I don't think that's your best line to date ! I don't think that Redford will pass it – though Lord knows he may be intimidated by now. I don't think Tree will have sense enough to do it – and Lord knows his performance would make one sick (Mounet-Sully was bad enough). Who then? If McKinnel had a little more poetry in his strength – if H. B. Irving were a little better. Trench and McKinnel seem the combination. Trench ought to be given a chance of doing his duty. Meanwhile let us proceed with a burlesque which Redford would love to pass Adipose – King of Greece (grease). Refrain for 1st chorus.

. . . But my spirit turns to the Ga–Iety and unto the strains of Yip-i-adi I.E. I.E.   Then we will write on the top of our notepaper – say it in any theatre almost you go into.

> If honour for such things be,
> Why should I dance my dance.

That's a great couplet.

Oh, it's a big play – I think you were right at first – McKinnel and Trench should be the combination.

I stay here till the 10th producing *Mine Pedersdotter* – which we call *The Witch* – and playing (Heaven help me) *Man and Superman* for the fortnight's rehearsals – then to raise a little money *not* for love of it – do I dance that dance, though after what you can see in London at the moment – well it's Homer to Alfred Austin.   This was to have been for Lillah – but as she has to play at the Duke of York's she'll only be here this next week for Monday.   On the 12th I hope to go to Berlin for a week.

It will be seen from the above letter that *The Witch* had its first production in Glasgow, without Lillah, though she saw the play, for she was engaged in Somerset Maugham's *Grace*, which opened in London on 15 October.

Earlier Barker had received a first play from a young dramatist, to whom he wrote a letter from Court Lodge, which provides an example of Barker's interest in young writers for the theatre:

August 2 [1910].

Candidly this is pretty bad – that is, viewing it as an achievement, but if you don't – and I'm not inclined to – then let me say that you can write dialogue – you can visualize things dramatically and when you've given over doing things for the sake of doing them and saying things for the sake of saying them – no matter whether they are – not true – but appropriate and reasonable, then, if you can write anything – that is if you had got anything genuine and simple and worthy in you to write – I prophesy (for what that's worth) that you'll be able to write a play.

Then Barker went to Berlin to see Reinhardt and his work; and wrote to Murray:

Berlin, Thursday [1910].

I am at this moment just off to see a rehearsal of *Oedipus* (Reinhardt production). . . .

It is now the afternoon and I have been and come back.   Going to be quite interesting and for the direct dramatic – almost violence of the

Oedipus – suitable. And the Germans make it more violent again – though they make it big. I feel I shouldn't quite like it for *Euripides* – I want more philosophy.

Nothing now against having *Oedipus* sent to the Lord Chamberlain at once is there – indeed a measure of precaution – before one begins to give thought to it? I leave here Tuesday or Wednesday and as soon after as may be I'll try to see you. Theatre here so alive and interesting – it makes me ashamed. But we have the potentialities I am sure – and of something even better than the Germans – something on a higher, serener plane. But it's their vitality we want first – Do you think it comes from so much food and drink? – the less good part of it yes – but the better from their thoroughness. I do admire the brutes.

On his return he writes again about the possibility of the Greek play being done by the Trench–Harrison management, and he breaks the news to Murray that he had accepted a music-hall engagement; he also touches upon the anxiety about a licence for *Oedipus*:

Thursday [December 1910].

Well – personally I rejoice for you and in principle I rejoice as one ought when a sword is turned to a ploughshare – But it was a very nice sword. Now, Uncle, as to *me*.

(*a*) Trench may not want me to produce at all. Then it is up to you. As far as I can make out he still does in production and casting what he is told – with sufficient emphasis. But you must judge what you think right and wise to tell him. (Doesn't that sound moral and condescending of me?)

(*b*) He may want me to produce and come to loggerheads over terms. If I ought to meet him at this point (though don't give a poor devil away by telling him (T) that he (I) expect to have to!) it will be easier for me to do it for a production in the middle of February. Cos' why? I shall be in London from about Jan. 10. I am going on the Halls! for four weeks – to turn an honest penny – much needed. Do not mention that abroad for the moment. I'll tell you more of it – not uninteresting! So I thought you had better know this. Having earned a penny – I must retire down here again to the everlasting "play".

But whoever does *Oedipus* and whenever it is done do warn Trench that there should be a clear two months' thought given to the preparation – the music and the selection and training of the chorus – that can't be hurried. May this time God help us.

When next you do write about the censor you must begin "To my countrymen". I feel like Prossy in *Candida*, "Silly old fathead" – Lord R!

I can't take no holiday this Xmas – but is there *no* chance of seeing you?

Sunday [1910].

What if the L.C. and his committee do refuse *Oedipus*? I suggest to you a public reading at the Queen's Hall – the play cast as it would have

I

been chorus and all – in fact a performance minus costume and movement – it would be most effective. I also should be rejoiced at a public declaration at the same time from you that you would not re-submit the play for licence. My fear is that the L.C. means to scotch opposition by making as many concessions as he can – we – the general body of opposers – are so rottenly divided on the question of principle – that it would be an easy job if he had the wit to set about it. Personally one will be glad to see the *Oedipus* through but – at once – everyone will bless the name of the committee and say that nothing more need be done.

Monday night [December 1910].
Thanks for your wire. Well if it's definitely not till after Xmas, that's all I want to know at the moment. What about the licence? Fisher White – well. Not ideal, but truly I don't see a better. I wish he hadn't a voice – though that's useful to an Oedipus.

By the way, Lillah reproached me for not having told you she'd embrace Jocasta with fervour. I think she's written now to you herself.

I think it's quite on the cards you know that Trench won't want me – so I'm not at all considering myself " there ". Oh Lawks – be careful about the music – Trench has been pretty bad so far. Meanwhile any chance of seeing you. I've interesting things – some – to tell about Germany.

From Gilbert Murray to Granville Barker

Dec. 9 1910.
The exact *Oedipus* situation is as follows:

Trench has got the Lord C's licence and writes to me that he cannot think of producing it " for months yet ". To this I have replied by asking for a definite date before which. To this he makes the natural retort of not answering my letter.

Meantime Tree writes asking my terms and saying that he had a plan in his mind which he is sure I shall like. It evidently is the Berlin plan of a performance in a circus with vast crowds and performing elephants. Whelen says it was very effective indeed in Berlin. But then it was Hofmannsthal's version: sure to be coarse and strong, suitable for laying on thick. Still, I am unprejudiced. Have you any view, and could you produce it in that style?

I have told Tree that I have asked Trench for a date and will write to him when I hear.

Of course I will urge Trench to have you. And also Tree, if it comes to that. I have taken that rather for granted with him so far, and have said that I want the same sort of production – with allowance for the larger stage and the different style of play – as we have had before. But I don't think there is much chance for Feb.

Granville Barker to Gilbert Murray

Tuesday [December 1910].
Well – that's like Tree's d——d impertinence and as to Trench – oh but we are beginning to know our Trench.

However, now that you've so charmingly insulted Tree by suggesting that he – he – HE – may be taking over Reinhardt's production we may have some pretty developments.   Anyhow several things are coming on to the tablecloth and somewhere soon we ought to meet and talk.   Is there any chance.   Don't you go a-tempting me with your furrin health resorts.   I took my busman's holiday in Berlin.   The temptation is though that Lillah ought to have one, and I wish I could get her abroad for a week or two.   But I fear it can't be done.   Will you be alone there then or with whom?

Damn it, Sir, what's the fare and do a young married couple travel as one?   I understood the French nation wished to encourage matrimony.

Jan. 4 [1911].

Having lunched with a real Theatrical Knight you are evidently too proud to write to me at all.   What is now the Tree and *Oedipus* position?

I go on the Music Halls as I explained and shall be in London all February and half March.   I produce the *Witch* for Lillah at the Court on January 31.

If by chance the capital for this *increases* in the process – not decreases – and if the perfide Frohman fails – what about *Iph:*?   though hardly at the Court – These be some of my lighter thoughts.   Join them with yours and so farewell.

Sat. [January 1911].

There ain't a circus left in London that I can think of.   Perhaps it's the Albert Hall – for I think there are possibilities in a production like that. Reinhardt's – as far as I could judge from the two rehearsals I saw – promised to be unnecessarily violent.   But I don't see H.B.T. wanting me to interfere – though Heaven knows for his own sake he'd better have *somebody* or he'll never learn *Oedipus*.   Well, let me hear more; it would be larks.

The production of *Oedipus* did not come off, however.   Another effort at prose-writing had been made during the previous year, when Barker started on a series of " Prison Studies ", in which he projected a number of short monologues by prisoners explaining to themselves how they had come to commit the crimes for which they had been convicted. One example of these studies entitled *The Bigamist* survives, but none was published.   He also wrote a preface to a volume of *Three Plays*, by Maurice Maeterlinck, published in 1910.   John Masefield, advising him about the fee he should get for the preface, said that he never got more than 3 or 4 guineas for a thousand words, and did not think either Yeats or Symons got more.   But he thought Barker on Maeterlinck would be such a draw that he might ask for 20 guineas.   In that preface Barker urged people to get into the habit of reading plays :

. . . the most vital of the literary arts. They are perhaps the ultimate test of an imaginative writer; they are certainly the ultimate test of an imaginative reader.

What he said then about the art of translating plays is well worthy of attention, for he was already having experience himself – in translating, or in working over a translation of, Schnitzler.

*

At the end of 1910 a matinée performance was organized at the Haymarket Theatre on behalf of the funds of the National Shakespeare Memorial Committee at which Shaw's *Dark Lady of the Sonnets*, written for the occasion, was performed. It had all the appearance of being written and produced in a hurry, except for the costumes by Charles Ricketts – a grey-cloaked Shakespeare, a silver-and-black Elizabeth, a scarlet Dark Lady. Barker played Shakespeare. " I want Barker," said Ricketts, " who of course wants to show his legs, to appear *at first* wrapped in a large grey coat, half statue and half Guy Fawkes; he can show his legs in that hose afterwards." The piece was a delicious trifle, and made an exciting contribution to the afternoon, though Barker was not at his best. Shaw sent him a postcard:

[Postmarked Nov. 25 1910.]

Forgot to warn you that you made an astonishingly XIX century start by saying " on the contrary " instead of " Far from it ". Remember " endless naughtiness to a gentleman as lewd as herself" and " high nature and fruitful industry " (or whatever it is: my last copy has gone). The costume was telling; there has been a great rally of the old adoration.

That year, 1910, was a crowded and important one in Barker's life. On his visit to Germany he not only saw Max Reinhardt and his theatres in Berlin, but Louise Dumont and Gustav Lindemann, who directed the Schauspielhaus in Dusseldorf, which impressed him deeply. He afterwards wrote two articles for *The Times*, the first appearing on 19 November, in which he compared the programmes of the theatres in London and Berlin, to the great disadvantage of London. He said:

One thing above all, the German Theatre has vitality; and vitality covers a multitude of artistic sins.

The visit confirmed his conviction that only a repertory system was of any use. He noticed, however, that there was a great difference in the attitude of the audience in Germany: " They listen attentively; they seldom laugh " – this was at a performance of *The Doctor's Dilemma*. He was critical of the quality of the acting, which he considered often very poor. In the second article, he said of Max Reinhardt's two theatres:

. . . this one organization, with its two houses . . . giving us in one week a greater variety of good drama than any two London theatres will give in a year.

A further article in *The Times* on the Theatre Exhibition in Berlin was very scathing. " The exhibition is worth a visit," he said, " though not a visit to Berlin."

In January of the following year, 1911, Lillah arranged six matinées at the Court Theatre of *The Witch*, John Masefield's adaptation of the Norwegian play, *Anna Pedersdotter*, by Wiers Jenssen. William Archer had seen the play on a visit to Norway a year or more earlier, and made a rough translation, which he sent to Lillah, saying that it had a fine part for her. She gave it to Barker, who sent it to Masefield, asking him to put it into shape, for he thought the play would appeal to him. In fact, it did not, and Masefield did little to it, though he gave it a new title. Archer was rather aghast, for he had thought of working at the play himself. However, no one would look at it, Shaw among others being against it, and at last, after the week at Glasgow, these matinées were done with Barker producing, Lillah making a powerful impression in a not satisfactory though highly theatrical part. A letter from Gilbert Murray to Barker mentions the play and says much about the coming Reinhardt production of *Oedipus* in London :

Feb. 20, 1911.

I enjoyed *The Witch* very much. A good, tight, well-made foreign melodrama, with some really fine scenes. I thought Lillah exceedingly good, better than in anything I have seen except possibly *Nan*. The long scene where she wished Absolon dead seemed to me really fine tragic acting, of the sort one hardly ever sees.

Now as to *Oedipus*. I trust you are in the inmost counsels of Ordynski and Whelen, and will be in those of Reinhardt. You are the only person on whom I can really lean this professorial head.

Ordynski writes to me as if all was practically settled. I have sent a book to Reinhardt at his request, and Stoll had gone to Berlin and " after his coming back will go in a hurry for prepare the work ". So Ordynski puts it. He also says R. will give me full authority over the words. As to this, I suggest that in the Albert Hall we shall have to cut largely. Speech there has to be very slow, has it not? Anyhow I am ready to consider cutting.

We must clearly have an English producer to act with Reinhardt, who cannot produce the speaking, etc. This should be you, if you can manage it. And of course me with you. We must alter the old method into something more formal large and spectacular. – Eh?

Further, I have had a cable from Coburn, " retain rights *Oedipus* ". (He has done the *Electra* quite a lot of times, about 24, sometimes with big houses. Casson says he was not so bad.) But if the Reinhardt business

comes off and is a success, R. might like to do the same thing in America.
What do you think? And we might even do the *Troades* in the same sort
of way, with an immense stage, and have a perfectly gorgeous time over
it. So I am not closing with Coburn till I hear something definite from
Reinhardt.

At any moment the Devil might suggest to him to cut Sophocles and
just get a translation of Hofmannsthal, or a new play of the sort composed
by Sir Herbert's secretaries.

Matinées of *Nan* took place the following month at the Court Theatre.
Then Lillah and Barker, with Nigel Playfair, appeared for four weeks in
the Palace Theatre variety programme in Barker's own version of Arthur
Schnitzler's Viennese playlet, *The Farewell Supper*. This was a successful
experiment, though not approved of by all their friends, with the exception of Shaw, who was entirely for it. Gilbert Murray wrote to Barker
on the 10 February :

Anatol seems to have been a success. Best congratulations, though in my
heart I feel, Not here, O Apollo, are haunts meet for thee.

There was now being discussed the Max Reinhardt production of
Oedipus with Martin Harvey. A proposal to do it at the Royal Albert
Hall had been turned down. Two letters from Barker mention the
subject; the Court reference concerns *Nan* :

Sunday [February 1911].
No – *Anatol* is pot-boiling – I've taken the trouble to devise a new sauce
to boil, that's all (metaphor gone wrong !).
Friday. Why yes – there'll be a seat kept for you. If you find you
can't come (Heaven forfend) send a wire to Drinkwater (Bus. man :)
at the Court March 4. I can't – I shall still be at the Palace – it may be my
last night there – if so I could come any night immediately after. It may
not (I shall know by the end of this week) in which case I could only come
on Sunday – impossible for you (?) I should really rather have more
news to-morrow. I have been writing out casts for them rather at
random. Reinhardt is undoubtedly keen and the Albert Hall miscarriage
is a scandal.

March 13th, '11.
Ordynski has now gone off to Berlin leaving the *Oedipus* arrangements
in Whelen's hands and he (W) is a little slow in the uptake of them. I
think it would be such a good matter to bring this performance off,
especially in view of the dunder-headed command performances with
which the English Theatre is to be insulted over the Coronation (*Money*
if you please). I hope you will keep actively enthusiastic about it; it
will egg them on.

Barker was displaying increasing restlessness. Unless the National Theatre was to be established – and there seemed no hope whatever of that – there was nothing for him but a hand-to-mouth existence all his life. His playwriting was proceeding slowly. Although a copious writer, his inventive powers were limited, with his critical sense acute, so that he would work at his plays over and over again, with the result that his final production was small. Among the plays upon which he was working was one entitled *The Village Carpenter*, afterwards called *The Wicked Man*, and a considerable amount of dialogue written on large sheets of paper survives. Among the notes for the dialogue for Charles, the hero of this play, are two sentences that deserve to be recorded:

The Devil is always offering you the kingdom of the world, but if you can't rule over it it's not worth taking, and I can't: I should be a slave on it.

We second-raters, we must decline the fight for we daren't be beaten.

In fact, except for translations, made in other circumstances, Barker finished nothing more for the theatre, except some trifles, until after the First World War. We shall come to that later. He was even talking about leaving England and becoming a naturalized citizen of a country where the theatre was treated seriously; for his visits to Germany had filled him with admiration for the attitude to the theatre in that country, so different from the casualness of the English theatre, with its utter commercialism and theatrically uneducated audience. There seemed no place for him in London either as actor, producer, or author. His wife shared this dissatisfaction; for the West End comedies in which she was in demand gave her no pleasure, moved as she was with the desire for poetry and for acting the great classic parts. But she had little difficulty in getting profitable engagements.

Early in 1911 Barker left the executive of the Fabian Society, as did Bernard Shaw, and after that dropped almost entirely out of the Webbs' circle. He had taken a keen interest in the society's work and had given many lectures on its behalf, usually on theatrical subjects; he resigned not because he had changed his mind about socialism, but because he was generally unsettled, and there was much dissension in the society. Referring to Barker's Fabianism, (Sir) R. C. K. Ensor wrote to me on the subject as follows:

He and I were elected simultaneously, and quickly found an attachment based originally, I think, on the fact that we were of exactly the same age. He was, to my thinking, remarkable good at common sense – a quality in which most of our colleagues excelled less than in many others. He particularly shone in this respect in contrast to G.B.S. Indeed, what I found most to his credit was that, after being introduced to the Fabian

Society by Shaw and induced by him to stand for the Executive, he had the independence of character to stand up against Shaw's charms and wiles, whenever (as was so commonly the case) Shaw was exerting them on behalf of some quite impracticable policy.

However, the connection between us did not last long, for after his first year or so Barker found it impossible to put in more than an occasional attendance at Executive meetings. He stayed on nevertheless, being re-elected on his theatrical reputation. In 1910 I myself resigned, not from any disagreement, but for twelve months, to give a chance for new blood to be elected. I urged others of my colleagues to do the same, but Barker was, I think, the only one to follow suit. Unfortunately, he never came on to it again, being convinced that he could not find the time. I myself remained an active Fabian for some time longer, but eventually had (like Clark long before) to desist when I became a full-time leader in it again, and so could not attend meetings.

*

About the same time, in the early months of 1911, the Barkers took a small flat over the newly opened Little Theatre, John Street, Adelphi. The existence of this theatre was due to the fashionable actress, Gertrude Kingston, who had it constructed out of an Adams' building once occupied by Coutts, the bankers. It was indeed a little theatre, seating no more than 278. Miss Kingston had opened it on 11 October 1910 with a version by Laurence Housman of Aristophanes' *Lysistrata*, which, strangely, the censor had passed. She had intended to run the theatre for feministic plays, but was not successful, however, and Lillah knew the building was available. So, with the determination to keep Barker in England, she went to Shaw, living a short distance away, and asked for a new play. "Get a theatre and the money," he said, "and the play will be there – a money-maker," he added. Then, without saying anything to anyone, she went off one morning to Lord Howard de Walden to ask for £1,000 to take the theatre and re-start Barker in management. She got the money, to which Shaw added £500, and her friend Lily Antrobus a similar sum, and Shaw handed her *Fanny's First Play*, with strict instructions that the authorship was not to be divulged. Thus Lillah took a lease of the Little Theatre and invited Barker to become its producer. On the condition that he could choose the plays himself, he agreed, and the Lillah McCarthy–Granville Barker management was inaugurated.

The Little Theatre was an attractive, if somewhat precious, little building, and the Barkers did something to make it more homely and democratic. There were stalls for 250, and seven boxes at the back. As there was no pit and no seats at pit prices, they made two rows at the back into pit seats at the usual price of 2s. 6d. They set up a drama bookstall in the spacious foyer. A. E. Drinkwater became manager and remained with the management until the end. The first production on Saturday, 1 March, was the Schnitzler *Anatol* dialogues in Barker's translation, produced by him, with himself in the name part, supported again by Nigel Playfair as Max, and the five ladies played by Gertrude Robins, Katherine Pole, Dorothy Minto, Lillah McCarthy, and Alice Crawford. The settings were designed by Norman Wilkinson of Four Oaks. This proved to be Barker's last public appearance as an actor on the London stage, and was a brilliant affair. Barker's light, ironic manner suited the part admirably, Playfair being a perfect foil, and the production had delicacy and wit equal to the writing.

The aim of the management being short runs, a fortnight later William Archer's version of Ibsen's *The Master Builder* was put on, with Norman McKinnel and Lillah McCarthy; but the run ended sooner than was planned, for McKinnel was under contract to play elsewhere, and had to be released. So the anonymous new comedy, *Fanny's First Play*, was hurriedly staged with no more than a fortnight's rehearsal on 19 April. The play was an instant and complete success. It had the form of a simple domestic comedy, except for the induction and epilogue, in which Fanny, the supposed author of the piece, was introduced, with her father and a theatrical manager and five representative critics. Had it not been for this audacity, there might have been a chance of mystifying the public about the authorship, for Shaw had written nothing so " easy " and nothing so transparently sincere. Shaw had a double reason for dissimulation. He wanted the management to escape whatever disfavour his name might arouse (for his previous two plays had been intensely disliked, especially by the critics); but more than anything his sense of the publicity value of curiosity about the authorship would, he guessed, yield dividends to the management and to him. " Let people think the play is by Barrie," said Shaw. Certainly there was much discussion, Shaw maintaining complete ignorance; but it was obvious that the play was his, and equally obvious that it was to the public taste. Shaw was besieged by Press-men who wanted to know the truth. " No," he told the representative of the *Pall Mall Gazette*; " nothing shall ever induce me to betray the authorship of *Fanny's First Play*. The performance last night was superb; and the audience enjoyed it as much as I did." Despite the too-short rehearsal, the production was first-rate, and the acting reached perfection. Barker attended no rehearsals except the dress rehearsal. It is, of course, a slight piece, what Shaw called " an easy play for a little theatre", and afterwards " a pot-boiler", but the players enjoyed themselves as much as the audience, not least those who represented the London critics. What the critics had to say is well represented by the enthusiastic notice in the *Pall Mall Gazette*:

Gentlemen, off with your hats! A great thing has happened. In three
delightful hours the Court Theatre of 1904-7 has come back to us, with
all the laughter and magic of the old days. Regrets have been poured
forth in bucketfuls over the collapse of that memorable enterprise
Well, here it is again, with many of the familiar faces, all the former
finished art, and the master spirit of the movement, Mr. Bernard Shaw,
with one of the most amusing plays he had ever written, one of the
wittiest and most audacious plays of all his attack on " the mean things
which men have to do to keep up their respectability ".

A. B. Walkley assisted in the make-up of the version of himself as Trotter,
and the other critics, Vaughan and Gunn, were easily recognizable, while
Flawner Bannel was typical of the popular Press. Lillah played Margaret
Knox, the rebellious daughter, Dorothy Minto was the unforgettable
Darling Dora, Cecily Hamilton the sympathetic Mrs. Knox, and Edmund
Gwenn one of the unhappy parents, while Fanny was Christine Silver,
and her perplexed father Harcourt Williams. None of the parts presented
any difficulty and the piece was wholeheartedly accepted by the public.

It was Coronation year, and the Little Theatre was filled at every
performance. Writing to Vedrenne two days after the opening night,
Shaw said:

When two or three are gathered together (by the way, you will not
recognize this quotation as you are a Catholic and do not read the Bible)
in the Little Theatre, they enjoy *Fanny's First Play* enormously. It is
like old times at the Court, except for the void left by Vedrenne. The
difficulty is to get in the two or three.

There was real difficulty to get in all who wished to see the play; but
the intimacy of the theatre added to the effect of this domestic piece, and
rarely were play, theatre, and company so happily united as on this
occasion. The theatre was crowded at every performance, and for the
first time Shaw allowed a run. He was uneasy, as the weeks went by,
and so was Barker, for here was something contrary to their experience
and their declared principles, but the play had such abounding life that
it was clearly unnecessary to take it off. On its 200th performance Shaw
said to an interviewer:

For the first time I have allowed a play of mine to run itself to death in the
usual commercial fashion. . . . What reason have you to doubt that if I
had allowed *John Bull's Other Island* or *You Never Can Tell* or *Man and
Superman* to run on in the same way at the Court Theatre in the great days
of Vedrenne and Barker, they would not have been running still?

Tuesday and Friday matinées of *Nan* were started on 16 May, with Lillah
in her original part.

*

When the Royal Society of Literarature was about to elect its first Academic Committee in 1911, Barker was nominated, but was not elected. His admirer, Sturge Moore, writing to W. B. Yeats on 26 April, said:

Barker is a man with a far truer intellect than Belloc, not that I want him elected. He is one of those painfully honest people who in time to come might defend a journalist who had dubbed a butcher " great " by giving that adjective a significance it never had before.

Neither Belloc nor Barker was among the thirty members elected. Soon afterwards Shaw and Barrie were put on, Shaw reluctantly, because he " was such a trouble on a committee ". Years later Barker became its President.

*

As part of the Coronation celebrations the Barkers' friends, the Prime Minister and his wife (Mr. and Mrs. H. H. Asquith), invited them to stage a performance at 10 Downing Street for the entertainment of Their Majesties King George V and Queen Mary. This performance took place on 30 June, when the third act of Shaw's *John Bull's Other Island* and Barrie's *The Twelve-Pound Look* were performed, produced by Barker, who played Larry in the Shaw play. Lillah McCarthy appeared in both plays, with the other players in their original parts. This was at a time when the Irish Question was acute.

Barker was mostly at Stansted, writing. He proposed to Gilbert Murray that they should collaborate on a book upon the Drama, and got the following reply from Murray:

July 8, 1911.

The drama is very tempting, but the real objection to it from my side is that I shall not have any time this year to write a word. And next year I go to America to lecture in the spring.

I have 1. to prepare lectures for next term: 2. to write my book on Greece for the H.U.L.: 3. to do an Oxford Book of Gk. Verse. 4 and 5 are complicated.

4 is that the other day at Overstrand I was poking the wall of a house with my stick in an absentminded way, when the owner asked me what the Dickens I meant. I said, like Artemus Ward: "I am poking it to see if I like it, because if I like it I'll buy it." And in a few minutes I found I had bought it. So now it has got to be furnished and there is generally the devil to pay (besides the lawyers). It may be described as a Nobleman's Cottage Residence with Pigstye, and we shall use it instead of lodgings.

5 is that my dentist has fallen into low spirits and says that nothing will cheer him except being allowed to take out all my top teeth at one sitting. I offered him two or three, but he says there is no fun unless it is ten at least. It will incapacitate me for lecturing for ever so long, so I have urged him

to try someone else. I am not the only possessor of teeth. You, for instance, have dozens of excellent ones – just the sort he likes.

So on the whole I do not see that I can promise to help in the drama book just now, nor let them advertise it. But we might keep the idea before us. It would be great fun to collaborate with you. By the way, Margoliouth has made out that Aristotle did really define Tragedy as " a representation of Felicity ". By Felicity – not a satisfactory translation – he means High Life, the sort of life one desires or considers good. Very interesting : and shows what an imagination the old fellow really had. E.g. the death of Crippen is not tragic, but that of a martyr is.

When we do write the book, we will write only what interests us and seems to matter. No history, no information : only we must pay great attention to the Irishry and Brieux and all that seems to affect the future.

Barker wrote to Gilbert Murray two months later and referred to the *Iphigenia*:

5 Sept. 1911.

I have been meaning to write to you for ever so long. First it was to say that I have been reading *The Rise of the Greek Epic* for, I think, the third time; and by Jove, it would be such an education to me to do anything with you, that you must not let the book on the Drama go right out of your mind. You really must not. I want to do it.

The second thing is, that Lillah has her eye on the *Iphigenia* for matinées, about November I should say. At least this is the position. They want to stay on at the Little Theatre after Christmas, but they don't know yet if they can. If they have to move to another, it might be a more suitable one for *Iphigenia*, and in that case better postpone until the Spring, – otherwise about November.

Granville Bantock now says definitely that he can't do the music. I have got S. P. Waddington to have a try at it. He is very interested, and if it comes off, it should be very right, because he is very anxious to put the verse and the meaning of the choruses first, and the music second. I hope you approve, but you are not committed. I am trying to cultivate a lieutenant for productions – at the present moment in the person of Harcourt Williams (he did Pompey), so the production might be by me and by him so to speak. Again do you approve? What about *Oedipus*? What is the meaning of your version and Courtney's?

The Greek play was the one Frohman was to have produced. The possibility of the production of *Oedipus* was approaching realization, as another letter a month later confirms :

Oct. 7, 1911.

We do move from the Little Theatre at Xmas and in all probability to the Kingsway, although this, until the lease is signed, is more or less private. No doubt therefore that the Kingsway is better ground for *Iphigenia* than this. No reasonable doubt that they should do it there in the Spring

'you are willing. I do not seriously suggest that Duncan might as well
e corybantic with one of the older ones. Why not the *Bacchae*!!
Just as useful to him and no interference with the poor pedestrian
Manager like us. What do you say?

The run of *Fanny* continued throughout the year. On 3 October a
ries of matinées of a triple bill started, including revivals of Meredith's
The Sentimentalists, Barrie's *The Twelve-Pound Look*, and Barker's farce,
ococo. Barker produced all three, and Lillah played in the first two.
The following month she took an engagement with Beerbohm Tree at
His Majesty's in *The War God*, but her departure had no effect upon the
un of *Fanny*, which continued as gaily as ever, her part being played by
Evelyn Weedon.

*

On Saturday, 25 November, news went round that the Lord Chamber-
in had appointed the dramatist Charles Brookfield as Joint Examiner of
lays. This was regarded as an outrage upon the dramatists who objected
o the working of the censorship, especially as Brookfield's *Dear Old
Charlie* had been one of the examples of questionable plays passed by the
ensor for performance. Moreover, it was in that play that Barker had
een recognizably referred to as "Mr. Bleater" and his play as *Sewage*.
The following Sunday evening a performance of Laurence Housman's
ensored play, *Pains and Penalties*, was being given by the Pioneer Players
: the Savoy. At the close of the first act, Barker and Gertrude Robins
ddressed the audience and proposed a resolution protesting against the
ppointment, which was passed by those present with only two dis-
ntients. The appointment was officially announced on Monday, and
arker wired to Gilbert Murray:

an you suggest anything to be done *re* Brookfield appointment censor-
ip. Suppose Raleigh and rest of committee won't resign as *Guardian*
ggests, but something must be done.

The reference to Walter Raleigh was in connection with the Advisory
Committee recently appointed by the Lord Chancellor to advise the
xaminer of Plays. The following Wednesday the Dramatists' Club had
e matter before it when Anthony Hope [1] proposed a resolution of protest
hich was carried by a single vote, several not voting.
Barker attended the Dramatists' Club and afterwards wrote to Murray:

Ve had a heated time at the Dramatists' Club to-day. Hawkins [1] put a
solution protesting against the Brookfield appointment and out of

[1] Anthony Hope Hawkins.

about 18 present, only 8 voted for it. It was carried because only 6 or
voted against.

Pinero sat in the chair and was dignified. But that of course puts a
end to the Dramatists' Club as being of any use but for a luncheon clu
which – Heaven help us! – nobody wants to attend. It seems unlikel
that the dramatists who do object will publish a protest over the
signatures because the dramatists who affectionately call Brokfiel
"Charlie" would probably reply with a manifestation in his favou
Individually, I fancy we may do something, and do you, please, do any
thing, and I should suggest writing to any members of the Governmer
that you felt you could. I think the row will go on, though there may b
no practical result, and the dramatists – to their shame – will have n
official part in it.

Brookfield was, of course, an early friend of Barker's, for the latter playe
for him, and Brookfield had introduced him to Charles Hawtrey, so tha
it was not easy for him to oppose the appointment as strongly as he fe
impelled to do. The Brookfield appointment was somewhat analogou
to the situation that had arisen in 1824, when George Colman the younge
writer of comedies and farces, one-time manager of the Haymarke
Theatre, and regarded as a " careless and immoral " author, was appointe
Examiner of Plays by his boon friend, George IV. Colman proved to b
a rigid censor, not allowing a lover to be called an angel, " damn " bein
" a pill he could never swallow ".

The Brookfield matter was raised on the adjournment of the House c
Commons by one of the Court Theatre dramatists, Robert Harcour
on 1 December, who asked that the appointment be cancelled, whe
Reginald McKenna as Home Secretary replied asking that judgment b
suspended until Brookfield had been given an opportunity of defendin
himself. Barker wrote again to Murray :

About the Brookfield business – you will have seen about McKenna i
the House yesterday, and look at the *Morning Leader* of this morning. Th
only practical thing there seems left to do for the moment is to get
discussion in the House of Lords, where Spencer is bound to answer fo
himself. Most unfortunately, I must go away on Monday morning
However, I will do what I can. Do you think that Gore would do any
thing? – a Bishop is the proper person on this occasion! – if he would, :
would be a great score.

I have had a talk to McKenna, who practically admitted that th
appointment was scandalous, and that the situation – if it had to do wit
an officer of the King's Household – would be impossible of defence. Bu
he won't promise legislation unless he is actually forced into it, and I thin
what we have to do is to get enough fuss made to force him. Do devis
anything you can.

The Home Secretary was not, in fact, forced, and nothing further was done, though by Barker as by others the Lord Chamberlain's action was felt to be an insult.

★

With *Fanny* becoming " the Charley's Aunt of the new drama ", as Shaw called it, and Miss Kingston refusing to continue the tenancy of her theatre except at what was regarded as an exorbitant rent (for now at last the Little Theatre had become popular), the play was continued at the Kingsway Theatre in Great Queen Street, which became the new home of the management. Lord Howard de Walden had for the first time found a theatrical enterprise to be profitable as well as pleasurable, and enabled a twenty-five years' lease of the Kingsway to be taken from its owner, another actress, Lena Ashwell. The Kingsway Theatre, though small, was much larger than the Little Theatre, seating 564. There was at this time no gallery, as it had been abolished by Lena Ashwell, and in reply to a letter of protest by an enthusiastic supporter of Shavian drama, Barker wrote as follows :

Jan. 10 1912.

It is a great pleasure to me to get such a letter as yours. But really what you must do if you want intellectual drama cheap – or any drama cheap that does not appeal to the great masses of people – is either to get it endowed or – to expropriate the London Landlords !

My wife put in half-crown seats at the Little Theatre on principle, though it was practically giving money away – and we have taken a few seats from the amphitheatre here and called it the gallery; though that is also giving money away, one does it on principle. One cannot afford (things costing what they do) to give plays to anyone for a shilling – that's all about it. I think you must say " thank you " for those two rows ! If we were doing the strictly business-like thing I'm not at all sure that we should not abolish them altogether.

At last, on 10 January 1912, *Oedipus Rex*, in Gilbert Murray's translation, was produced by Max Reinhardt at Covent Garden Theatre with Martin Harvey in the name part and Lillah McCarthy as Jocasta. Altogether it was a tremendous affair. *The Times* said of it:

Oedipus Rex undoubtedly held the audience last night spellbound, though they were no Greeks " of the best period ", or of the second-best, but just Londoners of to-day.

The critic comments upon the crowd of eminent politicians and fashionable women that made the brilliant audience, and goes on –

. . . there rushes in, pell-mell, another sort of crowd . . . loudly wailing and violently gesticulating; they shout for *Oedipus*, and from the bronze door at the back slowly advances a gracious white-robed figure to greet them – and from that moment until two hours later, when this same figure staggers out blind and bleeding, you are taken far away from 1912, away from yourself, away from the fashionable dames and the eminent politicians, away to 425 B.C. there or abouts.

"Germanization of the Greek tragedy," said the *Daily Express* . . . "more Reinhardt than Sophocles," the *Daily Telegraph* declared in a long and detailed account, "we are in no mood to limit praise", so Martin Harvey was praised for his "note of kindliness", "a most human king". Lillah "rose to the height of her opportunity . . . nobly tragic". But the critic, while admitting that Reinhardt had much success with the chorus (which was a large crowd, not the fifteen men of Sophocles), found their marches rather curious than impressive, "and on the whole we can but record that even he has failed to solve the problem of a Greek chorus in a modern theatre. Perhaps it is insoluble." Barker had nothing to do with the production, but had much to do with Lillah's part, for she asked him to help her. He had seen the Reinhardt production in Berlin, and talked to the German producer about it, and he rehearsed her in the part, after attending rehearsals at Covent Garden. Lillah made notes of his suggestions to her at the time, from which the following extracts provide an example of Barker's methods.

Jocasta enters the scene when the conflict between Creon her brother and Oedipus her husband is at its height; she says :

> Vain men, what would ye with this angry swell
> Of words heart-blinded? Is there in your eyes
> No pity, thus, when all our city lies
> Bleeding, to ply your privy hates? . . . Alack,
> My lord, come in ! – Thou, Creon, get thee back
> To thine own house. And stir not to such stress
> Of peril griefs that are but nothingness.

Barker's comments were as follows :

Should the door be open or closed on Jocasta's entrance? Ask this. If open, walk over to the further side by the door post; if shut, stand centre. Keep your voice low, calm, clear, and steady on the first words, having in mind the sorrow. Make no gestures as you stand speaking. Go to Creon when you address him.

Without going through the scene in detail, the following list of "don'ts" is characteristic :

Don't act.
Don't be melodramatic or break the verse.
Don't gasp.
Don't tremble until you have said, "I look on thee and tremble."

Don't be tired on "To one so fair of speed"; be majestic and beautiful.

Don't play to Oedipus from the time you say, "He has found his death" to "Dear lord long since". Stand still and erect.

Don't lift your hand to your face until the end.

Don't be agitated on "My lord methinks I too should know".

Don't move at all through Oedipus's long speech till you go up behind him and put your arms around him. Face audience and keep still, don't move a muscle.

Don't act during his long speech; leave it all to him.

Don't act or shout or bounce "Be sure of this he told the story so when he first came". You must be consoling and must comfort Oedipus.

Don't shout "Apollo!" – swell it.

Don't petition him; command him to cast off this curse.

Don't make gestures to Oedipus on "For God's sake, Oedipus, believe him". Stand upright, not one foot on step, but both feet together.

Don't petition Oedipus; command him.

Don't explain your story too much. Build up Jocasta in your mind before coming on the stage.

Keep everything and everybody at a distance.

Realize the position slowly: (1) Intense horror, (2) tragic despair, (3) intense agony.

Keep your brain busy all through. What you are thinking is the important thing, not what you are saying.

Listen with great intensity.

Lift your eyes and speak in a hoarse whisper, "Unhappy one, goodbye! Goodbye before I go: this once, and never, never more!" meaning before I hang myself. You cannot overdo the passion of "This once" and "never, never more". Abandon your thoughts to outer darkness, after "This once", draw in breath; the horror of incest is physical anguish.

These are no more than a selection from the notes. They indicate the concentration and attention to detail Barker brought to the subject. His suggestions were possible only because Reinhardt left the principals alone and Lillah was dependent upon herself. Of her acting in general, it may be said to have been powerfully glamorous; it had glow, and her full tones were expressive of deep feeling. She was essentially a leading player, and it may be gathered that she was inclined to do too much. Acting was, however, a sacred ritual to her, whatever the part, light or serious, and no effort was spared to get it right.

The production was a great occasion, and was well supported. Gilbert Murray wrote to Lillah two letters about her playing, which should come here, because Barker had so much to do with it, with one to him from her interposed:

Jan. 12, 1912.

I expect Harley has told you the sort of thing I had to say about Jocasta. First of all, I never saw you so good. Indeed I did not know that there

K

was any actress in England capable of looking and speaking the part
with that heroic strength and dignity. But I do run up against Reinhardt
here and there. You will consider with H. whether any modification is
possible, without spoiling his effect. (He is, I think, haunted by the
nervous, frivolous, jumpy Jocasta of old German critics. Hofmannstha
took her that way. My Jocasta is a stronger, calmer woman, schooled by
experience and suffering.)

In detail: at your first entrance I want more calm and authority. You
cannot make others calm except by being calm yourself. You mus
bring an atmosphere of calm authority.

I *don't* like the "The Seer? Pah!"

I should like you to be stronger than Oedipus, as a mother is stronger
than a child, and keeps a brave face to him. But this perhaps goes righ
against Reinhardt and cannot be considered.

I don't like your way of taking the Corinthian's line, "Then all thy
fear has been for nothing". Too excitable.

Perhaps in general too many movements, detracting from the value o
the big movements.

Your two longish speeches – "The Seer", and the prayer to Apollo are
magnificent. I got the feeling of stately beauty here, the essential quality
of a Greek tragedy, more than anywhere else in the play. It was a joy to
me. Something similar in the Messenger's entrance after all that tumult
and row.

This letter seems all fault-finding, when I mean it to be quite the
opposite. The whole thing is magnificent.

Thank you, too, for taking me in. It was a great pleasure to me to
spend a night at the flat. It is the quietest place in London, I think.

Lillah McCarthy to Gilbert Murray

Jan. 16, 1912.

Thank you so much for your telegram and good wishes last night; also
for your most kind letter with notes for Jocasta. I wish you had seen the
performance last night; it was a very different thing from the rehearsal
on Thursday. Harley worked with me for three hours every day –
Friday, Saturday, and Sunday, and knocked out all my superfluous
gestures, and got in a wonderful swing of the verse which helped me
enormously to bring out the value of the part. Do let me know when
you come up to see the performance; I shall be so glad to have a talk
with you after. Martin Harvey was quite up to his best form last night
and the whole performance seemed dignified and real. Of course I am
enjoying every moment of it, and now that the strain is over it is a
fortnight's glorious work in store.

I hope business will keep good; there was a crammed house last
night.

We so much enjoyed your little visit to us and hope when you are in
town you will stay with us at the flat whenever you can.

Gilbert Murray to Lillah McCarthy

Jan. 19, 1912.

I am still here, as I was suddenly caught by an old illness of mine, a cramp in the throat, on Tuesday night. However, I got up yesterday evening in time to see *Oedipus* again.

It gets better and better. *You* seemed to me better than on Tuesday, and so did Harvey. I enclose an inarticulate letter from Agnes, written in the train, which may please you.

I have one note only. " Come, I will tell you an old tale " should be said after a mental struggle and with effort. You are going to tell him something you have sedulously hidden from every human being till now, and can hardly bear to tell now.

Excuse pencil. My fountain pen won't write except in my waistcoat pocket.

It is a magnificent performance.

After an interview printed in the *Pall Mall Gazette*, in which he discussed the production, Murray wrote to Miss McCarthy a letter that indicates that he had been misreported, and what he thought about what had been done with the play :

Feb. 20, 1912.

Your *Pall Mall* is a great shock to me! I did not " read a paper ", I only talked in a private discussion about the whole production in our " Drama Society " and talked with all the freedom of conversation. But even at that the man misrepresents me. I spoke most warmly about your personal performance and made it quite clear that my criticism of R's conception of Jocasta did not apply to you.

I did think the absence of a proper altar and figure of Apollo a dreadful mistake. Putting down the trophy cup in a place where everyone had been walking did not and could not get the religious value of that scene, with Apollo's mocking answer to your prayer. This man has also got my remarks about the end badly wrong.

You will realize from reading the part with me and afterwards with Reinhardt how different our conceptions were. But I am annoyed that my remarks should have been reported in such a muddled way – with all the disagreeable sentences selected and put alone. I wish you had been there to take part in the discussion, and I am sure you would not have been hurt, as you naturally are by this report.

*

At the Kingsway Theatre Eden Phillpotts' first play, *The Secret Woman*, a version of one of his own novels, was announced for matinées in January, but was censored. Barker would not accept the censor's alterations; neither would the author; and it was proposed to give a series of six matinée performances open to the public without charge. Barker wrote to Gilbert Murray because this new action raised the whole question of the censorship again :

The Lord Chamberlain will only grant us the licence on condition that certain lines which I am marking in the copy I send you are cut out. Apart from the futility of cutting out these lines if he is going to license the play at all, we as management, that is to say I, particularly, feel that I am obliged to make a firm stand against any interference. Phillpotts is also prepared to make a stand, and the proposal is this – emanating from Barrie – that he (Barrie) you, Hardy, Kipling, and Shaw should invite another 30 or 40 people (eminent " gents " and ladies in literature) to form themselves into a committee to present the play here for six performances to the public, free, gratis, and for nothing.

We keep just the windy side of the law in doing so ; the committee of course are all right, and (privately) Barrie guarantees the nett cost. The reasons given are to be that it is impossible to expect men of letters accustomed to the freedom and responsibility of having direct access to the public through their books to give any sort of serious attention – to give their best work in any way to the theatre – if they are to be thus hampered. This is Phillpotts' first serious theatre job and it seems it would be an effective protest made both by us, the management, and more especially, by Phillpotts' fellow authors. Will you do this. Barrie wants me to ask you to save time. He is dealing with Hardy and Kipling. Shaw stands in. If your answer is (in principle) " yes " wire me, would you, the first thing in the morning. If you incline to the negative, which I much hope you won't, don't say " no " without having heard further from me, for I may have explained the matter rather badly.

Professor Murray was not altogether in favour of the proposal, and Barker wrote further to him :

About Phillpotts. I am not so in love with my own policies, though I may seem so, that your doubts do not cause me great uneasiness (though by the way it was Barrie's idea, not mine). On the other hand, what *are* we to do? Not to fight is a counsel of despair, and things being as they are, this is the only way of fighting. But what you say is quite important. A further idea. That is as soon as the play has been produced, and received by the public, to submit it again to the Lord Chamberlain's Office and say that granting, as they have granted, that the play can be done at all, do they still hold that these passages should be cut out – making our doing this as public as possible. I thought of getting Barrie and you four others who are signing that letter he has drafted to put something of this sort into it, saying that you would give the free performances, and then on those the play would be submitted again to the Lord Chamberlain. But Barrie seems to think there is no good object gained in mentioning this beforehand, that it will be possible to do it without this. Further, there is the incidental inconvenience of delaying this letter any longer. But does the re-submitting the play meet your objection in any way?

A letter was sent to *The Times*, signed by a number of dramatists who had read the play, protesting against the censor's action, and announcing the free performances to show how unreasonable the ban was. They said of the author:

Never in all these years of novel-writing has a word been breathed by any responsible paper or person against his fair fame, but the moment he has the ambition to write a play in the same spirit which inspired his novels he is at the mercy of an official who knows no better than to use him thus.

Then Lena Ashwell, owner of the theatre, applied for an injunction in the High Court to stop the free public performances, which the Judge did not grant on the undertaking by the management that the performances would be private. Two private matinées were therefore given, the first on 22 February, when the play was enthusiastically received by a distinguished audience. The enthusiasm was aroused more, however, as a gesture to the management and the author than by the merits of the play. All the critics were unfavourable. In fact, the piece was neither well cast nor well produced. It was a play of country folk, of whom Barker knew nothing, and was one of his more serious mistakes. A dramatization of a novel, it was by no means a first-class dramatic work. With tragic and gloomy elements, the leading part played by Janet Achurch did no more than make an approach to a tragic character.

After this failure, Barker was greatly preoccupied again by the censor-ship question. He found the poets troublesome in not seconding his efforts: Robert Bridges would have nothing to do with them; neither would Thomas Hardy, because " he quite dislikes Phillpotts' work ", as Barker complained to Gilbert Murray. He, Barker, considered applying for a summons against a music-hall working under a stage-play licence for performing a stage play without submitting it to the Lord Chamberlain. He thought that if a conviction could be got, the Lord Chamberlain's Department would be brought to a serious pass, for it could not examine and pass manuscripts of all music-hall turns. This, he thought, would force the Government to introduce legislation on the subject. But he did not get Murray's support, and the idea was not carried out, partly because it might have involved more expenditure than Barker was able to face.

*

While all this was going on, a version of Arthur Schnitzler's *Das Märchen* by Barker and C. E. Wheeler was presented by the Adelphi

Play Society on Sunday, 28 January, produced by Maurice Elvey, who played in it. Barker appears to have had nothing to do with the performance.

Preparations were actively in hand for the long-awaited production of Murray's version of Euripides' *Iphigenia in Taurus*, which at last was given at the Kingsway on 19 March, when nine Tuesday and Friday matinées started. Produced by Barker, the play was a marked success, Lillah having one of her favourite parts in Iphigenia, one of the most consistently fine things she had done, in John Masefield's opinion. Barker's mind was largely on the censorship while he was preparing for and rehearsing the play, as the following letters from him to Gilbert Murray show:

Feb. 19, 1912.

I cannot write you a very well thought out letter for we are in the middle of alarums and excursions with the Lord Chamberlain and his minions. But what I feel about the music and dancing is this. We must let the musicians make music and the dancers dance as we have engaged them to do, and when they have got it so far under way that they can tell us "this is the sort of thing we mean" then we can come in and modify it as much as we think well and find possible. But so far, the music is certainly not in a condition to be judged – the chorus are still squalling it like cats. And as to the dancing, I should say it hardly exists. Next week, however, I will be able to take it in hand, and I hope you will be able to see it too. But in a general way, I do repeat I think we are committed.

Yours under the harrow of the Lord Chamberlain.

Feb. 23, 1912.

I doubt if you will ever like either the sound or the sight of the chorus, but I am quite sure that if you saw them now you would have six fits, therefore, by Apollo, you shall not see them!!

When I have worked at them a week or so you may then get through the sight of it with only a fit and a half. When I have done with them I think on the whole that I shall like them very much, and anyhow I feel that we are not committed to the experiment. I promise you that like or dislike it shan't be a disgrace. The only real fault in the music is that he has pitched it rather tryingly high, but for the rest, it is designedly stuff that can be worked on, malleable stuff, conceived in the loosest form possible.

I hope to get the play cast and to start work on it about the middle of next week. For the next two or three days I shall be trying to find out what it means, and if in any important parts I fail, may I drop down on you sudden for a couple of hours' talk? Will you say if there is any time that you *can't* have me between now and say Wednesday.

Will you trust the casting to me? It will have to be experimental – that is to say there is no Orestes that is thoroughly good. At present I think it rests between Godfrey Tearle, Guy Rathbone (both too stockish and fat but of the right weight and intensity) and Arthur Wontner (he played the young man in *The Witch*, if you remember). He has good points all right but is rather " wankling ", won't stay " put ". The rest of the cast is of course not over difficult. Must stop now.

Feb. 29, 1912.

I have devised a plan over our production here, that we should always, if possible, acquire the country rights of the play we do, that I should have somebody by my side at rehearsals (as for *Iphigenia* I have Harold Chapin, who has been producing up in Glasgow) and that then when the Repertory Theatres want to do the play, we should send them our production, or scenery or its designs, our costumes – and *my* production – this sense – that my assistant should go down and rehearse the company from the prompt book he will have made under me, and that then I should attend the last two or three rehearsals and polish it up. This plan over the matinée was to make it more worth our while to spend all we reasonably wanted to on the production here in the hope that handing it on to the other theatres would help to repay us. We have not any country rights in the *Iphigenia* that I know, and you may not like the plan – and then there'd be no more to be said – but if you do, and could arrange for Dean (and later, perhaps, Casson or Wareing) to fall in with it, I should be, for various reasons, very glad. Chapin is quite good enough a man to exercise a lot of individual discretion in rehearsing other companies, but the thing that would remain would be the general scheme which I had worked out, one hopes more or less with your approval – but that's to show. I had thought too that it would be better for the author to have *one* work at his play when it first came out instead of perhaps two or three scrappy goes at it when it was done in various places.

There is to be a debate in the House of Lords on the censorship on March 13, to be opened by Lord Newton, who I presume, is still pro-censor (he certainly was on the committee). It is vitally important – don't you think? – that we should be strongly and well represented. *Do* bring any influence you can bear on possible peers to speak on our side. I suppose Gore is still unattainable? Has Curzon any opinions, did you gather? Anyway, do consider what is best to be done. Do you see, also, that the Managers are getting up a counter-petition to retain the censorship? This means that the thing Whelen is in charge of will need all the influential people it can get at the back of it. Altogether, though we may be in for another defeat, it seems that we are in for another battle!

Mar. 13, 1912.

My wonder is that you didn't throw the book at my head and forbid the performance altogether. But we have been working and I think and hope and pray we shall have something better to show you on Friday. We start going through the play at 12 sharp. Will that suit you?

The *Iphigenia* was so much liked that a special matinée was given at His Majesty's Theatre on 4 June as part of the Shakespeare Festival.

Also three afternoon performances were arranged at the open-air Greek Theatre at Bradfield College on 11, 14, and 15 June: Barker took the part of Orestes at these performances.

★

That summer there was talk of replacing *Fanny* at the Kingsway by another Shaw play – a revival this time – but Shaw preferred that something else should be done. "I should do a Barker", he advised, which was done, *The Voysey Inheritance* being revived. Barker was thinking of organizing a company to take to America with Shaw and Barker plays, and a series of Murray's Euripides' versions, for which he considered a single scene could be made to do. Shaw urged him to take *The Madras House*, "something strong", he said. But it came to nothing.

Barker was tireless in his search for new dramatists, and at the Kingsway, as previously at the Court and the Savoy, he gave much attention to the work of new writers that was sent to him. In this he was actively assisted by Allan Wade, who acted as his theatre secretary and had the same interests. As an example of his helpfulness to writers who showed some talent, there is a letter to H. F. Rubinstein, who two years earlier had sent him a play and now had submitted another:

June 8, 1912.
You ask too much of me – not the reading of your play, or twenty plays, nor telling you what I can about them, but to give you advice which might influence you in such a serious matter as (let me put it so) earning your living and acquiring your ultimate standing of citizenship. No, that is a matter which from beginning to end you mustn't ask me. But as to the play: I looked into it last night – I cannot say I read it for I hadn't time, but I read enough to confirm my former opinion. I believe that what you lack is still not only the skill but some of the instinct of the artist, in particular the selective instinct which makes him love the *form* of the whole thing rather than the amount of matter which goes to make it up. The idea, as far as I could judge it, to present a normal Jewish family and the revolt from its ideas, is as good as it can be; dealt with sincerely and simply and as unprejudicedly as may be, there could be few more attractive themes, so that I think the bread of your play is very good but "the butter is spread too thick". Now, can you see which is butter and which is bread? I wrote this because I have a very busy week or two before me, and I may not have time to read the play thoroughly until later, and I judge by your letter that you don't want to be kept waiting.

He wanted above all to concentrate upon his writing. This he did at Stansted, where he had quiet and could be undisturbed. At this small house, the Barkers by this time had a butler and his wife to look after them. The tables and chairs Shaw had had made for *Getting Married*

XXIX   Granville Barker reading a First Folio (Glasgow, 1910)

XXX *A Farewell Supper* (Little Theatre, 1911). Nigel Playfair, Lillah McCarthy and Gra~
Barker

XXXI *The Winter's Tale* (Savoy, September 1912). Lillah McCarthy as Hermione, and Henry A~
as Leontes

XXXII *The Winter's Tale* (Savoy, September 1912). Henry Ainley as Leontes

XIII *The Winter's Tale* (Savoy, September 1912). Costumes by Charles Ricketts, settings by
Norman Wilkinson

XXXIV *Twelfth Night* (Savoy Theatre, November 1912). Costumes and Scenery by Norman Wilkinson. Haydn Coffin as Feste

XXXV *Twelfth Night* (Savoy, November 1912). In the foreground Henry Ainley and Lillah McCarthy

found a place in the dining-room. They were fond of dogs and had as many as seven. The Shaws, Gilbert Murray, the Galsworthys, and other friends were constant visitors, but members of the acting profession were seldom among them. The American visit was put out of mind by a new development.

*

Nothing would satisfy Lillah McCarthy but to carry out her dearest wish, which was to perform Shakespeare. This had been considered when the Savoy season was on, but Shaw was altogether against it. Yet the idea was never absent from Barker's mind, too, not simply because his wife kept it there, but because he wanted to produce the great plays, which he had had no opportunity to do since *The Two Gentlemen of Verona* at the Court eight years earlier. On 13 February Shaw had written a serious letter to Barker, inscribed, " Here is a thing for you to consider ", suggesting that " the hour has come for a new audible Hamlet; and in my opinion, a feature of the new one will be (as in Poel's Juliet) youthfulness ". Gordon Craig had recently produced the play in Moscow. Why not collar Craig's production, suggested Shaw, " and play Halmet yourself "? Perhaps, he added, " Teddy would play the ghost of a lost soul ", while Lillah " could make a new thing of the Queen " – an instance of Shaw's insistence on the importance of secondary parts. As it happened, *Hamlet* was not done, a great loss to the English stage, neither were any of the great tragedies, though preliminary arrangements were made for at least two of them – *Macbeth* and *Antony and Cleopatra* – in both of which Lillah was intended to appear.

What made Shakespeare possible was that Lord Lucas called on the Barkers one morning to say that he had sold his pig-farm. " Here's the money for Shakespeare. . . . I like his pearls better than my pigs," he said to Lillah as he handed her a cheque for £5,000. Barker was in his bath, from which Lillah called him: he appeared wrapped in a towel, smiling, and said, " But you will have to add another £5,000," which was done, the second amount being treated as an investment. So a theatre was looked for, a lease of the Savoy Theatre taken, and the production of *The Winter's Tale* put in hand. This, of course, was to be no more than a beginning. The entire play was to be performed (only six lines were cut), a platform stage was to be used, and as for scenery, " I would have none of it! " declared Barker. The cast was carefully chosen, the leading players being paid a maximum of £10 a performance, no stars as such being recognized; it comprised Henry Ainley as Leontes, Lillah McCarthy as Hermione, with Léon Quartermaine, Arthur Whitby, Stanley Drewitt, Dennis Neilson Terry, Esmé Beringer, Cathleen Nesbit, and others. The " decoration " was by Norman Wilkinson, the costumes by Albert Rutherston, and the music was directed by Nellie Chaplin. "O Lady Fortune, stand you auspicious", quoted from the play, was printed on the announcement.

To say that the production startled London on Saturday, 21 September, was to put it mildly. The play was not well known. It had been seen (or part of it) at His Majesty's Theatre in 1906, with Ellen Terry as Hermione, and again six months later with a different cast. Prior to that, the last London performance was in 1887, when Mary Anderson played Hermione. Barker threw all conventional ideas of playing Shakespeare overboard. He broke out of the picture-frame by building the stage over the orchestra pit – not exactly a platform stage, but near to it – and he brought the actors forward throughout. The large apron was on a lower level than the permanent stage, the latter being used as something like the inner stage of an Elizabethan theatre. There was a single interval of fifteen minutes. At that first performance the critics had their breath taken away, and the audience was partly spellbound, partly bewildered. "It was not Shakespeare," bewailed the critics; "it was post-impressionism"; it was, above all, Barker – "too much Barker". The lines were spoken so quickly that there was grumbling that they could not be heard – "the poet's verse is killed by spiritless jabbling", complained the *Daily News and Leader*, which was nonsense, but critics and public were unused to having Shakespeare's verse delivered in the lively, urgent manner in which it requires to be said. The costumes were thought to be too brilliant, the decoration too confusing. Every possible objection was raised. A. B. Walkley in *The Times* found it "distinctly amusing".

On the other hand, there were those who recognized new factors in the London theatre – freedom from subservience to the actor-manager, freedom from elaborate staging, faithfulness to the text, and the conviction that Shakespeare was not a dead classic, but a dramatist for the twentieth-century theatre. To his friend, the actor, Harcourt Williams, who had seen the play, but was not playing in it, Barker wrote:

September 24, 1912

That really was a most cheering letter to get. To think that people can be enthusiastic with everyone carping and cavilling! But then – they don't really like Shakespeare, or poetry, or acting. But you do, and I am so glad you saw and felt what we were all up to.

Glancing through the papers on *The Winter's Tale*, I notice one of them (I think it was the *Daily Mail*) said that every actor or actress who had ever played in Shakespeare would loathe and hate this method of doing it. And that, with your letter on my desk, made me laugh.

Praise was indeed louder and more continuous than the heavy groans of the dissatisfied. The *Daily Mail*, in a column article, concluded by saying:

Thanks to the violent divergence of opinion about its merits, the public, with their attention captured by the railings of adverse critics and Mr. Barker's spirited rejoinders, were first amused, then speedily desirous of seeing the production and forming opinions of it for themselves. The theatre is filled, the enjoyment of the audience manifest.

Gordon Craig was interviewed so that he might condemn it, but said he had not seen the play, though he went on to say:

If I had produced it, I should have had the same material as Mr. Barker – that is to say undisciplined material.

Here was a marked development of Barker's genius, for what was displayed was not mere cleverness; the production was clearly not a stunt, designed simply to startle, or intended to turn Shakespeare on his head to draw attention to the producer, but a serious work, an effort to provide the basis for a new understanding of the play. It was a contribution to drama as unmistakably as it was a bright entertainment. Barker was thirty-five, a master at last, working with every sign of authority.

He put the whole of himself into the production and demanded everything of his players. He rehearsed the company until every member was worn out, and drove poor Henry Ainley almost demented. Left to himself at first and restricted in his movements, that experienced actor had no idea beyond reciting his part; only when Barker took him seriously in hand did he start to act and to put into his playing the passion that rendered him prostrate. Yet the result was worth all the pains. Every player added to his or her reputation. All were raised to the highest level; some to heights never before thought possible for them. There was no weakness in the playing anywhere. The real oddity was in the staging. In saying he would have no scenery, Barker left the *décor* in Norman Wilkinson's hands, and thus appeared to be giving more emphasis to the queerness of the setting than in fact he intended. There was no need then for the scenic economy practised at the Court, and this fact was evident also in the splendid costumes by Albert Rutherston.

All the same, public support was insufficient, a heavy loss was sustained, and the play was taken off after six weeks on 2 November, to be followed by *Twelfth Night* on 15 November, previously announced for the 9th.

The reception given to this favourite comedy was altogether different from that accorded to the tragi-comedy. There was hardly a breath of adverse criticism. In the main, the same players were engaged, for matinées of *The Winter's Tale* continued to be given. Henry Ainley was

Malvolio, Arthur Whitby Sir Toby, Léon Quartermaine Sir Andrew, Hayden Coffin Feste, Evelyn Millard Olivia, and Lilliah McCarthy Viola. To say that every player enhanced his or her reputation is to put it mildly. Everyone was praised, everything was delightful. It was agreed to be the most beautifully played and produced Shakespeare play ever seen upon the London stage. Norman Wilkinson was responsible for the costumes as well as the decoration, and Nellie Chaplin again had the music in hand. The engagement of Hayden Coffin for Feste, a part in which virtuosity in singing is demanded, was an inspiration. Young Nicholas Hannen had been offered the part, but was unable to take it; then it was given to H. O. Nicholson, who felt unequal to the songs; finally Hayden Coffin, who had called on Barker a few days earlier, was invited. This musical-comedy star was an immense success, and delighted in Barker's producing. He had to learn the pipe and tabor, also the virginal, and mastered them.

Played continuously in a black-and-silver setting by Norman Wilkinson, the play possessed an intimate atmosphere that was irresistible. There was a formal garden with a great staircase right and left, with drop curtains and a small inner tapestry set for the carousal. All traditional "business" was eliminated. Viola as played by Lillah McCarthy made the play her own (as indeed it is); Ainley's Malvolio was an idealized prig brought heavily down; it was not forgotten that Toby and Aguecheek were gentlemen, not boors; and the Clown was as sweetly melancholy as such a man should be. "I have never seen any Shakespeare production which approaches this", wrote H. W. Massingham in the *Nation*. "*Twelfth Night* is treated with bold disregard of the brutish superstitions that adhere to the production of a Shakespeare play", said John Palmer in the *Saturday Review*. A considered review in the *Sketch* said:

There is some difference of opinion about Viola; several suggest that she lacks humour. The fact is that she eschews deliberately the almost traditional humour of making fun of the equivocations due to her disguise. So much the better, for, in consequence, we have a truer and more womanly Cesario than before, and the play is helped greatly.

The best account of the play is contained in a letter to Barker from John Masefield, dated 26 November. It was, he said:

. . . much the most beautiful thing I have ever seen done on the stage; the play which has delighted me most, quite perfectly done. The speaking of the verse was beautiful: Lillah often got most exquisite effects with a sort of clear uplifting that carried us away, and I believe that the women scenes were never once allowed to drop to the dreamy and emotional; they were always high, clear, and ringing, coming out of a passionate mood. The men were equally good whenever they were called upon for poetry: the Duke once or twice failed to round out a cadence; but what is an accent or two in so big a thing? And Antonio was fine. . . .

You got the full flavour and power from it and made one feel that one was listening to one of the world's masters at his happiest. One saw a great man's intention and also his strength. If I were asked what made me see it most plainly I should say your sudden and inspiring bit of vision at the end, when you made Feste blaze out at Malvolio and Malvolio flame up in reply. That was a superb thing to have seen and it made me feel that Malvolio could play Lear, if you took him at his fences with similar fury. (I'm sure he could. You've discovered what Ainley can do.) Lillah all through was beautiful and it was a delight to see her success, real enthusiasm for her all over the house. . . .

The comedy was divinely done, and kept on the height of comedy all through; the letter scene of course much the best; and I liked the way you made the drinking scene a concert, another bit of seeing with W.S.'s mind; and your ceremony of the duel was superb. Feste ended the play divinely; and there was a fine touch when the blacks came down and shut the golden gates. W.S. does make one feel cheap. . . . If I hadn't got to make a living I would go to every performance; so would Con. My dear Harley, you have really done a most astonishing thing; intuition and sympathy and fine and poetical feeling; and you've given new souls to all your cast, and broken an ancient tradition. Bless you and thank you and may you enjoy great and long success.

The two Shakespearian productions put Barker into an unassailable position as the leading London stage producer: not manager or actor or dramatist, be it noted, but producer, the man in whose hands the play became not simply a practicable thing, but a work of art. Even those who did not like what he did admitted his great talents. The Barker star was high in the theatrical firmament. How much this was due to Lillah has not been measured. There can be no doubt that her untiring energy and enthusiasm, as well as her belief in Barker's genius, had everything to do with it. She combined with impulsiveness much practical sense, so that the management of the Savoy as well as of the Kingsway owed much to her. Everyone found Barker agreeable to work with, polite, considerate and self-sacrificing: he had no sense of the value of money, however, though he was capable of paying attention to detail – even the utmost detail of his productions – sparing nobody, least of all himself, yet he had little patience with the details of normal life. Lillah did much to make up his deficiencies. She not only looked after him in the theatre but she also gave him a home in which he could be himself, paid attention to his health, inspired him in his work, and did her best to relieve him of money worries. It is a fact that Barker always in all he did had to depend upon someone.

There is in existence a book setting out with meticulous care how the money went on the production costs of the plays. No doubt the figures look absurdly small to-day, but in the years before the First World War, while they were by no means negligible, they were certainly not extravagant. I have summarized the figures as follows:

	The Winter's Tale			Twelfth Night		
	£	s.	d.	£	s.	d.
Management	357	8	11		—	
Stage Management	108	18	3½	14	1	11
Printing and Advertising	544	18	11½ (a)	99	8	6 (e)
Wardrobe	746	10	4½ (b)	619	7	1 (f)
Electrician	132	9	11	10	2	9½
Properties	255	17	11½ (c)	165	7	11½ (g)
Scenic Artist	207	8	4	91	2	8
Carpenter	399	10	0½ (d)	190	14	11½ (h)
Stage Extension	7	17	8		—	
	£2761	0	5½	£1190	5	10½

(a) Including Press Agent and advertising.
(b) Designer, £65.
(c) Designer, £30.
(d) Designer, £30.

(e) Porters and Photographs only.
(f) Designer, £60.
(g) Designer, £30.
(h) Designer, £30.

*

At the end of June 1913 Shaw and Barker paid a visit to the Delcroze School at Hellerau, near Dresden, to see the theatre there. He afterwards wrote to Gilbert Murray:

Sunday.
Glory be – my dear G.M. but that's great news – we're all very glad – all being Lillah and I naturally (plus G.B.S. who is down here and says . . . but Good Lord what age is the man – he founded Toynbee Hall before I was born). I'm a week late in writing for I've just been over to Dresden to Hellerau to the Jacques Delcroze Academy of Eurythmics – *which you know all* about. Besides the Eurythmics there is a Salzmann Man with a system of staging and lighting which is the only modern artificial light staging possible for Greek plays (you know after Bradfield I swore – Never in a stuffy theatre again). But this – I'll tell you all about it – when, if ever, we meet. Will you not be this way at all – or ask us for an August week-end. But Salzmann – moaning and saying how good his lighting might have been if only he could have spent money on it but he had nothing – only a wretched 68,000 marks for the experiment. That's Germany. Damn, who wants to do *Rhesus*? Somebody there must who'll make a Greek play company – that and nothing else – And the Eurythmics would be the path to it. It wants that sort of foundation

not on artistic sense belikes (God guard us!). I want to grow a beard. I shall never write plays till I do nothing else. Are you at your H.U.L. Greek book?

*

The success of the joint management at the Kingsway caused the Barkers to look for another theatre for Shaw's new play, *Androcles and the Lion*, in which he had written a principal part for Lillah. There was no idea of finishing with Shakespeare, for there was still some of Lord Lucas's money left, and Lillah's ambitions were by no means satisfied. For the time being, however, the Shaw play took first place, and Lord Howard de Walden made possible a four months' lease of the St. James's Theatre from Sir George Alexander, and there, on 1 September 1913, a distinguished audience gathered. *Androcles* had been rehearsed by Barker, for Shaw was at the climax of his love affair with Mrs. Patrick Campbell. He admonished and instructed Barker by letter, but at the dress rehearsal he came along and found the playing too slow and re-strained, and turned everything upside down. "In the course of four hours, Shaw transformed the play from a comedy into an extravaganza", says Hesketh Pearson, who had a small part in the play. "He danced about the stage, spouting bits from all parts with folded arms . . . always exaggerating so as to prevent our imitating him, making us all feel we were acting in a charade."[1] Shaw, of course, was right. He left the theatre at eleven o'clock, telling Barker to pick up the pieces, which the latter continued to do until the early hours of the following morning.

At its performance the play was received with enthusiasm – its produc-tion highly praised, but the work aroused more bitter controversy than any other of Shaw's plays. It was not, however, the dramatist's im-morality or blasphemy that offended this time, but what was considered to be irreligious flippancy, so that the play was regarded as insulting by some Church people, though defended with fervour by as many others as a highly religious work, which indeed it was. Shaw had written it " to show what a play for children should be like " at a time when *Peter Pan* was supposed, erroneously, as he thought, to be the ideal children's play, and partly to show the real nature of religion. He thus had a double purpose: the Lion for the children and the Christian martyrs for the religious. For once Shaw was genuinely angry at the way in which his play was received. Yet there were those who understood what he was at, as did the critic of the weekly *Graphic*, who wrote: " Everyone in London who loves a jest or has the heart of a child should be turning his or her way to the St. James's this autumn." The play has proved to be one of Shaw's most generally acceptable works, but at the time some of

[1] *Bernard Shaw*, by Hesketh Pearson (Collins, 1942), p. 289.

the religious papers became hysterical in their denunciation. Despite the way in which it had been rehearsed, or more likely because of it, the production proved to be admirable. Lillah in the leading part gave an exquisite performance, and the entire cast, including Edward Sillward as the Lion, was excellent.

As the play is short, another piece was performed with it, a work entitled *Harlequinade*, written by Barker in collaboration with Dion Clayton Calthrop. This rather flimsy piece, produced with the finesse Shaw would not have in his play, was not immediately understood by critics or public, and gave only qualified pleasure, so that it did not help the programme, but somehow detracted from it in the eyes of all who were not enamoured of everything Barker did. " A theatre audience is in no mood for these subtleties ", muttered *The Times*.

A letter written by J. M. Barrie to Barker indicates the latter's state of mind ten days after the St. James's season opened :

Killiecrankie Cottage
11 Sept. 1912

My dear Harley,
    This house is lit by gas made in a mysterious shed, and it keeps blinking slow-fast blinks every third word or so. " The curtains will be lowered three times during each sentence to indicate that the gas man has gone to Pitlochry."
    You have been seedy, and that makes you more gloomy than you need be. What worries you is that things are getting better so slowly not that they aren't getting any better at all. In relief I don't doubt that *The Winter's Tale* and *Twelfth Night* will make all Shaksperian productions a little better for all time to come. But it is only a foot or two that is gained, and you are young and want so much. The thing that saddens me about all your efforts is that you have this beastly monetary ado to rend and disgust you. I know how it must hurt your sensitive soul and make you unhappy. I don't know whether it would be better for you to get out of it all and just become a literary man, but I certainly do know that you are doing good work.
    I'm coming up by the night train on Monday and hope to see you Tuesday if you are in Town. Plays seem very far away from me when I see Michael wondering without words whether I am satisfied with him to-day.

Yours always,
J. M. B.

Here we see one of Barker's most intimate friends encouraging his longing to get out of the theatre. The two plays were taken off on 25 October after eight weeks, a considerable loss having been made, though the average receipts were £850 a week. The following week, on 29 October *The Witch* occupied the bill, a gloomy play, it was generally thought despite Miss McCarthy's acting; its production was a mistake from the point of view of attracting the public.

*

One of the objects in taking the St. James's was to introduce repertory, a desire not satisfied by runs of plays, however good, and this was started upon at the beginning of December, when a three weeks' season was announced, every evening at 8.30 and matinées on Wednesdays and Saturdays. Five plays by Ibsen, Shaw, Galsworthy and Jenssen-Masefield, and Masefield and two short pieces by Molière and Maeterlinck were given during the period, the programmes being as follows:

	First week, 1–6 December	Second week, 8–13 December	Third week, 15–20 December
Mon.	*The Wild Duck*	*Le Mariage Forcé* and *Nan*	*The Doctor's Dilemma*
Tues.	*Le Mariage Forcé* and *Nan*	*The Doctor's Dilemma*	*The Wild Duck*
Wed. (Mat.)	*The Witch*	*Le Mariage Forcé* and *Nan*	*The Doctor's Dilemma*
Wed.	*The Wild Duck*	*The Witch*	*The Death of Tintagiles* and *The Silver Box*
Thurs.	*Le Mariage Forcé* and *Nan*	*The Doctor's Dilemma*	*The Witch*
Fri.	*The Witch*	*The Doctor's Dilemma*	*The Death of Tintagiles* and *The Silver Box*
Sat. (Mat.)	*The Wild Duck*	*The Doctor's Dilemma*	*The Death of Tintagiles* and *The Silver Box*
Sat.	*The Doctor's Dilemma*	*The Wild Duck*	*The Doctor's Dilemma*

The company was substantially the same as for the Shakespeare revivals. Miss McCarthy played in *Nan*, *The Witch*, *The Doctor's Dilemma*, and *The Death of Tintagiles*. Granville Barker did not play, but produced. The Molière piece, *Le Mariage Forcé*, had a permanent set with four doors designed by Albert Rutherston. *The Times* declared that the Shaw revival was "welcomed with enormous enthusiasm". Public support was good, though it might have been better, and money was lost – not much, but more than enough. On the Wednesday evening after the fifth production, Barker addressed the audience from the stage, in which he declared his beliefs in the necessity of real repertory – repertory for the sake of a healthy theatre. What he said was substantially as follows:

L

Many of our audience tonight are here not for the first time in these three weeks. . . . For we have been doing repertory, real repertory. I own I take a certain pride in the very word. . . . Let me apologize for our shortcomings. We have given you no Shakespeare, and without Shakespeare English repertory, is as Mrs. Jones puts it, "not quite itself". Circumstances have overbalanced our selection of plays more on the tragic side and more on the foreign side than I could have wished. We have been conscious sometimes, and I am afraid you have, of a certain lack of complete preparation in the performances: incidental, some critics have suggested, to any repertory theatre. No, it is not. Performance in repertory could be more perfect not less than other performances. But incidental to our setting out upon this adventure without adequate resources or equipment, relying on the loyalty of our staff and the enthusiasm of our company. . . .

Well, ladies and gentlemen, is this repertory to continue? I am prepared to stake whatever reputation I may have acquired in the service of the theatre that repertory, real repertory, is the only path out of the evils which beset the theatre, of which we have lately been reminded so often. Only in repertory is a manager able to present normally to a normal public a constant variety of plays, as a publisher is able to present to his public a constant variety of books. Only in repertory can you satisfy with equal ease the taste of the five thousand – ten thousand and twenty thousand, whose tastes are to be catered for. Only in repertory can the actors have that variety of work which sustains them in the honourable position of interpretative artists instead of (as other systems do) reducing them, however imperceptibly to themselves or you, to the level of artistic automata.

In Heaven's good time (but hardly within the next three years) we are, I hope, to have a National Theatre in being. But that is only an institution, however fine, and to-night I am pleading for a whole system. Besides, we must prepare for our National Theatre. If we do not, then when it comes, and we on our part are not used to its methods, and you on yours are not accustomed to its aims, it will be in danger of settling down as a mere museum of theatrical antiquities. No, if we are to save our dramatic souls we must begin to save them now.

He went on to ask again : "Is this repertory to go on?" They had the plays, they had the actors. "I do not think this company need blush beside any company of actors in Europe," he said. What they had to be assured of was public support, and he asked for 1,000 people to put down £25 each, and to guarantee a further £25 a year for three years, and the thing could be done.

In fact, he talked too long and, to some who heard him, without the necessary enthusiasm. Also there was a general feeling that the London theatre public could not be educated into accepting repertory, a feeling that still exists, though why playgoers should be so incapable of accepting what is the rule in opera, and has since become the rule in ballet, it is difficult to understand. However, the Old Vic has lately proved that repertory can succeed. Though Barker invited correspondence and offered to see anyone personally who was interested and to explain what was proposed, little progress was made. At the end of the year John Palmer published his book, *The Future of the Theatre* (Bell), which he dedicated to Barker, though in its pages he regarded his work to date as negative: the promise of *The Marrying of Ann Leete* not fulfilled. But he looked hopefully to him for the future.

*

In the meantime, repertory was continued at the Savoy in the new year until, on 6 February 1914, the third Shakespeare revival took place, *A Midsummer-Night's Dream*, with Lillah McCarthy as Helena, Christine Silver as Titania, Nigel Playfair as Bottom, and the company as before. "One's memories of this performance must always be golden memories", said *The Times*. "Individual performances were one and all excellent", remarked the *Daily Telegraph* in an enthusiastic review, though the critic protested at the fairies. "A Shakespeare nightmare", declared the *Daily Mail*, while the *Sunday Times* said, "It was a revelation", and the *Observer* asserted rightly that the production was "revolutionary in its attempt to get back to what the poet planned". Much controversy was aroused, especially over the golden fairies, a controversy which has persisted in the public memory, so that everyone who refers to any of the three Barker Shakespeare productions says at once: "You remember the golden fairies."

The production was a complete departure from the theatrical prettiness with which this popular play has been invested. Barker made no effort to meet conventional expectations. He maintained the same unqualified adherence to the spirit and intention of the play as in the two earlier productions. What he did was what he considered the play inherently required. Contrast was made between the severity and definition of the scenes in the palace and the soft, misty atmosphere of the woods. The scene for the fairies was a mound of green with a background of curtains in changing lights, the fairies being gilded from head to foot, including faces and hands, only four of them being small children; there were vivid costumes and masks, Puck being dressed in scarlet and a large wig with red berries in it. The result was a suggestion of non-human lightness, swiftness, and mystery. The speaking was fast, with full respect for the poetry. The comedians were comic, but not with the usual witless, knock-about silliness. The conflicting reception from the critics was no surprise, some hailing the production with enthusiasm, others calling it grotesque and irritating. What was most strange was that three London newspapers did not refer to it at all.

The features of all three Shakespeare productions were the entire text, the continuous stage action, the playing forward to the audience, the speed with which the lines were spoken, the value given to the poetry, the elimination of conventional theatrical business with which stage Shakespeare is overladen, and the sense created of the play as whole. I have referred to the restraint in Barker's producing methods, but in Shakespeare he went " all out ". To an actor who asked if he was doing too much, he replied, " Too much! You haven't begun! " In these plays Barker became a producer of European quality, a great artist and craftsman of the theatre whose equal did not exist on the London stage. Had the war not occurred, Shakespeare productions would have gone on, for Barker had not produced the great tragedies, which he was preparing to do.

Further money was expended, however, on preparations for the *Macbeth* and *Antony and Cleopatra* productions, which were never completed.

*

In connection with the Savoy productions, three paper-covered reprints of the plays were published by Heinemann (at 6*d.* each), each containing a short preface of eight or so pages by Barker, with a few reproductions of the costume designs. There were brief scene descriptions; otherwise the texts were a modernized version of the First Folio. As these were the first of his Shakespeare prefaces, they deserve to be looked at. In the first, *The Winter's Tale*, he said:

They are only the elaborated notes of the producer, who must view the play, first and last, as in action and on the stage.

Writing about *Twelfth Night*, he takes up the criticism of those who found the speaking of the players too fast in his first production:

I question a little their expertness of hearing, a little too their quickness of understanding Elizabethan English not at its easiest, just a little their lack of delight in anything that is not as they thought it always would be, and I suggest that it is more difficult than they think to look and listen and remember and appraise all in the same flash of time.

He goes on to compare the two plays:

The Winter's Tale, as I see its writing, is complex, vivid, abundant in the variety of its mood and pace and colour, now disordered, now at rest, the product of a mind rapid, changing, and over-full. I believe its interpretation should express all that. *Twelfth Night* is quite other. Daily as we rehearse together, I learn more what it is and should be; the working together of the theatre is a fine thing. But, as a man is asked to name his stroke at billiards, I will even now commit myself to this: its serious mood is passionate, its verse is lyrical, the speaking of it needs swiftness and fine tone; not rush, but rhythm, constant and compelling. And now I wait contentedly to be told that less rhythmic speaking of Shakespeare has never been heard.

In this preface Barker refers to two comedies, *Much Ado About Nothing* and *As You Like It*, also to *Henry V*, and says:

I confess to liking those three as little as any plays he ever wrote. I find them so stodgily good, even a little (dare one say it?) vulgar, the work of a successful man who is caring most for success. I can imagine the lovers of his work losing hope in the Shakespeare of that year or two.

As he speaks of " liking ", there is no arguing with him, but as for *Twelfth Night* –

I feel happy ease in the writing, and find much happy carelessness in the putting together.

The third preface, to *A Midsummer-Night's Dream*, shows the play divided into three parts, and Barker finds some fault with the play, but as to its stageworthiness he finds none. The texts indicate that only a few lines were cut in each play on the ground that they were regarded as having no present meaning.

*

Barker's playwriting received appreciation from two young Viennese living in London, G. Sil-Vara, London Correspondent of *Neue Freie Presse*, and Rudolph Kommer, a journalist and a theatrical impresario, who had seen *The Voysey Inheritance* at the Kingsway. Filled with enthusiasm, they made a German version, much to Barker's pleasure. It was published at once in Berlin, and though intended for production in Vienna, was never in fact done there. As will be seen from the following letter to Rudolph Kommer, Barker had tried to get them interested in *The Madras House* without success. Writing from the Kingsway Theatre, he said:

Dec. 18, 1913.

You write me the most interesting letter and there is much to be said. If I were writing Edward Voysey now I dare say I should write him a little different, but then I am not, and though you may patch up the details of a play years after writing it I am quite sure you must never patch up the characters. I too am sick of the eternal feminine drawing him upward on and on, but after all Alice does not do that in the last scene (as a matter of fact she is far more masculine than Edward is in the usual sense of the term). No, honestly, you have got hold of the wrong end of the stick there. He is the idealist and she is the practical person. If I had developed her more it would have been in the direction of making her considerably more like old Voysey in unscrupulousness.   At the worst she interprets Edward to himself.   You had better leave him with those cuts that I marked in the edition I sent posting after Sil-Vara.   You would patch up the characters I dare say as well as I should for you are probably not a much more different person from the G.B. of 1902 than I am, but there it is – characters are not to be patched.   If you really are not keen on *The Madras House*, please do not undertake it.   I made the suggestion to you because of course it is obviously much better in every way to keep the plays all under the one publisher and translator if possible.   On the other hand, nothing more vexing to both of us than you consciously trying to exploit wares which you equally consciously feel you ought not to be exploiting.   I do believe in *The Madras House*. It is far more universal than *Voysey* and incidentally far better written.

The friendship with Kommer lasted for many years.   He had come to London two years earlier at the age of twenty-four in connection with Max Reinhardt's production of *The Miracle*.   A short, burly young man, full of spirit, wit, and charm, a vivacious and intelligent personality.   He had a keen interest in English plays, and at a later date made German versions of plays by Galsworthy, Lonsdale, and Chesterton.   He spent the war years in the United States, " serving the cause of old Franz Josef ", as Alexander Woollcott says of him in an entertaining and admiring sketch in *While Rome Burns* (1934).   He translated into German there several American plays, including O'Neill's *Emperor Jones*, Clare Booth's *The Women*, and Woollcott's own play.   He died in New York in 1943.

*

Some letters from Barker to Gilbert Murray indicate how the repertory proposal progressed :

Jan. 1st, 1914.

I will tell you how you can contribute your twenty-five pounds ! *Prunella* is being something of a success in America and I am at last getting more than a few shillings in fees for it.   I have always thought I would like you to take back, if you would, some at any rate of the money with which you helped to launch it.   For the life of me I cannot remember at the moment how much it was, but we can find out.   There !

We simply must pull this repertory through, it is now or never.   One thing else you could do and, if you please, you really must.   Masefield had a brilliant idea that during one week of the repertory (which will last at the Savoy for another three) we shall each of us take a performance in this sense – after it, come in front of the curtain and make a short but moving appeal to the audience.   Really, my speech was a good tip.   It affected people in a way that letters to the papers don't, and as we will have our speeches reported verbatim we shall get the double advantage. We want nine people; there are you, Masefield, Shaw of course !! me, Galsworthy's away.   Then higgledy-piggledy I have in mind Wells,

Bennett, R. J. Campbell, Oliver Lodge, Garvin (who really does like literature and is going to run us hard, he says, in the *Observer* and the *Pall Mall*). I want a bishop; I want a literary politician; I want suggestions from you; I want nine people. I want to know what you think of it but it is now or never and think, oh, think G.M., of being able to do *The Trojan Women* to a normal evening audience, with clerks in the pit and dock labourers in the gallery. It is worth fighting for.

Jan. 12th, 1914.

Oh, that is indeed a blow. Why must you desert me, is it your health, or don't you think you ought to speak, or what? Reconsider it if you can – it is so important. Tell me this too: there will have to be trustees for the money, will you be one of them? I would try and make Barrie the other and find a third, but I would sooner have you than mere peers.

Feb. 10th, 1914.

I am off I think and hope about Saturday or Monday next to Moscow via Berlin. Why don't you come? After all, what is Oxford, even in term time. We could walk across the Hartz Mountains or any other Wald we could find and listen to the birds beginning to sing. If you won't do that (though you are a coward and cloistral if you don't), then Lillah and I propose going at the beginning of March to Spain or to Rome and sitting down somewhere there for two or three weeks. What about that?

Feb. 14th, 1914

Here are these two documents and the Trust Fund Deed is being drawn up for you three to approve and after that we must fire ahead.

How are you. Will you come to Spain or Rome or Algiers in the beginning of March? Say yes.

Barker went off to Moscow to see the work of Stanislavsky's Art Theatre. He saw *The Cherry Orchard* and other Russian plays, as well as Maeterlinck's *The Blue Bird*, and plays by Goldoni, Molière, and Knut Hamsun. What Barker thought of the productions is not recorded. Stanislavsky was then a producer-autocrat, for only in his last few years did he place the emphasis upon the playwright's intentions and the importance of the actor, which were Barker's leading ideas.

Before he went he prepared a statement of the repertory proposal which was sent to people interested, inviting subscriptions such as he had suggested at the St. James's, saying that the money " will be placed in the hands of trustees; the first charge upon any nett yearly profits of the Theatre will be to pay 5% interest on it; at the trustees' discretion, it will be repayable; and it is intended that at the end of three years any further and sufficient accumulation of profits should be used to continue the work ". He considered that the theatre could be brought into being within six months. Lord Howard de Walden, Sir James Barrie, and

Professor Gilbert Murray were to be the trustees. While he was away, Barrie wrote two letters to Murray, who was insistent that a trust deed should be prepared without delay and before any money was accepted:

21 Feb. [1914].

I think there is no doubt at all that you are right and that we should get a lawyer to go into the matter before we undertake the responsibility. However ignorant you may be about such affairs, I am more so. Your knowing that there are such things as trust deeds, for instance, filling me with awe – very likely you know what debentures are. I told Barker this, but he said it was all right. However, we might obviously get into trouble. I don't know when it is proposed to issue these prospectuses (I think Barker is in Russia); they may be out, but the correct course would be for us to have a lawyer's advice before the public is told we are to be trustees. I don't have a lawyer myself but could find one; knowing you have a good one can't we get him to go into the matter for us both at once?

26 Feb. [1914].

You are quite right. Barker consulted me on this very subject before he went off. Spence of *Westminster Gazette*, whose advice he had asked, had said it was a mistake for Mrs. Barker to be in it. I agreed with this view for reasons similar to yours and Spence's, and Barker seemed to take the objection as sound. But he had discussed it, I gathered, with Lillah and she was keen to be in, and I am far from sure that so far that does not hold. I'll talk to Barker about it when he returns.

The trust deed was prepared by the end of the month with the advice of E. F. Spence, and by the time Barker returned everything was in order. If by 31 July 1914 the money contributed did not amount to £10,000 the subscriptions were to be returned. It was proposed that the repertory should open on or before January 1915 and continue for at least three years, subject to the money in the hands of the trustees being sufficient for the purpose. The theatre was to be under Barker's sole management and control, and he was to be remunerated by 5 per cent. of the gross weekly receipts of the performances up to £1,000 and 10 per cent. of gross weekly receipts in excess of £1,000. Up to 5 per cent. was to be paid on the subscriptions each year, if earned. Response was, however, so small that nothing came of the proposal and the money subscribed was returned.

*

Barker had been brought back in a great hurry from Russia because in his absence, as she had done some years before, Lillah listened to a suggestion made to her that possibly another rich man in search of a title, this time a Canadian, might find £70,000 for the National Theatre, for it was in such a theatre that what Barker wanted could best be done. She was successful a second time, and wired to Barker to return; unfortunately, however, those responsible for these matters had to let her know that the money could not be allowed to be made available for the purpose. Neither the National Theatre nor the Barker repertory scheme was, in fact, practicable in face of public apathy.

King George V and Queen Mary came to see *A Midsummer-Night's Dream* on 15 March, and a few days later the Barkers went to North Africa for a holiday. Before going, he wrote to Murray:

March 11th, 1914.

Here are some spoils from *Prunella* and with luck there may be some more. It is pleasant to send it you after all this time.*

Is there any chance of getting you for a holiday? Lillah must go away – she is to be deported as early next week as possible. We thought of Algiers, and to sit in the desert for a week or ten days with a camel. I should like to see you on a camel. Is it at all possible? for we should fit in to anything really restful and sunny that you could propose. We thought of Easter at Seville, where they do a sort of Christian version of the *Bacchae* before the High Altar on Good Friday.

* How good of you G.M. to lend that helping hand. Please God one doesn't forget those things.

Telegram to Gilbert Murray

16th March, 1914.

Dash the repertory spend it on coming to the desert with us we hope to start Friday it will make a new professor of you do come.

A Midsummer-Night's Dream continued at the Savoy until the middle of May, when Shakespeare came to an end. The three Shakespeare productions were experiments in a new method, which convinced Barker and all who saw them that he was working on right lines. He had gone back to Shakespeare and to Shakespeare's stage, not for the sake of historical reconstruction, but to present the plays as living dramatic works for the theatre of the day. As he wrote later with justification, " Though Shakespeare was an Elizabethan playwright, he was – and now is to us – predominantly much much more ". Lillah had been actively finding more money for the other productions, and had succeeded in getting promises of another £10,000; but these prospects were to come to nothing with the outbreak of war only three months away.

In the meantime, on 3 July, the management organized a supper on the stage of the Savoy Theatre to celebrate the Shakespeare season, the invitations being issued in the names of Sir James Barrie and the Barkers. The entertainment consisted of a revue, compered by Frank Tinney, an American comedian appearing at the Hippodrome, with seven sketches, and concluded with " still another version of *The Adored One*, which will be subject to interruption ". Charles Ricketts wrote an amusing account of the affair in his journal. All the theatre stars were there, with Shaw, Yeats, Barrie, Chesterton, Rupert Brooke, the Asquiths, Marks', Laverys, Lyttons, Howard de Walden, and others. The day after, Barker went to Ayot with Barrie and others to take part in a cowboy film, for which Barrie was responsible, in which he appeared with Shaw, Chesterton, Lord Howard de Walden, and William Archer.

*

To return to the Kingsway Theatre, which all this time had been successfully kept open, John Galsworthy's *The Eldest Son* was produced by Barker on 25 November 1912 – not a great success – followed by a revival of *John Bull's Other Island* on Boxing Day, when Shaw made a written appeal to each member of the audience not to interrupt the performance by too much laughter and unrestrained applause. For the rest of the next year it was occupied by Arnold Bennett's *The Great Adventure*, produced by Barker, which had opened on 25 March 1913, and, after an uncertain start, when it was nearly taken off, had a first run of 673 performances, during which Henry Ainley added to his reputation and Wish Wynne made hers. The first performance ended at 11.40, and this made the critics cross, records Arnold Bennett in his journal. In the same journal, Bennett had written some years earlier about Barker himself. Under the date 19 February 1910, when he and they were staying together at the Royal York Hotel, Brighton, he wrote:

Granville Barker seems a simple man, half, I mean. . . . No general conversation. All art, and chiefly theatre. I should say deficient in humour. Very intelligent and nice. Neither of us says much of the other's plays. No worldly conversation. I mean no polite, insincere interest shown in personal things that come up. This is not from consciousness of strength, but from *manque d'usage*, I should say. Wife the same. She is a different woman when animated and fifty times better. . . . She tries to be interested in everything. I ought to have begun making notes of this woman earlier.[1]

On an evening of June 1914 Bennett supped at the Connaught Rooms in London with the Barkers to celebrate the 500th performance of *The Great Adventure* across the street. Asquith, the Prime Minister, arrived, to everyone's delight. "When I bet Ainley a quid that the play would not be running on September 1st", Bennett wrote in his journal that night, "Asquith took the stakes. He was in great spirits."

*

[1] *Arnold Bennett*, by Reginald Pound (Heinemann, 1952), pp. 215–16.

A " Dramatic Supplement " to the *New Statesman* appeared on 27 June 1914 with the first page blank except for the puzzling announcement :

We have been prevented at the last moment from publishing the article by Mr. Granville Barker which should have appeared on this page, owing to an injunction granted in the High Court by Mr. Justice Joyce on Friday afternoon, June 26th.

It appears that Barker, when asked for the article, had sent a draft to the Editor asking if it was what he required ; the Editor proceeded to use the draft, to which Barker objected. As the Editor refused to listen to his objections, Barker applied to the High Court to stop publication. A proof had been sent to him, from which it appears that the article was entitled " How Henry Ibsen Tchekoff Smith will rewrite *The Silver King* ". Henry Arthur Jones's popular piece had been given an all-star matinée at His Majesty's Theatre on the previous 22 May, and Barker put into dialogue a conversation about the play between the boy Smith, his father, and the writer. " Viewing the play with the historical eye . . . one may say – yes, with justice – not so bad for 1882," comments the father, to which the writer makes a vague remark, and the boy says nothing. " How would you rewrite *The Silver King*," the boy is asked, " in the light of thirty years advancing drama, under the shadow of those two whose unworthy namesake you are? " To which the boy's reply is : " I'd tackle it." That is about all. Not, it must be admitted, much of an article ; no wonder Barker did not want it printed.

On 27 June that year the Barkers were invited by Sir Philip Sassoon, one of their consistent supporters, to give a private performance at a party to celebrate his twenty-first birthday. Barker chose John Masefield's short piece, *The Sweeps of '98*, written in 1905, but not before acted, which was hardly a good choice for a joyful occasion.

*

When in August 1914 the First World War started, Barker was in the greatest dejection. He was without enthusiasm for the war, but consulted his friend, the Prime Minister, upon what he should do, and was advised to go on with his theatrical work. The Army, he was told, did not want him. He was still working at Stansted on *The Wicked Man*, and made notes for another to be called *The Committee*, but he could not get on with either. Masefield wrote on 26 August to ask him to bring what he had written to read to them. " One feels that ", he said, " the old order is dead. I suppose our individualism will be made less casual than heretofore ; and we are still young enough to give the new thing a shove."

At Murray's request, he signed a letter to the public Press about the war:

September 12, 1914.
I sign it and would sign it with my blood if anything were to be gained by shedding it, even that much of it. And I can only hope some neutral person has heard of me. My principal admirers are alien enemies. I do not gather whether you want me to procure any other signatures, but if you do send it back and I will do so.

An indication of Barker's state of mine is contained in a private memorandum he prepared that September on the effect of the war upon the theatre, the future of the Kingsway, and his own future. It is of sufficient importance to be given in full:

September 23rd, 1914.
I am concerned about the future of the Kingsway.

Quite apart from the special circumstances of the war it seems to me that we are reduced to a policy of Keep the Theatre Open. It is not only that we lack plays. I see no sign of any movement in playwriting either among known dramatists or " discoverable " ones which will provide us with any distinctive work or place in London on our present lines.

Without this we are but one among the other West End theatres and at our natural disadvantage of size and position.

Except Shaw, who is uncertain in his output and likely to be more so, our own lot of people do not produce worthwhile plays. Galsworthy's last three we have refused; Masefield's we have been compelled to refuse. We have had no new play offered to us which has combined quality with any chance of success.

The Keep the Theatre Open policy may be a good one. At any rate, I will urge nothing further against it than that it is one which I personally am constitutionally incapable of following. Don't let it be thought, therefore, that when I again suggest the possibility of my retiring from the management I am in any way launching a threat to compel, as an alternative, the adoption of a fresh policy of my own. The possibilities of managing a theatre like the Kingsway successfully are limited and it may well be that my restlessness outruns them. It may well be that it would be better for Lillah to re-assume the control she had at the Little Theatre and to centre the activities of the theatre more on herself. She has appeared very little at the theatre, so it is still fresh ground for her, her position with the public is certainly stronger than it was four years ago, and I think A.E.D.'s advice and mine (quite apart from her own common sense) would prevent such mistakes of policy as ruined the Ashwell management.

But if I am to continue to be intimately associated with the management I know that I shall be both unhappy and " difficult " unless I can see the theatre advancing to some end and serving some definite purpose which is not otherwise served.

I suggest that it might be possible for the Kingsway to take up the work of the Court Theatre, where the Court Theatre left it, avoiding its proved mistakes and improving on its policy. The Court Theatre worked in a basis of short (defined) runs and matinées. This had many economical advantages – but serious economic disadvantages. I proposed to Vedrenne the conversion of this system into one of "limited repertory". He would not agree, principally for reasons that our experiments with real repertory have since proved to be inadequate ones. "Limited Repertory" was to mean nine (or ten) performances a week of which six (or seven) were to be devoted to the main bill – the mainly advertised bill – two to another play and one to a third. The ideal in this was to have one play in favour, another coming into favour, and the third stepping out in favour. So regarded, it demands at least the nucleus of a stock company. It was a mistake at the Court – perhaps then an inevitable one – to depend too much on two people: Shaw and myself.

A limited repertory is the only way I see (except a real repertory) of giving any encouragement or putting to any test doubtful propositions in the way of plays. I think a more catholic choice might well be made than was made by the Court Theatre: we had a particular battle to fight then, which in a sense is finished now. On the other hand, foreign plays which we did try and failed over, might have a better chance now.

For a scheme of this sort at the Kingsway I suggest a directorate of five people: L.G.B., H.G.B., A.E.D., Norman Wilkinson, Lewis Casson. Some of the names are obvious, some represent necessary positions to be filled. L.G.B. and H.G.B. are so to speak the vendors. A business controller is necessary; an artistic controller, which we never had at the Court, is I think very necessary in view of the more poetic and decorative sort of play that one would hope to see done; a producer who is as in touch with the younger and cheaper generation of actors as I was when we started the Court is also necessary, I think. That these last two names ought perhaps to be Charles Ricketts and mine I am aware, but we have both, I fear, ceased to be modest people in our ideas and projects and this must be a modest scheme.

I propose that each director should contribute £1,000 to the capital and undertake to contribute £500 more. This is not impossible sum for people to find or have found for them.

Would it be sufficient capital? The function of the directors should be to control the general policy of the theatre, decide on the plays, advise as to the productions. The question of their actual powers is a more difficult one.

They should take as directors a *very small* percentage of the receipts – indeed I am not sure that they should take even this. For actual work done they should be paid agreed fees and salaries.

The capital should take 5% and the profits should be divided equally after allowing for a reserve.

The present management might for the goodwill and equipment of the theatre take a reasonable profit rental.

The cost of the performances (at nine a week) ought to be made to work out (nett) at £60 each. What this means on the front of the house side I do not know. On the stage it means much greater simplicity and economy than we have felt necessary to use. With the actors it means a strict limitation in salary; it means here indeed breaking new ground.

But on the bringing of the nett cost to £60 a performance would depend I am sure the feasibility of the scheme.

No one can prophesy what the effect of this war will be upon the English drama. If it has any that is not disastrous, it should be the strengthening of a taste for the simple and the serious. It may also bring about a weariness with the accustomed thing both in plays and acting. I think in any case that we should make up our minds and make preparations now either for a fresh start or for winding up.

If you ask me why I don't propose to start all this under the present régime, I reply that, as far as I am concerned, one cannot do a thing twice. I cannot recapture the spirit in which the Court Theatre work was done; my mind is upon other sorts of production and other sorts of work. Nor do I think that by merely engaging a man to act under your direction you can expect that spirit and enterprise and self-sacrifice which alone can carry through on the artistic side such a scheme as this.

There are other reasons.

There are indeed many things to be said for and against. I have only put down those for and – as one does, I fear – only those that most concern me.

But the others will come up in discussion.

                                                    H. Granville Barker.

This was a sensible document, but it shows that he was heavily discouraged. It was not merely his impatience; the war had changed everything, and while it removed the possibility of the National Theatre for which he had been waiting, he was prepared to put himself into any practicable scheme; otherwise all he could do would lead nowhere. He saw no prospect of anything maturing, however, and nothing but a precarious future.

*

As a contribution to the war effort, a matinée was organized by Miss Elizabeth Asquith at Covent Garden Theatre on 5 November, with an elaborate programme in aid of an Arts Fund for the relief of members of the artistic professions in distress owing to the war. John Masefield's verse play, *Philip the King*, was included, which Barker produced, and in which Lillah McCarthy, Henry Ainley, Norman McKinnel, and others took part. This was an extravagant production, with costumes and decoration by Charles Ricketts, and music by Gustav Holst. Much trouble was taken with it and many weeks of preparation went into it. Barker drew up a detailed plan for the crowds of Spanish citizens gathering in the courtyard of Philip II's palace, which was printed for the use of the

players, with their cues.   So badly organized was the whole affair, however, that the early part of the programme much overran the time-table,
and as Barker had allowed the play, the most important feature of the
matinée, to be placed at the end, many of the audience in the stalls had to
leave before it started, and there was a constant stream of people going
out, because of the lateness of the hour, during the playing.   None the
less, it made a deep impression.   Charles Ricketts, in a letter to Lillah
McCarthy, said:

Philip the King remains one of my favourite sets.   The Covent Garden
stage allowed scale and space, both rare in London theatres.   I remember
with pleasure the huge semicircle of curtains, the monumental doors
studded with coffin nails, the huge crucified Christ I painted in the manner
of El Greco.   Your jewelled dress looked austere and catholic.   Together
with *The Death of Tintagilles* I count *Philip the King* among the few successfully lit scenes I have witnessed; in each case this was due to Barker, who
is, in my opinion, the best producer we have had since Irving.   To-day
most plays are under-rehearsed, and all technical matters affecting scenic
production left to chance.

*

The Bennett play finished at the Kingsway on 7 November, and as a
further contribution to the national situation Barker prepared with
Thomas Hardy a stage version of the latter's great epic, *The Dynasts*, the
first performance taking place on 25 November.   It was in three parts,
something like one-tenth of the original being used.   A specially constructed stage was built and the piece was played in grey curtains.   At each
side there was an elevated seat occupied by women players as chorus.
In the centre facing the audience at the foot of converging steps there was
a lectern from which Henry Ainley in costume read the narrative.   On
the stage there were two side entrances, and an inner stage, slightly
raised, within which changes of scene were indicated.   The production
was highly impressive and was much praised, but public response was
disappointingly small, though no one who saw this exquisite production
ever forgot it.   As an example of how the play was received, " Captious
Critic " of the *Illustrated Sporting and Dramatic News* may be quoted
(19 December 1914):

There is no connecting story to link the various campaigns together, that
is to say, no British private casts a languishing eye on a Spanish maiden in
the Peninsular War, and marries her after he has been made a
Field-Marshal at Waterloo. . . .

Barker himself was altogether out of heart while the play was in rehearsal,
and by no means cheered up by the small audiences, which increased,
however, so that the play was continued till 7 January 1915.   To help the

audience, a twelve-page pamphlet on some of the lesser-known characters was presented with the programme.

This ends Granville Barker's work as producer-manager in the English theatre. After *The Dynasts* a company of Belgian players was given hospitality at the Kingsway, and in February *Fanny's First Play* was revived with Lena Ashwell in the leading part. Then in April Vedrenne and Eadie had it for a few weeks, after which it came back into Lena Ashwell's possession.

*

Before continuing the story, the moment has come to survey Barker's achievement as a producer; for apart from plays done the year after in New York, his intermittent return to the London stage later on, when he had given up the theatre, brought no more than a reflection of his qualities. "If one of you should prompt me by asking whom I considered to be the best director of plays I've know", says A. E. Matthews in his autobiography, *Matty* (Hutchinson, 1952), "I would unhesitatingly reply 'Granville Barker'." The actor was recalling two experiences of Barker, forty-five years earlier, at the Court Theatre. Such praise is characteristic of all who write or speak of him from their own stage experience. Barker, they say, was charming, flattering, the most intelligent and inspiring of producers, but the words leave hearers guessing at what caused him to be so remarkable. Matthews wrote after experience with Charles Hawtrey, "who taught me everything", and "the great George Alexander", and after working with almost every producer of eminence in London and New York, as well as after being a highly capable producer himself, so that his testimony is important. Desmond MacCarthy, the best dramatic critic of the first half of the century, called Barker "the best producer of his time".

His contemporary was Edward Gordon Craig, five years older, who had given up the stage in 1897, to return with a first production in London in 1900 of *Dido and Aeneas*, by Purcell, shortly after Barker's first London production. Then after half a dozen more productions in the next three years, including an Ibsen and a Shakespeare play, Craig ended his active work on the London stage. Undoubtedly Barker got something from him, for the aims of the two were akin, though their methods were different. What Craig demanded in the Man of the Theatre existed in Barker:

. . . a master in himself . . . capable of inventing and rehearsing a play; capable of designing and superintending the construction of both scenery and costume; of writing any necessary music, of inventing such machinery as is needed and the lighting that is used.

XVI *A Midsummer Night's Dream* (Savoy Theatre, 1913). Designs by Norman Wilkinson. Titania lays aside her crown and sleeps

XVII *A Midsummer Night's Dream* (Savoy Theatre, 1913). Two fairies and (*centre*) Christine Silver as Titania

XXXVIII *The Dynasts* by Thomas Hardy (Kingsway Theatre, 25 November 1914). Showing the built-out stage

These qualifications, save the musical one, Barker had. A different personality from Craig, his practical work continued longer, and developed further, but in the end he, too, was defeated, substantially by the same causes as those that defeated Craig.

It is to be noted, and perhaps this is the place at which to make the remark, that there was a seeming cleavage between Gordon Craig's point of view as a stage reformer and that of Barker. The latter started and ended with the play; the terms within which he worked were those of the play itself. Craig declared that he wanted the actor to " cease from being the marionette of the playwright ", he was " to develop his own powers ". This demand arose from his conviction that the drama originated with the actor, not the playwright. The cleavage was, however, more apparent than real, for though the actor may perform without the playwright, he cannot perform drama without him. Craig's plea was that actor and playwright should be one, or that at least the playwright should belong to the actor's company. That was Barker's own view. " Acting and drama were and are indivisible ", said Craig, and Barker used almost identical words. Yet the two men never came together and a chilly atmosphere of opposition between them was never dissipated.

What both men aimed at was total reform of the theatre, an aim voiced by William Butler Yeats at that very time; for, writing in 1903, he had written the oft-quoted words :

I think the theatre must be reformed in its plays, its speaking, its acting and its scenery. . . . There is nothing good about it at present.

So, too, thought Barker, and not merely thought: he felt in his soul. With that in his mind, he started on his first production in his early twenties for the Stage Society. Craig made his name at once with his above-mentioned production; not so Barker with his, a month earlier, though his work was received with respect. It was not until four years later, in the Vedrenne–Barker management at the Court Theatre, that his position was established.

Shaw was unquestionably the most potent influence in Barker's early career as producer, but Barker owed much to the two Germans who came to London at the end of the last century, when J. T. Grein had the idea of establishing a German theatre there. These men were the romantic actor, Hans Andresen, from the Karlsruher Hoftheater, and the character actor, Max Behrend, from the Berlin Stadttheater. Both were members of a company that Grein, with Carl Junkermann and H. A. Hertz (father of Margaret Halston), set up at the St. George's Hall, afterwards at the Great Queen Street Theatre (later called the Kingsway). Andresen became director of the German company, and Behrend its

M

producer. That Barker learned much of the technique he was soon to develop from these men there can be little doubt – Behrend in particular. It was said of the latter by an English admirer that he was the first stage manager in Europe. The features of his productions were team work and the care given to the smallest parts.

Though Barker's direction was always highly individual, it was not because he attempted anything that might be described as calculated idiosyncrasy. He was not concerned that his signature should be seen upon a production : he sought for the signature of the dramatist. As producer, his hand was evident in the way in which the action was built up, in what is now called the pattern of the production. This was achieved not merely by variation of tone, change of emphasis, or alteration of pace, but by the interaction of stage movement, so that the action was composed of layer upon layer of movement, speech, and silences held together in the completed form. Yet there were no merely clever tricks, devices, or cunning effects. The detail was endlessly contrived, always with significance; there was nothing introduced for its own sake. Indeed, there was something like austerity, so that bareness was a real danger; yet, again, not for its own sake, but so that anything not essential should be eliminated. In his immense concentration upon detail, Barker was in danger of reducing everything to miniature, making the stage smaller than actuality. Yet in seeking the full expression of unity in play, setting, and the voices and movements of the players, Barker showed his greatness as a producer, for the conception of unity is greatness in art, not excellence in one thing only.

What attracted people in Barker's productions and caused them to be so well remembered (as I among others remember them) was precisely their element of rhythm : repetition of the rise and fall of the action, variations in time, the relation of speech to movement – in fact, the action as a whole. Except in music, the existence of rhythm is hard to find in contemporary life, and even in music it often seems absent, for our times tend to be without meaning. Rhythm is an expression of meaning. As Barker sought to establish it in his productions, it was the meaning of the play. It is important to realize that rhythm is not a thing in itself; for it is not a cause, but an effect, and producers who aim at rhythm without knowing why achieve nothing.

When Barker spoke of the performance of a play as a piece of music he was thinking of its rhythm essentially, but those who seek to follow Barker's methods need not themselves think of music; they must think of the play, its action and end. Rhythm is the repetition and sequences of action, the expression of energy, and conveys the regularity of organic form, and without doubt it is one of the most important elements of drama. When working out a production, Barker would play the pianola for hours. This aided his sense of rhythm. Not that he imitated musical rhythms, but the rhythm in the music, the stresses, variety of phrasing, the balancing of one bar with another, and, above all, the sense of the musical piece as a whole influenced him in working out the action of the play. Dramatic action is movement – the movement of speech, thought, feeling, and the thing done, not merely physical movements, but how the sentences follow the thought and anticipate it, the counter-point, overlap, and change of speech, with variation in cue-taking, timing, emphasis, and appreciation of what is inherent in the situation. The rhythm contains the life of the play, and in Barker's hands the flow, the fullness, the direction of the dramatic action gave the play its being.

One of the objects of drama is to restore and to maintain rhythm in the life of man, which is one reason why drama is such an important social art; it explains why Barker was so anxious that the use of drama should be developed in education.

What was intended in the play, what was implicit in it, its content and dramatic meaning, Barker never went outside. That is why weak and shallow plays in his hands remained exactly what they were. He was not the sort of producer to make one kind of play into another. His failures were almost always the failure of the play. There are producers who pride themselves on being able to " get over " a play possessing no significant content or form by their own artifice and cunning. That Barker never attempted. It is indeed a dangerous practice, though all too common; for as likely as not it will lead to a play of quality being mishandled because the producer does not take the trouble to find out what it contains, thinking more about his own talents than about the play. Barker put the play before the producer, just as he put the part before the actor. The latter was as revolutionary a principle of stage management as the former, for actors took it for granted that the script of a part was there in the first place to enable them to display themselves, and, if they were star actors, to regard the entire play as no more than a vehicle for their personalities. With Barker, because the play itself took precedence, stars were not required.

At rehearsals Barker was wholly concentrated, and never shouted or lost his temper. He would go upon the stage, and, taking hold of the players, move them about into the positions he wanted. If he had anything important to say, he would take the player aside and talk to him, making suggestions and illustrating his meaning. He let nothing go by uncorrected, not always stopping the rehearsal but by explanations at the close. Actors who worked for him declared that it was an exciting experience, for he called forth the utmost energy of which the actor was capable. Barker was parsimonious with praise. He was sympathetic and encouraging, and took endless pains with any player who showed a disposition to learn; indeed, at times he went on long after it seemed obvious to others that there was no hope. But he did not perpetually say how brilliant the actor was or how delightful the actress, even when perhaps, the praise might have been deserved, though he could say that he was satisfied.

He had, in fact, great respect for the actor, not so much, perhaps, for particular actors as for the actor's art. This can be seen in all he wrote about the theatre. He considered one of the producer's main tasks to be to aid the actor, to enable him to work freely, but first to make sure that he understood the part in relation to the action as a whole. His aim was to get spontaneous playing, or rather the sense of it – that is to say, playing from direct inspiration from the actor's mind and heart – and to avoid the mechanical and mere repetition. Writing in the *New Quarterly* in 1909, he said:

. . . if acting cannot seem spontaneous, it is nothing. It can only seem so by the actor coming fresh to his work, his whole personality like a sensitive plate, which he exposes untouched to the light of his conception of the part. The image produced, valuable according to the rightness of the conception, will vary from time to time according to the condition of the plate, but each time it must be a fresh image.

From all this it can be seen that Barker's aims were to encourage imagination in the individual actor, and to secure ensemble acting, with emphasis not merely upon characterization, but upon the structure of the play. Thus his productions had the appearance of being more natural than anything to which playgoers had been accustomed. The forcing of playing for the sake of theatricality was not allowed on his stage, for movement and gestures, as well as the voice, were disciplined to the needs of the play. No concessions were made to conventional theatrical values. Yet Barker's aim was not simple naturalism. He aimed always at the dramatic or what should be called the poetic form. His object was to make the play convincing, but he did not attempt to present slices of life even in the most realistic scenes. This is proved by the fact that what each character had to do, even the smallest part, was exactly worked out, timed, and detailed. He created an atmosphere permeated with the personalities of the characters, an atmosphere of life in depth, having no resemblance to the contrived semblances of life characteristic of naturalistic stage productions.

It is a pity that in current criticism the difference between the terms "naturalism" and "realism" is not maintained. "Naturalism" is concerned with the illusion that what we see on the stage is actual life itself; it is aimed at the rendering of the model as it exists. "Realism" is concerned with the truth or vision of life, and presents us with a comment upon or criticism of life in which the forms of nature are employed as a means to an artistic end, which is the communication of the artist's vision, when natural forms are transfigured into a work of art. There is a subtle but essential difference.

These are inevitably inadequate notes upon a subject difficult to discuss and to explain. An artist's technical methods are implicit in his work, and to write of them apart from the work is neither easy nor generally profitable. Barker's attitude towards stage production was stated in *The Exemplary Theatre* (1922), which was a manifesto upon the principles that should be recognized in the National Theatre, for which he was hoping, and is also contained in his Shakespeare *Prefaces* and elsewhere. Indeed, it is implied in everything he wrote, in his plays as much as in his lectures and other works. He developed from the Court Theatre days, when he was tempted to be a dictator, as he said himself, to a maturity of manner in which he was recognized as a master. At that point, unfortunately, his art was checked. When he declared, as he did in the book referred to above –

. . . the constricting fault of most modern play production is to treat every possible moment with severity of regulation, and it is more to our main purpose to insist on the needlessness of nine-tenths of it . . .

there can be no doubt that he was thinking of his own early efforts, and especially of the work of those producers who attempt to emulate him. I am not sure that he worked out his ideas of direction theoretically at any time, though he was ceaselessly thinking about the function of the producer and how to express it. One of his best statements is contained in another quotation from the above-mentioned book:

To suggest, to criticize, to co-ordinate – that should be the limit of his function. The symphonic effect must be one made by the blending of the actors' natural voices and by the contrasts that spring from the conflicting emotions which their mutual study of the parts spontaneously engenders . . . but we must never forget that to put a play into action on the stage is to pour it into its mould; once there it tends very quickly to set. . . . But in nearly all plays . . . the physical action is extraordinarily unimportant, the mental, the emotional action all in all. Delay, then, in entering the physical phase should not trouble the experienced actor. He has no business to be agitating his mind at rehearsals (much less at a performance) over physical movements, unless they are such matters of gymnastic as fighting, dancing, or the rough and tumble of farce.

Barker did not meet Stanislavsky or see any of his productions until he visited Moscow in the summer of 1914, when his work in London was virtually over. His method was much nearer the French than the German, though one of his early masters was a German, for he was more concerned with the dramatist and the actor than with stage decoration. He had little in common with Reinhardt, and gave relatively small attention to the *décor* of his productions, for even in the Savoy productions of Shakespeare, apart from getting something like an open stage, he left the *décor* mainly to the designers. He was by no means an imitator, for he had at all times his own creative impulse and energy. His method of rehearsing everything in detail was the classic method, for the essence of the classical principle in art is that what is done can be repeated; and to have standards, as he had, is to have deep concern for efficiency. He left nothing to chance, and all that could be made mechanical was brought into mechanical perfection. That was for the sake of the fullness and elevation of the spirit, so that the free energy of creative action should transform the imitation of life. Only when every movement, gesture, and position of the actor is precisely rehearsed and mastered, so that the actor may not have to think about them (asking himself what he has to do) any more than about his words (asking himself what he has to say), can acting in the pure sense exist. Barker started not with the physical action, but with the inner conception of the character and its place in the play, for he wanted the character to come alive in the actor with the energy of the dramatic action; for that reason he banished the conventional routine of merely conventional stage business, and aimed at a disciplined technique to replace slipshod methods and short cuts. To quote once more from what he says about the actor:

His obedience must be asked to a stern and searching training of body, mind, and imagination. Next, he must turn his back upon all the attractive tricks which save him so much trouble and can earn him such applause. And, finally, he must be ready to surrender himself and to merge his carefully cultivated artistic identity in a company of his fellows.

Actors can play for their own hands, aiming at their own effects, with indifference to the other players, or they can so adjust their acting to their knowledge of the methods and personalities of those with whom they are playing that a smooth performance results: in both instances violence may be done to the play, its meaning may be distorted, and the creative energy that belongs to it may be misdirected and lost. The producer's aim should be to see that neither of these faults arises by maintaining the dramatic action and the balance of the characters, so that the effect intended in the play is got. The producer's is the production's controlling mind, which must be at the service of the dramatist, whose play is master.

Actors tend to use themselves superficially. It is often said that they can play parts they do not understand; what would be more correct would be to say that they play *in* such parts – they cannot play them. This may be true, however eminent the actor. Unless an actor understands a part, he cannot play it; he does something else. By " understanding " I mean intuitive appreciation of the character, entering into the " soul " of the person represented. If nothing but the manners, appearance, and tone of voice of the character are presented, the part has not been played. Barker aimed at such understanding and was not taken in by substitutes for it. He never allowed anything to be done on his stage merely because it was " effective ". Unless whatever it was – intonation, movement, gesture, look, timing, pause, or use of properties – belonged to the play and was necessary for its interpretation, he had no use for it. He was never at a loss for what had to take place at any moment of the action and would not let the actor be at a loss.

He was a drama producer in the true sense, in contrast to the theatre producer. Irving, Tree, Boucicault, even Barrie were theatrical producers and their work may be contrasted with his.

PART THREE

THE VISIT TO AMERICA AND THE
FIRST WORLD WAR

THE war that was to end war put off the National Theatre and all ideas of repertory to a remote future, and the drama itself was kept alive only in its simple theatrical elements. There was, however, an interregnum for Barker. Towards the close of 1914 he was invited by the Stage Society of New York to be responsible for a series of productions in that city. Earlier, Gordon Craig had been asked to go, but had demanded a guarantee of £100,000, which was tantamount to a refusal. Then Barker was invited, the sum of £25,000 having been found by a group of rich men. He was disposed to accept, as he was told he could choose his own plays and company, for it revived ideas he had entertained two years earlier, and he was unhappy in England; although war was still only a professional business, everything was going to pieces. But he wanted Lillah to go with him. She was then leading lady at the Haymarket Theatre, and received the suggestion without enthusiasm; but both Shaw and Barrie advised her to go for Barker's sake; so did Asquith when she consulted him. " Go to America," said the Prime Minister. " We don't want Barker as a soldier." And a professional visit to America was regarded as backing up the war effort.

So they went to New York, but before going Barker insisted upon arrangements being made for the lease of the Kingsway Theatre to be given up, an extraordinary thing to have done, but indicative of his despairing state of mind.

Among the millionaires who had guaranteed the cost of the American season were Otto H. Kahn and Archer M. Huntington. At a reception given to the Barkers at the Huntingtons', Barker met Helen Huntington, though it is possible that they may have met earlier when he and Archer went to New York in 1908, for Huntington was interested in the new theatre, for which Barker was then wanted. Anyhow, he and Helen met in 1914, and from that meeting much followed.

An English company was engaged in New York, and *Androcles and the Lion* and *The Man Who Married a Dumb Wife* were put into rehearsal. The season was to start at Wallack's Theatre, an old building due for demolition, and the intention was afterwards to tour the States. On

28 January 1915 the two plays were received as extreme novelties, the Shaw piece being described as " Shaw with Barker trimmings ". New York was startled by Barker's abolition of footlights, and by his spotlights in front of the balcony, not to mention Albert Rutherston's painted curtains. On 16 February, *A Midsummer-Night's Dream*, repeating the London production, created another sensation, and encountered much criticism, being regarded as needlessly provocative and exasperating. A critic writing in the New York *Nation* on 25 February said:

Obviously the producer . . . is concerned principally with two things; to create the fairy atmosphere of the piece and to ensure that full value shall be given by the players to Shakespeare's verse . . . in quickening the tempo of the piece he has unfortunately gone beyond the capabilities of his players. It is not too much to say that hardly a single performer is intelligible all the time, and many of them are unintelligible a good deal of the time.

It was thought by some critics that Barker had taken liberties with Shakespeare's lines, so unfamiliar were they with the play and with lively and rapid speaking of the verse; others scoffed at its simple stage setting. Shakespeare was followed by *The Doctor's Dilemma*.

What puzzled the New York public more than anything else was Barker's short-run system. It was thought the plays were taken off because they were not successful, and nothing would convince critics and the public otherwise. So people did not go to see them, as they might have done, because a supposed failure did not appeal to them. However, audiences were good, but the season came to an end when Wallack's Theatre was pulled down. There was talk of starting a repertory theatre, with Barker as its head, and promises of money were got, Lillah being very active in this, but nothing came of it. Writing to Gilbert Murray while this idea was in the air, Barker said:

Feb. 26, 1915.

Send me any inside news you can about things in England – newspapers are dry comfort. And tell me whether in spite of all the work in prospect here, and the good I really do think of being able to do keeping it going, you believe I still ought to be back there instead of here. It is good doing the work here when everything else seems to be tumbling down, but – one feels about once a day that the trenches would be a welcome relief to the crass anxiety of it all. Thank God Dennis got off with, I trust, a whole skin. It is the infernal stupidity of the business which still gets over me.

Funds were found to enable a performance of Gilbert Murray's Greek version of *The Trojan Women*, with Lillah McCarthy as Hecuba, to be done at the newly built Adolph Lewisohn Stadium at the College of the City of New York on 15 May. This was an immense auditorium, only part of it being used for the play. Here, however, it was possible to give the play under conditions that approximated to those of the Greek theatre, and the production was received with critical respect and great enthusiasm. An effort was made beforehand to get President Wilson to write a special preface to a theatre edition of the play, but he said that he "must detach himself from everything which seems to bear the character of an attempt to make opinion even in the general interest of peace", for the Barker visit was looked upon as British propaganda. Afterwards, *Iphigenia in Taurus* was performed at the Yale Bowl, Harvard, and Princeton, and *The Trojan Women* at Pennsylvania University. Both plays had settings and costumes designed by Norman Wilkinson and music composed by Professor David Stanley Smith of Yale. *Androcles and the Lion* went on tour, but neither Barker nor Lillah went with it. She might have gone, but he hated the idea of the tour. Mrs. Patrick Campbell, who was successfully touring in America, wrote to Shaw to say that she thought the Barkers were disappointed over the result of their visit; she thought they made a mistake in not themselves risking a summer tour.

In fact, there was trouble between the Barkers. Helen Huntington had formed an attachment to him, and Barker seems to have been captivated by this fascinating little woman, twelve or thirteen years older than himself. She was a poetess in a small way, having published *Folk Songs from the Spanish* in 1900, also a number of novels, among them *The Sovereign Good* in 1905 and *Marsh Lights* in 1913. The poems were slight, and both they and the novels were no more than women's magazine affairs, but the lady had an air of mystery, and Barker became devoted to her. His wife was distressed when told about the attachment by Archer Huntington, who was by no means pleased. Thus, whatever theatrical developments had been possible in America were brought abruptly to an end.

The Barkers left America in June 1915, Barker assuring Lillah that everything was at an end with Helen. They arrived in England on 28 June, and Lillah went straight to Stansted. Barker remained in London for a few days at the flat the Galsworthys had lent them, as they had no place in London, their rooms at 5 Adelphi Terrace having been let. He reached Stansted on 8 July. He was heavily depressed. He told Lillah that, so far as the American visit was concerned, "there is nothing for you or for me, not even our salaries". He felt that for him everything was finished: the London theatre given over to frivolity, and the war a war of extermination of young men. His state of mind at this time is indicated in a letter to Gilbert Murray, which shows how deeply indebted he was to his friend :

Give me your patience for a moment – and longer.

Still my balance sheets haven't come from America (oh these American business people) and I still do not know how much I owe you exactly. I have put in my notes at about £250. To pay this and many other things I have to raise money on securities – and I have to do this (through trustees and a Judge and God knows what red tape). And one can't raise as much money in these days as in others. *And* they won't permit me to raise any at all unless what I do raise will satisfy everybody. Now I may not be able to send you here and now your whole amount (it's a near thing anyway and I can't of course be sure till I know what the whole amount is). I may only be able to send you £100 or £150. Needless to say, I shall make it the last penny possible (nothing noble in that – someone has got to get it). If this is so, will you undertake – fairly formally – not to sue me even into bankruptcy for the remainder, but to wait until such time as I can more conveniently pay it.

Sorry to be such a nuisance – but Art was ever this sort of a jade when I walked out with her.

He joined the Red Cross and went to France, returning to prepare a series of lectures he had undertaken to give in America that autumn. In September he returned there, and on his way over on the White Star liner *Celtic* he wrote to Lillah a letter, part only of which survives :

. . . work – and am not months behindhand and irritable to get back to it – and when will that be?

Meanwhile I'd go to the country and breathe air and cogitate.

You're with Charlotte at the Albert Hall to-night – that's an interesting show I expect. I perceive this voyage is going to make me double-chinned and liverish – there's too much to be at and a beastly orchestra. However, I've a table in my cabin and I'll get through some work if I can.

Bless you, dear Lillah – my dear wife – I love you very much if you please – and I'm not very far from you. Distance doesn't mainly count.

Get a healthy time – breathe air and I'll be back soon. Bless you – I love you – my dearest.

H.

Oh – letters – well I don't suppose many will come. Any marked private must just wait – the others you might open but I don't expect you'll be able to do anything with them. Use your judgment, dear, if you will please.

The letter shows affection for Lillah, and his intention to return after the lectures. Nevertheless, in New York the friendship with Helen was resumed: in fact, she had been corresponding regularly with him during his absence.

Lillah at Stansted was devoting herself to making more out of their old house, despite the absence of money, preparing for Barker's return. She rehearsed the name part in Sturge Moore's one-act play *Judith* for the Stage Society, performed at the Queen's Theatre in January 1916. It was enthusiastically received, except by the Press, as Charles Ricketts, who was responsible for the costumes, noted in his diary, " as usual when they suspect anything of being art, or poetry, or any damned superior thing of that sort ". In a letter to the author about the performance dated 26 January, W. B. Yeats found fault with Barker for the production,[1] though, of course, he had had nothing to do with it. Yeats was very nasty about Lillah's performance, but Sturge Moore, when dedicating the play to her later on, referred to " the splendid actress and beautiful woman whose genius revealed, with its virtues, the faults of my play ". Three years later there was another play with the same title, a full-length work by Arnold Bennett, written for Lillah, in which she also played the leading part under her own management, but it does not concern us in these pages.

*

Here I approach the most difficult part of this work. The easiest way out of the difficulty would be to slur over the events of the next two years, to compress what happened into a few sentences, or to pretend that nothing really important occurred, but it is not possible to do so and make a coherent story, or to do justice to those concerned. The truth must be told as far as it is possible to ascertain it, and as far as it is fair to the memory of others to tell it. I do not set out to relate the complete story, much less suppose that I am able to tell it from Barker's point of view. Only he could do the latter, and he did not choose to attempt it; but I shall do my best, knowing that what follows has at least some omissions but as few inaccuracies as it is possible to hope for.

On 3 January 1916, before the performance of *Judith*, Lillah received a long letter from her husband, written from New York, saying that he could not come back; it was of no use, she must divorce him. This was a terrible blow. She went at once to Shaw, who said that he, too, had heard from Barker by the same post. She had received the letter in the evening, and in the version of her memoirs (referred to later), but omitted from the published volume, she described what happened:

I went, all frozen on a cold January night. . . . I found myself at the flat. . . . Shaw greeted me very tenderly and made me sit by the fire.

[1] *Letters of Sturge Moore and W. B. Yeats* (1953), p. 24.

I was shivering.   Shaw sat very still.   The fire brought me warmth. . . .
How long we sat there I do not know, but presently I found myself
walking with dragging steps with Shaw beside me . . . up and down
Adelphi Terrace.   The weight upon me grew a little lighter and released
the tears which would never come before . . . he let me cry.   Presently
I heard a voice in which all the gentleness and tenderness of the world was
speaking.   It said : " Look up, dear, look up to the heavens.   There is
more in life than this.   There is much more."

She had to go on with her rehearsals, but when the play was over, having
said nothing to anyone but Shaw, she went down to Stansted and would
see nobody.   In the meantime, Barker had returned to the Red Cross in
France without coming back to England.   Shaw wrote to her anxiously,
but could get no reply, and sent a letter to her father about her.   Then she
saw him, and he wrote the following letter to her :

10 Adelphi Terrace, W.C.
19th January, 1916.

Quite seriously, I have come to the conclusion that you had better get rid
of Harley.   He has gone to France ; and I have now no belief that you
and he will ever patch it up again.   If I am right, then the sooner you set
yourself free the better for you, and the more creditable for him, as you
are now at the height of your powers, and not soured or aged by your
disagreement with him.   I don't know whether either of you is to blame,
or, if either, which ; and it doesn't matter anyhow ; but it seems to me
that if you come together again you are more likely to drive one another
mad than to settle down happily.   I don't see why you should not be
happily married ; but I gravely doubt whether Harley is fit for married
life at all : and I certainly do not advise you to push the experiment
beyond the ten years in which you have already had the best of such
capacity for domesticity as he possesses.   I was struck by the way in
which, when he went off to America, you immediately recovered your
health and looked five years younger.   How do you feel about it *really*?
If he writes you a letter to say that he will not come back, making it
clear that it is not your fault, you can sue for restitution of conjugal rights
with the usual sequel.   It is in your power to demand your release ; he
cannot refuse it.   Of course he should undertake to restore your
settlement and to leave you everything but his personal effects.

Naturally I should not interfere in this manner if I had not become
persuaded that the only way in which you two can remain friends and
have a reasonably comfortable future is to release one another from the
only relation in which neither of you appears to be happy.   You are
both good enough to regard me, apparently, as the proper person to
meddle.

Think it over – though I dare say you have thought of hardly anything
else for a year past – and either let me know whether I can do anything,
or take counsel in whatever quarter you feel most confidence.   The

sailing to France instead of to England indicates that some understanding should be come to.

Yours ever,

G. Bernard Shaw.

This was the affectionate letter of one who knew them both, who was advising Lillah for what he believed to be her good. A few days later he wrote again, suggesting that she should get advice from another friend:

Ayot St. Lawrence, Welwyn, Herts.

23rd January, 1916.

My dear Lillah,

Forgive my meddling again, but there is something which I should have said the other evening which I may as well say now. Unless you feel quite secure in your own judgment, it would be as well for you to consult some friend on whom you can depend to see the matter from your point of view and deal with it sensibly: Arthur Ponsonby, Asquith who is in a responsible position and doesn't want to marry you himself. I am no use, because Harley had calmly made me his agent to procure a divorce, and apparently wants me to let him have the decree by return of post. I wish I could; for now that your artistic partnership is broken by his retirement from management, nothing but a sort of devotion on his part of which he is constitutionally incapable could make him a humble follower of your star. You need somebody whom you can carry in your pocket, and not a rival genius. I may be wrong; but that opinion makes me a very unsafe adviser for you: I am like counsel retained by the other side; and you clearly ought to have your own advocate. Your marriage suited me extremely well both from a personal and professional point of view: I was as comfortable at Stansted as in the theatre; and it is not at all likely that his next venture will be as pleasant for me. Nevertheless you cannot trust me; for I now feel somehow that the domestic crockery is too badly broken to be worth mending, and that it is better for both of you to exchange your present wretched terms for the romantic relation of two people who were once married to one another and are not at all ashamed of it.

Unless and until you come round to that opinion you will inevitably and quite rightly regard me as a hostile influence. That is why I urge you to take some other advice. Even a lawyer might be useful, though if you have a friend of the right sort at hand, the lawyer should come second. I told Harley that he ought to send you a letter that could be shewn to a lawyer. I have just heard that he has done so. When you have it you can consider whether to act on it at once or not: it does not bind you to anything: but it enables you to sue for restitution if you wish to, whereas at present you are helpless except at the cost of making public a long and intimate letter which does no sort of justice to your position.

I cannot express to you how futilely intrusive I felt the other night. But what could I do? An Englishwoman can have her case disguised from her and be consoled with a little sentiment; an Irishwoman (which is what you essentially are) does not want to be humbugged and resents extremely any attempt to do it in a really serious matter.   She has to fight it out with herself; and the wise man runs away from that battle, which, anyhow, he has no right to witness.   I have not communicated since, knowing that you knew where to find me if you wanted me.

Next month Barker returned again to London, and at last he and Lillah had an interview at Shaw's flat.   He had no arguments, but demanded his release.   She would make no decision, for she was convinced, whatever he said, that Barker was under the influence of an infatuation that would pass.   The following letter from Shaw carries the matter further:

Ayot St. Lawrence, Welwyn, Herts.
5th Feb. 1916.

My dear Lillah,

Harley came down here after his interview with you.   He had also had an interview with his dentist, who tugged at his tooth without succeeding in extracting it.   He went back to Boulogne with a toothache and a chill, and had a tempestuous crossing.   I heard from him yesterday, but only as to his arrival, the misery of his journey, and the return of a coat I lent him.

Of the interview he said that you had persisted in asking what *you* had done, whereas the point that you hadnt done anything, and that *he* was the delinquent, and didnt defend himself and couldnt help it.   He described you as acting with complete dignity and putting an end to the interview yourself, but giving him no hint of a decision of any kind.

When I met you on Saturday in the car, I had just arranged with him that we should go down to Ayot by the 5.49 train.   As I thought it would spoil your week end if you knew he was within reach, I suppressed the fact with smiling treachery.

I look forward to a Judgment Day for him.   As I imagine it, you will be the stately chatelaine of a handsome house; and you will give him tea and shew him your four beautiful children.   And your human husband will grin affably at him.

Ever,
G. B. S.

★

Barker was still in the Red Cross, having been given the job of writing a book to interest the subscribers to the fund, which was published under the title of *The Red Cross in France*: the book is of small consequence.   In an Author's Preface Barker says he was put into khaki and told what to do, and the book has every evidence of being written to order, as he points out:

Nor is this a critical account of what I have seen; it is written frankly from the Red Cross point of view.

Characteristically, it starts with a chapter in dialogue entitled " A Chat in Pall Mall ", and there is much dialogue throughout the book. This makes it difficult to read, for the dialogue is wearisome, and the book has a scrappy appearance. Only an oblique approach is made to its subject. The book gave little satisfaction to those who had commissioned it, for the author was too obviously presenting a case in which his heart was not. In an attempt to recover himself, he asks towards the end: " This war was to end war, wasn't it? " and replies, " But not all war; only this stupidest sort." He thought the war to be stupid and everything connected with it, especially his own part in it, and was consequently incapable of writing a straightforward account of what was distasteful to him.

The book did, however, enable him to travel constantly between France and England, and he spent much time with J. M. Barrie, also with the Shaws. At this time he wrote a preface to one of the volumes in the collected edition of the novels of Leonard Merrick, *One Man's View*, written during the war and published in 1916. The novel is about a faithless wife in London and New York who wanted to go on the stage and to be a playwright. In the course of the preface Barker used the words:

. . . seeking still a real world in which it will be both sane and fine to live . . . and, oh, the pity if the finding it quite breaks their dream.

*

He and Helen could not easily correspond; but she kept a diary of her thoughts and emotions, and he wrote long letters to her every day, sometimes more than once a day, which were despatched as he was able to send them. It was a painful time for both, and full of exasperation for him. Then he left the Red Cross and went back to America, where, in New Hampshire, he stayed alone. There he wrote another long-short story entitled *Souls on Fifth : The Slight Study of an American Hereafter* (Boston : Little, Brown & Company, 1917). The small book has a coloured frontispiece by Norman Wilkinson. It may be described as a piece of moralizing upon attachment to material success. Written in the first person, he supposes himself alone in Fifth Avenue before dawn, and sees " what seemed to be a shadowy drift of grey ", composed of small grey shapes, the souls of those for whom Fifth Avenue was the ideal in life. One September night he found the soul of the Rev. Evan Thomas " wedged in the shutters of a candy shop ". He dug him out, and a long conversation takes place in which, on the text from the Acts of the Apostles about a man who " died and went to his own place ", the soul of the popular preacher tells how he left his church in England for " a pleasant, comfortable church " in Fifth Avenue. He " set out to convert

XXXIX   New York: Granville Barker with Lillah McCarthy (1915)

XL   New York (1915): Lillah McCarthy and Granville Barker (*at left*), with Barker's Aunt
Evelyn and her son-in-law; his Uncle Charles Granville and wife; his Uncle Bernard
Granville and wife

XLI *The Trojan Women* by
Gilbert Murray. New York
(1915)

Fifth Avenue; it was Fifth Avenue that converted me". The greater part of the story is concerned with conversations with "a pretty oval shape", which he calls "the Little Soul", the soul of a young woman who had died at thirty-five, after "a bungled operation". This turns into something like romance. The Little Soul cries:

Love is often like this, you know – how is it that you don't know? Death to give, but always life to him that will dare take the offered love. And how gladly one dies to give it.

The story was written under emotional stress. It has not been published in book form in England, but was printed in the *Fortnightly Review* in two instalments in 1917.

Barrie wrote a number of letters to him in America that survive, and because they reflect Barker's mind and show what a good friend he had in Barrie they are given here:

Adelphi Terrace House, Strand, W.C.
8 Mar. [1916].

My dear Harley,
I have seen Lillah twice. The first time she was so emotional that there was nothing for me to send you in a wire. I saw her again yesterday, and as far as I can see her position is this, that she does not mean to take any action at present because she considered that your real love is for her, and all else is transitory and that you will yet want to return to her. She said she would not stand in your way if she really believed otherwise, but that at present she doesn't. In answer to that, I told her of course what you had said to me, that this was the one love of your life, but she said that was just an idea of yours. I spoke of the necessity of being open in such a matter and facing it squarely, but it always came back to that in the end that if she believed you did have a deep and lasting love for this lady she would take action, but that she doesn't believe it. I can't doubt but that she will act in the only sensible way that remains for her, but how long it may be before she changes her point of view I of course can't tell. She doesn't want advice from me tho' I have given it her, and she gets excited and thus a word may make her turn from me as she has done from Shaw, who seems from her account to have treated it in a light spirit, almost banteringly. If I am to be of any use to you or to her it must be by both feeling that I am the friend of both, and in this belief I shall continue to try to show her, in a measured way, that the right course for her is to dissolve things as soon as possible. Of course, I never was very close to her tho' I like her and I may not have much effect. I offered her to get the P.M.'s advice, but she feared his telling the family and I had to admit that I thought he would, only it's so much better people should be told openly than find out as it were covertly.
I'll write again when anything to say. I should add I told her your coming back to U.S.A. seemed to be a decisive action, but she didn't agree.

N

She is very anxious people shouldn't know and I told her some did and who, but she holds they must be the only ones, which they can't be. Probably if she was sure it was known she would then act, but this is guesswork.

Yours,

J. M. B.

23 Campden Hill Square, Kensington.
6th April.

My dear Harley,

I still don't have any news to tell you. Y'day after your second letter I saw Lillah, and I suppose put my point of view more clearly to her, or more strongly, with the only result I fear that she went away feeling I was not her friend. That is so very far from being the case that I don't think she can on reflection stick to it, but it may make her chary of discussing things with me. The fact is, as I see it, that quite naturally her nerves are all on edge and I feel desperately sorry for her and desirous to be kind to her, but I can't pretend to her that I see any way out except her taking action. I point out that this seems to me the obvious course for her own sake, and she replies that she is not thinking of herself at all, and then it is all back to the old argument that you don't know your own mind.

She is to be in an elaborate cast of *Crichton* for a war matinée in June, and I should be seeing her about that in any case at times, but at the moment she does resent me. I am far from being on a high horse about that, for she is brave and dear in many ways, and attempts by one who is only after all an outsider to put things sanely, and caring very much for you both, must often seem cold and unsympathetic, however warmly intended. And doubtless one who blunders and touches unwittingly on the raw. I wish I could do more and better.

Of course I'll let you know any moment I have anything to say. I am out here, as the school holidays have begun and I write in a clatter.

Yours,

J. M. B.

Adelphi Terrace House, Strand, W.C.
21 May.

My dear Harley,

You must always be so disappointed in my letters, as I never have anything to tell you, and naturally there is just the one thing that you want to hear of. So I have put off writing again and again, but it seems to me this may go on interminably. I see Lillah at rehearsals of *Crichton* (for a matinée), but have had no talk with her of the vital thing for a long time. I think the last time I wrote I said she seemed to have resented the expression of my views and that I didn't know whether she would talk of this matter with me any more. However, she was quite nice about it soon afterwards and reasonable too, and indeed it is the mixture of practical and utterly impracticable in her that leaves me at sea more than anything else. I have not had any real talk with her on the subject since then, but it has come up, and as far as I can see she still adheres to the idea that you are just going thro' some tummy and worry fit, such as you have sometimes had about work, and that you will wake from it, devoted to her alone, as she holds you have always been. This argument that you don't know your own mind stops all sorts of reasonable discussion, because unless this lady is the woman of your life (as I believe, because you tell me so) then I don't know you at all, and I am a blank about the whole business. But I do believe you know your own mind, and I think on this subject any man without a hundredth part of your capacity knows his own mind, and so the situation is clear to me. Even more you and this lady mean to be married, it is inconceivable to me that you and Lillah will ever come together again, but that does not seem to be her view, which is so much outside my experience of life that I can't argue with it. I have said my say and there is no more I can say. Of course I expect that she thinks and thinks and has many quite opposite points of view in a day.

From what Wheeler has written me, I gather you know that she has talked it over with the P.M., who advised her to do as she is doing. Naturally, however anxious she is to be fair (and she is), she puts it from her point of view. That is not really very material, it is so entirely a matter between yourselves. She likes an expression of opinion if it coincides with her own, and so do you, and so do all of us. But it does not in any case affect her actions, and that at present is apparently to do nothing, and so you must see, it may go on and on. She may suddenly act – and I don't know at all whether you have been communicating, or to what effect – but the policy of drift is one which once adopted in many matters is the easiest to pursue till the grave closes over us. The shortness and uncertainty of life is always before me. So I do think I should say that the fact of so very few people here knowing of the matter makes it much easier for her to let things drift. If they knew you were definitely separated it would be so much more difficult. Of course I see troubles arising before you if you take some steps of the kind, but this drifting may go on and on otherwise, and again I say life is so short.

She has times of acute unhappiness I am sure, but only age will assuage them if the drifting goes on, and I feel very much that it is all gnawing at your vitals. It does seem wretched that you should be alone in the wilderness.

Of course I'd cable or write if I had anything to say.

Yours always,
J. M. B.

When the Military Service Act of that year was passed, which made him liable for military service, he was still away. In a letter to Mrs. Patrick Campbell, written on 14 May 1916, Shaw says, referring to Barker: "Everything has gone to the devil."

Barrie wrote to him a further letter full of wisdom:

Adelphi Terrace House, Strand, W.C.
4th July 1916.

My dear Harley,

Your letter just arrived to-day. If there was only one of those two things to worry you I would advise you. First, the war. I think there is probably no other man I would advise about this. Long ago I vowed not to do it. But to you I would say, I think you should come over and join. I feel sure there is no halfway house, doing Red Cross Work, etc.; all that sort of post has passed except for the over-age man. It is the one thing or nothing. I fancy one can't train for an officer now. You go in simply as a private. Everything considered, I would say come, despite the monetary troubles.

I am trying to be brief so as to be plain.

If there were no war I should advise you to come and fight out the matter here. Rightly or wrongly, I have come to the conclusion that it will go on precisely as it is for an indefinite time – " for ever ", as mortals say – unless you are here to do something. What to do even tho' here may be a problem, but you will never move matters over there, and perhaps a good deal would be done here by your merely being on the spot and openly admitting that you and Lillah were definitely parted, and that this is so whether another lady is in the case or not. So far as I know, scarcely a human being except the few you have told and the few she has told know anything whatever about it.

The position is made much more difficult by the American point of view. There a divorce is arranged comfortably, while here the idea is more that a man and woman openly go together and defy the world. I am not saying which is the better way, but in England Lillah, I suppose, could compel publicity. I don't say she would; my idea is that she would not, but it does seem to be in her power. I don't think the non-payment of the trust money would move her. I don't see what is to move her very much but getting rid of this idea that you really love her. However incomprehensible this may be (and I admit is to me), it is the wall against which all argument breaks. I don't know that you can alter it by coming here, but I feel sure it won't alter while you remain there.

By the way, I know that she wants you to come and join the Army. I don't know how far the conscription net carries. Your lawyer of course knows far better than I. My idea is that everyone here somewhere in last August when we had all to sign a paper is included.

I haven't seen Lillah since *Crichton*. She is getting up something else. As you doubtless know, the Ad Terrace flat is let furnished to Millicent of Sutherland.

The net result of this when I read it over is that I don't advise you either way (which is best) but just put my ideas before you. I went to H.H.A.'s to dinner lately in the hope of having five minutes with him about it but he wasn't there. However, I think this of no importance.

As for the play, Butt is no doubt right that revues hold sway, and people probably go to plays only when they can't get seats at revues. Still, some light plays seem to do all right. *Cinderella* [1] has done very well and still doing so, but not, I think, as might have been in normal times. The Daylight Saving Bill has been bad for theatres, but won't be after autumn.

I expect you have seen distorted accounts of the Skeffington case. It was a tragedy, just showing that with mad passions on one side they may break out on another. The officer was apparently genuinely insane and is confined as such.

This country is making huge efforts and will not cease till the victory comes. That may easily be years hence.

Jack is all right. He is in Dardanelles.

Peter now at front in France! They are anxious times indeed.

Yours,

J. M. B.

The unhappy Lillah was playing in Somerset Maugham's *Caroline* at the New Theatre, in Barrie's playlet at the Coliseum, and in war matinées, not knowing what she was doing. Shaw wrote her a descriptive letter which gives a picture of Barker at the time and of herself too :

Ayot St. Lawrence, Welwyn, Herts.
30th July, 1916.

My dear Lillah,

A new accusation! I did not answer your long letter. It was just long enough to tell me that boxes for your war matinée were 20 guineas. As if I had 20 guineas to waste on such follies! I call it cheek.

I had hardly sent off my inquiry to you – my last one – when the subject of it turned up in person, very worried and impatient, and rapidly coming to your conclusion that it is all my fault, except that you blame me because he wants a divorce and he blames me because he hasnt got it. The situation is very unsatisfactory. Unless he goes back to America to deliver a series of lectures, he cannot meet his financial obligations to the settlement trustees and others, and must file a petition in bankruptcy. But as he is liable for military service, and has been passed by the doctor after three minutes' examination as sound in wind and limb, and is actually walking on as a super in the Royal Horse Artillery next Wednesday (he is at present spending the week-end in Devon with the Galsworthys) the chances of his receiving a three months' furlough to go to America at the end of the year, when his training will be complete, are pretty doubtful. However, if there is a winter lull at the front, it is possible that the Adjutant-General, whom he knows personally, may be induced to exercise his powers of granting furlough for the purpose of averting bankruptcy, in which case the lectures may be delivered, and before the same emergency recurs a year later the war may be over. But this seems the best that can happen.

He was not bound to return, as he was not on the register and had not

[1] *A Kiss for Cinderella* produced at Wyndham's Theatre, 16 March 1916.

been habitually resident here since the date in the Act; so he can claim to be a volunteer. He chose the Artillery on the advice of some military friend of Masefield who pointed out that the artillery has some use for intelligence, and that it is possible to become a cadet gunner and get a commission if you can do leading business.

On Thursday I was at the Opera, and found myself between the acts in a very animated discussion of your and his affairs in Lady Cunard's box. It seems that Lady C. is an old friend of his idol. This was the first time I heard the matter talked about with any knowledge of who she is. Lady C. is evidently attached to her rather affectionately, so, if you meet her, be generous if anything is said about her.

We managed to restore Harley's tone to some extent here – he stayed mostly with us – but the strain of the situation has not been doing him any good; and how you stand it I dont know. He has been all these months alone in Williamstown, a little university town in New Hampshire, with all communications cut off, waiting for that divorce. Finally it got on his nerves, and he could not work, and came back to this soldiering slavery. You, meanwhile, have been working off your anguish in public appearances which have been, by all accounts, unusually glorious. But you cant have been much happier than he. Why not make an end of it and set him free before you both suffer so long that the hatred this sort of relation engenders becomes a permanent condition? Any adept yogi will tell you that if you once concentrate on a particular state of the soul completely for ninety minutes it will become part of your consciousness for the rest of your life. Well, do you want your whole life to be a repetition of the last six months? If he were bound, and you free, there might at least be vengeance in it. But your slavery is worse than his, because he can stand loneliness much better.

It is frightful to meet you flitting round the Terrace in the moonlight like a beautiful ghost, answering in unreal far-away whispers when you are spoken to, until finally one runs away from you in terror, partly terror of the ghost, partly terror of being provoked into laying violent hands on you and convincing you that you are flesh and blood still until you are black and blue.

People will presently get tired of the affair and avoid you and Harley like the plague; and serve you right! Is any man, or any woman, worth making such a fuss about? What has become of our nobility? I shall end by feeling like a dog barking at three cats on the roof. These, too, are the best years of your life. However, I know it is no use *my* talking. Go on tormenting one another, just as the rest are killing one another in France; it is the nature of the human animal. I will go on with my play and leave you all to your devilments.

G. B. S.

The letter shows that the situation between Barker and Lillah was being talked about, which was only to be expected, though intolerable to them both. As he was compelled to do, Barker had returned, and had chosen to enlist in the Royal Horse Artillery; but he loathed the Army, and could not reconcile himself to the life it imposed upon him, so he applied for a commission, and was admitted to the R.G.A. Cadet School at Trowbridge in Wiltshire. While there he wrote to Gilbert Murray:

I never thanked you for subscribing to my education – It was a good thing you weren't asked if I could do sums and expected to reply truthfully – for the mathematics here – I suppose they are simple enough to Senior Wranglers. But to me!! However, I struggle on and *may* not be sent with ignominy back to the ranks. And I suppose I am serving my country – my country is at least teaching me some interesting things – quite unconnected with gunnery. I would there were a chance of seeing you all.

He wrote a sketch of life in the Cadet School entitled *Picket*, which remains unpublished. His week-end leaves were spent with the Shaws at Ayot or in Barrie's flat in London, and he was concerned to get leave to do some lecturing in America. Only part of his training as a cadet was completed, for in October, with the help of his friend, Maggie Ponsonby, he was given a commission on the General List for the purpose of special duties in the Intelligence.

Shaw wrote another letter to Lillah:

10 Adelphi Terrace, W.C.
24th Nov. 1916.

My dear Lillah,

I wish you would talk to me a little about your domestic affairs, as if I have to hear much more of them from the other side only, I shall certainly be driven mad. You must not write about them; and I suppose I mustnt either.

Put it that I only want to have a comedy scene with you; why shouldnt you play one to amuse me? I meet all the other people and know what they think; but it is Lillah here and Lillah there, and Lillah thinks that, and Lillah means the other; and all the time I have no notion what you are really like.

I am going down to Ayot tomorrow afternoon; and Harley will spend Sunday there, raging because the world does not instantly adapt itself to his requirements, and because if nothing happens before the end of next week, he will have to go off to America to lecture and thereby make it impossible for anything to happen for another six months. I know of course all that has passed; and how you would like to have your affairs arranged; and if I could bring that arrangement about I would play for it vigorously; but I cannot satisfy myself that it is possible; and I dont know why you believe it to be possible. I wish you would tell me why, or open my eyes if I am misinformed on any point.

I tried to get at you through A.E.D. but he very wisely will not take the responsibility of advising you. Then I heard that you had consented to see Barrie, and had stood that shy soul on his head. Also you appear

to be on speaking terms with Masefield and Galsworthy but they do not
get much out of you.   Why not have a go at me? you know that neither
of us can hold our tongues when once we get talking; and something
may come of it – something better than this exasperating uncertainty.
It is all very well to trample on me through the telephone and say you
have nothing to say to me and dont want to see me – which *must* be a
most frightful lie; we have never really been sorry to see one another –
but if I can get face to face with you you can trample away for half an
hour; I am sure to get something out of you in the end.

ever,
G. B. S.

All the past year there had been no decision from Lillah.   She was
determined not to give way, being convinced that all would come right;
but it was not to be.   At last she listened to Barrie's sage counsel and
allowed him to take her to Sir George Lewis.   On the latter's advice, she
agreed to do what Barker demanded.   Thus proceedings for restitution
of conjugal rights were taken in December, and Barker was able to go
off to America with that welcome knowledge.   After the necessary interval, a petition for divorce was presented, and on 19 April 1917 a decree
absolute was made.   Barker covenanted to pay Lillah £600 a year for
her life, an amount subsequently increased to £650 a year.   This annuity
was regularly paid during his lifetime, and after his death was redeemed
for a lump sum paid out of his estate.

All the time before the divorce, Lillah and Barker had not met except
for the one interview, and they never met again or had any further
direct communication with each other.   She sold the lease of Court
Lodge in 1917 and went back to the flat in Adelphi Terrace.

*

Before Barker (in the Intelligence) left for America in January 1917,
he had been discussing with Galsworthy the possibility of producing *The
Fugitive* in New York.   On 13 February at the Little Theatre there, under
the direction of Winthrop Ames, his adaptation of Stevenson and
Osbourne's *The Wrong Box* was performed under the title of *The Morris
Dance*.   Barker made the play open at the second chapter of the novel,
where the characters are discovered in Bournemouth lodgings.   There
are four acts and ten scenes with some black-outs.   The fantasy no doubt
appealed to Barker, but the quality of the novel is in its story-telling and
its feature is the plot.   He made little of it, and the piece rightly remains
unpublished.   The play opens with a characteristic apologetic prologue.
The Manager is made to appear before the curtain, when he is challenged
by a member of the audience, who argues with him about the play to be
seen, and the Manager than reads the following prepared statement:

The functions of the theatre are manifold. Grant it therefore the very widest scope for their exercise. It is the mission of tragedy, by symbolic means, to make the things of life and death more real to us than in the actual body of them they can ever be. Allow then to the spirit of farce an equal liberty with sacred things because of the very sense of reality it tries to give to you, of release from the moral responsibility of the work-a-day world.

He then visited Chicago, Los Angeles, San Francisco, and other places, and was back in New York at the end of March.

In America Barker had some correspondence with Shaw about the production of the latter's plays there. Shaw sent him news about Lillah, and told him that " there are serious official leanings towards an attempt to convince the neutrals of Europe that we can outdo Reinhardt when it comes to high art by sending out a specimen of our best, and that it is understood for a wonder that this conviction cannot be carried out by the admirers of Reinhardt or by Sir H.T.". He urged Barker to take the job if he were asked. In fact, nothing came of the idea. When he came back to London and was kept at office work in the Intelligence, he continued to write daily to Helen and she to him. She expressed her abhorrence of Shaw, and on 24 November she related how she threw A.E.'s book, *The National Being*, which Barker had sent her, into the fire because of his praise of Germany.

A letter written by Barker to Gilbert Murray on the subject of children performing in the theatre deserves to interrupt the narrative :

Nov. 10th, 1917.
You touch me very nearly on this point. I have always disagreed with the general reforming run of opinion that theatre life is bad for children. The right sort of theatre life would, I am convinced, be very good, and a valuable part of education. But of course eight or twelve performances a week is the wrong sort of life either for children or grown-ups. It makes it even worse when children are let in for that, and made to carry on with some pretence of schooling in between times. The Pantomime School, for instance, at Drury Lane is an absolute scandal.

What I would like to see would be children forbidden to appear in any theatre for more than a certain number of hours and on a certain number of days per week – this plan casting forward to a time when repertory will come to its own, and acting be a civilized life.

I would also like to see no child allowed to be employed unless he belonged to a dramatic school, that is to say, I would like to see a law which would compel the bringing into existence of some institute for training children who adopted (for their childhood, and might intend possibly to adopt for their adulthood) acting as a profession. Their whole education could be balanced in this direction and appearances at the theatre form a normal part of it.

(Isadora Duncan and Margaret Morris did really institute something of the sort, and I should say that apart from some of its blithersomeness Isadora's training was not a bad one. Certainly she has never driven the children to death.)

But failing some sort of regulation of this kind, I would willingly see everybody under fourteen or fifteen absolutely forbidden to appear professionally on the stage. It would be a great nuisance in a way but you will remember that I did *The Midsummer-Night's Dream* practically without children (I only had five): and *The Blue Bird*, of all plays in the world, was performed in Moscow without any children at all. For in Russia (at any rate in Moscow) they are forbidden to appear.

In November, Helen and Archer Huntington went to France. Their divorce was then arranged, she having apparently the same difficulty with Archer as Barker had been having with Lillah. Her petition against him for desertion was, however, presented in Paris in March 1918, and in due course was completed. Archer continued to be very good to her. When these divorces were first contemplated in 1915, Helen had told Barker she had a small income, and she had said to him that he could remain in New York producing plays there; but Archer settled a substantial income upon her out of his millions.

*

At this point something must be said about the Huntingtons. Archer Milton Huntington was the son of Collis Potter Huntington, who started business in the hardware trade, went to California, and made a mighty fortune in railway finance; he died in 1900 worth many millions. A large part of his fortune was left to his son, Archer Milton Huntington. His nephew, Henry E. Huntington, who was associated with him in his financial business, founded the Henry E. Huntington Library at San Marino, near Pasadena, California. Archer Milton Huntington was born in New York City on 10 March 1870. He was never a business man, but was deeply interested in Spanish art, and founded the Hispanic Society of America in memory of his father. He is described as a big, kindly, gentle man, and his treatment of Helen shows him to have been generous. In 1898 he published *A Notebook in Northern Spain* after a visit there, and several books of poems. He has received honorary degrees from American and Spanish universities.

On 6 August 1895 at St. George's, Hanover Square, Archer married Helen Gates Criss, described in the register as " single and unmarried ". His father signed the register, also Prinz Franz Hatzfeldt Wildenburg and Francis Lathrop. Helen was the daughter of Isaac Gates, born at Beaver Dam, Wisconsin. She had a happy childhood and at three years of age went to live with her parents at Elizabeth, near New York. Her mother

llen, lived to a great age and wrote little poems for magazines to the last.
Vhile still young, Helen married a salesman in a Roman Catholic book-
hop in New York, much older than herself, named Criss, who wrote
oems and other pieces, and aroused her ambitions as a writer; she said
hat she had not had a happy life with him. They had a daughter,
rought up a Roman Catholic. It seems that in the early 'nineties Archer
Iuntington intended to join a tour to the Greek Islands, and Helen's
husband applied to go with him as secretary, as he was interested in art
esearch. Archer asked him to call; at the interview Helen accompanied
er husband, and was invited to go with him at Archer's expense on the
our. Afterwards Helen divorced her husband. Then she and Hunting-
on came to London to be married; they went to Spain for their honey-
hoon, and on their way took part in the presentation to the city of
aris by Joseph Pulitzer, proprietor of the *New York World*, of a piece of
culpture celebrating the meeting of Washington and Lafayette, which
ad been executed by Bartholdi and was erected in a square named the
lace des Etats-Unis.

★

Barker and Helen Huntington were married in London on 31 July 1918
King's Weigh House Chapel, Duke Street, Grosvenor Square, accord-
g to the rites and ceremonies of the Congregationalists, in the presence
f the Wheelers and C. D. Medley. Helen described herself as an
author ", gave her age as forty-three, and added Edwin to her father's
ame, describing him as a " railway director ". Barker gave his age as
orty, though he was four months off that number of years; he was still
the Intelligence, and did not get his release from the Army until early
the following year.

Helen was small, slight, and always exquisitely dressed and made-up.
he was undoubtedly an introvert, a complete contrast to Lillah. No
oubt she appealed to the still high-spirited though disappointed Barker
ecause of her intellectual abilities as an author. There can be no doubt
hat he had a genuine and deep attachment to her. Through her con-
derable fortune, she gave him the freedom to do the work he most
vanted to do – to write plays and criticism – but she cut him off from his
heatrical friends and ended his intimacy with Shaw.

The latter did, indeed, write to his friend the month after his second
harriage a friendly if admonishing letter, saying:

would be convenient occasionally to know something about you. I
urmise that you are married; but it is only a surmise. It is desirable
hat your friends should be in a position to make a positive affirmation on
he subject. An affectation of ecstasy so continuous as to make you forget
l such worldly considerations is ridiculous at your age. So just send

along any information that ought to be public, however briefly. I have
refrained, with an exaggerated delicacy, from asking you questions for a
year or so. Now I do ask them bluntly. People ask me questions; and
there is not the same reason for not meeting them with a mystery that
there was formerly for not giving them too much information.

But there was to be little friendship between them.

*

The severance of her marriage with Barker was a disaster for Lillah.
She had to continue her work on the stage, but did so mechanically.
She had a season at the Kingsway, but could not work. To cheer her up
Shaw wrote and rehearsed *Annajanska*, which was included in the variety
programme at the Coliseum in 1918. Her last theatrical engagements
were with Matheson Lang in *The Wandering Jew* in 1920 and *Blood and
Sand* the year after, when she virtually left the stage. She was then
forty-six. She married on 27 March 1920 at Marylebone Presbyterian
Church, Frederick William Keeble, a distinguished biologist. The
register was signed by H. H. Asquith and her mother. She then entered
upon a new life, which proved to be a happy one. Although she devoted
herself to poetry-reading with John Masefield, and took a profound
interest in poetic drama in general, it was upon the art of acting as she
understood it, for which she had disciplined her life, that her heart was set.
Yet that was now all over. She maintained her friendship with the
Shaws, the Galsworthys, the Masefields, Barrie, and others, but hence-
forward she lived in poetry and gardening, sharing the life of her scientist
husband. He was knighted in 1922 and died in October 1952 at the age
of eighty-two. On his knighthood Arnold Bennett wrote to Lillah:

13 July 1922

My sweet Lillah,
    . . . it does me good to see a decent title for once. After all, it isn'
he who ought to be congratulated but the order of knights bachelor. So
I'm damned if I will congratulate him.

To complete the story of Lillah in relation to Barker, it is necessary to
say something about her memoirs, *Myself and My Friends*, published in
1933. The writing of that book no doubt presented difficulties. Most
serious, however, was the difficulty created by the Foreword written by
Bernard Shaw, for he chose to tell the story of the breakdown of her
marriage with Barker. The publisher, Thornton Butterworth, became
disturbed when he received Shaw's manuscript, and took a copy of it
with the proofs of the book to Barker's solicitor for advice. Naturally
the solicitor refused to advise him, but on reading Shaw's contribution
he said that in his opinion Barker would take all means to prevent it

publication. A copy of the Foreword, together with the proofs, was then sent to Barker in Paris, who went in haste to Ayot to see Shaw. Barker was very angry, and it was a painful interview. In the end, a new Foreword entitled " An Aside " was substituted. Barker had made it clear that there should be no reference whatever to himself anywhere in the book. With every mention of Barker, direct or indirect, eliminated, Lillah thought the book should not be published, and would have no more to do with it; but her husband did not agree and took over the book to re-write it, which he did thoroughly. Thus it came about that nothing at all was said in it of Barker's connection with the Court Theatre, or with the Shakespeare productions at the Savoy; even the fact that he and Lillah were married was omitted. In the revised version there was this reference to him:

When I was touring with Ben Greet in 1895 there was a young man who played Paris to my Juliet. I met him again at the Court Theatre in 1905. In April 1906 we were married.

But even that was cut out, for Barker finally demanded that nothing should be said of him at all.

WRITER

THERE can be no doubt that Granville Barker's natural bent from his earliest years was to be a writer not only because in his youth the profession of actor was looked down upon, while that of writer was esteemed : he had the urge to write. In fact, he started writing very early, chiefly playwriting, as we have seen, one of his first works being an attempt at dramatic verse. He never ceased to write, for his desk was a refuge when he was not wanted in or wearied of the theatre. He worked at many plays, made experiments in fiction, wrote lectures, and finished as a leading Shakespeare critic of his day. Writers were his most intimate early friends, Gilbert Murray, Archer, Barrie, Galsworthy, Wells, and, above all, Bernard Shaw.

Although his second marriage enabled him to follow his bent, and despite the fact that his second wife was against his stage connections, he did in fact do some producing up to a few years before his death, and his writing consisted of plays or other work directly concerned with the theatre. Helen had made it clear that she wanted nothing to do with Shaw, but the latter did, however, invite them shortly after their marriage, in December 1918, to a reading of part of his new play, *Back to Methuselah!* They went, and, in a reply to a letter from Barker, Shaw confessed that he was tired out when he read it, the Brothers Barnabas had " never " he said, " seemed quite as tedious before ", adding : " It was rather hard on Helen to have such a depressing beginning of my play-reading."

At this time Barker seems to have had some idea of entering into politics as an advanced radical, and making a political career, but he received little encouragement, and gave up the idea. He was, indeed, a conservative at heart and might have been called a liberal-conservative. He now hyphenated his name, and thereafter wished to be known as " Granville-Barker ". It may also be noted that both he and Helen had used in their correspondence before their marriage and afterwards placed on their books the symbol as shown on p. 193.

Before Barker was free from the Intelligence, he had been asked to produce Byron's *Manfred* at Drury Lane, in co-operation with Sir Thomas Beecham, for a Byron festival, with Charles Ricketts doing the settings and costumes. But nothing came of it. On 20 February 1919 *The Times* published an article entitled " Reconstruction in the Theatre ",

hich showed him occupied with the theatre, though turning in a new
rection.

As the article is of some importance in Barker's life, it deserves atten-
on. Its sub-title was "Up from the Soil", which suggests what was in

The symbol used by the Barkers on their books

ie writer's mind. He referred to "enterprise which may transcend the
:ofessional theatre altogether . . . bands of semi-amateur players, who
|uip themselves, nevertheless, very professionally, work constantly and
riously, the product of their work being considerable in quality and
iantity too ". He went on:

ow, if the spread of such a movement here is only a sign that the English
:ople are inclining once again to look upon the drama less as a pur-
asable show and more as a pastime, in which they themselves can be
tive – if, for instance, a time is in sight when a band of players will be
garized in a village, or small town, or among a set of young men and
omen, much as a cricket team is organized now, and be looked on no
ore strangely – the movement is one to be encouraged.

e was right, for the amateur dramatic movement, a spontaneous growth,
as becoming one of the most important cultural elements in the country.
iggestions were made for helping such enterprises: (1) a building is
quired, (2) there should be a "nucleus of professional help", and
) the work should be connected with the educational life of the district.
hen he emphasized the essential values of amateur drama to the com-
unity: that the people themselves take part, and that the art of acting
iould be understood to be, in externals, the art of public manners and,
. essentials, the art of self-expression. He went further, and urged the
tablishment in our universities of "something like a Faculty of Personal
xpression, which would have within its ken the neglected arts of
ietoric, dialectic oratory, the beauty of the spoken language, and would
ke into account certain aspects of music and even of dancing ". He
included by saying:

7ithout the power of expression, all knowledge is ineffective. It may be
ierely depressing to find an educated individual remain half-articulate;
it an inarticulate community should alarm us. For we are committed

to democracy. If its expression is to be limited to the retention or dis
missal of a few hundred bureaucrats by the periodical making of crosse
on ballot-papers, it seems likely that from time to time the people will b
revenged on that sham by expressing themselves catastrophically, i
strikes, in revolution. We must have subtler methods, a living State c
fully articulate human beings from whose very diversity can best b
moulded the concord of accepted purposes.

What adds significance to the above article is that in the autumn of th
previous year Geoffrey Whitworth had hit on the idea of forming th
British Drama League, inspired to some extent by the Drama League c
America, established as long ago as 1910. Whitworth got into touc
with Barker, who, when the League was formed in July 1919, becam
chairman of its council. This new organization promised to provide a
outlet for Barker's energies, and he threw himself into its work wit
zeal. He presided at a conference at Stratford-on-Avon in Augus
during the Shakespeare Festival, and a letter to Gilbert Murray writte
from Hyde Park Place refers to his new interest:

                                                              24.7.19
On Tuesday, Aug. 19, at 3 p.m. I take the chair and the Conference confer
on "Dramatic art in National Life and the case for a British Dram
League"!!!
Ellen Terry speaks. Will you? The B.D.L. thinks you are mor
likely to if I ask you. They are in a hurry to know because of printing
wherefore this telegram form to Geoffrey Whitworth is enclosed.
Do – if you are not absolutely set against it. For then either we migh
pick you up in a car in Oxford and take you to Stratford – or better – i
you – and Lady Mary if she could – would spend a night with us some
where near Stratford (I think we'll stay at Leamington or Warwick
we could have personal talk of the musical glasses (Shakespeare barred!)
As a matter of fact, we are coming you-wards to-morrow – we loo
at houses beyond Oxford and shall probably pass a night there – at th
Randolph. But I expect you may be out of Oxford anyhow.

Characteristically Barker drew up an elaborate series of committees whicl
were set up by the League to cover every branch of theatrical work; o
a number of these committees he served. He was a first-rate committe
man in the sense that he saw the point at once, but he had not mucl
patience with those who did not pick the matter up as quickly as he. He
lectured for the League throughout the country. The acuteness tha
Barker exhibited in ordinary affairs was that of a producer who saw how
thing should be said or done, and without his energy, quick mind
practical sense, and reputation the British Drama League would hardl
have become so well established. Support was readily offered, becaus
of him.

The Theatre of the Future — ④

Orlando.... Ex-Seminarist Smith
Rosalind ... Ex-Seminarist Robinson

II The Theatre of the Future: Orlando . . . Ex-seminarist Smith, Rosalind . . . Ex-
minarist Robinson. One of six unpublished cartoons by Max Beerbohm for Granville Barker's
The Exemplary Theatre

XLIII Helen Granville-Barker: a reproduction of a photograph Granville
Barker kept on the mantelshelf of his Paris library. It probably shows
Helen as she was at the time of her second marriage (1895) or earlier. No
other photograph of her is known

Only gradually did the League become the organ of the amateur dramatic movement, however, for while amateurs were regarded as a means of spreading interest in the theatre, it was the professional theatre with which it was at first most concerned. But its most substantial support came from amateur dramatic societies, no less than 700 affiliating to it the first year, so that it was inevitable that amateur interests should predominate. As the idea of the National Theatre was especially intended to be supported, Barker considered the League's main work to be to create an audience for that theatre.

Some years later he took an active interest in the preparation of the report by the Adult Education Committee of the Board of Education on *The Drama in Adult Education*, published in 1926. The place of drama in education, including especially the universities, was the phase of amateur drama Barker found to possess the greatest importance. His work for the League gradually diminished, however, and he retired from its chairmanship.

*

To resume the narrative, it is necessary to go back a few years, when, in the spring of 1920, the Barkers were looking for a country house. Helen favoured South Devon, to be as far from the London theatre as possible, and they found a home near Honiton, in a seventeenth-century house called Netherton Hall, at Colyton, a little market town in the valley of the River Axe. A letter written from Sidmouth to Gilbert Murray comes here:

9.4.20.

How are you all? Well, I hope. We are here – working in the mornings and in the afternoons trying to get into our home (a long job) and in the evenings reading Zimmern's *Greek Commonwealth* and other improving books. When we came the other night to the Funeral speech – well, I felt you must be right about them currant-growers after all. (Lord, perhaps they didn't grow currants then – Oh I ought to have been at Oxford. But I should have disgraced you!) Our affectionate regards.

Another letter to Murray while they were waiting to get into their house follows:

18.6.20.

It is a darned shame to bother you when you are teaching Oxford Greek and trying to make the League of Nations go. But any other Professor will turn me down upon this point without – not even a second thought – not a first, I feel sure; and you may find some wicked delight in not doing so – and – in short I always do bother you about such things.

When Tyndall (I can't get at books here, but I presume it was Tyndall

o

– Tyndale – not the late scientific gent) translated that passage in I Corin
thians, " Behold I tell (or better ' show') you a Mystery . . ." did he –
could he have had in mind that, as he had the next ticklish piece of meta
physics to explain, far the best way to make people understand it would b
to exhibit it to them in the form of a mystery-play? I do not sugges
that he had a prophetic vision of a divine harlequinade in which we shoul
all be changed in the twinkling of an eye. But if the word connated an
connection with drama at all, I could make a telling point of it in a ver
" high-class " book, Sir, that I am now up to upon the Theatre.

Forgive me – and if necessary tell a secretary to say " NO ". We sen
our affectionate homage. We wish we saw you sometimes. You
won't be in London June 23–26? No. We shall.

The book on which he was working was *The Exemplary Theatre*. Th
Barkers got into Netherton Hall in the summer. There Barker lived as
country gentleman, with liveried servants and some splendour. Few
people connected with the professional theatre were invited, thoug
Archer came occasionally, and the Whitworths; Gilbert Murray never
The car would be sent over to Dorchester for Thomas Hardy frequently
George Moore dropped in now and then for a week-end, and, although h
said, " I have never made a woman angry in my life. I have made me
angry – but never a woman," he sometimes made Helen very angry, no
so much because of his famous naughty stories, which she did not like
as for his free use, when in the mood, of forbidden words. So when th
county came to tea on Sunday afternoons, he was sent to his room t
have tea by himself, to prevent the risk of shocking the ladies.

Barker wrote to his Austrian friend, Rudolph Kommer, now again i
London, from Netherton Hall on 27 September:

I am now quite un-get-at-able you see. (The only way I have found .
am ever to do any work.)

*

We have seen that Barker was interested in translations of plays, i
which he invariably worked with someone else, as in the versions o
Schnitzler with Dr. C. E. Wheeler, and soon after his second marriage h
translated a piece from the French by Sacha Guitry, *Deburau* (though with
whom I do not know; perhaps with little help, for he had a fair knowledge of French). This was commissioned by C. B. Cochran, and first
performed at the Belasco Theatre, New York, on 23 December 1920,
afterwards on 3 November 1921 at the Ambassador's Theatre, London,
with Robert Loraine in the name part, and published the same year. This
comic play in verse about the stage is slight but agreeable, and raise
questions about translations which Barker touched upon in a brie
preface, in which he said that " the final effect to be made in the theatre "

has to be put by the translator before all else. He claimed that he had kept to every detail of Guitry's dialogue, and declared that cutting was indefensible, " for the play is too soon impoverished and its very structure weakened ". Barker's version is gay, light-hearted, and highly readable.

As Helen had acquired a knowledge of Spanish, due to Archer Huntington's interest in Spanish art, it was not surprising that the Barkers turned their attention to Spanish drama, and that between them they made a version of the popular G. Martinez Sierra's *The Romantic Young Lady*, which was produced by him (associating Helen as co-producer) at the Royalty Theatre in December 1920. This was a delightful piece of work in writing and production, and showed the producer's hand to be as skilful as ever. There was much in the writing of Martinez Sierra that appealed to Barker, for he wrote about contemporary life with the poetic lightness, the innocence, the gaiety and vitality of spirit that Barker most admired. Barker could make the characters and dialogue his own. The characters are well outlined, as in his own plays, and the dialogue is a subtle blending of simple words that makes a dramatic whole of great delicacy. The success of this piece led to the completion of versions of three other plays by the same writer, and a fourth later, followed by versions of eight comedies by the brothers Quintero, published in two volumes in 1927 and 1932. These were considerable achievements, for they read as original works.

*

Before his marriage to Helen, Barker had entered into a contract to produce Maurice Maeterlinck's sequel to *The Blue Bird*, entitled *The Betrothal*, which was rehearsed at the end of 1920, the first performance taking place on 8 January 1921 at the Gaiety Theatre, with the beautiful Gladys Cooper as the veiled bride (her beauty taken for granted) and Winifred Emery as a fairy. " Spectacularly, the piece stands outside the pale of criticism ", said the *Daily Telegraph*. Barker was called for insistently at the fall of the curtain, but did not appear, though the audience demonstrated for a quarter of an hour. This was his last full-scale production on the London stage. Miss Cooper writes of him in her intimate biography, *Without Veils*, over thirty years later :

I can see him now, on the stage at the Gaiety . . . walking away from an actress who couldn't do what she was told, and saying under his breath : " May God forgive that woman ; I never can."

All eyes were on the great man and everything he said was taken to heart. But he made it clear to everyone that he had left the theatre, so that thereafter he did no more than overlook the production of his own plays, when he usually came to London to give a hand. The fact that he should have given his attention to this highly sentimental piece of commercial theatricality, staged by George Grossmith and Edward Laurillard in their home of musical comedy, puzzled his admirers. Yet the production was a marked popular success. It was so much liked that a third matinée had to be put on each week to meet the demand. Charles Ricketts was responsible for the greatly praised costumes and settings and, with a large cast, money was spent like water. The run of the play was interfered with by a coalmining lock-out, and it ended somewhat suddenly early in April. It was a time of economic unrest, growing unemployment, the rebellion in Ireland, *The Beggar's Opera*, and frivolity. The intention was to revive the piece as a regular Christmas entertainment, but it was not done. It is doubtful if this last effort added to Barker's reputation. Whether it did or not, Barker in his Devonshire home was devoting himself to a large programme of writing. In a letter to Kommer he wrote:

21.3.21

The world is still pretty sick, isn't it? A long and wearisome convalescence to face – and I only hope it is one. I am trying to write plays – but neither sick ones nor convalescent ones satisfy me – and yet one should not be out of the world.

The Barkers went to the Salzburg Festival in August, and afterwards he wrote from Flims-Waldhaus, Switzerland, to Kommer at Salzburg, where the latter was working for Max Reinhardt:

22 Aug

My regards to M.R.   And will you take an opportunity to tell him from me what a pleasure it was to me to see him after these many years, and to visit him in his kingdom.

Waste had been licensed in 1920, when H. M. Harwood intended to produce it at the Ambassadors, but the production did not come off. When Shaw's *Back to Methuselah* was published, Barker wrote to his old friend at once:

7.2.21

After cogitation – I had better have been able to read it more carefully – I don't find I've anything very notable to say about the new Gulliver.
   I am very interested in the Swift parallel.   If Swift had had your diet – or you his!   If he had had Dickens, Blake, and Mozart behind instead of before him ——
   Part I. I'll confess leaves me cold.
   Part II. Exhilarates me.
   Part III. I hate. You seem to me to be kicking the wretched Asquith-

George long after he is spiritually dead, but rather it is true as if you were a fellow soul in torment trying to escape and kicking viciously because you can't. But it is all rather a vacuum to me – an empty space (philosophically) between the before and after.

Part IV. I like best of all. Perhaps because *I* am an elderly gentleman – was born one. But besides that the ingredients the satire the fantasy and the rest seem to me better mixed. The whole thing balances better dramatically.

Part V. is Gulliver in excelsis. But it raises one question – How far can one use pure satire in the theatre? For satire scarifies humanity. The theatre uses it as a medium and must therefore be tender to it. Now in part V it is quite possible that the automata would be the most moving and appealing figures, leaving the others – what? How do you practically proceed to adjust your scale when you are using living actors – i.e. automata all of them? If you degrade the token and you falsify your case – and if you don't ———!

One other point. Why do I so loathe the " newly born "? Why does she strike in me like a bit of bad Stravinsky in the midst of a Mozart symphony? Is it because – far from being an " all Shaw " writer as the common cant goes, you are a conscientious observer of men's insides – so that when you do observe wrong – or merely, rather, observe the outside the result is appalling you must so loathe the newly born (your tradition of manners not being hers. I did not know your mother for nothing – though you may have debauched them truckling insults to your English tyrants) that you just write down the common Stravinsky scream you hear – You don't look inside her – knowing perhaps it would be waste of time. But neither do you pass her through your consciousness. That would make her " all of a piece " artistically. I can't surely suggest the right solution, but I know there is something wrong. And I believe Part V should be " all of a piece ". As it has to be " de-humanized " and yet is to be played by human beings it perhaps had better be de-characterized. Perfect formality may be dramatically speaking what it will need.

I am ploughing slowly through my theatre book – which I wish I had never touched – I am unskilful in such matters.

Whether we shall drive the workmen out before they drive us crazy is still a question.

Shaw's reply to this letter does not survive. The book referred to by Barker was *The Exemplary Theatre*, which he regarded as his most important work, in which he discusses the function and organization of the theatre and the place he considered it should have in society. It is a plea for the National Theatre, made, however, with a divided mind; for he was drawn two ways – to the theatre and from it. All the same, it is an eloquent plea the force of which does not diminish. William Archer, who was sent the proofs, proved his friendship by careful reading, and by the ample notes he made for Barker. Archer, of course, was

highly critical, and argued for the unintellectual drama against his friend.
In a letter dated 7 January 1922, he said of the opening dialogue between
" The Man of the Theatre " and the Minister of Education :

I think your Man of the Theatre is too resolutely highbrowed. He
does not sufficiently admit and stand up for the function of even the best
theatre as a place – occasionally and even frequently – of mere harmless,
unpretending recreation. We can't always be listening to Bach – there
is also a time for Offenbach, that is his misfortune, not his merit, and he
oughtn't to make it a law and an ideal for others. . . . Don't say that my
plea for the Average Human Being is suggested by the fact that I myself
can only write trivial plays. I have stood up for the theatre as a place
which ought sometimes (and frequently) to be devoted to pure recreation
ever since I began to stand up for anything – forty years before I dreamt of
writing plays. Such is the inferiority of my taste that, much as I should
like to have written *Waste*, I'm not sure that I wouldn't rather have
written *The White-headed Boy* – and I'm quite sure that I'd rather have
written *As You Like It* than *Coriolanus*.

There was some perversity in this, especially as Barker was not averse
to mere entertainment. Archer must have realized it, for in another
letter five days later he praises the book highly : ". . . it is extraordinarily
good ".

A set of proofs was sent to Bernard Shaw, but what his comments were
I do not know. Barker and Shaw were not then in direct communication, but it is worth while noting that Barker added to p. 135 of the book,
on which he was comparing Shaw's plays with Tchekov's, the following
sentence not in the original page-proof :

And though we class his [Shaw's] plays mostly as modern comedy the
call primarily for heroic treatment.

A set of proofs went also to Max Beerbohm, who responded by a
series of five cartoons illustrating " the theatre of the future ". The first
showed " The Managing Director addressing the cast on the prior importance of civic consciousness ", a heavily-brained old gentleman
with a long white beard, three pairs of glasses, and Barker's nose. No. 2,
" The Call-boy ", an excessively large-headed, spectacled boy. No. 3,
" The Acting Manager (front of house) ", a long-haired, spectacled,
bearded, top-hatted Chadband. No. 4, " Ex-seminarist Smith and Ex-
seminarist Robinson ", as Orlando and Rosalind, respectively, each very
high-browed, solemn, spectacled creatures staring at each other. No. 5
" The Public ", a blank. All the characters depicted had Barker's nose.
Max also sent some verses :

To H.G.B.

The Theatre's in a parlous state,
    I readily admit;
It almost is exanimate –
    But then, when *wasn't* it?
It always *was*, will always be;
    God has decreed it so.
Canst thou rescind His grim decree?
    O, my dear Harley, No!

In Shakespeare's and in Marlowe's day
    In Congreve's, in Racine's.
The wretched Theatre murmured " I'm
    One of the Might-Have-Beens! "
" O May-Be-Yet! " the critics cried,
    " We'll teach you how to grow! "
And were their fond hopes gratified?
    O, my dear Harley, No!

The Theatre is Exemplary,
    Now as in other ages,
Of all a Theatre shouldn't be –
    Of all that most enrages
Right-thinking men like you and me
    And plunges us in woe . . .
Mightn't perhaps the L.C.C. –
    O, my dear Harley, No!

Shall cubits come by taking thought,
    And Drama gain her soul
By learning what she doubtless ought
    From dear old Mr. Poel?
Shall syllabi and seminars
    And blackboards all in a row
Somehow uplift us to the stars?
    O, my dear Harley, No!

        Max, Rapallo, March 1922.

On his own copy of the proof Max wrote, referring to the second stanza :

    I'd meant to write in my MS.
        " Time ", and wrote " day ", it seems.
    This error fills me with distress
        And haunts me in my dreams.
    A lover I'm of chime of rhyme
        And to vers libre a foe, –
    Shall such a man rhyme " day " with " I'm "?
        O, my dear Harley, No!

        Max, Rapallo, December 1922.

Barker had two copies of the proofs bound with the verses and photographic copies of the cartoons, sending one to Max, keeping the other himself.

*

At this point we are reminded of *Conversations in Ebury Street*, published by George Moore in 1924, in which there is a chapter devoted to a real or imaginary conversation with Barker, " a man of the eighteenth century ", Moore flatteringly termed him. After references to the plays and Moore's own plays, the conversation turned to the National Theatre idea and Barker's *The Exemplary Theatre*, when Moore attacked Barker for placing his argument for the National Theatre " on the educational advantage thereof . . . an altogether false basis ". They go on to other subjects, but, as the conversation is mainly Moore's it need not detain us, excellent as it is.

Among the plays discussed with George Moore was *The Secret Life*, upon which Barker had been at work since 1919. He completed it in 1922 and published it the following year. Moore thought it his best play. It is, indeed, a striking work, one of the most beautifully written plays of the present century. It has thirteen characters, and eleven scenes in three acts, and is about a politician, Evan Strowde, who goes off during a general election to see a young woman in America, who in fact has died (though he does not know it) before he starts. The short opening scene introduces the characters; at first only their voices are heard, a risky device, which Barker undoubtedly saw how to stage, but the entire play has a hidden and secret theme, hence the title. It is hidden because, in fact, the dramatist is in doubt, a state of mind in which his leading character remains throughout the play. Strowde admits that whenever a thought was precious to him he hid it away. He says to his sister :

. . . you have never found that the whole world's turmoil is but a reflection of the anarchy of your own heart?
No.
That's where we differ then.

A little later he asks :

Have you never gone adventuring . . . dear good Eleanor . . . in your secret heart?

But she does not answer the question. Two other characters are later discussing Strowde :

I want to find out how it is he has failed?

Has he failed, then?

Yes . . . and you'll have to comfort him for it if you marry him.

The same two speakers conclude the scene, the girl, who afterwards dies, saying :

But mind your prayers, Oliver. For innermost prayers are answered. . . . They must be . . . and in mockery sometimes.

Strowde when speaking to Oliver, who is his illegitimate but unacknowledged son, says :

I lived half my life in the happiness . . . and unhappiness . . . of a vision. One fine day I find that the world I'm living in is nothing like the idea of the world I've been living by.

There can be no doubt that the lines I have quoted are to be applied to Barker himself, and I think the play yields its interest only when read in its application to the dramatist's own problem. In that sense it is of immense interest; but despite the quality of its writing, it is a disappointment. Barker did not expect it to be performed. When William Archer read it, he wrote to the author :

. . . in this play you seem to be drifting away from, not towards the theatre that is understanded by the people – even the fairly intelligent people.

Barker replied :

I protest I never have – I cannot – write an unactable play, it would be against nature, against second nature, anyhow; I act it as I write it. But there is no English company of actors so trained to interpret thought and the less crude emotions, nor, as a consequence, any selected audience interested in watching and listening to such things. But that, believe me, human fallibility apart – mine to begin with – is the extent of the difficulty.

The protest was well founded. His final play, started in 1923, was completed five years later, entitled *His Majesty*. This might have been Barker's greatest work, for it seems to be projected on a scale to make it outstanding, but a perfunctory ending suggests that Barker got tired of it, and completed it only to get it out of the way. The piece concerns a King who abdicates in a revolutionary situation for reasons that are personal and honourable rather than political. There are twenty-one characters, and nine scenes in four acts, with several black-outs. It starts promisingly with the King in exile in Switzerland; he is back in his country in the second act, but has to sign an armistice, which his opponents do not intend to keep; but the armistice is broken by his own soldiers, upon which the King surrenders, and is made prisoner, but enabled to escape by the intervention of the British Minister. The characters are carefully drawn, the dialogue polished and witty, and there are highly effective theatrical scenes; but in the last act it seems as though the play will never end, the writing declines in force, and the dramatic action peters out. Until then, the action is lively, tension is maintained, and the King retains our respect, but the entire last act is unsatisfactory.

His Majesty's state of mind is revealed in two speeches:

There are two ways of looking at this world, aren't there? As a chaos that you fish in for your profit . . . you can always pull something up. Then there's the world of your idea . . . and some of us would sooner go on to the end, hoping that may come true. . . .

And the further the reality slips from you . . . the better you know the idea was true. I came back set not to fight . . . and with nothing I wanted to win. But I did come to think for a little that there was something for me to do here. I shall never do it. Who wants it done? Yet I've never felt so much a king as I do now.

There can be no doubt that the King is a final self-dramatization, and possibly the best. The King was in his forties, as was Barker, and is so described:

He is not a very handsome man, nor probably a very clever man; but he is shrewd. His courtesy is innate and he has an ironic, a mischievous sense of humour. He has charm. There are depths in him too; for at times, one may notice, he withdraws into himself, seems to withdraw altogether elsewhere.

This, perhaps, is how Barker saw himself, or as he wished himself to be seen. The play has not been produced, though at one time C. B. Cochran contemplated doing it with Nicholas Hannen as the King.

The last two plays show that Barker's is a subjective drama – the drama within the soul – which indeed is the only true drama. Subjective drama is the drama of reality as was the Greek classic drama and the drama of Shakespeare. Barker was not fully master of it because his own drama was unresolved, while the nature of drama as an art is that the problems it presents, always personal, are always resolved – in tragedy through death, in comedy by a comic reversal. Barker was obsessed by what he called factualness. In his struggle with the facts, attempting to bring them into order, he lost himself for want of a guiding principle.

*

At this point we should look at Barker's playwriting as a whole. For this purpose I ignore his work in collaboration, his very early work, and his later short plays, and no more than mention his translations : altogether a considerable body of work, for the translated German, French, and Spanish plays were made into English drama, as though by an original hand.   This work has all been mentioned in the course of the narrative.

There were six plays written between 1899 and 1923, which indicate that a dramatist of the first order was lost in Barker.   I say " lost " because although works of great interest they by no means represent what he might have done under other conditions.   All the plays have obvious relation to each other, and each has the theme of the difficulty of adjustment to the conditions of life, the difficulty being present in the first four, when Barker was still young, in young or youngish persons seeking to establish themselves.   In the last two it appears in middle-aged men, for it continued to be, as we see from his life, his own difficulty. It is impossible to resist the impression that Barker dramatizes himself in each play.   In *The Marrying of Ann Leete* he is the girl Ann, so that everything is in reverse, not only the sex, for a life of comfort is forsaken for a life of toil.   Edward Voysey, in *The Voysey Inheritance*, is a Barker who may not escape his destiny and must pay the price.   Henry Trebell, in *Waste*, is a Barker who sees himself wasted through a moment of folly. Philip Madras, in *The Madras House*, is a Barker who surrenders personal success for human service, though he remains confused.   And so it is, as I have pointed out, in the last plays.   The first play is the weakest, but contains the germinal ideas of the rest.   Those ideas, which make Barker, as I think, one of the most important dramatists of the century, are expressed in his treatment of the situations in which he places the leading character of each play, and are contained in the dialogue.   He enters into the heart of the situation, revealing psychic strains and thought processes. The characters are individuals, the situations those in which the men and women of this civilization find themselves.

He is regarded as an " intellectual " dramatist because the characters express their thoughts instead of offering a description of what is happening, and in the thoughts, so expressed, is contained an emotional revelation. The end of the third act in his early play, *The Marrying of Ann Leete*, provides an example.   The scene is a garden, in the evening, and Carnaby, who is Ann's father, has been wounded in a duel :

Carnaby.   Yes.   It's raining.

Sarah [*her sister*].   Raining !

Carnaby.   Don't you stop it raining.

Ann [*to her sister*].   And I curse you . . . because, we being sisters, I suppose I am much what you were, about to be married;   and I think,

Sally, you'd have cursed your present self.   I could become all you are
and more . . . but I don't choose.

Sarah.   Ann, what is to become of you?

Carnaby.   Big drops . . . big drops!

Ann [*calling to the gardener, who is passing*].   John Abud . . . you mean
to marry.   When you marry . . . will you marry me?

Carnaby.   Take me indoors.   I heard you ask the gardener to marry
you.

Ann.   I asked him.

Carnaby.   I heard you say that you asked him.   Take me in . . . but
not out of the rain.

Ann.   Look . . . he's straight-limbed and clear-eyed . . . and I'm a
woman.

Sarah.   Ann, are you mad?

Ann [*to Abud*].   If we two were alone here in this garden and everyone
else in the world were dead . . . what would you answer?

Abud [*still amazed*].   Why . . . yes.

Carnaby.   Then that's settled . . . pellucid.

Sarah [*as Carnaby rises*].   Papa! . . . there's no rain yet.

Carnaby.   Hush, I'm dead.

Ann.   Oh . . . oh . . . oh . . . !

Sarah.   Abud, don't ever speak of this.

Abud.   No, my lady.

Ann.   I mean it all.   Wait three months.

Carn⌐┐   Help me up steps . . . son-in-law.   [*He falls.*]

Abud⌐. ⌐ɪɪ carry him.

Ann.   Such a long day it has been . . . now ending.

This technique he developed.   The characters are thought out as human
beings, not re-modelled on recognized stage types.   The elements he
introduced into drama have by no means been fully taken up and worked
upon as they deserve to be.   Shaw gave him general ideas but did not
technically influence him; Barker's main technical influences were those
of Ibsen and Schnitzler.   But his contribution is to be regarded as original.

The first four may almost be regarded as one play.   I do not mean that
he wrote the same play over and over again, but the first develops into
the second, the second into the third, and so on to the end.   Indeed, they
have something of the form of a symphony.   A statement of the theme
is made in the life of a woman, lost in a world that has no place for her,
who has the courage to leave it for a new world, where, honour remaining

ost, she retains faith. In the second movement a young man is over-whelmed by destiny, and allows fate to take its course. The third pre-sents a man given a great opportunity, who loses it by his own mistake and destroys himself. In the fourth, a return is made to the possibility of a new life. The remaining two plays are a coda, the theme restated in experience.

The plays remind us of the actor Barker speaking Shaw's words as Jack Tanner in *Man and Superman* :

For mark you, Tavy, the artist's work is to shew us ourselves as we really are.

It is true that a writer puts himself into his work : that is, he puts into it his heart and soul – in other words, his aim and moral purpose; it is true, also, that the problem of the leading character in a play is the problem perceived by and felt by the dramatist. We can say that, in a sense, the leading characters of every play are aspects of the dramatist himself, as Hamlet, Macbeth, and Lear were of Shakespeare; but that is not to say that in these characters we have so many Shakespeares. Shakespeare was detached from his works and created characters that were not him-self. This detachment is the sign of the greatest artists. Barker did not possess it. He was not detached. He dramatized himself because he could not stand away from himself. That is why he was so deeply injured by the banning of *Waste* : he was too much involved in it. The description of the hero in the revision of that play is manifestly a self-portrait of the dramatist at a moment when he, himself, perhaps was prophetically conscious of personal waste.

William Archer considered that Barker's plays had a defect, " associ-ated ", he said, " with the great quality of his technique ". He went on to explain :

That great quality is the subordination of mere story to the portrayal of manners and character. He sees the necessity of keeping the interest of the story alive, and does so, as a rule, with extraordinary skill. Many of his scenes, I will even say most, are positively tense with essential drama. But he is more concerned about the living tissues of a play than about its articulation, its skeleton; and this habit of mind, excellent in itself, carries with it obvious dangers. When a dramatist's primary object is to show two or three characters moving through a cunningly-developed story, he is seldom tempted to run to great length; but when there are a large number of characters to be illustrated, and the desire to get on with the story is relegated to a secondary plane, there is, so to speak, no auto-matic check upon the temptation to discursiveness. It cannot be denied that Mr. Barker sometimes yields to it. He frequently writes a little too much. There are perhaps not many scenes in his plays that would not gain by certain compression, and some would bear a good deal. Moreover, he has never entirely shaken off that precosity of style, that over-rapidity and over-subtlety in the interplay of dialogue, which rendered his early and immature plays incomprehensible to me.[1]

This is good criticism as far as it goes; I quote it at length because Archer was one of the few who have given Barker's plays critical attention, but I think he did not go far enough. It is true that Barker was not oblivious of the necessity of maintaining the interest of the audience, but it is an exaggeration to say that the number of characters was the cause of the story having a secondary place. To Barker, the problem of the leading character, the idea, the moral struggle, had the first place, everything being secondary or incidental to that. This shows that Barker was a true dramatist. Where he was in error was, I think, that his leading character was never sufficiently heroic, or remained, shall we say, too personal. A play cannot successfully be written about a character fundamentally so life-like as to be unequal to life. The leading character may be defeated, when the play becomes a tragedy, or he may escape from his predicament, when it is comedy; but defeat must contain the essential achievement and a note of inner victory, and the escape must be complete. " In all the great tragedies ", wrote W. B. Yeats, " tragedy is a joy to the man who dies; in Greece the tragic chorus danced." There is insufficient joy in Barker's work, whether tragedy or comedy: his comedies are not far removed from what the newspapers wrongly call tragedy and his one tragedy is the simple failure of an unheroic hero.

A letter from his friend, Dr. C. E. Wheeler, the year of which is uncertain, offers an excellent criticism of another aspect of Barker's work, particularly, in *The Madras House* and *The Voysey Inheritance*, his treatment of love. As the letter is from a man who played a large part in Barker's life as a young man, and as practically nothing, apart from his medical writings, remains of this distinguished and lovable man, I give the letter in full :

Sept. 30.

My dear David,
    There's a great deal to say about the play – but I don't know how much of it would be at all helpful. You seem to me to have blended oil and water rather. What's the difference between a Street-walker and the average middle- or upper-class woman? Salutary question, demanding, I think, bitter *swift* comedy. What is the economic condition of the drapery trade – what about living in or out, what about trusts and business methods? Most interesting questions, but demanding

[1] *The Old Drama and the New*, pp. 362–3.

methodical documentary treatment. Yet you've blended them and I think they don't mix – of course you've interwoven them, but they don't blend : the strands are to me separate. All that, however, matters little. What's more important is that I'm not sure that you yourself understand properly either Love or Beauty or Art, which is the expression of Beauty. If you're going to create for us you *must* not be as the unseeing and the Philistine. They say that Love is *only* modified (more or less) appetite and Beauty a stimulus thereto, and Art a pander. Further, as a Puritan you're ashamed of your appetites. So you're had both ways. But let us distinguish a little. Of course if you honestly see no difference between Casanova and Shelley or Browning – I may as well spare my breath. To see the difference is like all really important things a matter more of grace than of will, but no one who has ever known either Love or Beauty in a high degree need go wrong – and for those who have not it's a case of " Father forgive them for they know not what they do ". I'll leave Love out for it's a long story, and if I can make clear what I mean about Beauty, you'll probably be able to apply the principles. Beauty is the expression of Life simply and truly, and the aim of the true artist is to achieve Beauty forgetting self. " Love of the World " is the pursuit of beauty, and if he can't himself create it, a man is well employed in tending the garden where it may grow. But the antithesis to Beauty is Luxury which is self-display and self-aggrandise-ment and by a curse those who pursue Luxury – *call* it Beauty and those who have never known real Beauty believe them – those who have, simply smile. *Non ragioniam di lor, ma guarda e passa!* Now, I don't think you make this clear – Jessica is a luxury-hunter, not a lover of Beauty, though she played Bach and hung Botticelli in her drawing-room, but Philip, who has the root of the matter in him if he'd look at it, allows her to claim her pursuit as that of Beauty and the absurd creature damns Beauty instead of exposing the fraud.

What's wrong with Philip otherwise is what's wrong with so many of your people. Because you're not sure of the difference between Love and appetite – you solve your difficulty by denying any value to Love and so get no good of either – why are your heroes and heroines all *afraid* to love? Ashamed to live almost?

Penelope[1] played " Alice " quite straight, but she was not afraid at the end to show that Alice *loved* Edward and *wanted* his love, all of it, his body and his mind and his spirit, not to make a selfish possession of it (that's like luxury – its called Pleasure and pleasure-hunting is damnable or, rather, is futile), but to join it with hers so that both should bring a double force to that understanding of Life that's marriage – never mind if the union lasts an hour or a lifetime – if it's genuine it means more life and that's the final test. The result was that I was moved profoundly by the scene as was the whole house. But *she* had to put it in – you had funked it and thought Alice was finer if she didn't *want* him. What Rot. However, that's beside the mark.

Well, I liked the play. Its workmanship shows no falling off. Act I

[1] Penelope Wheeler, his wife.

is a masterpiece. If I find the rest in parts disappointing it's for grounds here vaguely and verbosely set down. But do, my dear friend, take hold of life. Help us all to *live* – it's hard enough anyhow sometimes.

Addio

My love to you,
Christopher.

Wheeler knew Barker intimately. He knew, perhaps, that, affected by emotion and with the root of the matter in him, Barker did not allow himself to love. It is certain that neither of the leading characters referred to knew how to love. It seems likely that Barker himself was a poor lover, for he was not strong, his stomach was always troubling him, and his emotions were absorbed by his work. That he was attractive to women is a fact, and that he was not oblivious of them is reflected in his plays; but while he did not, as Barrie admitted *he* did, neglect sex, his approach was through thought rather than through the feelings, so that coldness enters into the scenes between lovers, even fear, especially in the otherwise fine scene between Edward and Alice in *The Voysey Inheritance* to which Wheeler referred.

In the artist this failure with the emotions is a defect in imagination, and leads to the conclusion that the primary cause of Barker's failure as a dramatist was preoccupation with his personal problem as a man and his inability to solve it. The dramatizations of himself were one attempt after another to think out and resolve the problem of his own life, which he never succeeded in doing. Here we see a difference between Shaw and Barker. Shaw dramatized his experience and ideas, and disposed of them, because he had digested his experience, and his ideas were recognized as gifts that he had to pass on. Barker did not digest his experience, but carried it within him undigested : his ideas were therefore presented much as the product of reasoning than the free gifts of intuition, or the unfettered lifting of his heart.

Although these plays have elements of poetry, Barker did not attain to poetic ecstasy, without which true tragedy is not reached or comedy either. Yet no one who saw him on the stage, still less anyone who knew him, could doubt that he knew such ecstasy. The tones of his voice conveyed it, even as a lecturer; so did his manner on the stage and privately when young, and his expression, at times, when old. It may be that Shaw must bear some responsibility for this; for his scathing onslaught on romance (see his earliest prefaces) probably affected the younger man, who might have seen, however, that Shaw in his own plays did not disdain romance to make them palatable; but his doctrine rather than his practice affected Barker.

Barker was influenced as a writer to some extent by George Meredith, much more by George Moore. Archer was a greater influence even than Shaw. But there can be little doubt that he made the Irishman George Moore, the greatest English stylist of his time, his model. Moore's plays lack theatrical quality, but they have literary quality. In George Moore, it has been remarked, the style was the man, and the same is true of Barker. Geraint Goodwin says Moore's style was " forged in the furnace of his own thought "; it came, as Moore himself said of St. Paul, " straight out of the heart by thought ". This can also be said of Barker. And what George Moore said further about his own writing might also be applied to Barker's: " you can think it a bad style or a very good one – both views are admissible. But of one thing I am certain – it is my own. Everyone writes as well as he can." [1] What John Masefield wrote about Barker's plays on 10 September 1909 was justified:

What I admire so much in your work is its fineness and precision, it is like fine metal-work, all certain and strong and lithe, all the unnecessary cut away. You get all round your people before you begin, and when you do begin they just walk out of prison and are henceforth free.

Barker worked at his plays over and over again, cutting and re-writing, never leaving the work alone, destroying much more than he preserved, for his self-criticism was severe. He aimed, as Masefield said, at precision : the right word in the right place, not merely how the word looked upon the page, but how it sounded. For, as he said himself, " I act it as I write it ". Thus his dramatic writing never lacks distinctive style.

It was, indeed, in the diction, the tone of his dialogue, that he made his greatest contribution. He was acutely aware of the values of spoken language. He aimed at a subtle rhythm, speech that had organic form, which is notable in his earliest plays and was the one thing he perfected in his latest plays. In these earliest plays the very short speeches, often monosyllabic, are not casual ejaculations, but the notes of a tune. Their phrasing was for the sake of the melody of speech, which is only another way of saying, " for the sake of the meaning ", which, in drama, is a way of saying, " for the sake of the dramatic action ". What eluded him was the direction and end of the dramatic action. My own opinion is that had he stuck to the stage he would have found that direction, and have become a great classic dramatist.

His style had urbanity. His characters are polite, felicitous, lucid, and unaggressive. He provides a model of civilized playwriting not to be surpassed in the English language in this century. He was not at home with rusticity in any sense. Neither was he a propagandist, except of urbanity, which was his cause.

---

[1] *Conversations with George Moore*, p. 69.

What is more important, his sense of rhythm was the elevation of the rational mind into the sphere of poetry and the transformation of mere knowledge into truth; it was the symbol of the inexpressible, and his means of living in the realm of truth. The symbol was, of course, intended to be apprehended by the audience, aware of its existence through the experience of listening to living speech. Such audiences, capable of such intuitions of meaning, have to be created – they do not exist as a matter of course. What he said in a lecture at the British Academy on 13 May 1924 entitled "From *Henry V* to *Hamlet*" shows that he intuitively perceived what was required. In this lecture he probed more deeply than at any other time into the essential elements of drama. *Henry V*, he considered, marked a crisis in Shakespeare's career:

He had learnt that for presenting the external pageantry of great events his theatre was no better than a puppet-show; and that though the art of drama might be the art of presenting man in action, your successful man of action did not necessarily make the most interesting of heroes. For behind the action, be the play farce or tragedy, there must be some dramatically significant and fruitful idea or it may hang lifeless.

Here he approached exposition of the very essence of drama. Referring to *Julius Caesar*, he said:

Drama was to lie only formally in the external action, was to consist of the revelation of character and of the inevitable clashes between the natures of man. And even behind these would be the struggle within a man's own nature; and the combatant powers that must be dramatized.

And in discussing *King Lear* he remarks upon the "greater storm that rages in the mind of Lear", without perceiving the conclusion to which it should have brought him.

*

His characteristics as a dramatist may therefore be summarized as follows. (1) He is always concerned with a moral or spiritual struggle, so that his characters question and doubt themselves, examining and re-examining their motives. (2) He is always trustworthy in character-drawing; there is never any exaggeration of character to fit preconceived ideas or merely for the sake of effect. (3) He enters into the minds of his characters, and the heart through the mind. (4) His dialogue has style.

Although Barker is regarded, as I have remarked, as an intellectual dramatist in the sense that he appeals to the minds of the audience (which is true), he more than once declared that he abhorred the "intellectual drama", as such. "Intellectual Theatre gives me a headache", he wrote in 1910. That was because he was concerned with real men and women:

he saw the drama grounded upon life, elevated upon the stage in the being of the actor. What Barker found distasteful was not the intellectual element, but vision or intuition expressed in intellectual terms other than those of drama, i.e. that the play could equally well be a novel or a treatise. He was protesting in the name of the dramatic artist for the sake of his art, for a work of art is such because it contains in a particular form something of the artist's personality or soul. That is what he meant by the word " magic ", which he often used, the idea of acted drama as the vehicle of inner truth; and he was always concerned with acted drama. He said the thing himself in his introduction to the Centenary Edition of Tolstoy's plays:

The teacher must have his doctrine pat, but the artist sets out to discover truth itself with each new book or play or picture he begins. In a single devotion to that search lies art's integrity; let him respect this, and though the result may make the simplest show, some flush of a deeper truth may be manifest through it. The search is never-ending, and the search itself is the thing.

The realism for which he was admired or found fault with was not an attempt to put life itself upon the stage; it was an interpretation of, or comment upon, or ironic criticism of life. His realism meant that he went to life for his sources, material, and themes, the plays being the imaginative presentation. That is to say he offered a copy of an imaginative image, not a representation of the thing itself. The fact that the play as written and produced by him appeared to be nearer to reality than the thing itself does not contradict what I say, but confirms it. Altogether his writing was on a much higher level than that of any dramatist of his time, Shaw only excepted. Indeed, there is in his plays the consciousness of what A. N. Whitehead called, when writing of religion, " some eternal greatness incarnate in the passage of temporal fact ".

George Sampson described him as " The most disappointing dramatist of the period ", which was a reasonable judgment, the grounds of which were that he aroused expectations which he did not fulfil. He appeared to have a new thing to say in a new dramatic form, but neither said it clearly nor perfected the form. But there is more to be said of his work, as I have indicated, than Dr. Sampson allowed. Barker was disappointing because the conditions of the theatre did not make possible what he wanted to do. He did not have a company of actors and a theatre on a permanent basis (for at the Court they lived from hand to mouth), and the theatre itself, with its picture-frame stage, condemned him to a form of playwriting contrary to his talent. The picture-frame stage is the stage of illusion, and Barker's drama was concerned with reality and truth. Never at any time, after his early youth, did he write for the commercial theatre, or show any disposition to do so; he never possessed the means for acquiring the theatre he wanted and was never able to acquire those means. This explains his great longing for the establishment of the National Theatre. Although he experimented with Shakespeare at the Savoy Theatre, the outbreak of the First World War put a stop to any development of that work, with the almost complete paralysis of his playwriting.

When George Sampson found Barker disappointing, he could not say what was lacking to put that gift to use. It can, I think, be summed up in these words: the images in Barker's plays, though not without emotional content, as those who saw them when originally produced can testify, lack the complete emotional energy of drama. This lack becomes marked when the plays are produced by others without his insight, and it was in fact observable in the productions with which he himself had something to do in his later years. Truth, the symbol of which is water, is a source of the purest energy, but the energy has to be generated by emotion, or, to be more exact, love. It is not done by adding truth to truth. A different centre in the soul has to be awakened to activity. It is not a matter of mere technique. That Barker had a sound and practical understanding of stage effect as well as of stage writing cannot be denied; and it is no less clear that he would not sacrifice the dramatic idea to it. In this respect he was a much more scrupulous dramatist than, say, Shaw, but he lacked what Shaw possessed, an instinctive knowledge of what makes a play. Without that instinctive knowledge (which might have become conscious in Barker, but did not), his plays remain unsatisfactory.

He was concerned with a poet's problems without the equipment, natural and acquired, to enable him to produce works of poetry. He had the disposition, but not the resources. It is significant that when religion is mentioned in his plays it is talked about, never as something experienced or to be experienced. The " complete ignoring of religion " was a fault found by Beatrice Webb in his work. Shelley's phrase, " the visitations of the divinity in man ", finds an echo in his work only in devotion to truth and in feeling for rhythm, which is the harmony of opposites, and belongs to the nature of divinity.

His plays are works of importance in the history of drama, and are likely to be remembered when all but a very few of the most highly regarded plays of the first half of the twentieth century are forgotten. When we have a National Theatre they should be played regularly for their particular values, for in my judgment they will remain in the repertory of English plays.

*

An outcome of the active part taken by Barker in the Royal Society of Literature was a paper read on 7 June 1922 to the society on " Some Tasks for Dramatic Scholarship ", in which he referred to a " half-formed project for the re-editing of Shakespeare ", what he called " a Variorium edition of a new sort, one that would epitomize Shakespeare, the dramatist ". He remarked on the serious fact that " an overwhelming proportion " of critical literature upon drama " is written by people who, you might suppose, could never have been inside a theatre in their lives ". It is serious because many of the problems of scholars would " elucidate themselves " if the plays could be seen or imagined in performance on the stage, and also because –

. . . those of us who wish to inform ourselves thoroughly upon these matters have to wade through a large amount of what is, frankly, rubbish.

He complained of the lack of any adequate criticism of the experiments of William Poel and pleaded for a new school of Shakespearian criticism based upon experiment with the plays in a theatre.

This brings us to the most ambitious of Barker's literary efforts. When the young Victor Gollancz became manager of the extension of the old-established Benn periodical and technical publishing business into general book publishing, he projected a series of finely printed illustrated books for collectors, and among them an edition of the plays of Shakespeare. The idea was to present the plays from the point of view of their stage performance with drawings and paintings by distinguished artists. There were two editions, one limited to 100 copies at 12 guineas each, the other limited to 450 copies at 4 guineas each. Printed at the Shakespeare Head Press at Stratford-upon-Avon, under the direction of Bernard H. Newdigate, one of the greatest printers of his time, The Players' Shakespeare was a splendid example of English book production. The first two volumes, issued in the spring of 1923, were *Macbeth* and *The Merchant of Venice*, followed the same year by *Cymbeline*. The fourth, *A Midsummer-Night's Dreame*, appeared the following summer, and later in the year *Love's Labour's Lost*. After an interval of more than a year, *Julius Caesar* was published in 1926, and *King Lear* the year after. Then the venture was abandoned. In fact, it was a complete failure. The more expensive edition, beautifully as it was produced, did not appeal to the fine book collector, and the less expensive edition was beyond the means of others. Much more than half the entire edition remained unsold, and the copies were remaindered in 1930. The failure of this project was not surprising, for while it was declared to have a practical aim, it was much too costly, and by no means suitable for a hard life in the hands of producers and students. Furthermore, from the start it was uncertain how far the edition was to go or to what expenditure those who bought the volumes would be committed to make their purchases complete. No wonder it failed.

The first volume, *The Tragedy of Macbeth*, contained, no doubt, the results of Barker's studies for the intended production of the play in 1914. His general introduction appears in this volume, and differs considerably from the introduction to the prefaces when they were published together later. In particular, the demand that the plays should be performed as Shakespeare wrote them on the kind of stage for which they were intended was much more positive than he afterwards made it. Although the aim was to present the plays in each volume from the point of view of their performance, this was found to be impracticable, except to a limited extent, as Barker explained:

In no case, however, is the complete plan of a production set out. There has not been, indeed, the collaboration necessary to this between preface-writer and designers.

This was obvious in the first volume, for the *Macbeth* designs by Charles Ricketts are not stage designs at all, but pictures for a book.

It was characteristic of Barker that in this admirable introduction he showed himself to be made uncomfortable by what he regarded as Shakespeare's " pornographic aspect ", and had to declare that he would omit all such dialogue. This was not a pose, but genuine, for there was never a more sensitive, even squeamish, man on such matters than Barker. Yet he agreed that " deodorizing " may be carried too far, and ended by saying: " one . . . inclines to say sharply that if people cannot suit their taste to Shakespeare's they had better do without his plays altogether ". Even topical allusions whose meaning has been lost must, he says, be handled cautiously, for although the dead wood had better be cut away, " The blue pencil is a weapon with which few are to be trusted ". What he says on this matter provokes him into declaring:

. . . amazing as the statement may appear – Shakespeare's case as a playwright has still to be fully proved, and the proving it must needs be a thorough process. His plays have had every sort of treatment. Actors have twisted them up into swagger shapes, scholars have rolled them flat, producers have immured them in scenery. They have survived it all, and to say so much is sometimes thought to be the greatest tribute we can pay them. But there is another and more needful tribute: the setting out to discover what, as plays, they essentially are.

This important statement is buried in this volume.

When we came to his first preface and the notes on *Macbeth*, it was surprising to find that instead of the First Folio text, printed in the volume,

Barker used for the purpose of the preface the academic Arden Edition. From that point he seemed to go astray. I well remember the amazement with which I read the preface, having first read the introduction with profound admiration. For instance, Barker regards the opening scene of the play as spurious, "almost certainly, this was not Shakespeare's", and holds to the "good opinion" that "we do not meet Shakespeare's true text till Macbeth's own entrance". He goes on to say that the lines spoken by the witches have "all the tang of the Hecate lines", and he would omit them altogether, "in line with the forthrightness of the play's whole action". Shakespeare's beginning was the second scene, he thought, though "mauled by Middleton, some stage manager, or the compositor", and the following scene should start with Macbeth. So he went on. It is no wonder that he regarded the whole text as "extensively corrupted". As an introduction to the play, nothing could have been more disappointing. He could not have been satisfied with it, for he did not reprint the preface later.

Cymbeline, with Albert Rutherston's coloured drawings of costumes and scenes, stage plans, and line drawings, was a much more workmanlike volume. Paul Nash illustrated *A Midsummer-Night's Dreame* with colour drawings of scenes and costumes in line and colour, and drawings of scenes in perspective – but cold studio work remote from the stage. Thomas Lowinsky was responsible for coloured drawings of settings and line drawings in the text for *The Merchant of Venice*. Norman Wilkinson of Four Oakes, for *Love's Labour's Lost*, used a framed stage, with an apron, and an inner stage, rather like the stage used at the Savoy Theatre, and designed a general setting, with plans and elevations for each act and drawings of the characters in the text and colour. Ernst Stern, the artist for *Julius Caesar*, ignored the proscenium frame, and used an open stage, with an inner stage with doors on each side, so designed as to be capable of being set within a frame. Paul Nash did the last volume, *King Lear*.

This ambitious editorial work, which promised to be so valuable, was misconceived; for designs for the setting of a play, to be useful, must be for a particular stage and an actual production must be visualised. To design for the printed page and for the stage are entirely different matters. It is odd that Barker allowed himself to be involved in an enterprise intended to build up a vision of a performance separating "the *essentials* from the *incidentals*", for he had already said in the lecture referred to earlier:

. . . it is difficult to describe the performance of a play. One can be accurate enough about scenery, costumes, and even grouping. But when one comes to the acting – the performance itself, that is – there is little to be done but to record the impression it makes upon each of us. Not that the impressions of a cultured critic are not valuable evidence. But they are sometimes more informing as to the critic himself than the performance.

Fortunately for his reputation, the prefaces were revised, and all except two, *Macbeth* and *A Midsummer-Night's Dreame*, were soon issued in a series of volumes entitled *Prefaces to Shakespeare*, by another publisher, Sidgwick and Jackson, Ltd. This workmanlike effort more than restored what the extravagant edition had well-nigh destroyed, and the general opinion remains that the prefaces make Barker's name secure and crown his life's work. The first volume was issued in 1927, the remaining four being published at intervals, the last just after his death. The prefaces in the first volume (*Love's Labour's Lost, Julius Caesar, King Lear*) were among those already published, but were much revised in the light of criticism they had received, " and of my own (I hope) better judgment ". The general introduction was almost entirely new. The volume was dedicated " to the memory of William Archer and to the producers and actors of the English National Theatre – when that shall exist", an acknowledgment of what he owed to his friend and an indication of a still living hope for the future. Each volume as it appeared was received with acclamation as a work of immense theatrical as well as critical importance. Scholars, critics, and men of the theatre united in their praise, which may be summed up in Dr. Dover Wilson's remark that these books began " a fresh epoch in Shakespearean criticism ".

Nothing equivalent had ever before been attempted; neither has anything of equal authority been published since. Whatever else comes to be written about the plays, these five volumes will hold their own as contributions to the study of Shakespeare of unique value, the outcome of a lifetime of study and experience by an artist of the theatre of great insight and craftsmanship. On the general principles set out in them, Shakespeare production for the past twenty years has with varying degrees of understanding been carried out.

*

This is not to say that the prefaces are beyond criticism. Their merit is that the plays are regarded as works for the stage rather than as literary works at the mercy of experts in textual and academic criticism. Yet it has to be said that Barker relies upon the scholars much too heavily. No one would seek to deny the importance of their work upon the plays; indeed, it is essential, for plays are literary products, and their texts require to be studied and established. But scholarship has a limited function, and cannot cover the full scope of any dramatic work. Barker was never tired of pointing out that plays are intended to be seen and listened to. On the printed page we turn back and read again a page at a time, and pause over the language; but the drama is intended to be received in the bodily presence of the actor as the action takes place, and reflection accompanies the action. The processes of reading and of participating in a performance are different, and the result is by no means the same. If what the drama does could be obtained by reading, the expense and trouble of performance would not be justified. Literary criticism is, therefore, but a step towards the appreciation of drama.

While Barker did in fact demonstrate the possibility of examining the plays as actors and producers have to look at them, it must be recognized that he wrote in his library, having given up the stage, and that he set to work with the edited texts in hand and the books of the scholars around him. He thus tended to become less and less an actor, and more and more simply a scholar, and got further and further from the stage. He followed the scholars in their absorption in problems of time, place, and character, the rationality of the plots, the characters as they exist in themselves, and so on. In short, Barker succumbed to A. C. Bradley, whose *Shakespearian Tragedy*, first printed in 1904, he admired with very little reservation, and wished that of such criticism " one had more ". Bradley had, indeed, the right intention, for he, too, said that he proposed to write " from a single point of view ", that of " dramatic appreciation; to increase our understanding and enjoyment of these works as dramas ". Barker accepted this statement, saying, " To Professor Bradley the plays are plays, and never cease to be plays ", not perceiving how quickly the Professor got away from the idea! What constitutes a play Bradley did not sufficiently consider, or perhaps even contemplate that there was anything to consider, though in his opening chapter he does ask, " What makes a Shakespearian tragedy? " In his answer, Bradley follows Aristotle and expounds that philosopher very well; but because the work of Aristotle is incomplete (a fact too often overlooked), and because since classical Greece we have had Shakespeare, which was Bradley's subject, Bradley's conclusion, excellent as far as it went, did not go far enough:

The notion of tragedy as a conflict, emphasizes the fact that action is the centre of the story, while the concentration of interest, in the greater plays, on the inward struggle emphasizes the fact that this action is essentially the expression of character.

Bradley never got beyond drama as " the expression of character ", and the greater part of his book is concerned with the characters in the plays as they may have been as living men or women, which takes him far outside the sphere of drama, and makes most of his commentary beside the mark and seriously misleading. When he is not concerned with the characters he is concerned with the storytelling. In fact, he got right away from the intention he had announced at the start. Barker argues respectfully with Bradley on particular points, and is obviously restless over his general point of view, but as he had no theory of the nature of drama he is not able to withstand the powerful Professor. That becomes the radical defect in Barker's criticism of Shakespeare. He, too, considers the characters as they are in themselves, saying :

. . . the action of a play being literally the fighting of a battle of character.

He thus gets involved in questions of psychological interpretation that have nothing to do with drama as such. Barker certainly pulls himself up from time to time, as Bradley never did, for his eye is on the stage and the actor, but he does not escape from what is irrelevant, although he may appear to do so when he says rhetorically :

A play . . . is a magic spell. . . .

As the prefaces were mostly delivered as lectures in universities in England, Wales, America, and Canada, we may say that in associating with professors Barker became (almost) one of them.

What I have said may be illustrated by an examination of his long preface to *King Lear*. Barker will not have it, of course, that the play is " too huge for the stage ", and robustly " justifies " its place there. As a stage technician, too, he tackles Bradley in a fundamental sense :

Dr. Bradley seems to assume that every sort of play, when acted, ought in a single performance to make a clear, complete and final effect on the spectator. But this is surely not so. We need no more expect to receive – lapses of performance and attention apart – the full value of a great drama at its first hearing than we expect it of a complex piece of music.

Or, indeed, on the first reading of any book we may read. Bradley's error (" as I am bold enough to think it ", says the respectful Barker before the august presence) springs from approaching the play merely on the printed page, as Barker should have realized. Then, turning from the Edwardian critic, Barker deals with the Georgian Lamb and his condemnation of the scenes in the storm, Lamb having come from a hopeless performance of the play on the picture-frame stage. Here Barker makes one of his most pregnant critical utterances about Shakespeare's art :

. . . this is the basis of his stagecraft, to make Lear and the storm as one . . . any actor who should try to speak the lines realistically in the character of a feeble old man would be a fool. There is no realism about it. No real man could or would talk so. But the convention enables Shakespeare to isolate Lear for the time from all pettier circumstance, to symbolize the storm in him, and so to make him the great figure which the greater issues of the play demand. The actor must make both himself, and, for the moment, the lesser Lear – the Lear of infirmities and humours – forgotten. . . .

The storm, says Barker (as he had already said in the lecture to which I have drawn attention), is in Lear's mind : Lear creates the storm. This might have led Barker to see that perhaps the entire action of the play was in Lear's mind. He did not do so, and thus missed a great opportunity of critical understanding. For drama understood as that which takes place in the hero's mind, being concerned with nothing else but the art of securing the spectators' participation, is an idea that would have transformed Barker's dramatic as well as critical work. Without it, he got caught up in questions of time and place, and the characters and their interplay, so that his perception of the dramatic action was overlaid with irrelevances. He did not realize that the Lear of the play is the hero's own statement of himself, a poetic vision which does not need explaining on a rational basis. The Fool he regards as " of incidental, of decorative importance ", not, as it assuredly is, of essential importance, but he is rightly against steeping the character in extraneous sentiment.

The long discussion in the *Othello* preface of the " ambiguity in time " in the play, and the endeavour to make the compression of time compatible with reason, is another example of Barker struggling in the effort to reconcile drama in the Bradleyan sense with its true function. He comes to the conclusion that –

. . . the overriding explanation of this show of Shakespeare's stagecraft is that he is not essentially concerned with time and the calendar at all.

That, of course, is the truth, but he goes on to defend the dramatist when no defence is necessary :

He may falsify the calendar for his convenience ; but we shall find neither trickery nor anomaly in the planning of the battle for Othello's soul. And in the light of the truth of this the rest passes unnoticed.

Had natural time anything to do with the play, this would be mere special pleading ; but it has not, and Barker's defence is beside the mark. The play is a poetic work, a vision or contemplation of events ; the action is simultaneous, the beginning and end being one, and no questions of days, months, or years arise.

It will be worth while to look a little closely at the *Hamlet* preface, which has a volume of 329 pages to itself, and was regarded by Barker as the most important of the ten prefaces. That he had given years of study to the play there can be little doubt. He never acted the part or produced the play, and it must be considered a great loss to the stage that he did not. He regards the play as " a tragedy of inaction ", and thinks, as editors love to do, that Shakespeare made more than one attempt at the character – Romeo, Richard III, Jacques, and Brutus among them. He thinks that Hamlet suffers from indecision and lethargy, being weak, self-conscious, introspective, and attitudinizing. This hardly indicates any independent view. His discussion of the nature of the action is occupied with the division into acts, and the play's place-structure and time-structure. Shakespeare, he says (not sufficiently observing the significance of the remark), " uses clock and calendar or falsifies or neglects them just as it suits him ". He devotes pages to these problems, and ends by saying : " It comes to this, I think. Shakespeare's true concern is with tempo, not time." As the essence of drama is action, the thing done is what the play is concerned with and the discussion of " time-structure " is unnecessary, for the action is removed beyond time.

The nature of the action in this play is, I suggest, how Hamlet saw himself in a situation in which his affections were involved, including hatred for his uncle ; a situation, complicated by the visitation of the ghost, in which he felt he had to kill that uncle in revenge for the murder of his father, though he knew that as a civilized man and a Christian he could not do it, but how, in the end, he does kill him with a good conscience. Barker finds nothing of this. Hamlet is " A philosopher misgivingly impelled to action . . . a man at war with himself". " Ought we ", he remarks in a sort of perplexity, " to be able to ask so many – quite intelligent – questions? " about the play. The fact that the dramatist makes this possible is perhaps part of the explanation of the greatness of the play, but Barker finds it to be a serious fault. The " effective opposition of character to character . . . is certainly lacking ", he says, riding away on one of his own hobby-horses – that drama is character opposed to character – and he finds the character of Hamlet to be unsatisfactory. This displeasure with Hamlet as a man is not surprising when we find Barker dividing the action of play into three movements: (1) The taking of the oath. (2) The delay. (3) The fulfilment. He thinks it was Hamlet's " perverted scruple " about killing Claudius at his prayers that " opens the way to all the ills to come ". Nothing could be more simple, and no criticism could be more false ; it is no wonder that Barker disliked the play and the characters, for were it no more than a melodrama it would be a pretentious one. Barker appeared to see no more in it. Of Hamlet he says :

He never regains a natural spiritual health, nor does he reach self-understanding. His loathing of life only hardens to indifference.

Yet to justify attention to the play the confession is made that Hamlet's

" trouble is very much our own ". That is true enough, though Barker does not explain why, except that " Hamlet is a man adrift from old faiths and not yet anchored in new . . .", which seems to be nonsense.

That this preface, like the others, is written with much art, making it a literary work of distinction, does not remove its weakness as criticism, for justice is not done to a play that means something to every audience in every country throughout the world. The problem of Hamlet is, in truth, the problem of Everyman, for it is the problem of conscience, and Barker rightly finds a key passage in the lines that begin, " Give me that man that is not passion's slave . . .". The action of the play is occupied with Hamlet's struggle with conscience and with resistance to the fate that involves him in a task of vengeance, which, if yielded to, would have made him " passion's slave ". Yet Barker sees a young man unfit for his task in life, one who plays " false to what common sense would expect of him, and to what he once might have expected of himself ". This is to accept the point of view of the editors, who consider that Hamlet had a duty to revenge his father's murder, and who seek for naturalistic explanations of his difficulty in carrying out that supposed duty. The turning-point of the play is thus discovered by Barker to be when Hamlet postpones his vengeance on the King because it would not be sufficiently cruel to kill him at his prayers ! This takes him far away from the play's true action and the state of mind in which it was written. The real turning-point is when Hamlet makes the mistake of killing Polonius, acting without thought, as " passion's slave ", which involves him in his own death. In short, the play is not to be interpreted on the level of naturalistic storytelling, but on that of tragic drama, which is a different thing. That Barker did indeed see, but not so clearly that he was able to realize the play's true values; instead, he follows Bradley and is lost.

That Barker was seriously dissatisfied with this preface is indicated by a copy of the book that contains extensive revisions. More than a third, perhaps half, of the entire last chapter is cut, and it may be assumed that he intended to revise the book as a whole, but did not complete it. To judge from the handwriting, the revision was started not long before his death. Twenty-eight of the forty pages about Hamlet himself are crossed out and the last words of the chapter are made to read :

If a new age of faith or reason should succeed, or one for a while too crushed by brute reality to value either, we may well come to wonder what we – and Hamlet – ever found to make so much fuss over.

This shows an uneasy mind about the conclusions to which he had come, but a mind at least approaching perception of the play's dramatic action, as the revision, in his handwriting, of p. 310 indicates; it is worth giving *in extenso* for readers who care to compare it with the original:

Such over-introspective characters are neither truest to themselves in solitude nor likely to be happiest in the intimacy of love – with their egoisms overfed if they are the more loved, if they were the more loving, starved. But they may find relief from the warping tyranny of self in the generosities of friendship. With their friends they can be confidently and forgetfully and transparently themselves. And while the play may seem to be but one long opportunity for Hamlet's self-expression, a juster measure of him, of his faults and virtues, is reflected – paradoxically – from the few moments' self-forgetful praise of his friend than lies in all the searchings and scoldings of the soliloquies. He did not – that was there and then plain – really envy the player his facile emotion; he used it simply as a stick, with which to hit himself. He knows he is no coward, he has physical and moral courage both, and has proved it. He does not in the least wish that he were Fortinbras; his only interest in the sight of him, " with divine ambition puffed ", being that it is an occasion which " informs " against him – and which he can improve. He teems with intellectual pride; and his self-depreciation – the commonest of traits in the sensitively proud – is only a token of it. And upon all these points the soliloquies, taken at their face value, exaggerate and distort and mislead. But even as the qualities for which we love our friends are witness to what we would be ourselves at our best and are humbly conscious that we are not, so Hamlet's praise of Horatio –

> As one, in suffering all, that suffers nothing:
> A man that fortune's buffets and rewards
> Hast ta'en with equal thanks; and blest are those
> Whose blood and judgment are so well commingled
> That they are not a pipe for fortune's finger
> To sound what stop she please

reflects a far juster judgment upon himself. He has, as have all men, the strength of his weakness and the weakness of his strength.

> Give me that man
> That is not passion's slave, and I will wear him
> In my heart's core, ay, in my heart of heart,
> As I do thee. . . .

There is his moral ideal. His implied consciousness of his own failure to achieve it with the appeal to his friend, by the title of his love for him, to strengthen his weakness at this crisis. A generous spirit, a truth-seeking mind, of that there is no doubt. Had his lot been different, cast among loyal friends and faithful servants, not amid treacheries and disillusion, could he then have readjusted the balance in him? Or had his mother lived spotless and his father died of old age would he still have proved, by some other token, the man of blood and judgment so *ill*-commingled that he must always be his " passion's slave "? Is the

" vicious mole of nature " in him, of which he is so cripplingly conscious, rooted too deep? There can be within the limits of the play no answer to the questions. But by setting him for a moment or so under the clear sky of this strong and strengthening friendship, Shakespeare contrives implicitly to put it to us in all its pathos. . . .

In the United States two volumes of the prefaces were published by the Princeton University Press in 1946, and in an Author's Preface dated New York, May 1945, Barker said:

For various reasons the publication of an American edition has been delayed until now. In preparing it I have made only a few changes (there are some of comparative importance in *King Lear*, and one in *Julius Caesar*). Not but that I could – as I hope – have improved upon the earlier work. But I should have been tempted to re-write it altogether; and this would not have been practicable.

The last of the prefaces, *Coriolanus*, was first given in the form of lectures at Trinity College, Toronto, in 1942, revised and completed in 1946, a few months before Barker's death, and published in London the year after. It is very much an academic work; on that level excellent, but below the level of such a man of the theatre.

That Barker got further from the stage and more deeply settled in his study as time passed the *Prefaces to Shakespeare* as a whole make evident. It was to be expected, for he had put himself on the wrong side of the curtain to complete the work he had set out to do. He was working on other prefaces when he died, though his work had slowed down owing to continued illness. He did not publish the revisions of two of his original prefaces, but no doubt intended to do so, and to include more plays; but what he left has been lost.

*

Among the friendships Barker had retained from his theatrical days was that of Cuthbert Headlam, who was not a theatrical man, but had acted as secretary to the Parliamentary Committee on the Censorship in 1911 when on the staff of the House of Lords. They had become friends, as Barker had acted as a sort of manager of the case against the censorship, and they had kept in touch with each other since. Headlam was soon to become Member of Parliament for Barnard Castle; he later became a Minister, Privy Councillor and baronet, altogether a distinguished man. He wrote to Barker when they were both in Italy at the end of 1922, and received the following letter written from Portofino:

How pleasant to hear from you and to know that we are within a biscuit-throw – so called. But let us offer you one at close quarters. Won't you and Mrs. Headlam come and lunch on Tuesday at one? It would give my wife and me great pleasure.

We struggled up here yesterday in the pelting rain – our luggage following after in pitch darkness too. If it is *dry* by Tuesday, and you can come – and may both things be – I recommend the garden way by the iron gate at the end of the Molo Umbuto Primo – a pleasanter path – *when* it is dry.

*

There was little correspondence with Gilbert Murray at this time, and no meetings, because Helen, who tolerated Murray because of his academic eminence, found that even he was too much associated with the theatre. After the publication of *The Secret Life*, there is the following letter to him from Netherton Hall:

25.11.23.

We shall be in town Dec. 3–7 at the Connaught Hotel, Grosvenor Square – on our way abroad for the winter. And if you *do* find yourself in town that week and *can* make time to lunch (1 or 1.30 at your choice) it would be good to see you. *And* if Lady Mary should by chance be there too that would be even better.

Needless to say, you hit the nail of my *Secret Life* clean on the head. It is an experiment in technique, consciously so. Too much of one, I dare say; but I care for my craft. Thank you, though, for seeing the good side of that.

Affectionate remembrance to you from us both.

Both the Barkers were writing in their Devon home, and during 1923 Helen's long novel, *Ada*, was published; it was about a middle-aged American who once had been a lovely creature. " Why are not more novels written about the middle-aged? " one of the characters asks; and towards the end are the words:

He asked himself if it were really true that women are still children – precocious, gifted often, full of potential power – but children, most wisely treated when treated as such.

A letter to Lady Mary Murray says:

Oct. 14, 1924.

My dear Lady Mary,

When and if any leisure comes to you you must read Helen's book if you will – for its " like " her and *I* think, good writing. So I'm telling them here to send it to you.

It was good to see you both the other day and to have that familiar, kind, wise " voice " making this world and the Greek world one again – for an hour.

As ever, then,

H. G. B.

Earlier in the year Barker wrote to Shaw about a visit to *Saint Joan*, produced in London on 26 March 1924. The Barkers saw it a few days later, and he wrote to the author as follows:

12.4.24.

Well, we burned a candle to St. Joan as we passed by. For me she covers a multitude of Heartbreak Houses and Methusalahs. I believe it might be tagged " A Ratiocinative Mystery " play. The century of its subject is the century of its art – not in the Wardour Street sense! As theatre art just as – well, *I could say* crude, but let's say simple. The only difference is between God and a comic devil cheek by jowl and the divine and the comic all rolled into one. But the approach to it is, I believe, just the approach of the author of the Chester Plays – though in addition, of course, the ratiocinative – the Platonic dialogue touch. And personally I like that scene better than any – the Protestantism scene between the three men. Matter and method seem here to come together there to give the actors their best chance. All three good, and Swete excellent there – and no use at all in the later scene – so ask yourself why.

That would be my complaint – if I weren't too grateful for the whole to press it. Monotony of method in the acting and I think the methods of the parts' writing is to blame. They all, so to say, begin at A and speak straight on to Z. And all so steadily occupied doing and saying that what they are —— !!? Oddly enough, this is hardest, to my mind, on Joan. Because it must have been what she quite silently *was* which impressed people – Oh, far more than anything she said. I don't believe she was as glib as that – peasant girls (even saints) aren't glib. And then suddenly she turned Candida (with the Bastard)! Her last speech though in that church scene is magnificent – and Miss T. did it magnificently. Oh, if that had been the first time she really found her tongue! Otherwise, as far as Joan is concerned, the trial scene for me.

I am all for the Epilogue of course – though there again, I could wish it had been done differently. It would have been mere tactics to make the actors play a new tune to refresh the ears of an audience that could not but be tired. Casson had to – and what a difference that made. Thesiger half-tried to; but it needed co-operation. Though I see you did not want the usual dream stunt.

And that division in the trial scene to mark the turning did need someone to do what you'll never bother to. As long as your meaning gets over, what do you care? A composer conducting! But the acting very sound on the whole. But Lord! The sheep that had style and the *goats* that hadn't.

Are you well – and Charlotte? We are and glad to be back – though Algiers was a success. I did a preface and nearly all the first draft of a play – then called away suddenly with the news my mother was dying. But she didn't – made an amazing recovery – so having watched it we came on back – with some lost time to make up for.

Have you read Shane Leslie's *Doomsland*? If not, do.

★

He maintained his friendship with J. M. Barrie, for Helen was able to tolerate the dramatist: he was very distinguished. They often visited him at his country home at Stannay, near Broadway, in Gloucestershire. Lady Cynthia Asquith, in her book, *Portrait of Barrie* (James Barrie, 1954), presents a portrait of Barker when they first stayed with Barrie there in the summer of 1924:

Granville Barker has not – as I'd heard said that he had – lost his charm and personality – how could he? – but he does strike me as the worse for wealth. A certain sleeking of spirit and mind, as well as of body doesn't become him. He looks less like a poet and not wholly unlike a butler. According to Barrie, and Elizabeth Lucas (who had just "decorated" his house), his daily life is over-organized by his wife, Helen. The notice "WORKING HOURS NINE UNTIL ONE" hangs on the door of his writing-room . . . Barrie tells me Helen is determined not to let him have anything to do with the theatre.

The Barkers travelled a great deal, and he became an authority on the best hotels throughout Europe. Helen was restless, and he hated the Devon house, its servants, and its isolation. They had an apartment in London at Hill Street, Mayfair, but were more often at the Ritz Hotel. An indication of Barker's state of health is given in a letter to Gilbert Murray on the following 27 November, in which he says: "I'm now at my 10th doctor (counting them all in). And they're still talking."

On 13 May of the following year, Barker gave a lecture on Shakespeare for the British Academy at King's College, London, when the Earl of Balfour was in the chair. It was a magnificent, a beautifully read, lecture, and after Sir J. Forbes Robertson had proposed a vote of thanks, Bernard Shaw got up to second it. The latter, in common with others present, was much moved, and, telling the story afterwards, Shaw declared [1] that when he arose to speak the devil entered into him and, after praising the lecture to the skies, he said that Barker's retirement from active work in the theatre was a public scandal. What happened then, according to Shaw, was that he felt such a violent pain in his spine that when he left the hall he could not bend down to get into a taxi, and had to walk home on foot; there he lay flat on his bed until his wife arrived. He was incapacitated for some days, but suddenly the pain left him and he recovered. Whether he was suffering from lumbago or influenza or not, it pleased Shaw to blame Helen. She was sitting directly behind him as he was speaking, and he concluded that he had been bewitched! There are various versions attributed to Shaw of the same story, all different, but all substantially accounts of the effect of what he called an

---

[1] *G.B.S.*, *A Postscript*, by Hesketh Pearson (Collins, 1951), p. 159.

evil eye, for Lady Colefax told Shaw that, sitting next to Helen, she observed the latter fixing her eyes on the back of his skull.

★

A letter to Cuthbert Headlam, who at that time was in the House of Commons, comes here with a rare comment from Barker on political affairs:

30.7.25.

That's first-rate and thank you. Anyhow, it will be a protest. They need not have knuckled under at all, I dare say; but even so to let the brutes (obviously) re-draft the clause for them and swallow it whole! I fancy Lord E.P. will reward you with a wan smile. A precious reward. You must be – wearied to death. And, by Jove, what a chance the Enquiry Report gives Mr. B. if he could sack his duds and take on a Cabinet of " Young Tories " all. The Y.T. – I'm not sure he hasn't been the characteristic and gallant figure from Falkland down, and, though shot at Newbury, his soul goes marching on. But Shinwell to right of you and Bennett to left of you (R. Bennett – Secy. to Primrose League. Helpful fellow in a crisis. Statesmanlike mind!), you must wish sometimes you were writing history instead of making it. But I cheer you on!

In October 1925 Barker's mother died in the South of France. She had been living in Monte Carlo for many years.

A revision of *The Madras House* was completed and produced at the Ambassadors, with Nicholas Hannen as Philip Madras, and Barker wrote to Murray from Paris:

23.12.25.

A shameful confession that *The Madras House* has kept me till pretty near now from the House of Atreus! How good that with all else weighing on you, you still can translate them. I'm not the only person surely who see, though, how this play fits in with all else and reads the preface as dated from Geneva: " O praise persuasive gentle-eyed . . . wise are they and have found the way of peace." But when you depreciate the trial scene a little, may I remind you, sir, that a trial scene is always a " go " on the stage? Yes, from Aeschylus to Galsworthy – and Shaw – it never fails. This is not only thanks but a Xmas card with good wishes from us both to you all.

Next year a version of Jules Romains' *Doctor Knock*, made in 1924, was produced at the Royalty Theatre on 27 April by Dennis Eadie, and the year after Helen's collection of stories, entitled *Wives and Celebrities*, was published. It contained six sketches of women married to celebrated men, set in London, New York, Paris, and elsewhere, all well-off: a painter, a writer, a soldier, an old retired actor, an archaeologist, and others. The last words of one story read:

Well – she must just be patient, for didn't she love him, look up to him! In all essentials he was far above her. He had the mind of a scholar, a genius. He had weight. She sighed – as if Oswald's weight oppressed and afflicted her. If only she had been a little bigger and he not quite so big!

Another letter addressed to Cuthbert Headlam comes here:

7.6.28.

There is (as you may remember!) a case against the Lord Chamberlain, and it'll have to be fought out some day. But we don't want to whip up a full-dress row upon a side issue leading nowhere; a departmental blunder too, I expect, not intended to have logical consequences. But as to your Jix; by the paper to-day, he himself will " his quietus make with a bare (faced) Bodkin " if he don't look out.

Yes, indeed we are on the road to Dartmouth. Take us going or returning. Is your date fixed? You go to pat cadets on the head, do you? Helen is writing to Beatrice.

It's like you – and right, I'm sure – to stick to your guns and your miners. I'll be sorry if you chuck politics, but not surprised. And all the bright young men (of whom you are still one) are going into the City now. Good for the City. In fact, it is going to solve the social problem by making commerce and finance public spirited – aristocratic. If we don't keep an aristocracy of some sort alive we're damned.

*

Several letters to Murray written from London towards the end of that year provide evidence of Barker's activities:

3.11.28.

Be kind and find a moment to give me some advice.

The Royal Society of Literature are doing a set of ten papers on the 1870's, to be put in a book under my editorship – a not uninteresting lot, and I want to " top up " with Oxford in the 70's and Cambridge ditto – more or less from the literary point of view. W. L. Courtney was to have done Oxford, now he never will. With two O. men at lunch, I got seven names jotted down from which to find a substitute. Would you – without finding it too much a plague, add any that come to your head – and annotate these. Yes – sick or *No*. The paper to be read some time between now and April (but for the very aged it can be read. Saintsbury's is being read by Squire). Ten golden guineas the fee.

You will see me – hardly see me – humbly in the shade of Crewe and Newbolt on Tuesday.

8.11.28.

Very many thanks for the 1.2.3. About the Intellectual Co-ops, this strikes me. If you don't get money from the Government and are at a loss for it, or for some stuff and shelter I don't see why the R.S.L., properly handled, should not do something in that line. There would need to be some "handling" – in the first place of Crewe, who's president and Charnwood, treasurer; then of the Council (man-handling in this case, possibly). But the fact is, the R.S.L. has no real job (that it does, a dozen it could do) and it has some money. This also struck me. A lot of scientific co-oping is apparently being done; the lack is on the educational-literary side. That lets the R.S.L. and its clique in. I think it would like (bless it!) to "represent" Literary England. The real job, I suppose, will be to co-ordinate other jobs and stop overlapping. That might be incidentally done. All rather round-about, and the "Handling" could be a nuisance. But if you're really at a loss, the possibility may be worth exploring. The next Council's on the 21st and I'll go (for the last time this year) and report on the I.C. meeting. That letter from the F.O. could be useful. They rise like trout to letters from the F.O.

22.11.28.

Crewe was in the chair at the R.S.L. Council yesterday. I reported upon the I.C. meeting. Our Tories (we're very Tory) were silent. But C. himself was benevolent, though (quoting experiences with the Paris establishment) a little sceptical of practical results. I then quoted you (discreetly, I trust) upon the greater need – therefore! for British co-operation. C. seems full of benevolent beans and disposed to take his R.S.L. obligations and the like seriously enough. So, if occasion serves, you might think it worth while to get into personal touch with him – about the I.C.

As the letters show, Barker had become much interested in the Royal Society of Literature, and during his presidency the year after, in 1929, he had its publications put on a much more ambitious footing than had hitherto been attempted. He became responsible for a volume of papers on the eighteen-seventies, which came out in 1929, when Barker contributed a preface and an essay on "Tennyson, Swinburne, and Meredith". He took part in two other volumes, and the *Eighteen-eighties* (1930) contains possibly the most light-hearted essay he ever wrote, "The Coming of Ibsen".

The impression Barker created on those who met him for the first time at this period of his life is very well expressed in a letter by John Van Druten:

I met Barker in the very early nineteen-thirties (or it may have been in 1929) at a dinner party given by Constant Huntington. . . . I think I had asked to meet him. He was a figure of importance and also of romance to me. As a playwright he had fired my imagination and spurred on what talent I may have had, especially by the first act of *The Madras House*. I had seen and intensely admired his *Anatol*. I had heard many stories of him as a truly great stage director in the years before the First World War. I had a mental picture of him as a young actor. A lot of my admiration was based on things told me by Miss Auriol Lee, who had played with him and admired him. I had envisioned him as a slender, gentle, highly-keyed man who had once been described to me as " taut and quivering like a violin string ". I was intensely keen to meet him.

I will admit to a considerable shock when I saw him. The tense and sensitive young man had turned into a thick-set and reddish-faced man who suggested a farmer to me. I was, in any case, extremely shy of him, and I think that I deliberately avoided any real chance to talk to him. But one fragment of conversation remains with me. We were discussing the recognized translations of Ibsen's plays. I was objecting to them and, remembering the praise I had always heard of Barker's 1905 production of *The Wild Duck*, and my own admiration for what he had done to Schnitzler in *Anatol*, I asked him why he did not do the same thing to Ibsen, and paraphrase or retranslate his plays as he had done Schnitzler's.

Barker's reply was that that would be impossible and that the gritty, pebbly style of the current versions was essential to conveying the quality of Ibsen's prose. He was wholly against my suggestion. I remained in doubt of the truth of his statements.

During this period, too, he took in hand a revision of his first published work, the " Blue Book " on the National Theatre prepared with William Archer. Before Archer died they had been talking about an up-to-date revision. The new book, which appeared in 1930, was an entire recasting of the original: in fact, a new work. Much of the argument was omitted, and the details were brought up to date. Although he had a number of people to help him, every line of the new book is obviously from Barker's hand. He ended the preface with the words: " It really looks as if the National Theatre were on its way." But appearances were deceptive.

*

When Harcourt Williams was in charge of productions at the Old Vic from 1929 to 1934, he was in constant touch with Barker, and within the possible limits carried out what the latter had indicated in his *Prefaces*. The one on *Julius Caesar* " fired me with an ambition to do the play on his lines", he said. Barker's letters to him contain certain suggestions for the producer, among them the following remarks on other plays :

                                                                    5 Aug. 1929.
The only important thing about drinking the potion is, I think, that Juliet is forced to disobey the Friar by her father settling the marriage for " to-morrow morning". This, at any rate, is all that is dramatically evident. The rest of the calculation is lost in the general confusion and in the particular confusion that Friar John creates.

As to the dance, you will notice that the Quarto stage direction for the previous scene reads, " Enter Romeo, Mercutio, Benvolio with five or six other Maskers". I fancy that *only* the Maskers dance with the invited ladies who come out with Capulet. This rules out Tybalt and may partly account for his bad temper. Romeo stands out because that is his mood. I think the fun is that the unknown guests dance with the ladies and leave the men who have had legitimate invitations to the party out of it altogether; cf. Henry VIII invading Wolsey's little At Home (though I have to dictate this without looking it up, so I may be wrong).

Yes, certainly Romeo asks one of his own torch-bearers who Juliet is. He would not risk making himself known to Capulet, would he?

5.11.29.

I only got to see half the *M. of V.*, I am ashamed to say – from the Casket scene on. But I'm very glad I saw that and I have been wanting to write to you ever since. Everything pointing in the right direction I think; I should guess (though I'd not been there since I saw a bit of *A. and C.* and fled) that you have raised the general standard very appreciably already. A common method of verse-speaking: that's what I felt they most needed, and to let the verse seem to carry them along, not they to be carrying it – and not, some of them, to be so damned explanatory. I'm saying, I expect, what you have been shouting at them for weeks. But some of them speaking it very well all the same.

I liked immensely the arrangement of the trial scene. It justified itself. The action clinched and obliterated the Duke at the right moment and then parted to give him his place again. This is just what W.S.'s own stage management must have been. I rather wish (though this W.S. possibly didn't – couldn't – do) that you had tried the important entrances and exits R.I.E. They seemed to slide on and off rather too much.

Some of the acting quite good. I thought (I'd be grateful if you'd send me a programme; I couldn't get one) Portia played with real skill and judgment – though of course she could not give the fairy-princess touch to the earlier scenes. Shylock "utility" and one wants more; but – thanks to you, I expect, he "nothing common did nor mean". Bassanio rather solid, seemed to have no faith in his poetry. Antonio good, if a little timid. Nerissa first-rate. Lorenzo, Jessica, Gratiano – all the right stuff in them. Don't let this seem carping. I know you don't want more polite phrases. Well, the best of luck. Get the round pegs into the round holes and you'll win through.

25.1.30.

I strongly suspect that Lady Macbeth sat on the usual "state" in the inner stage and that the table was a long trestle brought on the main stage with Macbeth's seat left in the middle, pretty well bang in front of Lady M. But the "groundlings" were standing up and the masking would not be bad – nor would they consider this overmuch anyhow. The advantage of the arrangement is that it brings the main action well forward and keeps everyone's face to the audience. However, but for the danger of tying the whole affair too tightly in the background your separate sketch seems to me excellent.

But I see you've got the other arrangement noted too (except that you put Macbeth at the end which is useful for the short entrance, but probably (traditionally) wrong) and this – if the state is high enough and you can get the table far enough forward is very good surely. And both are quite legitimate. The large open space and the tables at the side : that would *not* have done, probably at the Globe, and I didn't think it good anyhow. But of course I haven't looked at the play carefully for a long while; and my preface to it is full of blunders.

I was so glad to see such a good account of your *Julius Caesar* in *The Times*. And it was most generous of you to quote me. You do seem to have got the thing on the move. It has been collar work I'm sure. But how good when you do feel the load moving.

6th June, 1930.

Nothing that is experience – proof – and I suppose you are wanting something that is – comes into my mind for the moment. Of Elizabethan drama, some people at Chipping Camden about twenty-five years ago revived Jonson's *New Inn*. I did not see it, but I was told it turned out very well. William Archer always used to say that Bjornsen's big historical dramas were very fine things – but of course the history is strange to us. He also used to tell me that Holberg, of whom he thought highly, would never translate into English (though, for all that, I believe he once tried). But I never could quite understand why. There is a lot of fun in Tolstoy's *Fruits of Enlightenment*, but it is not finally a first-rate play. This is all that comes into my mind for the moment. If anything more does I will write again.

I was fairly certain that you had made good at the Old Vic. – from the various criticisms I had read – not from the praise in them, because one can earn that – Alas ! – in all sorts of undesirable ways – but from the particular things that were said of the productions. And now from what you tell me I am quite certain. The thing is to keep the best of the company together and power in your hands. I hope you find no difficulty here. I saw something of Gielgud at rehearsals once, and he struck me as having the real thing in him. A trifle too much finesse, perhaps. A little apt to let his sword blade turn just before he made the stroke (I expect there is a better metaphor in golf, but I don't play it): he was, in fact, not quite crude enough for his youth. But having to play big parts in which mere finesse won't serve him, and having had your eye and mind upon him, will about have doubled his value already, I should say, and I believe he may go far.

★

As they were too much out of the world in Devonshire, the Barkers were in Paris in 1930 looking for another home, and eventually took an apartment at 18 Place des Etats-Unis, at the corner of rue Galilee. There, except during the German occupation, they lived for the rest of their lives. This was a handsome and commodious apartment on the first floor, overlooking the gardens, in which stood the statuary presented to

Paris by Joseph Pulitzer in 1895. On the ground floor, facing the gardens, Barker had a large room, used as a library, with a separate entrance and a small sitting-room where he used to rest. They had a spiral staircase constructed between the floors. There was a staff of eleven, including Barker's Swiss secretary, who acted as majordomo of the establishment, and a chauffeur. Most mornings he would take an hour and a half's exercise, walking or riding in the Bois de Boulogne, and, after breakfast, shut himself up in his library, writing. Helen, too, was not to be seen until luncheon, for she spent the morning resting and getting ready for the afternoon. In the early afternoon he often walked in the Bois with Helen, and the rest of each day was devoted to social activities with her. They moved chiefly in the diplomatic and wealthy American sets, and made a good many distinguished French friends, among them Madame Clara Longworth de Chambrun, authoress of a number of books about Shakespeare in both French and English. Helen had the ambition to found a literary *salon*, but she lacked the personality and Barker was unwell, and also much preoccupied with writing.

That year, 1930, he was appointed to give the Clark Lectures at Trinity College, Cambridge, which he liked very much, Helen also being highly pleased with this academic recognition. He made a great impression at Cambridge, for he excelled as a lecturer. His voice was in fact the interpreter of the best in him: intelligence, expressiveness, sincerity, excitement in his subject, and depth of conviction, also impetuosity and (one must add) the tendency to go on and on. The lectures were published the year after, entitled *On Dramatic Method*, " a fascinating, challenging and very English book ", said *The Times Literary Supplement*. Sending a copy to Gilbert Murray, he got the following reply:

May 25, 1931.
I ought to be doing honest work and your wicked book on *Dramatic Method* had seduced me and made me not only read it, but also want to talk to you about almost all of it. In the Shakespeare part, I think you are a little unjust about metre. Some of the effects which you specially admire are, to me, metrical effects. Metre to be exact need not be wooden; and verse to be fluid or musical need not be irregular . . . at least that is how I should like to argue. I agree violently about the Restoration Drama. But are you not a little harsh on rhyme? Shakespeare wrote rhyme badly, just as Jonson did. He always jingled it. But take *Epipsyciddion*, or some of Browning. . . . Or even me. Is my verse really as bad to speak as the Restoration people? You ought to know, and of course I can't. I should have hoped that, while it did sound strange or foreign – or outside the regular English tradition – it did get certain dramatic effects. Though I confess I don't know of any satisfactory original English play in rhyme. As to the Cassandra scene,

your account is very interesting, but you seem to miss, or not to think worth mentioning, one chief characteristic of the scene. C. is under a curse, the curse not to be believed, and she knows it. There is a regular progression. First, the vision, growing steadily in clearness. Then her effort to warn the Chorus, which is first only conveyed through the riddling, prophetic language. Then at 1178 she pulls herself together, drops the lyrics, and tries to convince the Chorus by first showing them that she knows the past. She mentions the curse, and they say, " Not at all. We believe you all right." She warns them in prophet language – in a new paroxysm – and they don't understand! 1242. At last she gets the statement quite clear, 1246. They can't help understanding, but say it is impossible. Then comes her last paroxysm, which leaves them as it were paralysed, not actually disbelieving, but just unable to think or act. The dramatic interest is to see the prophetess warning the Elders to stop the murder, and the curse working to prevent her words from having effect. But of course there are other strands woven in, or other vistas behind.

I am rather angry that the pornographers have got the Cambridge Theatre to do the *Lysistrata* " in a less Bowdlerized version than has ever been seen on any stage ". It is a fine play in itself. Given the phallic festival as an institution, and given a bitter war against which the Comedian is protesting at the risk of his life, it is a magnificent play. But under modern conditions it is merely an exercise in obscenity. Damn them !

His answer to Murray was as follows :

31.5.31.

What is wanted (besides other things in this wicked world) is that the Council of Intellectual Co-op : should appoint a sub-ctte " to determine whether the peace of the world will be better advanced by the development of the static or dynamic drama " consisting of you and me (or I : it could settle that too). Then I could really thresh out to my profit at any rate that business of rhyme and regular metre *v.* blank verse and rhythm.

But oh – the nincompoop I was to overlook (it was just that) the primary scheme of the Cassandra scene – especially as it does not really vitiate the rest of my contention. Thank you for the lesson. I was on the point of sending you the thing before I finally printed it, then I thought : No, Geneva and overwork apart, this is not fair. A man must make his own blunders and suffer for them.

I much agree about that Cambridge Theatre in its present phase. There is a tall, thin man with a soft, sleek beard – but that will do when we meet, if we do.

Thank you again.

An attempt by Malcolm Morley to get him interested in a revival of *The Voysey Inheritance* at the Everyman Theatre failed that year. Morley had been playing with the idea of getting hold of the Court Theatre and reviving its glories; it is not surprising that Barker saw nothing attractive in the notion. Two letters to Morley, written from Vittell, touch upon these matters:

4.7.31.

All I have against the Court Theatre is the innate difficulty in making it pay the expenses of first-class work. But if you can solve that problem, good – and certainly it is a better place than the Everyman.

As to *The Voysey Inheritance*. There's nothing against its revival there, *if the cast can be made a satisfactory one*. But I fear I don't attach enough importance to the matter to constitute myself its responsible producer and to return to England for that purpose. If I *were* in England (but it is uncertain when I shall be), I'd certainly come and superintend a few rehearsals; I could not promise these.

But I have advised (I gather you must have seen or heard of the letters) against beginning a new enterprise at the Court with its revival. This would be crying – I will not say Stale Fish, but certainly Old Co'. You need, surely, something more immediate and arresting.

10.7.31.

My advice upon practical matters is nowadays not worth having. But I have a stray feeling that the price the " intelligent " playgoer can afford to pay nowadays and pay fairly often – an important point – is at the most 5s. and there are many for whom 2s. 6d. or less is nearer the mark. If you can live upon these – and there are not so few – then your financial problem is solved. Anyhow, good luck to you.

I've not time to tackle Pasteur, I fear. But it is a fine thing of its sort and should not be difficult to do.

If you find yourself in association with Loraine and he would care to play my re-written *Waste*, that would be of some interest to me. It was re-written for a revival by H. M. Harwood and the contract lapsed. I have never moved much further in the matter, for I hardly know any actor whom I should care to see in the part. Loraine, however, is one of the few. But, of course, the whole play wants solidly casting – and I fear expensively casting. That is in general the want of my plays. They suit neither the aspiring youngsters nor the older men, who are the " left-overs ". And rather than do them weakly it is far better to leave them alone.

If and when you get your plans cut and dried, by all means write to me about this or any other matter if you still want to, and I'll do my best to meet your views.

I shall be here only till the 19th. My home address is always the safest.

*

He had become president of the Shakespeare Association in 1930, succeeding Sir Israel Gollancz, who had been its founder and president until he died in June; Gollancz had run the association as one of his hobbies, and left it with some money in the funds. Although it was thought that the presidency was vested in the professorship at King's College, London, which Gollancz had held, it was finally decided to invite Barker, who accepted on condition that he should not be merely a figure-head. Professor (as he now is) G. B. Harrison, who was secretary of the association at the time, says in a letter:

Soon after, we met, and it was clear that G.B. intended to make things move, if he could. He was keen that the association should cease to be merely a sort of cosy lecture club, catering for a few old ladies and gentlemen who liked to listen to an occasional lecture – but a real Shakespeare Society. He had a number of ambitious plans: they included a study of the Elizabethan private theatre, and a general index of the works of E. K. Chambers. The index was ultimately made, but the private theatre book never came off: it was to have been a team venture. W. J. Lawrence gave the first lecture (to have been the first of a series of studies); this was followed by a lecture on the economics of the private theatre by T. W. Baldwin. After the latter had finished, Lawrence got up and in his brogue remarked that " if the rest of the chapters of the book were to be so bad as Baldwin's contribution the book was not going to be worth much ". That venture never came to anything.

It seemed that Barker had no hope of doing much through the Shakespeare Association and its council of elders, so Harrison suggested to him that if a survey of the state of Shakespeare studies – one of Barker's many projects – was to be of any use it would be better if they did it themselves. " To my surprise and delight ", says Harrison, " he agreed."

As a result, *A Companion to Shakespeare Studies* was taken in hand in the spring of 1931. The planning of the work was done in Paris by Barker and Harrison. He insisted that it should be a book, not just a collection of unco-ordinated essays, and to signify the unity of aim, each member of the team was to receive a share of the royalties so long as the book endured: the Cambridge University Press, which had agreed to publish the book, was much opposed to the idea of sharing the royalties among so many, but Barker insisted and it was carried out. The two editors drew up the scheme of chapters and list of contributors, and Barker invited the proposed contributors to a luncheon at the Garrick Club. Putting the proposal before them rather nervously, for the scholars at first were cold, he charmed them into warm interest, even enthusiasm. Barker was then, as always, a perfectionist, and G. B. Harrison relates what happened:

I was the channel for all contributions and criticisms. As each chapter came in, I sent it off to G.B. in Paris, and it came back with his demands for revision. The standard was uneven, as is inevitable in a composite work, but we found that the bigger the man the more co-operative he was over changes. One or two contributors were very sticky about re-writing, but G.B. was insistent. The merits of the book, such as they are, are largely due to his persistent demands for revision until he had more or less what he wanted: though in the end I was of the opinion that had we written the whole book ourselves, it would have taken half the labour – for I was the buffer, and G.B. would relieve pressure upon me and I had to pass on his comments and then receive the injured protests of the writer.

I saw a good deal of G.B.'s methods. He was never satisfied with his own efforts and would go on re-writing and polishing right up to the page-proof stage and even beyond. I believe he would have done better work in criticism and certainly have left more of it had he been more content with his own first drafts; but that was not his way.

The second paragraph exactly states Barker's way with all his writing. He was never satisfied; though he wrote copiously, his output in both criticism and dramatic work was much reduced because of this persistent self-criticism. The book came out in April 1934. It was a first-class piece of practical work, setting out what is required in the preliminary contemporary approach to Shakespeare, providing information and guidance to students and stage workers; it is still going strong and has recently been included in one of the popular series in the U.S.A. Barker's own contribution was on " Shakespeare's Dramatic Art ".

*

His friend Headlam had become Parliamentary Secretary to the Ministry of Pensions in 1931, and a year later, when he was moved to the Ministry of Transport, Barker wrote as follows:

14.9.32.

I'd hoped they might push you into " Education " in the Commons – with Irwin in the Lords. After all, you've *been* educated (which can't be said of all) you even *are*, in a measure, educated (which can't be said of many). If the Nat: Gov: is going in there ought to be a shifting round and shaking up. Were you a real politician, I suppose you'd now be taking a cure at Aix and teaching Mr. S.B. how to do cross-word puzzles.

Yes, indeed, I see: if there is nothing better than Pensions going and a couple of directorships could be found, an unmuzzling for a couple of years before the next G.E. might pay. I have a feeling, Cuthbert, any-how, that we ought to strive to be at our best between 60 and 80. We shall be calm and perhaps wise, and ready to take the world as it is, while post-war youth will be middle-aged and pettish and disappointed. Then they may turn to us and say: Well, come in now, if you know —— Can I serve you in New York – we go there to-morrow. I wish you were coming. I'd like to show it you. (If I *could*, write to me at the Savoy-Plaza Hotel – beastly name! – Fifth Avenue at 59th Street till Oct: 10th.) We shall be back in London at the Ritz, I suppose, from

about Oct. 15–25th.   When really we shall count on seeing you both.
For, after all and on second thoughts, we mayn't live to 80.   Beatrice is a
bad correspondent – it comes of having too many secretaries.   But Helen
forgives her from time to time, and even speaks of her with affection.
And there is a spare room here looking out on the backyard, it is true,
but with bathroom attached, and everything else fairly handsome about
it.   You'd be put up in the hotel round the corner and allowed in for
meals.   Anyway, you are both asked.

God bless you.

Do you know the story of the international committee on Elephants –
I must run to another sheet.   Each nation represented had to bring a
paper on the subject.   The English man brought: Elephants I have shot.
The Frenchman brought: La Vie Amoureuse de l'Elephant.   The
German brought two volumes entitled (I shall get this wrong): Ele-
phantismus: ein kleines bibliographie.   The Pole brought: 2 Elephant
et la question Polonaise.   And the American brought a magazine article
called Bigger and Better Elephants!

*

Harcourt Williams, still directing at the Old Vic, proposed to Barker
the following year the possibility of doing *His Majesty*, to which he
replied:

19.10.33.

His Majesty.   It would be pleasant to find myself working with you.
Well done all round, and rather more than this in the parts which matter
the play might make its mark.   But I have held it back, and shall, from
every other rut of chance.   Hannen remains the best man I know of for
the King.   Charles Laughton would get full value out of the *real-politik*
revolutionary.   The Queen?   I put down Miss P.T. and Miss F.C.
Fauts de mieux, and because they [1] do attack their parts emotionally – to
this extent from inside out, not with that tight cleverness which tries to
work from outside in.   F.C. the last time I saw her, had finally resolved
into the minor key – and that's no good.   I last saw the other as an ageing
Q. Elizabeth.   It was pure "tushery" – and yet the woman can "act".
Something absurd about her – and melodramatic.   But there was that
about the Queen – though she never knew it.   Nor would Miss P.T.
have had to know it!   Miss W. [1] I saw play Charlotte Brontë.   More
brains than the other two multiplied by twenty; but she plays from
outside in.   She'd have to calculate her absurdities.   And when it comes
to the breakdown at the end, where the woman, and she alone, really
suffers and we must feel sorry we have laughed at her – that is the
"moment": if the actress can't bring that off, better not begin!   Still,
the thing may have to be played "objectively" in the event.

But the fact is that I now know nothing about casting – I doubt if I
have seen five English plays these last two years.   I may well have lost

---

[1] Miss P.T. = Phyllis Neilson-Terry; Miss F.C. = Fay Compton; Miss W. =
Diana Wynyard.

my producer's touch. And, for that matter, the stuff itself may be " out of date ". It will have to wait to become historical.

However, there was no escape for Barker. The rebuilt Sadler's Wells Theatre, just opened, was being used by the company for plays, and Harcourt Williams proposed to do *The Voysey Inheritance*. Barker could not resist his old friend, and, in fact, took great interest in the production, considerably revised the play, and came over from Paris to supervise it. In a preliminary announcement it was explicitly stated that he had not returned to the stage:

Mr. Granville Barker has no intention of renewing his connexion with the stage as a producer, but for the sake of a cause with which he sympathizes he has for the past fortnight directed the rehearsals of *The Voysey Inheritance*, which he has specially revised.

Writing to Harcourt Williams after the dress rehearsal, he said:

May 3rd.

This is not a letter of thanks: I owe you more than a scribble. Where would the play and I now be without you! Well, I know where I should be: in the doctor's hands again. Besides, you'll be able to keep it alive, and human, and intelligent. For you know what it is about: and they need – most of them – *telling* what it means. (You must expect to find that its moral and mental processes are Greek and Hebrew to the younger critics.) And you have an intimate touch with the people which I have lost. Bless them; they write well and courageously: but they are strangers to me, and I'm not sure we speak the same language.

Trenchard is very good: distinguished individual (a little more white in the hair – a white lock? – might tell!) Don't let him drag or get *ponderous*. A little danger of that; which disappeared when you got next to Edward. See you are not too badly masked by Hugh (his head is outsize). If you both lean forward on the table it helps; and you can lean a little nearer your mother. A trifle of impatience as you wait – and then will wait no longer – at the door. I am a little afraid of the whole thing dragging. If it does they must *not* merely hurry, for if they can't get the thing understood it is fatal, i.e. they must not bustle through the " capital " scenes. But they must brisk up the *ensemble* bits. Also watch Hugh and Beatrice; B. especially. But tonight if I feel it dragging I'll send you round a note. I shall be in the Board Room between the acts: could they put a couple of chairs there?

These enclosed notes for the cast: important – as soon as they (the cast) reach the theatre they should have them.

All my thanks to you. Good luck.

H. G. B.

Curtain cues. They want to be very smart on these, and if the curtain itself can fall a *little* quicker it will be to the good.

Act I.   Ring on Mr. V.'s.   Don't brood.

Act II.   I gave them the exact line: halfway through Mr. V.'s speech.

Act III.   Ring on Alice's "It would delight him" – *not* on "And I shouldn't".

Act IV.   Clarence's exit.

Act V.   Ring as they start to say the *second* "Till tomorrow".

May 3.   7 p.m.

I wrote a long note this morning to "Edward" and "Alice" and I mustn't inflict another on them.   But there is one danger point at the end of Act III to which *you* might call their attention.   Say we agree about it, or what you like.   I *did* just mention it to Alice: but it may escape her.

When he says "Then there is nothing more to be said, is there?" and she replies "Not now.   But there will be" (the "But there will be" is almost to herself), they must be in relations of *closest comradeship*: but *not lovers*.   For, if they seem so, nobody will understand how it is that in Act V they are *not* "engaged"; and the love-scene and her proposal to him will be very puzzling.

The production on 3 May had something of the Barker finish, and was received with much respect, even enthusiasm; but there was disappointment, for the revision had not strengthened the play, rather weakened it; and the first performance, which started at 8.30, was so slow that it did not finish until close upon midnight.   It was not surprising that one of the critics referred to the play's "tedious and now demoded chatter", though the *Daily Telegraph* spoke of it being "absorbingly interesting . . . a pure joy".   In fact, Sadler's Wells was too large for such a play, which required a certain intimacy with the audience.   Indeed, the new theatre was soon considered to be unsuitable for any plays, even Shakespeare, and they ceased to be performed there, the theatre being given over to Old Vic opera and, later, to ballet.   The play was transferred to the Shaftesbury Theatre on 25 May, where it had a short run.   Gilbert Murray wrote to Barker about the production:

I wonder what you thought of *Voysey*.   I gathered from some criticism that the younger generation had rather forgotten what really fine and delicate production was like, and were shaken in their self-satisfaction by the sight of your technique.   If so, it will do great good.   I do not know when I shall be in Paris again, but will certainly let you know beforehand.

The answer to Murray's question was contained in a letter to Harcourt Williams:

June 15, 1934.

Well, there it is! another ploughing of the sands – and I fear not worth the trouble and fatigue it was to us all.   Things have not changed in

40 years. For our sort of play and our sort of attitude to the theatre –
yours and mine – *real* repertory and a permanent company are the only
solution.

*

An invitation to participate in a theatrical conference in Rome in the
following October, organized by the Reale Accademia d'Italia, was
refused in the following letter:

23rd June, 1934.

I am most honoured by the invitation you send me to attend the Volta
Congress. But I fear that I ought – though with great regret – to decline.
For the last twenty years I have been out of touch with the active theatre;
I could not, therefore, be of the use to the Congress that you are good
enough to suppose. It is also very doubtful whether my present work
would permit me to come to Rome in October.

But once again, I am most honoured to have been asked; and my wife
asks me to add her thanks for her share in the invitation.

This was followed by a more explanatory letter:

11th July, 1934.

It is most kind of you to write to me, and I owe you a fuller explanation
than I was well able to give in my answer to the official invitation.

The congress is, I understand, to be upon the theatre not the drama.
I appreciate the intimate connection between the two, but there is a difference in the angle of approach. The problems of the theatre are practical
and each nation has its own. And I cannot hope to speak upon the
English problem with the authority I might have claimed twenty years
ago.

The other difficulty would be in my relation to the rest of the English
delegation. I do not know, of course, of whom this will consist. But
they will be in touch with the immediate English problem, and I should
be out of touch with them as with it. Yet I might feel compelled to
oppose their views. In England itself this would not matter; but at
Rome, at an international congress, it would, I fear, make an unfortunate
impression and lead to confusion.

I remain then most honoured by the invitation and touched by your
generous insistence upon it. I am always happy to find myself in Rome;
but I think that at this congress I should be out of place.

*

Settled in Paris, Barker did what Gilbert Murray urged him to do, and
joined the branch of the League of Nations Union:

Oct. 26, 1934.

I dutifully joined the committee of the L. of N. branch here. The first
meeting I'm called to is to decide whether we ought to go on or dissolve.
Have you any "dope" (as the Americans and, I have no doubt, the
English now say) to impart to me on the point? Or to save you trouble,

R

is there anybody in Paris whose opinion you think would be a good guide? For a first meeting won't make the situation very clear to me; yet I shall have to vote.

This may not find you in time; for I see the meeting is on the 30th (Tuesday next). In which case don't even bother to answer.

But look us up, again, *please*, when *you* are here.

As Murray had to go to Paris to attend meetings of the Union, in which he was deeply interested, Barker pressed him to stay with them:

Oct. 31, 1934.

Why don't you – Helen bids me say – let us put you up for those three days? You ought to come:

a because we'd so much like to have you.

b because this is a much healthier part of Paris in December than down by the river.

c because you can have a quiet room and a latchkey and come and go as you will.

d because you will be properly fed. *I* am on a *régime* which calls for a public analyst as well as a cook!

e because you can then more comfortably read us the *Seven against Thebes*.

f because I could then read you my Preface to *Hamlet* – but no, you may think that a reason for not coming.

However, I have lots more why you should. So do. And meanwhile our affection to you and yours.

That year Helen's novel, *Come, Julia*, was published in London. Written with distinction, it is about London, Devonshire, and Spain, and people with money. It was praised for its delicacy, which was just praise. Gilbert Murray mentioned the novel in a letter to Barker:

Dec. 31, 1934.

Come, Julia was a great pleasure. I quite agree about the " quiet beauty " which runs through it. There is a delicacy of touch and observation and a complete abstinence from the obvious effects. I cannot help wondering how Julia got on when she arrived at León. I think it must have been rather a shock to her. But the book was a real pleasure to me.

By the way, when you have time look at *Agamemnon* 1060, p. 46, in my translation, where Clytemnestra says to Cassandra:

" If, dead to sense, thou wilt not understand . . .
Thou show her, not with speech, but with brute hand."

What do you think the business should be? Does Clytemnestra address the Leader, as I say, or some attendant of her own who has come out? The Leader seems either to stop the attendant or to refuse to act himself, but it is a little puzzling.

Helen produced two other novels in 1932 and 1935, and in 1936 an anthology entitled *The Locked Book*, containing quotations from English, French, and other authors, including the Old and New Testaments and Plato, alluding to angels. These quotations, she said, had been collected in the course of her reading. The book contains an introduction, which ends with the suggestion that it " may be laid down with something of wonder, doubt, and, perhaps, a desire for mysterious beatitudes ".

*

During Barker's connection with the British Drama League the National Festival of Community Drama had been founded, and the great development of drama festivals throughout Great Britain had got well established. The drama festival had spread to other countries, and in Canada the Governor-General, Lord Bessborough, took great interest in the idea, and made a practice of getting the best adjudicators he could find for the annual final performance. This was continued by his successor, Lord Tweedsmuir, and in the spring of 1936 Barker was asked to act as adjudicator in the finals at Ottawa. He had taken no active part in the festivals in England, but this invitation appealed to him, and he accepted. He and Helen were the guests of the Governor-General; he kept himself very remote. It appears, too, that he was not at all liked as an adjudicator, for he sat on the stage speaking as at a lecture, which was highly interesting to those who knew him, but not the sort of critical appreciation and analysis of their work the amateurs desired. One of the plays included in the festival was Shaw's little piece, *Overruled*, which Barker disliked, and said so, though the report is that the performance was by no means a bad one. Helen did not care for the affair at all, and looked displeased throughout.

*

All these years there was one play Barker's admirers never forgot, for it had never been publicly performed, the one-timed censored *Waste*, since revised and accepted. During Anmer Hall's tenancy of the Westminster Theatre, his young producer, Michael MacOwan, conceived the idea of getting Barker's permission to allow the play to be done, so he paid a visit to Paris to try to persuade him. Barker was only too pleased to see his visitor and to hear about his plans, but when his own play was mentioned he declared with emphasis, " Impossible ! " It could not be cast, he declared, and he would not entertain the idea. None the less, he was gratified to be asked, and at last, with many reservations and conditions, agreed. That he was troubled about it can be seen in a letter he sent to Harcourt Williams :

Sept. 21, 1936.

The Westminster Theatre is proposing to do my re-written *Waste*: that is – I have made this a condition – if they can find a Trebell (the chief part) who can really be relied upon to carry the thing, the whole four acts of it, on his shoulders. I'm not much help to them with suggestions, as you may guess. I don't know if you saw the play or have ever read it: but can you suggest anyone whose work I may not know, who could really dominate a performance when all the parts around him had been as " heavily " cast as possible? If anybody does come to your mind I'd be grateful for a word about him.

How are you and yours? My best remembrances, please.

We went to Salzburg for our holiday. The best of the music magnificent. Reinhardt – I make reserves, the *Everyman*: very dashing in its way. But all sin and no redemption! The banquet magnificent, but the Mass a foozle. No; that is unjust. The thing is very well done and yet – and yet! At no moment did I want to go on my knees. And I could hardly keep from it when Old Poel first did it – the real thing; not Hofmannsthal – in the St. George's Hall years ago. As to his Faust, though, I make no reserves, that is *wrong*.

I hope – if *Waste* does get done – that you may want to come and play (if you're free by chance at that moment) what they will want to offer you. I have to let them cast as far as they can from their company. But when I talked to MacOwan (who does things there) that didn't seem to take us very far.

A cast for *Waste* was agreed upon, and Harcourt Williams played the Doctor, the leading part being taken by Nicholas Hannen: it was a good cast. Barker stipulated for five weeks' rehearsal, one week for MacOwan to do the preliminaries, while he would, perhaps, do the rest. In fact, he worked at the play for four weeks, so that the production practically became his own. He seemed bursting with energy, and all were in great awe of him, attempting to give heed to every detail of his instruction. Indeed, detail was added to detail to such an extent that not until the dress rehearsals was there a run-through of any act. He would let nothing alone and would pass nothing that did not seem to him exactly right. In fact, he put more into the production than the players could digest, the result being that at the first performance the play moved very slowly and the effect at which he aimed was not achieved. He was meticulous about starting rehearsals to time. One morning the three opening players of the act to be rehearsed were not present at 10.25, when the rehearsal was timed for 10.30, but Barker insisted that the rehearsal should start to the minute, the understudies of the absent players being used. On another occasion MacOwan asked him how he thought the piece was going, and he replied with his hand on MacOwan's shoulder, " We are in a precarious position." He gave everyone a bad time. As usual, he gave little or no praise, but was adored. Every property was carefully specified, and when it was suggested to him that there were too many pieces of furniture in a set to allow the actors to move with comfort, he retorted that that was the idea : they were not to move for the sake of moving. At the dress rehearsal, says Michael MacOwan, he had the position of a chair altered in the second act : when reminded that the original position was important and that a number of players would be likely to be upset by the unexpected change, his reply was that he was aiming at that very thing ; they need shaking up, he said. The company was delighted with him, but the result was not up to the Barker standard though above the best of the London stage.

The Barkers stayed at the Ritz, and Helen came to fetch him for luncheon, sometimes also in the late afternoon, and whether she was waiting in the car or not, as soon as the chauffeur appeared, Barker stopped, grasped his bowler hat, and was off. Helen never came into the theatre. This was Barker's most considerable labour on the stage for a long period.

*

Barrie had got him made LL.D. of Edinburgh University when he was Chancellor : Barker did not dislike being called " Doctor ". It was natural that he should take great interest in Barrie's last play, *The Boy David*, when it was put into rehearsal in London in February 1936. There was much trouble over the play, as Elisabeth Bergner, who was to play the title part, fell ill, and it was not until November that it was given a fortnight's run in Edinburgh. Barker went to see it. Barrie was ill and unhappy ; so was Barker, though he cheered up his friend by appreciation of the play's merits, which he considered to be great, and was much disturbed by its poor public reception when it came to His Majesty's Theatre in London on 14 December. Barrie died on 19 June the following year, and Barker wrote a preface to the published version of the play, in which he declared that " The English theatre to-day owes much to the encouraging influence of Barrie's originality ", and about this particular play he said :

Barrie is not transcribing a chronicle. He is taking an old tale for a theme, interpreting it anew, treating it as a parable for the expression of the idea he finds in it, readjusting it for the better expression of the idea.

Acknowledgment of Barker's scholarship was made by Allen Lane, who, shortly after he started the 6d. Penguin Books in 1936, asked Barker to edit Shakespeare's plays and poems in separate volumes ; he refused, but suggested G. B. Harrison for the job, who was invited to do it, with the result that the Penguin Shakespeare is the best available text of the plays. How it should be done was discussed with Barker, who offered his ideas and approved the general layout and methods proposed by Harrison.

The B.B.C. had asked him several times to broadcast on Shakespeare or the National Theatre, but he had steadily refused. He had been invited by George Barnes (now Sir) to make a selection from Shakespeare for a broadcast, and replied on 31 July to say:

The first thing that strikes me is that of William Shakespeare you should only read sonnets and lyrics. Plays are not meant for reading aloud, more particularly over the wireless.

That, indeed, was an opinion then shared by many. Asked for his advice, Barker gave a warning that " if you turn on the tap of advice, you may find it hard to turn it off again ". He made, however, many suggestions, and said he might be willing to give a talk himself on how " the film can be fitted to W.S.", also upon Shakespeare on the air. " This ", he said, " is the problem. These are its chief factors. Can you deal with *them* and solve it? "

The outcome was that on Thursday, 25 February 1937, he gave a twenty-five-minute talk entitled " Alas, Poor Will! " It was broadcast from Paris, as he could not come to London, and was regarded as one of the best radio talks ever given. Originally intended to take twenty minutes, Barker wrote twice as much as was required, and the time was extended by five minutes because what he had written was so good. The talk was downright criticism of film and radio performances of Shakespeare. He declared that the cinema adds too much to the plays while the radio subtracts too much. He went on:

There is far more to our enjoyment of a play than the mere looking and listening. Its performance, both on our part and the actors, is an exercise in social and human relationships.

Printed in *The Listener*, the talk was replied to rather disdainfully the following week by Alfred Hitchcock writing on behalf of films. One suspects he must have read Barker's talk, not listened to it, for the real Barker quality was in the voice and manner, perfectly conveyed on the radio. The film producer declared flatly that " the cinema has come to Shakespeare's rescue ". The screen improves Shakespeare, he asserted, and turns " a lot of nonsense " (by which he meant the poetry, which " spells considerable gloom to the average mind of to-day ") into pleasing fare for the housewife. Defending radio productions, Val Gielgud more modestly pleaded for the hundreds of thousands of listeners who had never seen a Shakespeare play.

After this experience, Barker was pressed to broadcast again, but refused:

I really cannot afford to do any more broadcasting. The net result for me was a spate of begging letters; from people who thought I was dead – but, being thus unexpectedly alive, might be good for £5. So my fee vanished – twice over.

All the same, he did want to broadcast once more, this time on the work of the British Institute in Paris, of which he had become Director.

*

For some years the British Embassy in Paris had been considering the creation of a British Institute in the city. There had been an English Guild since the 'nineties, carried on by teachers of English at the Paris schools, which in 1902 had become the International Guild. In 1927, after its usefulness had been demonstrated, it was decided to take over the Guild as a tutorial college; an ambitious scheme was inaugurated, and the British Institute was set up in January 1928 as part of the University of Paris, in premises occupied by the Guild at 6 rue de la Sorbonne. Although under the highest auspices, the British Institute did not secure the funds its work required, despite much enthusiasm and able work put into it, and despite an increasing number of students. In fact, the direction of the Institute proved unsatisfactory. Then in 1937 the Embassy suggested to the joint French and English committee that Granville Barker might be approached to become its Director. This was agreed; and Barker accepted the position, and became part-time Director of the Institute. He took up the work with characteristic energy, and his offer to the B.B.C. was with the object of getting the British public interested; but the offer was not accepted. He set about getting the interest of important people, however, especially people with money, and he succeeded. In fact he set out to " produce " the Institute as a place of learning, devoted to preparing French and English students for the university examinations of both countries, and especially to making English literature better known in France. A letter to Murray tells him the news:

April 24 [1937].
How like you to mention casually in a postscript that you have just finished a critical edition of the Greek text of Aeschylus. When you find *time* I can't think. But I expect that Athens is a welcome relief from Europe 1937.
It reminds me of St. John Hankin's remark to me about you – before I knew you, I think. What are you to say of a man who starts a book on Greek Literature with " To read and re-read the scanty remains now left

to us of the Literature of Ancient Greece is a pleasant and not a laborious task . . ."?

But this is to tell you two things (a) I'm now Director of the British Institute in the University here. My accession to the post not a world-shaking event; but the work may be interesting if I can fit it in with my own work. And (b) we shall be here in Paris at the end of June, and will hope to see you.

Although he worked there only in the afternoons, Barker established himself in a handsome room, which he beautifully decorated and furnished at his own expense, where he gave his mind to his task. He had competent heads of departments, and was himself the grand gentleman. Normally, he did not see the students or the tutors, and gave instructions in writing, and while he inspired great respect and confidence there was no intimacy with staff or students. He looked at one, it was said to me by a member of his staff, as through spectacles, or as though one was not there, so that people were conscious of being on a level different from his: indeed, he made them feel uncomfortable. Then, by a word, or glance, or gesture, he would put them at ease, and immediately and for good changed their attitude to him. Thus there are not many people who speak or write slightingly of him, for what I have referred to was rarely missing in his personal contacts. He was by no means an easy man with whom to work, however, for he expected perfection – everything had to be just right. He was very sparing of praise. Occasionally Miss Maud Burt, to whom the Institute owed much, head of the English Department, or J. M. Cocking, whom he appointed as his deputy, would be asked to make up a luncheon party at the Barkers', and occasionally Cocking was invited to the Château de Grégy, the Barkers' country house about an hour's ride from Paris, for Barker seems to have been fond of the young man upon whom he came greatly to depend, but this was as close as any personal contact with those who worked at the Institute went.

At 5.30 in the afternoons he fascinated large audiences by a series of lectures at the Institute on Shakespeare's dramatic poetry, the memory of which continues: he also lectured on *Hassan*. Throughout his director-ship he organized public lectures at the Sorbonne by distinguished people from England, the first by Lascelles Abercrombie, while Hilaire Belloc, John Masefield, W. H. Auden, Professor Ernest Barker, Cyril Norwood, Charles Williams, Desmond MacCarthy, G. M. Young, and Geoffrey Faber were among other lecturers. At one reception at the Sorbonne on behalf of the Institute he took pains to have railed off part of the handsome drawing-room for the leading guests, which was something the French did not understand. He started a monthly bulletin, which had only a short life, from November 1937 to April 1939; Barker did not write for it. Under him the Institute occupied more and more of the extremely unpretentious building in which it was housed, for the number of students steadily increased. Barker would have liked much better premises, and was in process of getting the money to make a move possible; he did in fact find money to add two floors to the building, one of which housed the library; but even that was not enough. Then, to complete the story, at Easter, 1939, he resigned. The war atmosphere was gathering and he became dispirited. Also he became seriously unwell.

*

As the Stage Society was in difficulties during the 'thirties, it was not surprising that an approach was made to Barker for help, and he replied to W. S. Kennedy, who had served with him on the council, declining to do anything, in a characteristic letter from Paris:

Jan. 8, 1937.
My impulse: 1. to do what you ask because you ask it, and one likes to please, and 2. to be and feel good natured, 3. to do something for old times' sake for the S.S. But I check myself; asking whether if the S.S. can't finance itself through its membership its mandate is not exhausted. I don't remember which way my vote went in 1904; but I have certainly thought since that incorporation of such a society is a mixed benefit. It may retain its body when it has lost its soul. Asking besides whether none of the new abundant experimental societies and theatres will do these plays, and if not, why not? *Are* there plays which it is left for the S.S. to do?
I haven't in any case £ s d which I ought to spend in such a way. But – and don't think second thoughts merely churlish – should one even spend 50s.? I know no better on these grounds, if I'm right, than to say No. Again, don't think me merely churlish.

*

John Gielgud had first met Barker some years earlier in 1928, when Anmer Hall was producing *Fortunato* and *The Lady from Alfaqueque*, in both of which he played, and Barker had seen him at the Old Vic the year after, being much interested in his playing. When Gielgud was preparing to open his season at the Queen's Theatre in the spring of 1937, he wrote asking if Barker had a preface to *Richard II*, which called forth the following reply dated 16 June 1937 from the Ritz Hotel, after Barker had seen *Romeo and Juliet*:

How pleasant to hear from you.
R. and J. Yes, I liked it much. I could have made reservations, but I'd do that of a performance by archangels. But it was far the best bit of Shakespeare I'd seen in years.
Richard II. I've done no preface to it, nor none am like to do.

My advice! I can't imagine it can be of much use to you. But if a talk might serve any sort of purpose, and if you're within reach between now and Monday night (when we leave London), why it would be jolly to see you again at a less distance; so do fix a time to come in.

They met, and later that month Gielgud asked his opinion about going into management on his own account, and got sound advice in which the writer comments on his own experience:

June 27, 1937.

I fear I shan't be in England again till – heaven knows when! But – in case you come over – we shall stay in Paris till the end of July; then I hope for the mountains and Salzburg.

It would be very pleasant to see you and to talk. I am only afraid that my counsel – such as it would be – might increase and not lessen your distraction. For distracted – if I guess right – you must be, between two aims: the one, which is really forced on you, a personal career, the other, the establishing of a theatre, without which your career will not be, I think you rightly feel, all that you proudly wish it to be. It was Irving's dilemma; he clung on to one horn of it for a number of glorious years; then he was impaled on the other, and it killed him. It was Tree's; and he would have died bankrupt, but for *Chu Chin Chow*. George Alexander, thrifty Scotsman, replied to me when I congratulated him on the 25th anniversary of his management: Well, I've not done much for the drama (though in a carefully limited fashion he had), but I've paid salaries every Friday night without fail, and *that's* to my credit. And it was.

I won't say that there too was my dilemma, because I never had such a career in prospect, I should suppose. But I pinned my faith to the theatre solution; and finding it – with a war and a " peace " on – no go, I got out. It must be your dilemma, I think; for you have rather the Irving than the Alexander conception of your job (by the way I never saw your Hamlet, I wish I had). The question is; have times changed? can you yet hope to establish a theatre? if not the blessed " National " Theatre (but names mean nothing) [then] such a one as Stanislavsky's or even Reinhardt's of 30 years back? For that you'll gladly sacrifice as much of your personal career as need be – this I see; but naturally you don't want to make the sacrifice in vain.

Is a compromise practicable? I don't know. Everyone English will be for compromise, just because they are English. And even the work has to be done in England. Perhaps one must accept there the fruits of the national virtue and failing combined. It makes for politics, but bad art. And so it is, you see, that the question (for me) opens up: no longer for me a practicable question, therefore, I can still say *theatre or nothing* and not suffer. For you a devilishly practical one; so, who am I to counsel you? Only I'd say: do not expect to pluck more than a few grapes from thistles, and don't expect them always to be of the best quality!

Barker went to see *Richard II*, and afterwards the two were together at luncheon, with Helen, at the Cassons': one of the very few actresses Helen could tolerate was Sybil Thorndike, whom she liked very much. The next day, on his return to Paris, Barker wrote a letter of detailed criticism to the actor which, long as it is, deserves printing in full:

Oct. 15, 1937.

. . . But I'll now tumble out my impressions of *Richard II* for you, and if you pick anything useful out of them for a future time, good. Remember, though, that I haven't looked at the play's print for a fairly long time and my memory is a sieve.

I applauded you at first sight for so unselfishly hiding yourself in a corner. But I fear you were wrong to do so. I fancy W.S. thought of the scene as a meeting of the Privy Council – Richard presiding (the P.C. and the Star Chamber, the King absent, were the courts of the day for State affairs) probably raised on a dais at the end or centre of the table, formally presiding. And after letting the discussion rip – and actually, I dare say, playing cup-and-ball or reading Froissart or the *New Yorker* during the dull parts. But the point is that while W.S. doesn't begin to *write Richard* till he comes back from Ireland (till he becomes himself, a *man* and not merely a King), he does keep one guessing and wondering what sort of a man he is up to that point, and what the devil he will do next, and the more we see of his cryptic face the better. You got that admirably during the Lists scene – as good a piece of Shakespeare staging as I can remember. But I'd like it done from the beginning. Richard, of course, carries too much sail for his keel and so swings violently from side to side at any puff of wind. But his stillness and silence in between – which W.S. intended, I think, though he had not yet discovered how to make such things positively effective (as Othello's silences are) – show us the poet who is not really living in this practical world at all, but in one of his own imagination.

All the " plastique " of this part of the production and the blending of the scene (but not a word of the D. of Gloucester could I hear. I fancy she was getting her emphasis all wrong) all that scenic invention excellent. Gaunt's death scene particularly, and the colloquy afterwards (though damn all that crossing and genuflection and *Dies Irae*) first-rate.

. . . I understand you not stressing the sexual-pervert part of Bushy-Bagot-Green – though of course the suggestion is there: but very delicately done by Shakespeare, an *ex post facto* one, only brought in at their dying moment, cf. Gaveston in *Edward II* by a man who wasn't a sensitive dramatist – but I think they might be more gorgeously dressed than the others, to show that they are the caterpillars of the Commonwealth, whereas Bolingbroke and Mowbray and Aumerle should be " rich not gaudy ". But why is the poor D. of Y. (who is by the way rather a Polonius – a first study for him? – your man lacks distinction) so shabby?

But my chief grouse is about the verse. It is a lyrical play. W.S. has not yet learned to express anything except in speech. There is nothing much, I mean, in between the lines, as there is in *Macbeth* (for an extreme example). Therefore – I am preaching; forgive me – everything the actor does must be done *within the frame* of the verse. Whatever impression of action or thought he can get within this frame without disturbance of *cadence* or *flow*, he may. But there must be nothing, no trick, no check, beyond an honest pause or so at the end of a sentence or speech. And I believe you'll seldom find that the cadence and emphasis – the mere right scansion of the verse does not give you the meaning without much of any further effort on the actor's part. The *pace* you may vary all you like. Clarity there must be, of course. But here, it is really the breaking of the rhythm which destroys it, for, as I said, Shakespeare has written one tune and his words are playing that in the treble (say); if one tries to play another tune with them in the base – naturally we can't understand the thing.

Variety of pace – tone – colour of speech; yes, as much as possible, but within the *frame*. You must not turn W.S.'s quavers into crochets or semibreves – or semiquavers for that matter. And I think each character ought to have his own speech. I thought during the first half of the play they were imitating each other; then I found they were imitating *you* and your taste for sadder *sforzandi*; good enough for Richard and clearly indicated for " Down – down I come –" and " No lord of thine, thou haught insulting man –" appropriate to him but quite wrong for Augustus Caesar-Bolingbroke or Mowbray or the " Tenor " gallantry of Aumerle.

The thing got – I began to swear – more and more hung up as it went on, and you began to play more and more astride the verse instead of in it. The scenic invention of the deposition scene was again admirable. B. on the throne, you wandering about below like a lost creature – admirable (but oh if you'd have let the marvellous and sweet music of that verse just *carry you along with it*). The *tune* of that " bucket and well " bit (again the business admirable) and even more of the " No deeper wrinkles yet . . .". It is like an *andante* of Mozart. Shakespeare has done it for you. Why not let him?

Yes, scenic invention here again admirable, but I fancy that this is meant to be a scenic repetition of the opening, with B. taking his place on the very throne on which we saw Richard sitting then.

And your holding up the whole play (progressively so) obliged you to cut the Aumerle conspiracy, the dramatic point of which is merely that it is a swift and excited interlude between the *slow* (this good again, I thought) farewell between Richard and the Queen and the slow, philosophical death scene. " I have been wondering how I may compare . . . etc.", the pace of which is changed by the arrival of the groom and goes to the rapidity of the death – but that ought to be a hell of a fight. Note that for all the action suggested in the play there has been no single stroke of violence till then. It has all been done by politics – B. finessing the old D. of G. and taking you without a struggle, to when at the end that politician gets his dirty work *done* for him – it should be very dirty.

Then he comes in – the hypocrite – and condemns Exton. He feels in a sense what he says. But this is why the B.'s of this world are successful; they can feel that way.

An admirable criticism, applying the writer's stage treatment of verse – that the actor must play within it, not ride away on it, the rhythm of the poetic-dramatic significance being one. The letter brought a reply from the recipient in which Gielgud defended his method of acting the part, which, he said, was based to some extent on what C. E. Montague had written about F. R. Benson – but he showed how much he had taken Barker's criticism to heart by the night after shortening the play by eight minutes, without cutting a word, " simply by speeding up : and how it improved the performance ! " to use the actor's own words. This response deserved the letter he at once received from Barker:

Oct. 19, 1937.

Bless you – for you really are a most satisfactory person to write to, and it pleases me no end that you should have been able to turn all that talk to some practical use. For I repeat, I know how comparatively easy it is to criticize and how hard to *do* the thing right.

First to clear away that Benson business. B. *was* good and God knows he wasn't always, and he did let the thing carry him away – though still and progressively not at the pace it might have. But if he played the " jewels . . . beads " passage slowly it was probably because he could not remember his words. (Never shall I forget the performance from that point of view. I had just been playing Richard, so I happened still to know it, and when B. *started off* with

> Old John of Gaunt, time honour'd Lancaster
> Hast thou, according to the oath thou swear'st
> Brought hither Henry, thy rebellious son . . .

and so on . . .!)

And Montague was a good critic; but I doubt if he had much technical knowledge; nor perhaps has Agate – good Shakespearean critic though he is – about the best among the few I read – as much as perhaps he thinks. And his criticism now lapses rather often into the " This sort of thing gives me the pip . . ." method. And after all, for a foundation of criticism technical knowledge is needed. Don't let him worry you. And don't let me worry you either.

I appreciate that difficulty, of avoiding reciting, in giving life to a conventional form, of getting sense and music combined. I believe the solution may lie in doing the things separately at first, sitting round a table – *if* you have a company accustomed to working with you and to follow – and one day working out the sense, and the next singing the music, and then, when first you go on the stage doing nothing but the movements (the words merely muttered). Then when all three are so fixed in the mind that you don't have consciously to think of them – but not till then – letting the whole thing rip. Of course it won't come right at the first go off, but you could discuss what is proportionately wrong. Care for *which* third it is that is harming the other two-thirds and correct this. But it might give the spontaneity – the appearance of it – that is needed. And if you could impress on people; take all conscious pains possible at rehearsal, i.e. at the partial rehearsals: for sense, for music, for movement: at the full rehearsals, getting these three combined, learn to " let yourself go " and only keep enough self-consciousness to enable you to correct faults (well, you know all about that duplicate consciousness which only an actor, and a *real* actor, seems to understand). The plan might not work. But for a play like *Richard* – and for a good deal more of W.S., it might be worth trying.

I believe *Richard* plays quickly because in moments of excitement he thinks devilish quickly. He has the " artistic temperament " which we get furious with because so many people sham it. But with him – and with W.S.: it is far more autobiographical than *Hamlet* – he genuinely either can think or not. This explains those cryptic places in the earlier part.

But when I say *think*, I mean *imagine*. He does not think in the scientist's sense. But once his imagination is lit up, the thoughts come at a rush, and he never lacks words – or rather, images for them, cf. Shelley – another of that kidney. And, since he is an artist, painful feelings are as interesting to him as pleasant ones, in fact more so, because – a sensitive creature – he can feel more keenly. But here are pages running away over Richard, of whom you know a darn sight more than I do.

The writer then went on to refer to other plays:

As to the *Merchant*, I've never really liked it as a whole. It hasn't the true thrill in it – except, partly, for Shylock. It is elegant accomplishment – and *how* elegant WS. could make it – and skilled construction. But his heart was never in the thing. That is why, I think, both Antonio and Bassanio are really empty – Morocco is as human as they – and though Portia is a pretty fairy tale, she never *quite* comes to life. He *does* get something into it once he has two stories running together in the Trial Scene – and thereafter in the last bit at Belmont – which gives us the best of Portia, the most lovely and alive. Of course, there is Shylock. Shakespeare got him – but not thoroughly until the Tubal scene (in prose: a sign that he was writing elegant artificial verse for the rest, when he let go, it was into prose): and not in tune. He meant him to be a contemptible character, the sordid villain of the play and it was too late to change all the values without ruining it. You'll do an interesting S., I'm sure – and why not try it. My fear would be that you'd spoil the balance and the scheme which I see as Magnificent and *Stately Venice*: even the young men stately: and *real* this side of the story, i.e. real for a fairy tale. Belmont magnificent and quite childishly unreal. The contrast to both these – Shylock, the sordid little *outsider*, passionate, resentful, writhing under his wrongs – which are real – and the contempt of the Venetians. We dislike him thoroughly and are meant to. *But* when you are a Shakespeare how much more you *pity* people you dislike (your conscience tells you to) than those you like : you give your love to them, they don't *need* your pity. If Antonio and Bassanio had been made live characters, they'd have pitied S. too. As they are not – our pity goes out to him a bit more. But I think he mustn't bate one jot of his unpleasantness to gain our pity. He must either earn it as a most objectionable creature, or not at all. Will you do this : that's the question – for me.

Have you ever tried Malvolio? You could do something very good with him. For he had imagination : the imagination, though, which is swamped in egotism and so becomes purely ridiculous. You see a lot of them about – in Chelsea, I expect in velvet coats (they used to wear) instead of yellow stockings, painting sham pictures and writing sham poetry and being dreadfully solemn about it. But there is a tragic side to the man, and again, as with Richard, this comes out with misfortune, and he acquired dignity.

But your leading lady isn't a Viola – alack – only an Olivia – the dainty child – a princess weighed down with splendour. For Viola you want something really boyish – a Miss Bergner who can speak English *and* beautifully.

But some day do this : a picture of two great Elizabethan Houses (both alike in dignity, both that W.S. knew something about by this time. In *R. and J.* he had it all wrong – Capulet is an old Alderman, like Papa) – for that is what they are, and *all* well-bred, down to Fabian. Feste outlawed, Sir Andrew a gallant idiot, even Sir Toby, only a drunkard but not spewing drunk.

As to me – oh, no. I have to put it all into books now, and as quick as I can before my time is up. I doubt if I'd *be* any good as a producer any longer – other reasons apart. I doubt if I've energy and patience left.

But an argument with me – just the two of us – might clear your mind sometime, and mine. And, you see, you have *got* it in you.

It is no wonder that the actor had been tempting him with the idea of producing again ; but Barker was adamant.

Later that year John Gielgud played Joseph Surface in *The School for Scandal*, produced by Tyrone Guthrie, at the Queen's Theatre under Gielgud's management, and the actor received the following letter :

Nov. 30 [1937].
I have, thank God, no self-granted moral responsibility towards Sheridan, so I was able to sit back and enjoy myself, which I did, and came away feeling the lighter in heart with the world to-day, a little easier – which, I take it, is how one ought to feel after seeing the *S. for S.* With the rather fine pleasure too of having seen the best J.S. I remember or am likely to encounter. Forbes-R. was good, but even then, elderly, and the more inexcusable. I liked your dandy-ism, and shallowness. Just – for me – the right value.

The humanizing of the whole thing – even the sentimentalizing of it is justifiable. For after all what S. did was to sentimentalize upon the Congreve tradition. This " man of sentiment " being a man of sham sentiment. Charles and Sir Peter and Sir O. being the genuine senti-mentalists. But I'm not sure that so much *bon ton* need have been sacri-ficed. Lady S.'s salon a bit of a bear garden, and the edge taken off Sir Peter. C.'s softer bits and the fall of the screen, how good, though; one forgot, *for a moment*, the loss of the rest. And one always knew that Rowley well played and not cut would be not half a bad part.

But I'm beginning to meander into criticism – I thank you for a good evening that's really all I wanted to say.

★

Because of his successful broadcast earlier in the year, Barker was asked to give the National Lecture, which took place on 13 October, the subject being " The Perennial Shakespeare ". This broadcast was again much praised. In it he declared that Shakespeare was –

searching for some more universal truth which lies behind the ever-shifting appearances of things, some key to their meaning . . . it is the part of a great poet to transcend circumstances for us and to abolish time.

He went on to put forward " the doctrine of Shakespeare's stage for Shakespeare's plays ", in the course of which he said :

we do not want to restore what may be called the " accidentals " of Shakespeare's stage, or to present the plays in a replica of the Old Globe.

This was good doctrine, which he went on to make more explicit :

the essential of Shakespeare's stage . . . upon which his craft as a play-wright *did* depend (were) . . . the things about it which gave him free-dom in time and space, and the plays their swift mobility of action; the intimacy of the actors with their audience, which makes soliloquy effective and justifies the familiarity of the clowns; the neutral back-ground which lets him, when he will, paint his scenery in poetry.

He found fault with the prevalent " monkeying " with the plays on the stage, and the talk concluded with an outline of the task of a National Theatre. This and the earlier broadcasts indicate what a brilliant speaker he was.

Much of Barker's writing was prepared for lectures, yet he was never pedagogic or professional; he never rapped his lectern to recall the audience's attention. He was a fascinating lecturer, speaking very fast (for he always had too much to say), his expressive eye holding the audience. He did not domineer. He was persuasive and considerate, he wooed his audience and sought to establish communication. Not that he was self-forgetful, far from it; but he wanted so sincerely the listener

or reader to understand what he was putting forward that he assumed he
was not persuasive enough and appealed almost for forgiveness in an
earnestly confidential manner. He was never rhetorical or declamatory.

A characteristic feature of all his writing, in whatever form, was that
it had the nature of conversation, depending upon tone and inflection, so
that it is always better when spoken. To this was due its involved,
parenthetical, and repetitive style, and the impression that he was a man
thinking aloud. That he sought to create such an impression is certain,
but with the result that much of what he wrote appears to be inconsequential and tentative. No doubt the best writing has qualities of good
conversation, but when a conclusion is expected a positive point of view
has to be declared, which Barker seems to have sought to avoid. This
was in the attempt to appear to be undogmatic, and suggests a humility
he did not in fact possess.

★

After Barker had left the British Institute, John Gielgud asked him in
June 1939 to give some help in his playing of Hamlet in preparation for
the production of the play at Kronborg Castle, Elsinore, which Barker
did. After attending a rehearsal at the Lyceum, he invited the actor to the
Ritz and gave him notes from 10.30 in the morning until 1.15, and the
next day, Sunday, they rehearsed all day, to try out and improve what
Barker had suggested. Barker then wrote:

June 26, 1939.
Your telegram came, and thank you for it. Thank you too for trusting
somewhat in my preface. And if, beyond this, I have been of use to
you at all – it gladdens my heart. Besides which, that rehearsal showed
me more than one point I had missed till now. Thanks yet again
therefore.

I'm sorry my notes were unusable, but you are sending them I gather
to Copenhagen – where they may do what they will with them for me.
They should, however, acknowledge Sidgwick and Jackson's rights in
the matter. And if you want to place any substitute for them in the
Lyceum programme, better collaborate with Frank Sidgwick: telephone
to him at Holborn 7927.

We're off again by the Ferry to-night. Good luck on Wednesday.
I expect you are, by chalks, the best Hamlet going to-day. And that is
something to say of any man!

★

When war appeared imminent in the spring of that year, British Actors'
Equity Association had prepared a memorandum at the suggestion of
Humbert Wolfe, at the Ministry of Labour, on the situation that might be
expected to arise in the theatre should war occur, which was circulated
to the various theatrical bodies concerned. In that memorandum it was

S

suggested that there should be formed a National Theatre Council, a wartime theatre council, to consist of representatives of artists and managements to look after the interests of the theatre and to undertake theatrical productions in London and throughout the country. Although favourably received by the management side of the business, as by others, including the Ministry, though with some hesitation by Equity, the management bodies threw over the proposal when war actually started; but in the deep gloom that settled on the theatre in those early months of the war a scheme for an Actors' Theatre on an independent basis was prepared by Equity. Though blessed by the Coalition Government, that scheme was never put into operation; had it been carried out it might, perhaps, have formed the beginning of the National Theatre. Having been responsible for these schemes, I sent a draft of the Actors' Theatre proposal to Barker, who took deep interest in them. He wrote to me from St. Germain-en-Laye, and said in a long undated letter:

I am sympathetic and to that extent "understanding", and I did once know something about the matter, and the larger questions involved are the same. . . . The unemployment itself is the grave matter. I fear it may be the only one which you will be able to convince the Government *is* so. They acknowledge little duty to art of any sort and to the drama (as we know) none. . . . Well to remember also that a prejudice exists (*a*) against all co-operative work (*b*) against all enterprises run by artists.

The Government did approve, however, and when promises of the initial £50,000 had been received, he was asked to become the director of the theatre, but, as was feared, he refused:

Feb. 15.

Thank you for thinking of me as Director. But I fear that is out of the question. It is no longer my job. And I have enough other work mapped out for my declining years to see me to the end of them. And I fear more.

In fact, of course, he was by no means well enough for such a task.

Indeed, it appears that he had already been invited to take an active part in the wartime theatre by John Gielgud. Not to overburden this chapter with events that only slightly concern Barker, it may be related that just before the war E.N.S.A. was formed with the object of providing entertainment, including plays, to the troops, without, however, any provision being made for civilian entertainment. During that fatal September, when it was clear that the theatre had to keep itself alive as best it could, Barker wrote to Gielgud from France on 15 September: "If this war is to go on for long, something should be done to save the theatre from falling into the pitiable state (from the point of view of the drama itself) into which it fell during the last. And I think you are a chief among those who can do this." He then proposed a scheme that actors should be called up as part of the National Service system (apart from those who went into the Forces), including over-age men and women, and formed into a company to perform plays on a non-profit-making basis, which, in fact, was the entire essence of the Equity scheme. Gielgud replied that such a scheme could succeed only if Barker would become head of it, which he refused to consider.

*

Barker was, however, to make another contribution to the London stage. During the spring of 1940, when the Actors' Theatre already referred to was still in embryo, not yet still-born, he was invited to direct a production of *King Lear* at the Old Vic, the name part to be played by John Gielgud. This he agreed to do on condition that his name was not mentioned in connection with the production, and that Lewis Casson, who was to play Kent, should be the acknowledged producer. Casson accepted the suggestion with some hesitation, but he was ready to do anything to get Barker back into the theatre. Barker immediately came over from Paris and spent a fortnight with Casson and Gielgud working out details of the production, which Casson then took in hand. Of course, it became known at once what Barker was doing. In the meantime, he wrote constantly to Casson letters that later became a war casualty. He came to London for two weeks' rehearsal and worked with all his old skill and fire up to the first dress rehearsal, after which he suddenly returned to Paris and saw the play no more. In fact, his name was printed on the programme as joint producer with Casson. The first performance took place on 15 April; the day before, Barker wrote to the actor :

> Sunday morning [14 April 1940].
> Lear is in your grasp.
> Forget all the things I have bothered you about. Let your own now well self-disciplined instincts carry you along, and up; simply allowing the checks and changes to prevent your being carried *away*. And I prophesy – happily – great things for you.

He wrote two further letters while the play was running :

> April 29 [1940].
> Did we ever agree as to the precise moment at which Lear goes off his head.
> I believe that Poor Tom's appearance from the hovel marks it. The " grumbling " inside, the Fool's scream of terror, the wild figure suddenly appearing – that combination would be enough to send him over the border-line. Do you mark the moment by doing something quite new?

Difficult, I know, to find anything new to do at that moment. But something queer and significant of madness, followed (it would help) by a dead silence, before you say (again in a voice you had not used before)

Didst thou give all. . . .

I don't doubt you have devised something. But thinking over the scene this struck me – ought to have struck me before; perhaps we did agree to it – so I drop you this line.

You're having an interesting, if exhausting, time, I am sure, and I fancy a most successful one. Congratulations.

April 30, morning.

I think I have it:

. . . show the heavens more just.
   Lear remains on knees at end of prayer, head buried in hand.
Edg : Father . . . poor Tom.
   make much of this : don't hurry it : give it a " Banshee " effect, lilt and rhythm. At the sound Lear lifts his head. Face seen through his out-spread fingers (suggestion of madman looking through bars). The Fool screams and runs on : business as at present. This gets Lear to his feet. He turns towards the hovel watching intently for what will emerge. Dialogue as at present.
   Edgar's entrance and speech. Away . . . warn thee, much as now. And Lear immensely struck by it. cf. Hamlet–Ghost. Just as it is finishing (Edgar not to hurry it) stalk him to present position for Didst – thou . . . *and as he turns for the speech at B. we see that he is now quite off his head. N.B. Once Edgar is on he, Kent and Fool must keep deadly still so that those movements of Lear may have their effect. Translate the Hamlet–Ghost business into terms of Lear and it will about give you the effect.*

I believe this may be right . . . worth trying anyhow.

May 6th, 1940.

Your letter of the 2nd arrived this morning. I'll take thought and answer it to-morrow.

Meanwhile, here's a trifling point:

In the last scene Lear quite ignores (as you now do) the " 'Tis noble Kent, your friend " and merely gives a general answer : " A plague upon you, murderers, traitors all." And later when he looks at him and says, " Are you not Kent? " it should clearly be in a highly indignant " How-dare-you-enter-our-presence-after-I-have-banished-you " tone. And when Kent answers, " The same your servant Kent ", before he can go on to the rest of the line, the old gentleman should repeat, rather feebly, the magnificent " out of my sight " gesture with which in the first scene he banished him. " He's a good fellow. He'll strike. . . ." clearly refers to the Caius impersonation and the tripping up and beating of Oswald. Perhaps we did work this out.

The production had a mixed reception, and one member of the audience at one performance got up from his seat and protested against it. There was little of the real Barker quality, for the production was uncertain and confused, also very slow.

*

While *Lear* was being done, Gielgud had an offer to go to the closed but still equipped-and-seated Lyceum Theatre for a Shakespeare season of his own, and wrote to Barker asking for advice. He was anxious not to set up in management so near the Old Vic, and Barker showed that he had the scheme of the Actors' Theatre in mind (though not for himself), for both Treasury finance and a sum from the Pilgrim Trust had been available had that scheme matured. Barker did not like the Lyceum or " that dreadful Old Vic ", and thought that such a building as His Majesty's Theatre should be secured, but only a non-profit-making concern should be considered. He went into details, and wound up with suggestions about plays :

Othello. I should say that you and Emlyn Williams would make an admirable combination. You'd do an Arab Othello and he a robustly conscienceless Iago very well (from the one thing I've ever seen him do). And if I could be useful to you, a quiet day or so in Paris with you both going through it as we went through *Lear* on my first visit – to that you'd be welcome. But to more than that I fear I must say, No. To begin with, you don't need it. Once you have the flavour of it, the play is dead simple to stage. *Lear* really is difficult, next door to impossible, and perhaps I did lessen its impossibilities a little; one cannot say more, nor could much more have been done, things being as they were. But with *Othello* there are no such fundamental difficulties.

Why the deuce don't you do *Twelfth Night*? A really elegant performance; no clowning allowed. It records William's glimpse of a great household (or let us imagine so). He must have been asked down to Penshurst or Wilton for the week-end. Can't you see him going and buying two new ruffs for the occasion?

You'd make a first-rate Malvolio. Hannen as Sir Toby; a gentleman – Olivia's uncle, mind, who disdains to be drunk on anything but vintage burgundy (of which the cellars are naturally full). Haggard for Sir Andrew; an amiably foolish *knight*, with a real chance, he thinks of marrying Olivia. Hawkins an excellent Antonio, and his wife – if she'd only learn to speak! – quite good for Olivia. Does Edgar (I forgot his other name – Robert Harris, of course!) sing well enough for Feste? You must have a singer. If not he is a possible Orsino, although Orsino is your middle-aged romantic (Forbes-Robertson, aged eternally 40, is probably now playing it at the Theatre Divine, Paradise) or he'd be an excellent Sebastian. And of course you want a boyish Viola with a low, gently vibrating voice, and a mischievous mite of a Maria.

But a performance with all the elegance that we try to give to the

School for Scandal plus romance. A dish, believe me, that you can serve perennially. One no more tires of it than of Mozart's *Jupiter*.

I believe that *Julius Caesar*, played swiftly and ruthlessly for the sake of its action, always comes fresh too.

Nothing came of the Lyceum idea, however, nor, of course, of the Actors' Theatre, and the theatre in England was abandoned to what became the most abounding commercial prosperity it had ever enjoyed.

★

When the Germans invaded France in 1940 the Barkers got with some difficulty into Spain, leaving their apartment in the hands of an American attorney, established in Paris, the American Chargé d'Affaires being asked to look after the library especially. Arriving in Portugal, Barker wrote to Sir Cuthbert Headlam from Curia on 1 July telling him something of their experiences:

A ray of light amid the gloom was the news – in a 10-day-old *Times* – that you had won the seat. I will not say that it *quite* compensated me for the French collapse, but very nearly, Cuthbert, very nearly.

Anyhow, now that you are at the centre of affairs again and daily, I know, telling the Treasury Bench what for, give me some advice. Our recent history will be patent to you from this address. But we are safe and sound, and have had not too hard a time, although Helen is pretty well done in: she stands up to things finely from a moral point of view, but physically only in the end goes under the more.

We've not been to Lisbon yet, but as soon as she is better and it perhaps less packed with refugees, I'll get her there, and we must decide on our homeless course. *Ought I to bring her back to England ?* It is the place for me now, I feel. But what can I do there when I come? Are the men over 60 – and literary gents at that; yet I have *some* energy and competence left ! – now anything more than mouths to feed?

Send me a line of advice. We have been cut off from news for weeks now; and I haven't any idea what the real situation is. Send your letter by air-mail or the F.O. bag – or I'm little likely to get it. I haven't tried any of our people at Lisbon yet – nor do I even know who they are. But when the rush is over I hope to find them less " sticky " than they are likely to be now. But the Portuguese may not let us stay anyhow. The Spaniards gave us a (rather grudgingly enlarged) 4 days to get through.

Our love to Beatrice. It would be jolly to see you both again. The parting with our France was a sad one.

At the end of the month, still unable to get accommodation in Lisbon, he wrote again to Sir Cuthbert: the importance of what he says justifies its being printed in full:

July 30.

My dear Cuthbert,

We had polite permission to go to Lisbon for 4 days – and there at the Embassy about the 24th your letter of the 14th fetched up with me – also procured me, I expect, the honour of an interesting half-hour with the Ambassador. I told him in turn what I thought of your election and that the Conservative Central Office would probably think twice before it tried such conclusions with you again. But I fear diplomats don't understand such things. I do, however, just a little. And pretty plain it is that only by taking such a stand as you took and being justified of it *is* English Parliamentary Govt. to be prevented from going to the devil – as the French has gone. And let the wire-pullers and the toadies take warning in time!

I am thankful you are back in the House, and glad, as things now are – that you are not in office, since it would probably be some minor office – a mere muzzle. Whereas with a knowledgeable and watchful eye and an occasional flick of the tongue you can do much. And I only wish I sat by you as member for Grampound (those were the days!). With my oil (and your vinegar), not to say vitriol occasionally, dear Cuthbert – we could make a good salad-dressing. Why the devil should you be an air-warden? But you are needed as a watch-dog.

As for me, I hear it in unison; from Oxford (the V.C.), Cambridge (Sheppard of Kings) The Law (my Medley), the H. of C. (you) that I am *not wanted* in England. So it looks as if we should sail for New York about the end of the month, where I hope indeed I may be of some use – frustrated desire to do something is fretting! – when I really believe I might be along the lines you indicate if I could be officially or semi-officially set in the proper channel. At present my only touch is with the Consulate, N.Y. (Godfrey Haggard the C.-G. who was in Paris is a near friend and a sort of cousin of mine), and if they don't find me anything I must try Canada.

If you ever get the leisure to write, send me from time to time an " appreciation " of affairs for my guidance. The thing to be *done* at the moment – and for long ahead yet, is simply, of course, to beat the Germans. We over-sixties can't take any direct part in that, so we have to concern ourselves with the past (if we can learn any lesson from it) and the future (to plan for it, but not, oh *not* to talk much of it while men are actually fighting and dying).

The French collapse – their *moral* collapse – yes, you are right, a fearful shock; yet *too* great a one to be fully felt at the moment. I could write you pages of diagnosis of it, even though the facts are still obscure. But that is now the past. The *present* task is to fill up the strategical gap left. I sit in my ignorance puzzling at how that is to be done. If it is to be it will rank as the great diplomatic-military achievement of the war. God send us brains and character in due proportion for dealing with it. The future? (1) (*a*) The French are in for some years of physical and intellectual suffering (they are of a nature to suffer intellectually and profit by it). (*b*) They'll monkey about with their Constitution a lot more yet –

by Revolutionary precedent. (*c*) The more the Germans sustain these present people, the less, one would say their chance of survival (once the mailed fist is lifted). (*d*) Will the Germans foster anarchy in France to lessen her chances of recovery, or will they, by the time this becomes practicable policy, be too afraid for it among themselves? (*e*) Is the blockade going to lead to a starving Western Europe? From that query one could go on through the alphabet. But (2) will be for me that nothing will finally make the French people Nazi-minded; that they will remain one of the corner-stones of civilization – of what is left of it; that they'll do better for the cause of civilization in defeat than they did in victory; but we must do or say nothing now – " say " rather for we shall have to " do " much – which will make relations with the new France impossible, which will help them to prefer the Germans.

You agree? Of course it is all a platitude. But the thing needs watching.

Well, don't let us lose touch. This address should find us till near the end of August. After that try British Consulate, New York. And C. D. Medley will know the last.

Good luck and our love to you both.

I wish we could really smash the Italians. It would make a lot of difference in these latitudes.

The Portuguese are really most courteous to one – and they are wise to keep everybody from rushing to Lisbon at once. But – it is naturally irritating.

Barker did some work at the university of Coimbra, but they had decided to go to New York as soon as a passage could be got, which at last they succeeded in securing on the strength of Barker being taken on the staff of the British Consulate-General in New York. They sailed for the United States in an American ship on 6 September 1940, and on arrival in New York they established themselves at the Mayfair in Park Avenue, where they lived in great style. He did some unofficial work for the British authorities at once.

*

In the following October John Gielgud completed a book on *King Lear* with Hallam Fordham, who wrote a detailed account of the production, and he wrote to Barker about mentioning his work in the play, also about a proposed *Macbeth* production. Barker replied from New York:

Oct. 27, 1940.

Your letter of September 29th arrived the day before yesterday. By airmail this *may* reach you more speedily. About the Hallam Fordham book: no, I'd rather, please, that *all* mention of my share in the business were omitted. The record of the performance itself (and I cannot, of course, object to a copy of the programme being reprinted) may perhaps be of interest to those who take a technical interest in such things. But as to the rehearsals – that is another matter altogether. We were all doing our best, under the circumstances, and this meant many compromises and much that belongs to the occasion only. I came over merely to give some friendly advice, and, as you know, with many misgivings as to its applicability. I do not want it therefore to " go on record" (as the American phrase goes) nor anything that I do not write and print, and so make myself directly responsible for. I have written the substance of this to Miss Gilder. Thank you for consulting me. I hope my decision will not throw the whole book into the discard. But I do decidedly object to anything – as far as I am concerned, being given to the public, which was not given to the public. (When I'm dead and can't contradict you, do what you like !)

As to *Macbeth*, I fear I can't be very helpful. I have a five-year-old draft for a " Preface " here – a solitary copy which I managed to bring away. But when I shall be able to return to it I don't know. I remember making up my mind that much of the Witch scenes were spurious. But, except for Hecate – which is clearly either Middleton or the prompter – we have to accept the stuff as Shakespeare's since it probably replaces what Shakespeare wrote. No – don't cut a line of the Macduff–Malcolm scene. It is meant, I think to illustrate the demoralization which the Macbeth-sort of tyranny spreads even among wholly innocent people like Malcolm – you need an interesting Malcolm – in distrust of himself and of everybody else. (Even the doctor and E. the Confessor, though you may be justified in cutting this *piéce d'occasion* save for contrast, i.e. scepticism and faith.) This theme of demoralization and moral cowardice runs all through. Banquo Ross, Macduff. The murder of the plucky little child, young M. marks the turning point (or rather the news of it when brought to Macduff).

I've never seen one of Rylands' productions. He *may* only be cut out for the control of amateurs. But *discussion* with him could only be helpful and illuminating. And I've always heard that his men speak their verse excellently. You'd get admirable ideas from him and I should guess that he'd welcome any sort of collaboration that he could manage. He is a first-rate and most " humane " scholar and individual. I'm glad that things are so far comparatively well with you and that work is still possible. I am, for the time being, an Honorary Professor at Yale. I'm told this is of use, and other jobs of the sort and other work is in prospect, as much, I expect, as I can tackle. But I'd be happier digging trenches on the Norfolk coast, although I'd dig them badly.

The *Macbeth* preface, a revision of his first attempt for the " Players' Shakespeare ", has never seen the light and almost certainly was destroyed.

From May 1941 he served in the British Library of Information, without salary, as head of the Speakers' Section, where he looked after visitors from Great Britain who had come to lecture in America. He wrote to Gilbert Murray :

May 21st, 1942.
I am now (if you please!) in charge of the co-ordination of British speaking and lecturing in America. A nice little job! I am begging for a human individual "opposite number" in England, whose mind one knows, whose language one speaks, who knows the difference between *first-class* men (for a few of whom the U.S. is hungry – and for the information they can give as to what England is really like to-day) and second-class (whom they no longer want and who are a real danger to us, some of them) so press this on the Powers that Be next time you see them.

Murray's reply was as follows:

July 23, 1942.
It was a great pleasure to see your handwriting and have a short word from you. You must have a peculiarly difficult job. I always think that among difficult undertakings censorship of plays is so difficult as to be beyond human power, and the service of information a close second; broadcasting perhaps third. Whatever you say, there are dozens of reasons against saying it; and whatever you conceal, an equal number against concealing it.

It is no use writing news because you know it all beforehand. I am kept busy writing and broadcasting and sitting on international committees about co-operation in the Beastly Old World which is to follow our success in the war. I have also partly translated and partly invented a fragmentary comedy of Menander, which might possibly amuse you. It is certainly a very interesting landmark in the history of drama. But publishing and printing is a very slow matter now.

It must be very difficult for you to form any conception of American public opinion. It is difficult enough in this small island, but one thing that forcibly strikes me is that the people who are doing solid work haven't the time to speak or write, while those who for one reason or another have been unable or unwilling, fill the air with their demands and conferences.

He afterwards served in the British Information Service till 30 June 1942, when he was relieved of his official work, and regarded himself as having been shabbily treated by the British authorities; but he retained formal connection with the office. He was rather badly ill in New York with eczema, which he had had for some years, causing him to wear white cotton gloves, and on and off he spent a good deal of time in hospital. None the less, in New York he learned to use a typewriter, a useful accomplishment for a man whose handwriting was never easy to read.

At the beginning of December 1942 he went to Toronto, where he delivered the Alexander Lectures at University College on *Coriolanus*. In the middle of September the following year he received a card from Shaw telling him that Charlotte had died: "You will not, I know, mind my writing this to you", he concluded. Charlotte Shaw (eighty-six when she died) had been very fond of Barker always, and felt the severance of their relations very much.

An effort was made by Professor Dover Wilson during 1943 to get Barker to think of establishing himself in Edinburgh after the war and to take charge of a proposed Barrie Memorial Theatre; but, of course, he was not in a state of health to consider anything of the kind. That year it was proposed to make a combination between the National Shakespeare Memorial Theatre Committee and the Governors of the Old Vic; but quarrels about policy arose, and Barker was asked, privately, by Lord Esher to write a strong letter advocating a combination between the Old Vic tradition and modern repertory, which called forth a long letter from Tucson, Arizona, where the Barkers were staying; a reference is made to Stratford-on-Avon at the start:

Feb. 24 [1943].

Stratford, I have long thought, ought to aim at becoming a Shakespeare Academy, giving – besides the necessary elders – youth its chance, and developing the classical spirit; and as there was nothing "classical" in the usual sense about the Elizabethans (except for Ben Jonson) this would not make for dullness. As to the Old Vic, it must change its name, and shed the rest of the silly sentiment which helps to keep it third-rate. And as to our National Theatre – if the Civic theatres are to come into being elsewhere, even unwieldy old London won't wait – and now will be its time, or possibly never. A good thing, at any rate, if you can get rid of that ridiculous South Kensington site. Excellent for a pillar-box – or for the statue of W.S., for which, don't forget, you have to provide out of old Badger's (was that his name?) money, but no use for a factory of drama. Ask Nuffield what are the requirements for a factory, and then translate what he says into the terms of the theatre – it is as simple as that. For the public; they must be able to get there cheaply and easily, with special allowance made for wet winter nights. That means a site adjoining one of the big traffic centres, with underground access if possible. My last hopes were for the Surrey side of the new Charing Cross Bridge – and the time will come, I still think when the railway company will no longer be allowed to hold up a whole city – the National Theatre on one side and the National Opera House on the other, with underground access to the transformed Waterloo Station. In default of this something of the sort by the new Waterloo Bridge might not be bad. But you must have ample space for the building – enough room in the factory for all its essential machinery, unless the manufacture of the article is to be extravagantly costly – and above all you must have your two auditoriums and be perfectly prepared to argue for three. I get cross when people who ought to know better speak of the two "houses" as if they would be a sort of luxury, not to be indulged in until the whole affair was a great "success". They are a sheer economic economy and necessity, as things now are – and indeed always were, as W.A. and I

ought to have seen in the year of grace 1903 – oh, Lord! Anyhow they
have now become an absolute economic necessity. For why? You must
aim at a triple elasticity: as to the sort of play you do; as to the size of
audience it will attract, and (in consequence) as to the number of performances you give of it. And you cannot afford to waste the actors and
their time or the theatre and its space – for these things cost money, and
nowadays a great deal of money. A National Theatre Training Company would be now very advisable. Impossible to produce a fair specimen of the real thing right away. Either it would be very inferior, or
to give it quality there would be a temptation to engage " star " actors
at ridiculous salaries. The result of that would not be good in itself.
Further, the National Theatre must come to depend on its team work,
ultimately on its tradition, and be an example of the truth that in these
and similar affairs the whole is greater than the sum of its parts. And you
must go for quality, first and last. I personally would not give a straw
for a National Theatre which did not set out to be *better* (just that) than
the theatre round the corner. I don't know whether this Training
Company idea would be of any use now. For its accommodation,
Stratford might be borrowed for the chief working period. For trying
out the work it could tour – or even come to London for a strictly
limited time. If the Old Vic had accommodation to offer, it might go
there. But I cannot as I write see any other grounds of collaboration
between National Theatre and Old Vic. The Old Vic is a VOLKSTHEATER
– and of no reliable quality at that. And it is at quality, I insist, that the
National Theatre must aim. If the right theatre building already existed,
National Theatre and Old Vic might go in as joint tenants for a bit. Or
if Old Vic could put forward any claim and guarantee any ability for the
job, it might act as a trainer for the inceptive National Theatre Company.
But I fear that would only result in a muddle – a face-saving muddle.
There is ample room for the two institutions. But how you are to get
them under one roof, each preserving a separate identity, I do not see.

The best thing, for me about the new outlook is the association with the
C.E.M.A., for the theatre is for the first time admitted to the fellowship
of the Fine Arts. You know, don't you that there had to be a legal
decision about this. If you don't Kenneth Barnes can tell you all about it.
And Keynes in the chair, who knows something about economics and
also cares something about art, and you on the board, who have been
known to look at a picture occasionally and even to go to a concert and
are now, damn it, a theatre expert, no less (from nothing has the theatre
suffered as from the people who knew or thought they knew all about it
but certainly knew nothing about anything else) – really it looks as if
something might be done.

I fear this wont be what you want . . . and I'm sorry it is so long, but
I have had no time to make it shorter. But perhaps you can extract
something from it which may serve some purpose.

Let us have some news of you all. We have been here since December,
curing – I hope – our various small ailments. And as I am now quit of
the Information Services (whether they happier to be rid of me or I of

them I do not know; I only a little restless at having no " war job "). I have been for a change doing my own work. Otherwise we have been reading, largely Parkman and Trollope . . . get down your first edition of the *Vicar of Bullhampton* and have another go at it. But oh, but oh, I'd give a lot to be in England for a bit.

Why in God's name is Winston Churchill letting Anderson and that little pip-squeak of a C. of E. make fools of him and Morrison and Bevin over the Beveridge Report? Can't they see that it is a damn' sight more than a financial question? And all the anti-New Deal people here chuckling. Reaction after the war; return to common sense. If they are counting on that – God help them. Beveridge has offered them political salvation on a dinner plate, and they haven't the sense to take it. But was Winston Churchill ever any good over such matters?

Harvard appointed him visiting lecturer on English literature from 1 November 1943 to 29 February 1944. He also lectured at Princeton University the latter year, the substance of the three lectures being published the year after as *The Use of the Drama*. In those lectures he found the educational use of the drama in self-expression. Through education, " the simple and complex, trivial and mighty, art of the drama " has its influence in the state and in industry. And the influence of the arts in general, he said, is that:

It gives a man poise, a point of view, sets up for him a general standard of quality. It helps refine his faculties, mature his perceptions, gives balance to his judgment.

He went on to discuss how the drama should be used in education and how plays should be studied. He found something incongruous in such a discussion " when this most destructive of wars is still raging ", but concluded with the reflection that " Art is not mere entertainment. . . . It is a moral exercise. . . ." While at Harvard he proposed a scheme for the study of Shakespeare in the University – ten to twenty selected students, advanced graduate students possibly, to take one of the important plays and spend a year co-operatively studying it, and under the lead of a *rapporteur* to prepare a report covering everything from text to the staging of the play. He wrote to Professor Dover Wilson suggesting that he should get something of the kind put in hand at home. " Why not ", he asked, " put a little polish on our Shakespeare studies? " In October 1944 he arranged to return to England, but had to go into hospital instead. He lectured at Harvard at Easter, 1945, while waiting to go back to England, and, as they intended, to Paris.

*

During these years in New York Barker worked for a time with W. Somerset Maugham, and there, too, he thought about the war that twenty-six years earlier had caught him in its grasp, bringing him to that city and changing his life. He was then not forty, still young and eager, and with a sense of the future. Now he was feeling old and sick, and his back was turned on the future. Those who met him found a charming and thoughtful man, but withdrawn and uninterested in the self-destruction of the world. On 30 April 1944 he wrote to Sir Cuthbert Headlam:

I have never been so slow and empty of ideas, and generally demoralized in my life. But what does that matter, except to me . . . and not much even to me.

Helen's last volume was published in London in September 1944, entitled *Nineteen Poems*, containing verses written during their stay in New York, though one is dated 1935. The last poem reads:

" Our reign among men seems over,"
Said a thrush to a rose.
" Now there is none to heed us,
Only a battle-array
Man's violent heart beseems.
Hard are his loves and brief.
No time he finds for dreams.
In place of my true notes
He listens for shriek of shell
And roar of gun. Instead
Of your breath, the smell of powder
And smoke is thick around him.
Resistless furies have found him
And ravished him from this pleasance,
These clean and verdant places.

" But not for that must we falter.
Let ours be a holy trust !
The voice, the beauty, we cherish
Must serve of their age-old altar :
Your bloom light up and ward
Forsaken places. Your petals,
Perfect in death as life,
Fall in fair patterns
Upon the unkempt sward ;
And I will sing my song
For ever over and over.
Hymn of poet and lover."

The Barkers arrived back in England late in May 1945 and went again to Sidmouth. He was asked to broadcast, but refused. He was also asked to be chairman of the amalgamated National Theatre and Old Vic, but of course had to refuse. He still wanted the Old Vic productions treated as "preparatory" for the National Theatre. He was in London when the war with Germany ended in 1945 and that evening had dinner with John Gielgud at the latter's house. Barker criticized Gielgud's Haymarket Hamlet and said he did not remember having seen him in the play before. This is referred to in the following letter to the actor. "V.W." is Virginia Woolf, who had written in the *New Statesman* about Ellen Terry after her death.

August 15, 1945.

Here is the V.W. article and thank you. Very good; though she doesn't add much to the book itself. However, who could? The best of its sort I know.

Interesting: it brings up a subject she broached last night. "I cared more for love and life. . . ." But if she had not she would not have been a great actress. The convinced mummer, who is nothing but a mummer does not, I am convinced, give you the best work. The artist "in spite of yourself" he's your man. The mummer the easier to deal with (managerially). You only have to feed him continual popularity. The rebellious artist whom his art has to conquer – that gives you your E.T.

I am ashamed that I had forgotten the "Lyceum" (your) performance of Hamlet. I knew that I *had* seen you at it before but I could not remember when, and that "extraordinary" occasion escaped my memory. It don't think I told you last night how much and well it seems to have matured. All the difficult bits. The Ophelia, Gertrude, R. and G. ones. These especially which seem so easy; I suppose there's no one at present who can touch you at them. All that it struck me to criticize was the late saner parts: from the Gravedigger (how good he is the simplest and best I've seen!) scene onwards. I'd like the intellectual continuity kept clearer (he is now past dispute, " sane "). I was troubled now and then by the sudden outbursts of rather (?) forced emotion, passages on the brass: they spoil what a musician would call the melodic line, in this case they break into the intellectual continuity. We can be held – at least, you, I am sure, can hold up – by quiet, or at any rate *controlled* tension. And of course I'd like you as detached from the back-ground as possible, you as much among us, so that we share your thoughts. He has his problems out, is pretty cold-blooded about them now (the King must die "a man's life . . . to say One") and R. and G. remorse-lessly "go to it". And he is ready to die himself. All quite cool and calm. Only that sudden, vain, heartrending pang for Ophelia and all that is gone. Yes, I'd say: take full advantage of the change from student's age to the stressed "thirty".

You gave us a delightful evening. Good luck in India.

You'll find the Indian Shakespeare scholars very nippy.

From a hotel in Sidmouth, Barker wrote to Gilbert Murray:

Jan. 9th, 1946.

So you're So! – and I gather that if you didn't go out of your way to tumble downstairs no one would suspect it.   But I began to claim quite a long acquaintance with you.   Do you remember the one-armed Pathan who did a turn of pretty sound work for you some time in the last century at Glasgow?   Sir, was that not I?   And though my memory isn't what it was (I'm more eightyish than you I suspect) I can look out of my window here and be appropriately reminded of

> Bird of the sea rocks, of the bursting spray
> O Halcyon bird!
> That wheelest crying, crying on thy way . . .

– though there I may stick.   A good chorus!

You've really mended, I hope and that the news is even better than that. We were at Oxford the other Sunday and I was nearly looking in on you: but you weren't receiving.   We're in refuge here till the English and the French governments between them will let us go back to Paris and our possessions there (5 years in our trunks!).   Lady Mary's well, I hope. We both send her, and you too, our very warm regards.

*

Then the Barkers returned at last to Paris in the spring to find that their apartment had been well looked after by the *concierge*, M. Emile Magdelainat.   Everything was intact, except the linen.   After the entry of the United States into the war, they had no longer been able to have funds sent to Paris for the rent.   The apartment was occupied by various tenants, first by a member of the American Embassy, afterwards by a Frenchman, who was arrested by the Gestapo for protecting and camouflaging enemy property (the Barkers') and detained in prison for two months.   The Hungarian Consul-General, who had given a certificate of protection, also got into trouble.   The Gestapo took special interest in the library, of which an inventory was taken in September 1942, together with that of all the other property.   In November 1943 it was arranged that the Hungarian Commercial Attaché, with his wife and two children, should occupy the apartment, and after he had to leave, owing to more trouble with the Germans, the Hungarian Cultural Attaché went there until the Liberation.   The Barkers were, in fact, lucky in their Paris friends.   After the Liberation, Paris became very crowded, and a member of the American Red Cross had the apartment for a time.   It was then occupied by the first French tenant until 31 March 1946.   Buildings in the Place des Etats-Unis had become the Gestapo and S.S. Headquarters, and the Paris Brown House of the Nazi Party was there.

Resettled in the apartment, Barker went on with his literary work, but he was a sick man. Punctilious in replying to correspondents who wrote to him about Shakespeare, his handwriting was very shaky. Asked to do a broadcast for Shaw's ninetieth birthday, he replied on 14 May:

Thank you; but it must, I fear, definitely be " No ". A stupid little illness prevents me doing any immediate work. Later on if there is anything suitable I can do for you of course, I will, should you want me to.

Then he appears to have had a fall, broke two ribs, and developed pneumonia, and a month later had a violent, nearly fatal cardiac attack. He seemed to recover, and on 10 July wrote to George Barnes at the B.B.C.:

Don't think I have really been dangerously ill; I have been quite out of keeping – so you may guess.

He also wrote to Gilbert Murray, referring apparently to his last Shakespeare preface, *Coriolanus*, which had a preface dated March 1946. It was published the following year:

July 14, 1946.
No, I think you can give C[aius] M[arcus] C[oriolanus] – W[illiam] S[hakespeare], anyhow – that credit.
    There's the preparation in the episode of the poor man (got from Plutarch, and I dare say it suggested the rest). This at the very moment of victory:

> He cried home; I saw him prisoner;
> And then Aufideus was within my view
> And wrath o'erwhelmed my pity.

And, of course, there is the significant " sentence " (W.S. came to like " sentences ") as the crisis nears:

> Not of woman's tenderness took
> Requires no child nor woman's face to see . . .

(interrupted here to go out and look at the new aeroplanes flying over Paris; not the last interruption of the sort possibly!)
    No; but for the chink in his armour, the " weakness " which is his death, I don't believe W.S. would have been interested in him.
    Aufideus a parallel case, but done with *bitter* irony; pity turns sour in him.
    Let's meet before you go if possible.

At this time he was suffering from delusions and was very unhappy. The Embassy chaplain was sent for and had several distressing interviews with him. He died rather suddenly at his apartment on 31 August 1946 at the age of sixty-eight: the cause of death was arterio-sclerosis.
    On the day after, Desmond MacCarthy paid a tribute to him on the

T

B.B.C. Home Service radio, which has not hitherto been printed, in the course of which he said:

Harley Granville-Barker will figure in every history of the stage which deals with the twentieth century. He has also won a permanent and special place among Shakespeare scholars. He was pre-eminently what the French call *un homme de Theatre*. . . . As an actor, he excelled in the expression of lyrical emotion . . . the poet in him was uppermost. As a playwright it was the psychologist who endeavoured to see human emotions in relation to a moral or social order who was in control . . . as a man he was both critical and kind, and fastidious without being censorious, and that he was as enthusiastic as a man can be who has no illusions. Both his manner and appearance were inevitably charming, and his arresting voice – it was at once gay and melancholy – expressed a great friendliness with detachment. His gifts and knowledge were ever at the service of disinterested artists and scholars.

When Bernard Shaw heard the news on the radio, he murmured to Miss Patch, who was with him and related the incident to me, that he had always hoped they might come together again. A pathetic letter from him was printed by the *Times Literary Supplement* in which he said:

The enclosed photograph of Harley Granville-Barker, taken by me forty years ago at the Old House, Harmer Green, when our collaboration, now historic, was at its inception, may interest your readers.

We clicked so well together that I regarded him as my contemporary until one day at rehearsal, when someone remarked that I was fifty, he said, "You are the same age as my father." After that it seemed impossible that he should die before me. The shock the news gave me made me realise how I had cherished a hope that our old intimate relation might revive. But

> Marriage and death and division
> Make barren our lives

and the elderly professor could have little use for a nonagenarian ex-playwright.

The photograph was reproduced on the front page of the *Supplement*. Afterwards he wrote of him that as a young man " He was self-willed, restlessly industrious, sober and quite sane ", going on to say:

Altogether the most distinguished and incomparably the most cultivated person whom circumstances had driven into the theatre at that time.[1]

Among the tributes to him was one from Vice-Admiral C. S. Holland, who wrote in *The Times* of his life in Paris:

[1] *Drama*, Winter Number, 1946.

The first time I met him I found an irresistible attraction in that broad, sturdy figure, that open, kindly face, those friendly eyes, that quiet, charming voice. I was lucky enough to discover that he liked walking in the Bois in the quiet hours before it was taken over for the day by the children and nurses. And there many mornings each week we would do our round of roads and paths while he asked questions, gave his views, and argued his points. He had that extraordinary aptitude of being able to talk to and with the unscholarly without making them feel ashamedly ignorant and unread. For me listening to him was a veritable joy. His voice had that wonderful quality of a beautiful instrument which made such an attractive background to his eloquence and speech. What a delicious sense of humour he also had!

He died unhappily. One day in the last months he was walking with their two dogs in the public garden, under the shade of Bartholdi's work, and said to a friend who was with him, "I feel my life is useless." And one thinks of him, before his accident, lying crying in his little sitting-room, while Helen upstairs heard nothing. He was alone, because he never discovered himself.

His body was embalmed and buried in the large cemetery, Père Lachaise, where the body of Oscar Wilde also lies, with Jacob Epstein's memorial. The grave is marked by a plain stone bearing only his name and dates. Helen was against erecting anything more. His will was proved at £10,395, which included the value of his library, copyrights, etc., out of which had to be paid the debts, duty, and costs, including the sum paid to Lillah in redemption of her annuity. In 1929 the Barkers had made wills in each other's favour, he bequeathing his entire estate to her, she bequeathing hers to him, with bequests subject to the discretion of the survivor. When Barker died, his widow promised to give the books he had left to the Mayer Sassoon Library at the Institut Britannique, but afterwards she refused, as she could not bear to have his library disturbed. She consented, however, to students at the Institute making use of the library, but little or no advantage was taken of this permission. There was talk of a scholarship being established in his memory, but nothing was done. For some years Helen gave a donation of £200 a year to the Institute's library for the purchase of books, however. On her death a thousand or more books were offered to the Institute. Barker had also left books to the British Museum and the British Drama League, but they received none. Most of the manuscripts he left of partly finished works have disappeared.

Helen Granville Barker died on 16 February 1950. Shortly before, she had made a will in her own hand and deposited it with a notary. Her body was buried beside that of her husband. It appears that during her last years she became increasingly difficult. She was always exceedingly mysterious about herself. Her exact age at the time of her death is unknown; it was possibly eighty-six, but she looked younger. Everything about her was mysterious, however. There is some uncertainty even about her name, for she sometimes added " Manchester " (one of her mother's names) to her own Christian names. One of Barker's main interests throughout their married life had been to prevent anything from hurting her, and he went to all lengths to observe this. The year before she died, she went to St. Moritz, where she and Barker had spent their honeymoon; the evening she arrived she insisted on going out for a walk alone, and did not return. A search was made for her in the mountains, and she was found at midnight, unconscious and half-frozen. She did not recover from the effects of that episode.

EPILOGUE

FROM the point of view from which I am writing, to say that a man's life is tragedy is to acknowledge greatness, for it is to speak of him in relation to spiritual values, in which sphere tragedy lies. Only of heroes may the word "tragedy" be used. Suffering or failure, unexpected, even undeserved, is not in itself tragic; it is only a sad story. The hero makes tragedy. To say that a man's life is a tragedy is to say that it is a work of art. Tragedy does not belong to nature but to human consciousness. That is how I see the life of Granville Barker and why I think his life important. I do not say the tragedy is clear, but it is certain, and to contemplate it is highly worth while and will occupy much attention in time to come.

That there was greatness in Barker is suggested by the fact that he has become a legend so soon after his death. He is the myth of the twentieth-century English theatre. The impression of his personality was such that his memory is held in devotion by everyone almost without exception who was brought into touch with him, and the revolution in the theatre of which he was the figurehead has put him in a place unchallenged by any other theatrical figure of the century in this country. A candid examination of his life establishes the basis of the legend and justifies the myth. The large content of his work as a whole contains the most creative element in the theatre that this century can show. It was creative because it pointed to the future, and the theatre that is to come will be built by those who owe their inspiration to him.

When his life story is contemplated, it is seen to be of a piece. The young, shabby Barker, who could not always afford a bus fare, remained the same when, well-dressed and well-fed, he charmed the intelligentsia of London, Paris, and New York. In the fact that he did not change lies the explanation of his story. His handwriting may be noted in evidence, for he wrote precisely the same hand in his sixties (except for the last year) as in his twenties. His eye had the same look, his appearance (except for increasing fullness) remained the same; so did his handshake, for, like many highly sensitive men, he did not grasp heartily and strongly the hand held out to him, but put out his own hand for the friend or acquaintance to take. Neither did his mind change, for the theme of his first play was that of his last: voluntary exile following admitted defeat. His work indicates preoccupation with the idea of failure. His vision of the world reflected in his plays and criticism was his vision of his own life. In a sense, though it is an imperfect metaphor, it might be said of him that inwardly he was like a chrysalis who did not break out of his cocoon into the sun.

A chief weaver of the threads that bound Barker was Bernard Shaw. The two were closely associated in Barker's early twenties, and their reactions to each other affected their lives throughout – Barker's most of all, he being the less mature man. Shaw had a clear mind and firm determination; he was immensely active, highly informed, a burning fury of contradictions, possessing amazing competence, making every day and every thought in the day a drama. Deeply concerned with the theatre in which his real life lay, Shaw's vision ranged over the field of human life, and Barker saw society largely through Shaw's eyes. Barker was ever feeling his way, sensitive, even timid, the very opposite of Shaw, who detached himself from his innate shyness. Shaw detached everything, so that he could see clearly, and did not attach himself even to his immediate surroundings. It was this detachment that made Shaw so annoying and caused so much misunderstanding. Barker saw everything in immediate relation to himself, which is why he had little of the clarity of vision characteristic of his friend. This attachment he did not like, and his life was a continual effort to extract himself from and to avoid involvements; his fear of commitments fostered the air of aloofness that more and more surrounded him. His extreme volubility and frequent obscurity had the same origin. "I prefer addressing minorities", he said as a young man; "one can make them hear better." He was happiest alone, and craved solitude, being most himself when with himself; indeed, there was much of the narcissistic element in him, a terrible obstacle to one possessing a natural fount of generosity and affection.

There was not only Shaw; there were William Archer and Gilbert Murray, outstanding among other friends. All were rationalists, partly destructive in ideas, but imaginative, with creative impulses. The energy of their lives and the intellectual level of their conversation and aims made the greatest possible appeal to Barker, who was powerfully stimulated by them, and viewed himself on their level. But their rationalism was a negative influence that drove him in upon himself, and increased his inability to overcome the world.

When Barker was young it was the thing to be a writer, while to be an actor was to belong to a despised profession. He never grew out of that state of mind. Even when he was active in the theatre, his friends were not actors, not even the actors in his own company, but dramatists, poets, artists, and politicians. Among the visitors to his home at Stansted, at the height of his youthful career as a producer of plays, actors were rarely included. Even the leaders of the profession were not among his intimate friends. So it is not surprising that, when his second marriage caused the break with the theatre, there was little disturbance of theatrical friendships, because they hardly existed. When actors met him afterwards, as they did from time to time on his brief and casual visits to the theatre or on other occasions, they regarded him with awe. He was at a distance always. Indeed, while actors who worked with him speak of him with reverence, usually with enthusiasm, I have never met one who claimed intimacy with him.

He gave the impression throughout his life of a man seeking to catch up with the deficiencies of his cultural equipment. His lack of early education appeared in his eyes to be a greater drawback than it really was. He once declared that life was the real educator, yet he felt acutely the disadvantage of having no other school but that of experience. It is, of course, a real handicap to a man whose interests are set among those who are highly educated, and who himself appreciates academic distinction, that he lacks formal education. Therefore, Barker worked ceaselessly at himself in his effort to overcome this handicap. It would have been better had he spared himself, or, rather, worked at himself in another manner.

Although he mixed freely with men of birth and ability and of many different temperaments outside the theatre, and although he gained immediate admiration and respect, he was always reticent and everywhere a man withdrawn. At an early age he appears to have turned in upon himself to escape from the world. Thus he did not escape from himself, but became the prey of his fears, so that he was never able to overcome them in imagination. His heart was given to the true, the beautiful, and the good, but devoured by doubt, so that he had no help in the effort to live by these ultimate realities.

This may lead us to think it likely that Barker was influenced by the man who most influenced Bernard Shaw, Samuel Butler, though there is no reference to Butler in Barker's works. If so, it was Butler's scepticism and questioning that counted. Shaw was essentially a believer, a challenging and troublesome man of faith. Butler was essentially a disbeliever for the sake of disbelieving, and made all faith seem absurd. It was Butler's irony arising out of the disbelieving state of his mind that influenced Barker most. Butler's natural earnestness was disguised by irony, and Barker's mind took on the same tone. This is marked in the irony of his plays. Irony is never liked because it always implies a certain superiority. The ironic person perceives incongruities by which he himself is unaffected, or, if affected, to which he is superior. " Irony ", said Barker in his preface to *King Lear*, " the fine mind's weapon which blunts itself upon the stupid." Some part of the irritation with which Barker's plays were regarded at the time of their first production was due to this element. Usually irony hides a sense of inferiority. It is all the same strongly objected to. Irony becomes sharpest when a man achieves what he set out for, but finds it worthless. Thus it may be said that the ironic element in Barker was prophetic, for what he finally achieved he found to have no value. Yet irony was in his work from the start. The situation of Ann Leete, Edward Voysey, Henry Trebell, Philip Madras, Evan Strowde, to say nothing of the King in his last play, was deeply ironic, and there is no more ironic character in drama than Anatol. The disturbing irony of Barker's plays was in the fact that the characters perceived their situation, but, with many gifts, of which this power of perception is not the least, they were unable to rise above it. Had Barker been able to invest his characters with that power, which is nothing else than the self-possession of those spirits capable of the exercise of free will, he would have written tragedies instead of comedies. Had he possessed it himself, he might have avoided tragedy in his personal life, or, at any rate, have lived to the end on a different level.

Barker's friends being rationalists, there is no ascertainable religion in his life or work. In fact, he practised no religion. He was, however, essentially a moralist, and reacted against Shaw's professed immoralism. His moralism and rationalism went hand in hand, and he was much nearer to the Webbs' personal standpoint (which was by no means irreligious) than was Shaw. In an article in the *English Review*, July 1910, he declared:

I think this normal drama is noticeable for its Puritan spirit, for the fact that, good-naturedly, portentously, industriously, or light-heartedly, it somehow makes for righteousness. And by that sign more than any other, I judge that the theatre is to be a power in England.

From this we may get the indication as from his work as a whole that Barker regarded art not as a wholly free activity in the sense of the artist being able to do as he pleases. He would have agreed with the idea that art has a function, and that the artist is limited by that function. Each particular work of art, each play, has a function, which the artist must observe. He would have agreed that it is its function that gives art social validity, otherwise it would be, as the philistine thinks it to be, of no account.

There is a surprising remark in the ast act of *The Voysey Inheritance* when Edward Voysey says, "I've never shirked the truth about myself. My father said mine was a weak nature," and Alice retorts: "You have a religious nature." He replies, astonished, "Oh no!" and she goes on:

Therefore you're not fond of creeds or ceremonies. Therefore . . . as the good things of this worldly world don't satisfy you, you shirk contact with it all you can. I understand this temptation to neglect and despise practical things. But if one yields to it one's character narrows and cheapens.

An oblique reference is made to religion in *Waste*, written a few years later, contained in the exchange : " What is the prose for God? " " That is what we irreligious men are giving our lives to discover." Writing to Gilbert Murray about the play in the autumn of 1909, when the enquiry into the censorship was on, Barker referred to his hero as :

The man of no religious ideas who when he got one at a great crisis in his life is so superstitiously possessed by it that it drives him monomanical and kills him.

He adds " I have not done it ", as indeed he had not, were that not very clear statement in the letter to Murray a description of what he intended. But that his aim was a moral one is clear enough.

Even the much earlier *Prunella*, cynical and seemingly amoral, is essentially a moral play, the action being presented from the point of view of an innocent and simply instructed girl.

When dealing with the actor's art in *The Exemplary Theatre* (1923), Barker made the generalization : " We are, indeed, interpreters all. Creation is not man's prerogative." A remark that perhaps indicates some degree of consciousness of having avoided the responsibility of creation in his own life as an artist, for he was then cultivating the academic mind. The moralism of the plays may account for their present neglect, and for the fact that when they are revived either on the stage or radio, neither producers nor actors know what to do with them. For in our society, moral presuppositions such as these characters make are not accepted and such scrupulously-minded heroes are not credible.

The irony to which I have referred was Barker's escape from the dilemma into which his moralism led him. Perceiving his situation, he did not face it, for he did not succeed in understanding himself. Although he was driven inwards, he neither knew himself, nor had he a sufficiently firm grasp of himself as a being to be able to understand himself in the sense of having a starting point in his own being. He therefore seemed to be a lost man, for a man who does not understand is lost. And to lack understanding of oneself is to be lacking in knowledge. A man may have any amount of learning, scholarship, even technical accomplishment, and still be devoid of knowledge. It is true that technique is a kind of knowledge, for knowledge always concerns something done, but facility in the way of doing a thing is not equivalent to doing it. Barker had not, in this sense, knowledge of himself. That was the cause of his failure.

What happened when Barker reached the turning-point in his career was determined by his past, by the influence upon him of his friends and others, by the situation in which he found himself, as well as by his own will to the extent that he was free. He was heavily discouraged. His theatrical work was giving him no satisfaction, his plays were not successful, and he was desperately fearful of the war. There was little prospect of the freedom to be able to devote himself to writing for which he craved.

It has been said that Barker's tragedy was that the theatre as it existed in England and America had no place for him, that he was forced into exile from it. While the fact cannot be gainsaid, such a situation does not constitute tragedy; it was a disaster for him and for the English-speaking theatre, which is another matter. His incapacity to find a place in it was an irreplaceable loss, but it would be a misuse of the word – a misuse that is unfortunately frequent – to call what happened to him for that reason a tragedy. A similar incapacity was experienced by his contemporary, Gordon Craig. That the English theatre should have lost two such geniuses is sufficient condemnation of the conditions under which it was (and is) conducted. But tragedy does not arise through the inability of genius to accommodate itself to the actual world; it arises in the causes in genius itself that make it unable to survive. It belongs to the nature of genius to overcome the world; that is the reason for its existence. If it fails, it is useless merely to blame the world, which cannot be other than it is. As a natural phenomenon, the product of the natural man, the theatre cannot be other than the instrument that it is. Only civilized men can make it different, only they can make it a supreme work of art, and if they do not choose to do so – if they are too uncivilized, shall we say? – the fault is in man. If genius succumbs, it is a disaster; to the genius itself it is a tragedy only if while facing the situation he compromises, or strikes his flag, or, as Barker did, self-exiles himself from his task.

Both Shaw and Barker had this in common, that they feared poverty. Even when Shaw was a very rich man he was constantly talking of being poor – he had a perpetual dread of it. Barker never had any money. He came from a home in which money was short, and had to start earning his living at the age of thirteen. Although he became artistically successful, he was always hard up. He never in fact understood money, either how to make it or how to look after it; only how to spend it.

It is beyond dispute that he and Helen were deeply in love. It may be that until he met Helen he did not know what love meant, and that for the first time, perhaps, he found it possible to be in love. Yet to say that love was the sole cause of what happened is not possible. Neither can it be said that he married Helen for the sake of the fortune she would have settled upon her. It is true that when he knew her she lived in a sphere of great wealth and that he married a rich woman. Taking account of his discouraged state of mind, it is impossible not to see that Helen offered him security such as he had never known before. But the money as such meant nothing to him, he could not have thought of it for a moment; but he did think of security, even soul security, certainly the security that would enable him to be free as an artist. He sought the outward conditions of inner activity, as a peaceful world is sought as a guarantee for mankind's future. There was nothing gross in his choice, and his motive was high and disinterested. He knew what was in him to do, to write, and he craved to do it without a vain struggle for the leisure in which, he considered, writing should be done. His love for Helen offered him those conditions. All the same, the choice was disastrous, for security is not to be bought at any price. It is not to be bought at all. In the effort to gain it, one may give up every desire, even perhaps one's work, but it is not found, as ascetics and saints have discovered, for it is not in the air the creative man must breathe.

It is said that Barker had planned his life to be ten years an actor, ten years a producer, and ten years a writer. That, indeed, is more or less what happened; but though it is true that from first to last he wanted to be a writer, he was in fact a man of the theatre. His true place of work was there as producer and dramatist, and he deserted it. When he shut himself out of the theatre he lost his vocation, and died as an artist. Afterwards he wrote no plays that had stage life; when he lectured it was the voice of one whose heart was chilled; and his Shakespeare prefaces were an echo in the language of mere scholarship of the artist he might have been. The praise given to the prefaces is deserved; yet they are to be read not with joy but with a heavy heart. To praise them without acknowledgment of the price paid for them, or to suppose that they are on the same level of creative achievement as his stage productions, is to do his reputation no justice.

Barker sacrificed himself to an illusion. No one is to blame but himself, for he defeated himself. It is a testimony to his genius that the defeat did not cause him to lower his aim for the sake of popularity or success, yet his creativeness withered away. In the last three decades of his life he completed a great volume of work, which contained evidence of the flame that burned in him, but the flame was no more than alive. For himself, there was unhappy death, for he reaped no harvest of internal harmony. His contradictions were not reconciled. His inward-looking was into his own private universe, which (as with everyone) is a field of darkness; he did not bring his conflicting personality under observation in the light of which nothing remains hidden. Thus he became increasingly negative. The snobbishness that became pronounced in his later life, not always covered by inherent charm, was evidence of continued insecurity, for the snobbish person feels insecure.

I have used the word "genius" of Barker, and the question arises: Was he possessed merely of an exceptional talent or had he genius? His work was broken, but I think few people who knew him would question that he had in him that flow of original creative energy rightly called genius. John Masefield, writing to him in 1910, said: "People have come to regard you as a kind of god." That was by no means an exaggeration. It was not mere talent, certainly not cleverness, not even intellectuality that impressed people most, but an innate quality of life to which even those who did not always like him or his work responded. That he had jeopardized his fame must be admitted, but genius is not contradicted by mistakes, even by so fatal a mistake as Barker made.

In truth, Barker represents the subjectivity of the age. His life may be read as a revealing presentation of the state of man. The age's sickness and despair were reflected in him, and his disgust with the poisonous atmosphere of the theatre was the same as the general disgust with the manner in which we consider ourselves forced to live. The anxieties, digestive troubles, and sexual disorders of individual lives are repeated in the false political tensions, profound economic troubles, and perpetual international conflicts of our generation. We live at the mercy of our reflex actions and lack the self-direction of free beings.

As in this book we are concerned with the theatre, it is possible to remark that the same impotence rests upon dramatists and workers there as is experienced by artists everywhere. The drama is the mirror of the age, and the task of the dramatist is to reveal inner tensions and their resolution. English and American dramatists of the present day are playful like Fry, or naturalistic like Rattigan, or merely confused like Eliot, or quite lost like Eugene O'Neill and Tennessee Williams, devoid of the seriousness that possesses the French dramatists in whose work the tensions are stark, but equally without resolution. In all three countries drama is regarded as mere conflict, and no audience is invited to participate in a play in which the form and pressure of the time is shown to yield to anything but compromise or to any conclusion bolder than an uneasy shrug of the shoulders. The poetic imagination slumbers and is starved.

Barker pointed to what was required to put the theatre into its rightful place – social responsibility for the institution and dedication in those who serve it. He wanted the theatre related to the common good and incorporated as an institution into the social order. The idea can be perceived in him in his earliest days and persisted throughout his life. He thought more of the drama as a means of the enlightenment of man as a social being than of its value as entertainment (though he did not ignore that element), still less did he think of it as a means of advancing his own name or position. That caused him to write as one attempting something that was worth doing and gives his plays seriousness. He was, that is to say, a disinterested artist who never by mere cleverness in the use of the technical means in which he was accomplished employed that accomplishment contrary to his integrity as a man and an artist. In the contemplation of his life our affections are engaged, and upon the complex story there remains a glow that may not be subject to the dissipation of time in the wilderness of existence. He was a Moses who sensed the future, but did not enter it. Looking with his eyes, the promised land is seen, but it will be better to learn from his failure the essential conditions of the courage required to possess it.

Barker wrote the equivalent of his epitaph more than once in his own works, but never more conclusively than in the last lines of the preface to his sick friend Barrie's last play, *The Boy David*, when he said :

If not in life, then in death, the wheel comes full circle, and the great things are no greater than the small.

APPENDICES

APPENDIX I

CHARACTERS PLAYED

THE first time Granville Barker appeared in a particular part is included and subsequent revivals are ignored. As a boy he played in Sarah Thorne's Company, and as a young man in various touring companies, and in many plays in Ben Greet's Shakespeare and Old English Comedy Company, but no record of the parts he took exists; neither is it important.

Date	Theatre	Play
21 May 1891	Spa Rooms, Harrogate	Dr. Grimstone in *Vice-Versa*
19 May 1892	Comedy	The 3rd Young Man in *The Poet and the Puppets*
5 December 1892	Comedy	Claudie in *To-day*
17 October 1896	Haymarket	Major-domo in *Under the Red Robe*
(–) July 1897	Kingston-on-Thames	Hastings in *She Stoops to Conquer*
20 February 1899	Kennington	Gordon Jayne, M.D., in *The Second Mrs. Tanqueray*
22 February 1899	Kennington	Antonio Poppi in *The Notorious Mrs. Ebbsmith*
15 May 1899	Kennington	Frank Misquith, Q.C., in *The Second Mrs. Tanqueray*
19 June 1899	Kennington	Selim in *Carlyon Sahib*
11 November 1899	Lecture Theatre, Burlington Gardens	Richard in *Richard II*
15 November 1899	Prince of Wales	Albert Bailey in *The Canary*
7 March 1900	Royalty	Lieutenant Maxon Wendowski in *Magda*
25 February 1900	Vaudeville	Erik Bratsberg in *The League of Youth*
10 June 1900	Vaudeville	Robert in *The Coming of Peace*
1 July 1900	Strand	Eugene Marchbanks in *Candida*
21 August 1900	Prince of Wales	Earl of Rochester in *English Nell*
16 December 1900	Strand	Captain Kearney in *Captain Brassbound's Conversion*
22 February 1901	Comedy	Paul Raymond in a translation of *Le Monde où l'on s'ennuie*
29 March 1901	Comedy	Napoleon in *The Man of Destiny*
16 May 1901	Wyndham's	Fergusson Pybus in *The Case of Rebellious Susan*
27 August 1901	Prince of Wales	Mr. Wenham in *Becky Sharp*
5 January 1902	New Lyric Club	Frank in *Mrs. Warren's Profession*

288

Date	Theatre	Play
3 July 1902	Lyric	Orsino in *Hamlet*
22 February 1903	Imperial	Basil Kent in *A Man of Honour*
26 April 1903	Imperial	Barend in *The Good Hope*
10 August 1903	New Theatre (Oxford)	King Edward in *Edward II*
8 April 1904	Court	Speed in *The Two Gentlemen of Verona*
23 April 1904	Court	Romeo in *Romeo and Juliet*
24 May 1904	Lyric	The Messenger in *Hippolytus*
1 November 1904	Court	Keegan in *John Bull's Other Island*
23 December 1904	Court	Pierrot in *Prunella*
7 February 1905	Court	The Lover in *How He Lied to Her Husband*
2 May 1905	Court	Valentine in *You Never Can Tell*
23 May 1905	Court	Tanner in *Man and Superman*
17 October 1905	Court	Hjalmar Ekdal in *The Wild Duck*
28 November 1905	Court	Adolphus Cusins in *Major Barbara*
12 February 1906	Court	Edward Voysey in *The Voysey Inheritance*
20 November 1906	Court	Louis Dubedat in *The Doctor's Dilemma*
14 October 1907	Savoy	General Burgoyne in *The Devil's Disciple*
23 November 1907	Queen's	Dick Dudgeon in *The Devil's Disciple*
24 November 1907	Imperial	Henry Trebell in *Waste*
30 December 1907	Savoy	Sergius in *Arms and the Man*

When, later on, *Arms and the Man* was taken on tour he played Bluntschli.

24 November 1910	Haymarket	William Shakespeare in *The Dark Lady of the Sonnets*
13 February 1911	Palace	Anatol in *The Farewell Supper*
11 March 1911	Little	Anatol in the *Anatol* sequence

On 30 June 1911 at 10 Downing Street he played Larry in *John Bull's Other Island* (Act III) and on 11 June 1912 he played Orestes in the open-air performance of *Iphigenia in Taurus* in the Greek Theatre at Bradfield College.

APPENDIX II

PRODUCTIONS

THIS list gives the first performance of a production and no account is taken of revivals, or when plays were taken on tour. Although Bernard Shaw's plays were usually produced by himself, Barker had much to do with them at the Stage Society, at the Court, and elsewhere; in fact, it can be said that he shared the productions with Shaw, but these shared productions are not included here.

Date	Theatre	Play
29 April 1900	Globe	*The House of Usna*, by Fiona MacLeod
		Interior, by Maurice Maeterlinck, translated by William Archer
		The Death of Tintagiles, by Maurice Maeterlinck, translated by Alfred Sutro
22 March 1901	Comedy	*The Revolted Daughter*, by Israel Zangwill
26 January 1902	Royalty	*The Marrying of Ann Leete*, by Granville Barker
7 June 1903	Imperial	*The Waters of Bitterness*, by S. M. Fox
		The Admirable Bashville, by Bernard Shaw
31 January 1904	King's Hall	*The Philanthropists*, by Brieux
8 April 1904	Court	*The Two Gentlemen of Verona*, by William Shakespeare
24 May 1904	Lyric	*Hippolytus*, by Euripides, translated by Gilbert Murray
26 June 1904	Court	*Where There is Nothing*, by W. B. Yeats
15 November 1904	Court	*Algavaine and Selysette*, by Maeterlinck, translated by Alfred Sutro
23 December 1904	Court	*Prunella*, by Laurence Housman and Granville Barker
7 February 1905	Court	*The Voysey Inheritance*, by Granville Barker
28 February 1905	Court	*The Pot of Broth*, by W. B. Yeats
28 February 1905	Court	*In the Hospital*, by Arthur Schnitzler
21 March 1905	Court	*The Thieves' Comedy*, by Gerhart Hauptmann
11 April 1905	Court	*The Trojan Women*, by Euripides, translated by Gilbert Murray
26 September 1905	Court	*The Return of the Prodigal*, by St. John Hankin
17 October 1905	Court	*The Wild Duck*, by Henrik Ibsen
16 January 1906	Court	*The Electra*, by Euripides, translated by Gilbert Murray
6 February 1906	Court	*A Question of Age*, by Robert Vernon Harcourt

Date	Theatre	Play
6 February 1906	Court	*The Convict on the Hearth*, by Frederick Fenn
27 February 1906	Court	*Pan and the Young Shepherd* and *The Youngest of the Angels*, by Maurice Hewlett
25 September 1906	Court	*The Silver Box*, by John Galsworthy
23 October 1906	Court	*The Charity that Began at Home*, by St. John Hankin
8 January 1907	Court	*The Reformer*, by Cyril Harcourt
8 January 1907	Court	*The Campden Wonder*, by John Masefield
5 March 1907	Court	*Hedda Gabler*, by Henrik Ibsen
9 April 1907	Court	*Votes for Women*, by Elizabeth Robins
16 September 1907	Savoy	*You Never Can Tell*, by Bernard Shaw
24 September 1907	Savoy	*Joy*, by John Galsworthy
14 October 1907	Savoy	*The Devil's Disciple*, by Bernard Shaw
22 October 1907	Savoy	*The Medea*, by Euripides, translated by Gilbert Murray
24 November 1907	Imperial	*Waste*, by Granville Barker
30 December 1907	Savoy	*The Convict on the Hearth*, by Frederick Fenn
22 May 1908	Royalty	*The Tragedy of Nan*, by John Masefield
16 June 1908	Haymarket	*The Chinese Lantern*, by Laurence Housman
9 March 1909	Duke of York's	*Strife*, by John Glasworthy
21 February 1910	Duke of York's	*Justice*, by John Galsworthy
1 March 1910	Duke of York's	*The Sentimentalists*, by George Meredith
9 March 1910	Duke of York's	*The Madras House*, by Granville Barker
3 May 1910	Duke of York's	*Helena's Path*, by Anthony Hope and Cosmo Gordon Lennox
31 January 1911	Court	*The Witch*, a version by John Masefield of *Anna Pedersdotter* by Wiers Jansen. This play had been first produced by Barker under weekly repertory conditions at the Royalty Theatre, Glasgow, on the previous 10 October
February 1911	Palace	*The Farewell Supper*, by Arthur Schnitzler, translated by Granville Barker
11 March 1911	Little	*Anatol*, by Arthur Schnitzler, translated by Granville Barker
28 March 1911	Little	*The Master Builder*, by Henrik Ibsen, translated by William Archer
3 October 1911	Little	*The Twelve-Pound Look*, by J. M. Barrie
3 October 1911	Little	*Rococo*, by Granville Barker
22 February 1912	Kingsway	*The Secret Woman*, by Eden Phillpotts
19 March 1912	Kingsway	*Iphigenia in Taurus*, by Euripides, translated by Gilbert Murray
21 September 1912	Savoy	*The Winter's Tale*, by William Shakespeare
15 November 1912	Savoy	*Twelfth Night*, by William Shakespeare
25 March 1913	Kingsway	*The Great Adventure*, by Arnold Bennett

U

Date	Theatre	Play

There was a private performance on 27 June 1913 at 25 Park Lane of *The Sweeps of '98*, by John Masefield.

Date	Theatre	Play
1 September 1913	St. James's	*Androcles and the Lion*, by Bernard Shaw
1 September 1913	St. James's	*Harlequinade*, by Dion Clayton Calthrop and Granville Barker
1 December 1913	St. James's	*Le Mariage Forcé*, by Molière
6 February 1914	Savoy	*A Midsummer-Night's Dream*, by William Shakespeare
5 November 1914	Covent Garden	*Philip the King*, by John Masefield
25 November 1914	Kingsway	*The Dynasts*, by Thomas Hardy
16 September 1920	Royalty	*The Romantic Young Lady*, by Martínez Sierra
8 January 1921	Gaiety	*The Betrothal*, by Maurice Maeterlinck

After this date Barker had a hand in a number of productions in London of his own plays and translations, also of one Shakespeare play, but these can hardly be called in any complete sense his productions, with the exception of *Waste* in 1936, which had his name on the programme as co-producer with Michael MacOwan, and *King Lear* in 1940, when his name appeared with that of Lewis Casson. They included Sacha Guitry's *Deburau* at the Ambassador's, 2 November 1921, Martínez Sierra's *The Kingdom of God* at the Strand, 26 October 1927, *The Voysey Inheritance* at Sadler's Wells, 3 May 1934, *Waste* at the Westminster Theatre, 1 December 1936, and Shakespeare's *King Lear* at the Old Vic, 15 April 1940.

The following productions took place in the United States of America. Though the plays, with one exception, had already been produced in London, they became new productions in America, the Greek plays being performed on open Greek stages:

Date	Theatre	Play
27 January 1915	Wallack's	*Androcles and the Lion*, by Bernard Shaw
27 January 1915	Wallack's	*The Man Who Married a Dumb Wife*, by Anatole France
16 February 1915	Wallack's	*A Midsummer-Night's Dream*, by William Shakespeare
25 February 1915	Wallack's	*The Doctor's Dilemma*, by Bernard Shaw
(–) May 1915	Adolph Lewisohn Stadium	*The Trojan Women*, by Euripides, translated by Gilbert Murray
15 May 1915	Yale Bowl	*Iphigenia in Taurus*, by Euripides, translated by Gilbert Murray

A LIST OF WRITINGS

COMPILED BY FREDERICK MAY AND MARGERY M. MORGAN

Note. This list comprises published material mainly; the final sections record unpublished plays and typescript copies of published plays. Certain classes of material have been omitted from its scope: reissues of plays in anthologies of drama; production editions, unless known to contain matter written by Barker; and ordinary letters to the Press. For general convenience, all editions known are listed. Different versions of texts are distinguished by the use of small roman numerals in round brackets, variant editions, or editions with variant imprints, by the small roman alphabet, and separate issues, when it has been necessary to distinguish these, by parenthetic arabic numerals. Description has had to be reduced to a minimum: the terminology of printer's sizes is used; the finer details of binding are not described; preliminary pages, when these are unpaginated and do not contain text-matter, are indicated by the use of round brackets; the number of the last page of the text follows, whether it is in fact numbered in the volume or not, and final blank leaves and advertisement matter are not taken into consideration. The form of the author's name is not repeated with each separate item; the hyphenated form is usual after 1918, although there are occasional exceptions to this rule, particularly in American publications. Items that have not been personally examined by the compilers are listed, but not described. When these are recorded in the Catalogue of the Library of Congress, the card-number is given at the end of the present entry. The place of publication, when not otherwise stated, is London.

Use has been made of the only separate bibliography of Granville Barker known, a "Reading List on Harley Granville Barker", by Mary L. Davis, *Bulletin of Bibliography*, VII (Boston, 1912–13), pp. 130–2. The compilers are further indebted for invaluable help to a large number of persons, librarians, publishers and others.

This list is incidental to the preparation of a full bibliography, and the compilers would be grateful for corrections of present statements and to learn of any unnoticed items.

PUBLISHED WORKS

A. ORIGINAL PLAYS

1. *Three Plays: The Marrying of Ann Leete; The Voysey Inheritance; Waste*
   a Sidgwick & Jackson, Ltd., 1909.
   Cr. 8vo; dull red cloth boards; pp. (viii) + 342 + cast lists.
   The plays were also issued separately (see 2, 3 (i), 4 (i)).
   The fourth impression (March 1913) and subsequent impressions contain a revised text of *The Voysey Inheritance* (see 4 (ii)). No indication of this change is given on the title-page, or elsewhere in the fourth impression.
   b Also published by Brentano's, New York, 1909. [Congress: 9-21843.]
   c Also published by Mitchell Kennerley, New York [1911].
   Cr. 8vo; brown cloth boards; pp. (viii) + 345 + cast lists.

2. *The Marrying of Ann Leete* (1899)
    a Sidgwick & Jackson, Ltd., 1909.
    Cr. 8vo; pp. (iv) + 79.
    (1) Purplish-brown wrappers/dull red cloth boards.
    (2) A special issue of fifty copies printed on hand-made paper, numbered, and signed by the author; grey cloth boards, half-vellum; issued in a case with companion volumes of *The Voysey Inheritance* and *Waste* (see 3 (i) *a* and 4 (i) *a*).
    b Also published by Little, Brown & Company, Boston, 1916. [Congress: 16-92951.]

3. *The Voysey Inheritance*
    (i) The original version (1903–5).
    Sidgwick & Jackson, Ltd., 1909.
    Cr. 8vo; pp. (vi) + 83–210.
    (1) Purplish-brown wrappers/dull red cloth boards.
    (2) An issue of fifty numbered copies uniform with 2 *a* (2).
    (ii) A revised version (1913).
    a Sidgwick & Jackson, Ltd., 1913.
    Cr. 8vo; purplish-brown wrappers/dull red cloth boards; pp. (vi) + 83–209.
    b Also published by Little, Brown & Company, Boston, 1916. [Congress: 16-9294.]
    (iii) The final version (1934).
    Sidgwick & Jackson, Ltd., 1938.
    Cr. 8vo; bright blue wrappers; pp. (viii) + 118.
    (iv) A German translation of *The Voysey Inheritance*, entitled *Die Erbschaft der Voyseys*, by G. Sil-Vara and Rudolf Kommer.
    Berliner Theater-Verlag G.m.b.H., Berlin, [1913].
    Cr. 8vo; pp. 126; unbound, stapled, with turquoise blue paper strip gummed to spine.
    Acting edition; not for sale.

4. *Waste*
    (i) The original version (1906–7).
    a Sidgwick & Jackson, Ltd., 1909.
    Cr. 8vo; pp. (vi) + 213–342.
    (1) Purplish-brown wrappers/dull red cloth boards.
    (2) An issue of fifty numbered copies uniform with 2 *a* (2).
    b Also published by Little, Brown & Company, Boston, 1916. [Congress: 16-9296.]
    (ii) Second version (1926).
    Sidgwick & Jackson, Ltd., 1927.
    Cr. 8vo; grey wrappers/light blue cloth boards; pp. (viii) + 115.
    A prefatory letter to H. M. Harwood contains the statement: "I doubt if one scrap of the old dialogue survives."

5. *The Madras House*
    (i) The original version (1909).
    a Sidgwick & Jackson, Ltd., 1911.
    Cr. 8vo; purplish-brown wrappers/dull red cloth boards; pp. (viii) + 144.
    b Also published by Mitchell Kennerley, New York, 1911.
    c Also published by Little, Brown & Company, Boston, 1916.

(ii) Second version (1925).
  Sidgwick & Jackson, Ltd., 1925.
  Cr. 8vo; grey wrappers/light blue cloth boards; pp. (viii) + 140.

6. *Rococo: Vote by Ballot: Farewell to the Theatre*
  a Sidgwick & Jackson, Ltd., 1917.
  Small cr. 8vo; light blue cloth boards; pp. 118.
  Title on spine-label is: *Rococo and Two Others.*
  The plays were later issued separately (see 7, 8, 9).
  b Also published by Little, Brown & Company, Boston, 1917.
  Cr. 8vo; brown cloth boards; pp. (viii) + 86.
  Title on spine is: *Three Short Plays.*

7. *Rococo* (1911–12?)
  The date of composition given in the published texts is 1912, but the play was
  performed at the Glasgow Repertory Theatre on 20 November 1911.
  a Sidgwick & Jackson, Ltd., 1925.
  Small cr. 8vo; grey wrappers; pp. 43.
  b Also published by Samuel French, [n.d.]
  Cr. 8vo; pink-mauve flecked wrappers; pp. (ii) + 29.

8. *Vote by Ballot* (1914)
  Sidgwick & Jackson, Ltd., 1925.
  Small cr. 8vo.

9. *Farewell to the Theatre* (1916)
  Sidgwick & Jackson, Ltd., 1925.
  Small cr. 8vo.

10. *The Secret Life* (1919–23)
  a Chatto & Windus, 1923.
  Cr. 8vo; black cloth boards; pp. viii + 160.
  b Also published by Little, Brown & Company, Boston, 1923.
  Cr. 8vo; brown cloth boards; pp. (viii) + 125.
  c Also published with the imprint of Sidgwick & Jackson, Ltd., 1923.
  Sheets of *a* were taken over from Messrs. Chatto & Windus.

11. *His Majesty* (1923–4)
  a Sidgwick & Jackson, Ltd., 1928.
  Cr. 8vo; light blue cloth boards; pp. viii + 131.
  b Also published by Little, Brown & Company, Boston, 1929.
  Cr. 8vo; brown cloth boards; pp. (vi) + 127.

B. PLAYS WRITTEN IN COLLABORATION WITH LAURENCE HOUSMAN OR D. C. CALTHROP

12. *Prunella, or Love in a Dutch Garden*, by Laurence Housman and H. Granville
  Barker
  (i) The original version in three acts (1904).
    a A. H. Bullen, 1906.
    Pott 4to; purple wrappers/pale mauve cloth boards; pp. (viii) + 89 + cast
    lists (90). With a frontispiece by Laurence Housman.
      Sheets of *a* were also issued with the imprint of Sidgwick & Jackson, Ltd.,
      1906.
    c Also published by Brentano's, New York, 1906. [Congress: 7-1292.]
    d Another edition, Sidgwick & Jackson, Ltd., 1907.

Cr. 8vo; purplish-brown wrappers.
e Another edition, with text re-set, Sidgwick & Jackson, Ltd., 1910 (April).
Cr. 8vo; purplish-brown wrappers; pp. 86.
f A re-issue of *b*, with frontispiece by Housman, in fcap. 4to Library Edition, 1911; oatmeal cloth boards, decorated with design of a sampler in blue and red; including two sheets of Moorat's music for Pierrot's Serenade, unpaginated.
g Also published by Little, Brown & Company, Boston, 1916.
(ii) Second version (1930), with an additional act (the third).
Sidgwick & Jackson, Ltd., 1930.
Cr. 8vo; grey wrappers/light blue cloth boards; pp. (viii) + 111.

13. *The Harlequinade* (1913), by Dion Clayton Calthrop and Granville Barker
a Sidgwick & Jackson, Ltd., 1918.
Fcap. 4to; oatmeal cloth boards; pp. (vi) + 84; with frontispiece and decorations by Lewis Baumer.
b Also published by Little, Brown & Company, Boston, 1918. [Congress: 18-5865.]

C. ENGLISH VERSIONS OF FOREIGN PLAYS

14. *Anatol*, by Arthur Schnitzler
a Sidgwick & Jackson, Ltd., 1911.
Cr. 8vo; purplish-brown wrappers/dull red cloth boards; pp. (viii) + 125.
b Also published by Mitchell Kennerley, New York, 1911.
Cr. 8vo; brown cloth boards; pp. (x) + 125. The text has apparently been set up from *a*, but is not printed from the same plates.
c Also issued with the imprint of Little, Brown & Company, Boston, 1916.
d Extracts from Barker's paraphrase of *Anatol* were published under the title, " The Little Theatre's Newest Play ", in *The Green Book Magazine*, VIII (Chicago, November 1912), pp. 818-24.

15. *Deburau*, by Sacha Guitry
a William Heinemann, 1921.
Cr. 8vo; bright red cloth boards, decorated with gilt mask design; pp. xii + 173.
b Also published by G. P. Putman's Sons, The Knickerbocker Press, London and New York, 1921.
Cr. 8vo; dark green cloth boards, decorated with gilt mask design; pp. (ii) + 226; with a frontispiece photograph of Lionel Atwill as Deburau in the Belasco production.

16. *Doctor Knock*, by Jules Romains
a Ernest Benn, Ltd., 1925.
Cr. 8vo; dull red wrappers/dark blue cloth boards; pp. (iv) + 95.
b Also published by Sidgwick & Jackson, Ltd., 1927.
Cr. 8vo; light blue cloth boards; pp. xii + 65.

17. *Six Gentlemen in a Row*, by Jules Romains
Sidgwick & Jackson, Ltd., 1927.
Cr. 8vo; bright blue wrappers; pp. (ii) + 30.

D. ENGLISH VERSIONS OF SPANISH PLAYS, IN COLLABORATION
WITH HELEN GRANVILLE-BARKER

(1) *Plays by Gregorio Martínez Sierra*

18. *Collected Plays* (*The Kingdom of God; The Two Shepherds; Wife to a Famous Man; The Romantic Young Lady*)
    a   Vol. 2 of the *Plays* of Sierra, published by Chatto & Windus, 1923.
    Demy 8vo; dull red cloth boards; pp. (viii) + 297.
    b   Also published by E. P. Dutton & Co., New York, [c. 1923]. [Congress: 23-26436.]
    c   A re-issue of b with the addition of an Introduction by the translators, [February, 1929].
    Large cr. 8vo; bright blue cloth boards; pp. xviii + 297.
    This is entitled: *The Kingdom of God and Other Plays.*

19. *The Kingdom of God*
    Sidgwick & Jackson, Ltd., 1927.
    Cr. 8vo; bright blue wrappers/light blue cloth boards; pp. (viii) + 105.

20. *The Romantic Young Lady*
    Sidgwick & Jackson, Ltd., 1929.
    Cr. 8vo; bright blue wrappers/light blue cloth boards; pp. (viii) + 77.

21. *Take Two from One*
    a   Sidgwick & Jackson, Ltd., 1931.
    Cr. 8vo; bright blue wrappers/light blue cloth boards; pp. (viii) + 89.
    b   Also issued with the imprint of Samuel French, New York, Los Angeles, London, and Toronto, [n.d.].
    Cr. 8vo; vivid blue cloth boards; pp. (vi) + 89.

22. *The Two Shepherds*
    Sidgwick & Jackson, Ltd., 1935.
    Cr. 8vo; blue wrappers; pp. (viii) + 59.

(2) *Plays by Serafín and Joaquín Álvarez Quintero*

23. *Four Plays* (*The Women Have Their Way; A Hundred Years Old; Fortunato; The Lady from Alfaqueque*)
    a   Sidgwick & Jackson, Ltd., 1927.
    Cr. 8vo; dark red cloth boards; pp. xviii + 296. With an Introduction by the translators.
    The plays were also issued separately (see 24–7).
    b   Also published by Little, Brown & Company, Boston, 1928. [Congress: 28-8377.]

24. *The Women Have Their Way*
    Sidgwick & Jackson, Ltd., 1927.
    Cr. 8vo; orange wrappers; pp. 77.

25. *A Hundred Years Old*
    Sidgwick & Jackson, Ltd., [1927].
    Cr. 8vo; orange wrappers; pp. (ii) + 79–171.

26. *Fortunato*
    Sidgwick & Jackson, Ltd., 1927.
    Cr. 8vo; orange wrappers; pp. (ii) + 175–217.

27. *The Lady from Alfaqueque*
   Sidgwick & Jackson, Ltd., 1927.
   Cr. 8vo; orange wrappers; pp. (ii) + 221–96.

28. *Four Comedies* (*Love Passes By; Don Abel Wrote a Tragedy; Peace and Quiet; Doña Clarines*)
   a Sidgwick & Jackson, Ltd., 1932.
   Cr. 8vo; dark red cloth boards; pp. xxiv + 311. With an Introduction by the translators.
   The plays were also issued separately (see 29–32).
   b Also issued with the imprint of S. French, New York and Los Angeles, 1932.
   Cr. 8vo; black cloth boards; pp. (iv) + ix–xxiv + 311.

29. *Love Passes By*
   Sidgwick & Jackson, Ltd. [1932].
   Cr. 8vo; orange wrappers; pp. (ii) + 71.

30. *Don Abel Wrote a Tragedy*
   Sidgwick & Jackson, Ltd. [1932].
   Cr. 8vo; orange wrappers; pp. (iv) + 75–176.

31. *Peace and Quiet*
   Sidgwick & Jackson, Ltd. [1932].
   Cr. 8vo; orange wrappers; pp. (iv) + 179–239.

32. *Doña Clarines*
   Sidgwick & Jackson, Ltd. [1932].
   Cr. 8vo; orange wrappers; pp. (iv) + 243–311.

E. SHORT STORIES

33. " Georgiana ", *The English Review*, I (February and March, 1909), pp. 420–31, and 690–99.

34. *Souls on Fifth*
   a Little, Brown & Company, Boston, 1916.
   With a frontispiece by Norman Wilkinson. [Congress: 16-8475.]
   b Also published in *The Fortnightly Review*, CI (1917), pp. 336–47 and 525–36.

F. THEORY OF DRAMA AND THE THEATRE

(1) *Books*

35. *Scheme and Estimates for a National Theatre* (in collaboration with William Archer)
   a First issue, privately printed, 1904.
   Cr. 4to; greenish-blue wrappers; pp. xxiv + 177.
   The authors' names do not appear on the title-page, but a preliminary note, p. (vi), is signed " W. A. " and " H. G. B."
   b *A National Theatre. Scheme and Estimates*
   Duckworth & Co., 1907.
   Cr. 4to; navy blue cloth boards; pp. xxxii + 177.
   The body of the text is identical with *a*. A preliminary note and a further preface, in the form of a letter from Granville Barker to Archer, have been added.

c Also published by Duffield & Co., New York, 1908. [Congress: 8-5141.]
(See also 37.)

36. *The Exemplary Theatre*
    a Chatto & Windus, 1922.
    Demy 8vo; royal blue cloth boards; pp. xvi + 288.
    b Also issued with the imprint of Sidgwick & Jackson, Ltd., 1922.
    c Also published by Little, Brown & Company, Boston, 1922. [Congress: 22-11544.]

37. *A National Theatre*
    A complete re-writing of 35, bringing it up to date; by Granville Barker alone.
    Sidgwick & Jackson, Ltd., 1930.
    Demy 8vo; pp. xvi + 135; with a folding plan.
    (1) Grey-blue boards, quarter oatmeal cloth.
    (2) A private issue; grey wrappers.
    (See also 55.)

(2) Published Lectures in Book or Pamphlet Form

38. *On Dramatic Method*
    Sidgwick & Jackson, Ltd., 1931.
    Cr. 8vo; blue cloth boards; pp. (viii) + 192.
    The Clark Lectures for 1930.

39. *The Study of Drama*
    Cambridge, at the University Press, 1934.
    Fcap. 8vo; dark red cloth boards; pp. (viii) + 93. Half-title, p. (iii): Cambridge Miscellany XVI.
    A lecture given at Cambridge, 2 August 1934, with notes subsequently added.

40. *On Poetry in Drama*
    Sidgwick & Jackson, Ltd., 1937.
    Fcap 8vo; light brown wrappers; pp. 42.
    The Romanes Lecture, delivered at the Taylor Institution, 4 June 1937.

41. *The Use of the Drama*
    (i) Princeton University Press, Princeton, 1945.
    Demy 8vo; grey cloth boards, with title on spine in gilt letters on purple ground; pp. vi + 91.
    One of a series of Princeton Books on the Humanities.
    Based on three Spencer Trask Lectures delivered at Princeton University in 1944.
    (ii) A slightly revised text.
    Sidgwick & Jackson, Ltd., 1946.
    Cr. 8vo; bright red cloth boards; pp. 78.
    (See also 59.)

(3) Articles

42. "Repertory Theatres", *The New Quarterly*, II, No. 8 (November 1909), pp. 491–504.

43. *a* "The Theatre: the Next Phase", *The English Review*, V (April–July 1910), pp. 631–48.
Delivered as a lecture to the Times Literary Club, 9 June 1910.
b Also published in *Forum*, XLIV (New York, August 1910), pp. 159–70.

44. "The Theatre Exhibition in Berlin", From Our Special Correspondent, *The Times*, 7 November 1910, p. 16.

45. "The Theatre in Berlin", From a Correspondent, *The Times*, 19 November 1910, p. 6, and 21 November, p. 12.

46. "Two German Theatres", *Fortnightly Review*, N.S. LXXXIX (January 1911), pp. 60–70.
On the Deutsches Theater and Kammerspielhaus and the Düsseldorfer Schauspielhaus. Originally delivered as a lecture.

47. "The Golden Thoughts of Granville Barker", a Letter to the Editor, *Play Pictorial*, XXI, No. 126 (1912), p. iv.
In justification of the mounting of his production of *Twelfth Night*. (This number of *Play Pictorial* also includes photographs of the production.)

48. "Reconstruction in the Theatre", From a Correspondent, *The Times*, 20 February 1919, p. 11.

49. *a* "Notes on Rehearsing a Play", *Drama*, I, No. 1 (July 1919), pp. 2–5.
b Also published in *Theatre*, XXX (New York, September and October 1919), pp. 142, 236.

50. "'Max', Mr. Granville-Barker and the National Theatre", *Drama*, N.S., No. 27 (April 1923), pp. 121–2.
An open letter from (Sir) Max Beerbohm, with a reply from Granville Barker.

51. *a* "The Heritage of the Actor", *Quarterly Review*, CCXL, No. 476 (July 1923), pp. 53–73.
b Reprinted in abridged form, with a biographical note on Barker, in *Actors on Acting*, edited by T. Cole and H. K. Chinoy (New York, 1949), pp. 366–73.

52. (i) "Notes upon the Prize Design for a National Theatre", *Drama*, N.S., No. 40 (July 1924), pp. 229–33. Illustrated with designs by W. L. Somerville.
(ii) *a* "Plans for a National Theatre", *Drama*, Special National Theatre Number (December 1929), pp. 43–6.
A slightly revised version of (i). (This number of *Drama* also quotes Barker, p. 38, in a collection of "Personal Opinions on the National Theatre".)
b Also published in *Theatre Arts Monthly*, XIX, No. 8, British National Theatre. A Special Issue (New York, August 1935), pp. 635–8.
The last two paragraphs are printed in reverse order from *a*.

53. "A Village Shakespeare Stage", *Drama*, N.S., No. 43 (December 1924), p. 257. Illustrated with designs by E. Ravilious.
(An editorial note, p. 256, quotes a paragraph by Granville Barker on preserving the essentials of the Elizabethan theatre.)

54. *a* "The Future of the Comédie-Française . . . A Letter to M. Copeau", *The Observer*, 1 September 1929, p. 11.
b Also published as "A Letter to Jacques Copeau", *Theatre Arts Monthly*, XIII, No. 10 (October 1929), pp. 753–9.

55. " A National Theatre ", *The Times*, 10 February 1930, pp. 13, 14, and 11
   February 1930, pp. 15, 16.
   Extracts from Chapter I of *A National Theatre* (37).

56. " The National Theatre ", *Drama*, IX, No. 3 (December 1930), pp. 34–6.

57. " Le Théâtre Britannique d'aujourd'hui ", *France-Grande Bretagne*, No. 135
   (Paris, April 1934), pp. 105–17.
   The abridged text of a lecture delivered at the Sorbonne, 23 February 1933.

58. " The Canadian Theatre ", *Queen's Quarterly*, XLIII (Kingston, Canada,
   Autumn, 1936), pp. 256–67.

59. " A Theatre that Might Be ", *Theatre Arts Monthly*, XXIX, No. 6 (June
   1945), pp. 370–77.
   Extracts from *The Use of the Drama* (41).

G. THEATRE HISTORY

60. " A Note upon Chapters XX and XXI of *The Elizabethan Stage* ", *Review of
   English Studies*, I, No. 1 (January 1925), pp. 60–71.

61. A Review of *Designs by Inigo Jones for Masques and Plays at Court*. With
   Introduction and Notes by Percy Simpson and C. F. Bell, in *Review of
   English Studies*, I, No. 2 (April 1925), pp. 231–5.

62. A Review of *The Physical Conditions of the Elizabethan Public Play-Houses* and
   Pre-Restoration Stage Studies, by W. J. Lawrence, in *Review of English Studies*,
   IV, No. 14 (April 1928), pp. 229–37.

63. (i) " The Coming of Ibsen ", *The Eighteen-Eighties*, Essays by Fellows of the
   Royal Society of Literature, edited by Walter de la Mare (Cambridge, at
   the University Press, 1930), pp. 159–96.
   (ii) Also published in *Theatre Arts Monthly*, XIV (October and November
   1930), pp. 866–74 and 931–39.
   A slightly abridged version of (i).

64. (i) " Exit Planché–Enter Gilbert ", *The Eighteen-Sixties*, Essays by Fellows
   of the Royal Society of Literature, edited by John Drinkwater (Cambridge,
   at the University Press, 1932), pp. 102–48.
   (ii) Also published, in a slightly different version, in *London Mercury*, XXV
   (March and April 1932), pp. 457–66 and 558–73.

H. SHAKESPEARE
(1) *Acting Editions of Shakespeare's Plays, with Short Prefaces*

65. *The Winter's Tale*
   a William Heinemann, 1912.
   Cr. 8vo; light buff wrappers, decorated with costume designs; pp. x + 123.
   Illustrated by Albert Rothenstein.
   b Also published by W. H. Baker Co., Boston, 1913.

66. *Twelfth Night*
   a William Heinemann, 1912.
   Cr. 8vo; light buff wrappers, decorated with costume design for Malvolio;
   pp. xi + 96. Illustrated by Norman Wilkinson.
   b Also published by W. H. Baker Co., Boston, 1913.

67. *A Midsummer Night's Dream*
    William Heinemann, 1914.
    Cr. 8vo; light buff wrappers, decorated with costume design for Puck;
    pp. x + 85. Illustrated by Norman Wilkinson.

(2) *Prefaces to the Players' Shakespeare*

The volumes of the Players' Shakespeare were published by Ernest Benn,
Ltd. The series was produced under the art-editorship of Albert
Rutherston, and the preface to each play was written by Harley Granville
Barker. The texts of the plays followed the Folio of 1623. There
were two issues:

(1) 450 copies for sale and 50 not for sale.
    Binding: pale grey boards, quarter oatmeal linen.
(2) 100 copies for sale and 6 not for sale.
    Printed on hand-made paper and bound by Zaehnsdorf in vellum/oasis
    morocco; signed by the General Art-Editor, the Illustrator, and the
    Author of the Preface.
    Size: $12\frac{1}{2} \times 9\frac{1}{2}$ ins.

68. *a* General Introduction to the Players' Shakespeare, in *The Tragedie of
    Macbeth*, 1923, pp. ix–xxiv.
    b Reprinted in *The Shakespeare Stage*, No. 2 (September 1953), pp. 11–21.

69. *a* Preface to *The Tragedie of Macbeth*, 1923, pp. xxv–lix. This volume is
    illustrated by Charles Ricketts.
    b Reprinted separately by Ernest Benn, Ltd., 1923.
    Demy 8vo; dark grey wrappers; pp. xliii.

70. *a* Preface to *The Merchant of Venice*, 1923, pp. ix–xxxviii. Illustrator:
    Thomas Lowinsky.
    b Reprinted separately, 1923.
    Uniform with 69 *b*; pp. xxviii.

71. *a* Preface to *The Tragedie of Cymbeline*, 1923, pp. ix–lvi. Illustrator: Albert
    Rutherston.
    b Reprinted separately, 1923.
    Uniform with 69 *b*; pp. xl.

72. *a* Preface to *A Midsommer Nights Dreame*, 1924, pp. ix–liii. Illustrator:
    Paul Nash.
    b Reprinted separately, 1924.
    Uniform with 69 *b*; pp. xxxv.

73. *a* Preface to *Loves Labour's Lost*, 1924, pp. vii–liv. Illustrator: Norman
    Wilkinson.
    b Reprinted separately, 1924.
    Uniform with 69 *b*; pp. xxxviii.

74. *a* Preface to *The Tragedie of Julius Caesar*, 1925, pp. ix–lxxvii. Illustrator:
    Ernst Stern.
    b Reprinted separately, 1926.
    Uniform with 69 *b*; pp. lix.

75. *a* Preface to *The Tragedie of King Lear*, 1927, pp. ix–xcix. Illustrator: Paul
    Nash.
    b Reprinted separately, 1927.
    Uniform with 69 *b*; pp. lxix.

(3) *Prefaces to Shakespeare, Collected and Published in Book Form*

76. *Prefaces. First Series*
    Prefaces to *Love's Labour's Lost, Julius Caesar, King Lear,* based on revision of 73, 74, 75.
    (i) Sidgwick & Jackson, Ltd., 1927.
    Demy 8vo; dark blue cloth boards; pp. xl + 231.
    Re-issued in cr. 8vo, Sidgwick & Jackson, 1945.
    (ii) An extract from the Preface to *King Lear,* revised and rewritten, was published in *Shakespeare Criticism* 1919–35. With an Introduction by Anne Bradby (World's Classics, O.U.P.), 1936, pp. 109–51.

77. *Prefaces. Second Series*
    Prefaces to *Romeo and Juliet, The Merchant of Venice, Antony and Cleopatra* and *Cymbeline,* the first and third based on lectures given at University College, Aberystwyth, the second and fourth being considerably revised versions of 70 and 71.
    Sidgwick & Jackson, Ltd., 1930.
    Demy 8vo; dark blue cloth boards; pp. xii + 345.
    Re-issued in cr. 8vo, Sidgwick & Jackson, Ltd., 1944.

78. *Prefaces. Third Series*
    Preface to *Hamlet.*
    Sidgwick & Jackson, Ltd., 1937.
    Demy 8vo; dark blue cloth boards; pp. x + 329. Reissued in cr. 8vo, 1944.

79. *Prefaces. Fourth Series*
    Preface to *Othello,* based on lectures given at Harvard College, in memory of Winthrop Ames.
    Sidgwick & Jackson, Ltd., 1945.
    Cr. 8vo; dark blue cloth boards; pp. x + 223.

80. *Prefaces. Fifth Series*
    Preface to *Coriolanus,* based on the Alexander Lectures delivered at University College, Toronto, in 1942.
    Sidgwick & Jackson, Ltd., 1947.
    Cr. 8vo.; mid blue cloth boards; pp. viii + 195.

81. *Prefaces to Shakespeare* (2 vols.)
    Princeton University Press, Princeton, 1946–7.
    Vol. 1: Prefaces to *Hamlet, King Lear, The Merchant of Venice, Antony and Cleopatra, Cymbeline;* vol. 2: Prefaces to *Othello, Coriolanus, Romeo and Juliet, Julius Caesar, Love's Labour's Lost.* [Congress A47-347 rev.*]

(4) *Shakespearian Studies Edited in Collaboration with G. B. Harrison*

82. *A Companion to Shakespeare Studies*
    Cambridge University Press; and Macmillan, New York, 1934.
    Demy 8vo; mid greenish blue cloth boards; pp. x + 408. Editors' Preface: pp. ix-x.

(5) *Articles and Published Lectures*

83. (i) a "From Henry V to Hamlet", *Proceedings of the British Academy* 1924–25, XI, pp. 283–309.
    British Academy Annual Shakespeare Lecture for 1925.

  b Also issued separately, in pamphlet form, by Humphrey Milford for the British Academy, [1927], pp. 29.
  Ryl. 8vo; grey wrappers; pp. 283–309. An off-print of *a*.
 (ii) Reprinted, in corrected form, in *Aspects of Shakespeare*, edited by J. W. Mackail (Oxford, at the Clarendon Press, 1933), pp. 49–93.

84. (i) " Shakespeare and Modern Stagecraft ", *Yale Review*, XV (New Haven, July 1926), pp. 703–24.
 (ii) " The Stagecraft of Shakespeare ", *Fortnightly Review*, N.S., CXX (July 1926), pp. 1–17.
 A variant version of (i).

85. " *Hamlet* in Plus Fours ", *Yale Review*, XVI (October 1926), p. 205.
 A single paragraph, postscript to 84 (i).

86. *Associating with Shakespeare*
 Humphrey Milford for the Shakespeare Association, 1932.
 Ryl. 8vo; grey wrappers; pp. 31.
 An address given to the Shakespeare Association at King's College, London, 25 November 1931.

87. *a* " Progrès du drame shakespearien ", *Cahiers du Sud*, X, No. spécial, *Le Théâtre Elizabéthain* (Marseilles, June 1933), pp. 25–8.
 Translated into French by Olivier D. Picard.
  b Reprinted in *Le Théâtre Elizabéthain. Études et Traductions*, edited by Georgette Camille and Pierre d'Exideuil (Les Cahiers du Sud, Marseilles, and Librairie José Corti, Paris, 1940), pp. 44–7.

88. " Shakespeare's Dramatic Art ", in *A Companion to Shakespeare Studies* (82, above), pp. 45–87.

89. " The Casting of *Hamlet*. A Fragment ", *London Mercury*, XXXV (November 1936), pp. 10–17.

90. " Alas, Poor Will ! ", *The Listener*, XVII, No. 425 (3 March 1937), pp. 287–9.
 The text of a broadcast.

91. *a* " The Perennial Shakespeare ", *The Listener*, XVIII, No. 458 (20 October 1937), pp. 823–6 and 857–9.
 Described as the Nineteenth of the Broadcast National Lectures, given on 13 October 1937.
  b Reprinted and issued separately in pamphlet form by the British Broadcasting Corporation, 1937.
 Cr. 8vo; bluish-green wrappers; pp. 28.
 Described as the Twentieth of the Broadcast National Lectures.

92. Review of *The Frontiers of the Drama*, by Una Ellis-Fermor, in *Review of English Studies*, XXII, No. 86 (April 1946), pp. 144–7.
 Devoted mainly to a discussion of *Troilus and Cressida*.

93. " Verse and Speech in *Coriolanus* ", *Review of English Studies*, XXIII, No. 89 (January 1947), pp. 1–15.
 Published posthumously. The proof was not corrected by the author.

H. OTHER CRITICISM

(1) *Critical Studies edited by Granville Barker*

94. *The Eighteen-Seventies.* Essays by Fellows of the Royal Society of Literature. Cambridge; at the University Press, 1929.

Demy 8vo; dark sea-green cloth boards; pp. xiv + 284.
Editor's Preface: pp. vii–xiv.

(2) *Articles*

95. "J. M. Barrie as a Dramatist", *The Bookman*, XXXIX, No. 229 (London,
    October 1910), pp. 13–21.

96. (i) "Tennyson, Swinburne, Meredith and the Theatre", in *The Eighteen-
    Seventies* (see 94), pp. 161–91.
    (ii) "Three Victorians and the Theatre", *Fortnightly Review*, CXXV (May
    1929), pp. 655–72.
    An abridged and slightly revised version of (i).
    (iii) "Some Victorians Afield", *Theatre Arts Monthly*, XIII (April and May
    1929), pp. 256–64 and 361–72.
    An abridged version of (i).

(3) *Critical Introductions to the Following*

97. *Three Plays*, by Maurice Maeterlinck.
    Gowans and Gray, Ltd., London and Glasgow, 1911.
    Fcap. 8vo; dark red cloth boards; Introduction: pp. v–xi.
    The plays are translated by Alfred Sutro and William Archer.

98. *One Man's View*, by Leonard Merrick.
    Hodder & Stoughton, [1918].
    Cr. 8vo; dark blue cloth boards; Introduction: pp. v–viii.
    This volume forms part of a uniform edition of *The Works of Leonard
    Merrick*.

99. *Little Plays of St. Francis*. First Series. By Laurence Housman.
    Sidgwick & Jackson, Ltd., 1922.
    Cr. 8vo; oatmeal cloth boards; Preface: pp. vii–xv.

100. *a Plays*, by Gregorio Martínez Sierra, Vol. I. In English versions by John
    Garrett Underhill.
    Chatto & Windus, 1923.
    Dmy. 8vo; red cloth boards; Introduction: pp. xi–xix.
    b This volume was also published, with the Introduction, by E. P. Dutton
    & Co., New York [1923].
    c The Introduction was reprinted in *The Kingdom of God and Other Plays*
    (see 18 *c*).

101. *Plays*, by Leo Tolstoy. Translated by Louise and Aylmer Maude.
    Humphrey Milford for the Tolstoy Society, 1928.
    Cr. 8vo; dull orange cloth boards; Introduction: pp. vii–xxii.
    This is Vol. 17 of the Centenary Edition of The Works of Leo Tolstoy.

102. *Little Plays of St. Francis*. Second Series. By Laurence Housman.
    Sidgwick & Jackson, Ltd., 1930.
    Cr. 8vo; oatmeal cloth boards; Preface: pp. vii–xiv.

103. *Portraits of a Lifetime*, by Jacques-Émile Blanche. Translated and edited by
    Walter Clement.
    Ryl. 8vo; buff cloth boards; Introduction: pp. vii–xiii.

104. *The Boy David*, by J. M. Barrie.
    Peter Davies, 1938.
    Cr. 8vo; blue cloth boards; Introduction: pp. vii–xxxii.

J. MISCELLANEOUS WRITINGS

(1) *Books*

105. *The Red Cross in France*
a   Hodder & Stoughton, 1916.
Cr. 8vo; bright blue cloth boards; pp. xii + 168.
With a Preface by Sir Frederick Treves.
b   Also published by George H. Doran, New York [1916], with a Preface by Joseph H. Choate. [Congress: 17-26174.]

(2) *Articles and Published Addresses*

106. " Some Tasks for Dramatic Scholarship ", *Essays by Divers Hands*, N.S., III (1923), pp. 17–38.

107. " On Translating Plays ", *Essays by Divers Hands*, N.S., V (1925), pp. 19–42.

108. " William Archer ", *Drama*, IV, No. 13 (July 1926), pp. 176–8, 182.

109. " Help for ' Unpopular ' Literature ", *The Author*, XLI, No. 2 (Winter, 1931) pp. 56–7.
Extracts from a speech made at the Annual Dinner of the Society of Authors.

110. " On Translating Greek Tragedy ", in *Essays in Honour of Gilbert Murray*, edited by J. A. K. Thomson and A. J. Toynbee (Allen & Unwin, Ltd., 1936), pp. 237–47.

111. " The Spirit of France ", *The Times*, French Number, 19 July 1938, pp. 3, 4.

112. *Quality.*
Humphrey Milford for the English Association, November 1938.
Ryl. 8vo; grey wrappers; pp. 17.
Presidential Address to the English Association, 1938.

113. The text of a speech at a Complimentary Dinner to Dr. C. E. Wheeler, *British Homoeopathic Journal*, XXIX, No. 1 (January 1939), pp. 65–66.

114. " A Pleasant Walk ", *Cornhill Magazine*, CLXII, No. 967 (April 1946) pp. 52–57.

115. " University Drama ", *Drama*, N.S., No. 1 (Autumn, 1946), pp. 11–16.

(3) *Interviews with Granville Barker are Recorded in the Following*

116. *Report from the Joint Select Committee of the House of Lords and the House of Commons on the Stage Plays (Censorship)*, Parliamentary Papers, No. 214 (H.M. Stationery Office, 1909), pp. 70–86.

117. *Report of the Oxford University Drama Commission* (Geoffrey Cumberlege, 1945).

K. UNPUBLISHED PLAYS

(1) *Plays Written in Collaboration with Berte Thomas*

118. *The Family of the Oldroyds*
A play in four acts; written *c.* 1895–6; not produced. The typescript is in the British Museum, a recent gift from Mr. Herbert Thomas. Press-mark: C.116.h.10. Each act has its leaves numbered independently and is enclosed in its own stiff paper folder. The recto of the first leaf in each folder is inscribed with Barker's name, this and the numerous corrections of the text being in his own hand. Size: 4to; ff. (ii) + 36; (i) + 20; (i) + 22, (i) + 11.

119. *The Weather-hen*

A comedy in a prologue, two acts, and an epilogue.

(i) Original version, written 1897; first performed at a special matinée at Terry's Theatre, 29 June 1899. The typescript is at the Lord Chamberlain's Office, the date of licence being: 21.8.99. Each act has its leaves numbered independently and is enclosed in its own stiff paper wrapper. The recto of the first leaf is inscribed with Barker's name in his own hand and also bears the stamp of the typewriting office, dated: 21 August 1897; the verso of the last leaf of the play is stamped with the date: 23 August 1897. There are some ms. corrections by Barker. This version has the alternative title: *Invertebrata*. Size: 4to; ff. (iii) + 27; (i) + 24; (i) + 24; (ii) + 20.

(ii) Revised version, later than the production of the play. The typescript is now in private possession. The prologue and the first act of the original text have been considerably revised, and Act II and the epilogue have been largely re-written. This version has not been produced. Each act has its leaves numbered independently and is enclosed in its own stiff paper wrapper. There are a few ms. corrections by Barker. Size: 4to.

120. *Our Visitor to " Work-a-Day "*

A play in five acts, written 1898-9; not produced. The typescript was presented to the British Museum by George Bernard Shaw in 1947. Pressmark: C.108.f.4. The play is bound in reddish-brown morocco, gilt-tooled, by K. Adams, and is contained in a case; the leaves are gilt-edged. A fly-leaf inscription by Shaw explains how the text came into his possession. Each act is separately foliated and bears the stamp of the type-writing office, dated: 8 May 1899. Barker's autograph signature appears on the recto of the first leaf of each. Size: 4to; ff. (iii) + 29; (i) + 20; (i) + 16; (ii) + 21; (i) + 11.

(2) *Plays of which Barker is Sole Author*

121. *Agnes Colander*

A play in three acts; written 1900-1; not produced. The typescript has been recently acquired by the British Museum from the Library of the Institut Britannique, Paris; pressmark: C.116.g.9. Bound, by W. H. Smith, in olive-green cloth boards, quarter dark purplish-red leather, and with gilt top edge. This volume originally belonged to Barker's own library and has his book-plate (designed by " Max ") pasted inside the front cover. The recto of the first leaf bears Barker's autograph signature and the date: January 10 1901. Size: 4to; the acts are separately foliated: ff. (iii) + 23 + 32 + 20.

122. *A Miracle*

A one-act play in verse; written 1902(?); performed at a matinée at Terry's Theatre, 23 March 1907 (Literary Stage Society production). The typescript, unbound, is at the Lord Chamberlain's Office, the date of the licence being: 21.3.07. Size: 4to; ff. (i) + 9.

123. *The Wicked Man.* A Fragment

Two completed acts, in manuscript, towards a full-length play, together with a collection of manuscript notes, made during the process of planning and composition, are in private possession. The earliest of the notes seem to have been written *c.* 1910, when the play was to have been called *The*

x

Village Carpenter. The two completed acts were probably written in 1914 and are contained in an envelope which bears that date in Barker's hand. These acts are written on small 4to leaves of lined paper, and there are 42 leaves to each act.

124. *The Morris Dance*
A dramatic adaptation of *The Wrong Box,* by R. L. Stevenson and Lloyd Osbourne. First performed at the Little Theatre, New York, 13 February 1913. The typescript, showing considerable ms. revision, was formerly in the Winthrop Ames Collection, Little Theatre, and is now in the New York Public Library. (Seen in a microfilm copy.)

(3) *In Collaboration with C. E. Wheeler*

125. *Das Märchen*
An English version of the play by Arthur Schnitzler. It was produced by Maurice Elvey for the Adelphi Play Society, on Sunday, 28 January 1912. No copy has yet been traced.

(4) *In Collaboration with Laurence Housman*

126. *The Pied Piper*
The scenario for an entertainment to be acted by children. A typescript copy is now in private possession.

L. TYPESCRIPTS OF PUBLISHED PLAYS

127. *The Marrying of Ann Leete*
British Museum pressmark: C.116.g.8. Recently acquired from the Granville Barker Collection, Institut Britannique. The typewriting office stamp is dated: 12 Dec. 1901. This typescript shows some slight differences in text from the published version of the play and includes a preliminary Note upon the Costume, which was not printed. It seems to have been used as a production copy and includes manuscript annotations by Barker. The recto of the first leaf of each act bears his autograph signature. The volume is bound in olive green cloth boards, half dark red morocco, by W. H. Smith; the top edge is gilt. Size: 4to; ff. (iii) + 26; (ii) + 29; (i) + 13; (ii) + 25.

128. *Waste*
British Museum pressmark: C.116.g.11. From the Granville Barker Collection, Institut Britannique. Barker's name and address and the date, August 1907, are typed on the title-page. The text is substantially that of the first version, as published, but contains numerous alterations and some lengthy (deleted) passages that do not appear in the printed text. This typescript has been used as a production copy (for the Stage Society production at the Imperial Theatre, November 1907) and is extensively spattered with manuscript notes, stage plans, *etc.,* by Barker. Bound in dark olive green cloth boards, quarter orange leather, by W. H. Smith. Size: 4to; ff. (viii) + 6 + (i) + 7–8 + (i) + 9–24; (v) + 35; (vi) + 6 +(i) + 7–10 + (i) + 11–33; (iv) + 23 + final ms. sheet.

129. *The Voysey Inheritance*
British Museum pressmark: C.116.g.10. From the Institut Britannique. The text is that used for the Sadler's Wells revival of the play and is substantially that of the third published version, though with variant passages.

Production notes and plans, corrections and deletions, in Barker's hand, appear throughout Acts I–IV. Act V, which is bare of such notes, appears to be from a duplicate copy that was not used in production. Bound in paper boards, marbled green, blue and gold, quarter dark blue morocco, with gilt top edge. Size: 4to; ff. (iii) + 22; (i) + 35; 31; (i) + 27; (i) + 32.

Addenda

130. "The School of 'The only possible Theatre'", *The Drama* (Magazine of the Drama League of America, Chicago, May, June, July, 1920). [Not seen.]

131. "Hints on Producing a Play", *The Amateur Dramatic Year Book* (1928–9), pp. 6–16.
A distinct item from 49 above.

132. "J. E. Vedrenne", *The Author*, XL, No. 3 (April 1930), p. 75.

INDEX

DATE DUE